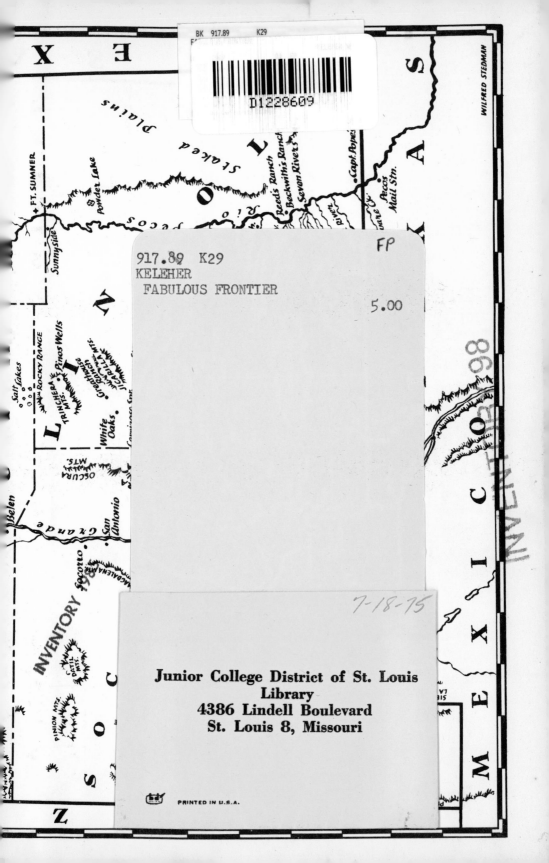

THE FABULOUS FRONTIER

WILLIAM A. KELEHER

The Fabulous Frontier

TWELVE NEW MEXICO ITEMS

revised edition

1962

THE UNIVERSITY OF NEW MEXICO PRESS

BOOKS BY WILLIAM A. KELEHER

Maxwell Land Grant,
a New Mexico Item.   1942

Turmoil in New Mexico,
1846-1868.   1952

Violence in Lincoln County,
1869-1881.   1957

Manufactured in the United States of America
by the University of New Mexico Printing Plant
Albuquerque, New Mexico
Library of Congress Card Catalog Number 62-19919

Dedicated to my wife
Loretta Barrett Keleher
and my children
Mary Ann Keleher Rogers
William Barrett Keleher
Michael Lawrence Keleher
John Gorry Keleher
Thomas Franklin Keleher

ILLUSTRATIONS

Captain Joseph C. Lea 37

White Oaks in the 1890's 41

Lincoln, New Mexico, in 1886 59

Pat Garrett and Associates 78

Pat Garrett Family Grave Site 90

W. W. Cox 95

Thomas Benton Catron 127

James John Hagerman 193

Albert Bacon Fall 223

Major Fountain and Staff 237

Oliver Milton Lee 261

James Robert Gililland 263

County Courthouse at Hillsboro 265

Charles Bishop Eddy 283

William Ashton Hawkins 303

New Mexico in 1880. Endsheet Map

CONTENTS

PREFACE TO REVISED EDITION   ix

PROLOGUE   3

1. DOWN THE PECOS, UP THE TULAROSA   29

2. ABOUT JOHN S. CHISUM   56

3. PATRICK FLOYD GARRETT   67

4. FRONTIER LAND PROBLEMS   102

5. THOMAS BENTON CATRON   117

6. WRITING MEN   141

7. JAMES JOHN HAGERMAN   180

8. ALBERT BACON FALL   208

9. ALBERT J. FOUNTAIN   233

10. OLIVER MILTON LEE   244

11. CHARLES BISHOP EDDY   278

12. WILLIAM ASHTON HAWKINS   299

EPILOGUE   322

SOME SOURCES AND REFERENCES   326

INDEX   331

PREFACE TO REVISED EDITION

ALMOST TWO DECADES have elapsed since publication of "The Fabulous Frontier." In the interim, a new generation of native born New Mexicans has reached maturity, many of whom may be interested in the history of southeastern New Mexico. In the interim, also, New Mexico's population has been substantially increased by the emigration of people from other states and countries. Many of the new arrivals, finding here their heart's desire, have become permanent residents and truly dedicated citizens of New Mexico.

The atomic bomb explosion in 1945 changed for all time to come the face of vast areas of land in southeastern New Mexico, altered the use to which the land had been put since time immemorial, and profoundly influenced the thinking of the inhabitants. The explosion of the bomb served to bring into sharp focus the historical background of the Old Lincoln County country, and to demonstrate the vast changes that can come over the spirit of man's dreams in the proverbial "twinkling of an eye."

The text of the first and second printings has been followed except in minor instances. The revision consists principally in the insertion of facts and information not formerly available, together with a recitation of events and incidents believed relevant, which have taken place subsequent to initial publication, marked by an asterisk (*) for identification.

Many people helped to make this book possible. My renewed gratitude to George Fitzpatrick of Santa Fe, and my sister, Julia M. Keleher, for reading the original manuscript and evaluating it; to Ilda B. Sganzini and Ellis Dean Neel, for secretarial assistance; and to D. L. Jackson of White Oaks, for the use of his file of *The Golden*

Era. Since the material for "The Fabulous Frontier" was gathered, and subsequent to first publication, many people who contributed generously of their time and recollections, have passed away. Among them are the following: Marion L. Fox, William Clifford Reid, Mrs. A. B. Fall, Cesario Pedragon, Oliver M. Lee, William A. Bayer, George L. Ulrich, Frank Worden, Mr. and Mrs. H. G. Graham, George Curry, Andrew H. Hudspeth, Will Robinson, Lucius Dills, James M. Hervey, E. D. Tittmann, Roy A. Prentice, Dr. W. C. Field, Judge Colin Neblett, Charles C. Catron, H. B. Gerhart, Isidoro Armijo, Monsignor Jules N. Stoffel, Percy Hagerman, J. M. Hawkins and J. R. Gililland. In fact, most of those who furnished material for the book have died. This volume is a legacy to readers everywhere from all of them. Most of them belonged to an era in southeastern New Mexico now gone forever. Each one of them had personal knowledge of some one or more of the events described in the book; many of them had personal, sometimes intimate, acquaintance with one or more of the characters delineated. Fortunately for posterity, their testimony was taken while still available. Their names are here recorded in grateful appreciation.

The Fabulous Frontier is an attempt to recapture some of the atmosphere prevailing in Territorial days in southeast New Mexico. For decades that part of New Mexico was marked "The Staked Plains" on government maps and shunned by Apache, Spanish colonist and Gringo alike. Although some were born subsequent to 1860, many men of prominence in early day southeast New Mexico were veterans of the Army of Occupation of 1846, or men who had seen service during the Civil War either in the California Column or some other contingent in the Federal or Confederate Army. Most of them were lovable old rascals, colorful, adventuresome. Influential political ties in the States obtained for some of them posts of honor and importance in New Mexico. Some of them came as "carpetbaggers," but later learned to love the Territory and proved their loyalty by residing in New Mexico until death. The New Mexico of a half and three quarters of a century ago was decidedly a bit of the last Western frontier.

Murder was a common offense. Stagecoach robberies were nothing to get excited about. It was nothing unusual in the seventies and eighties for outraged ranchers in New Mexico to run down a horse thief, cut off an ear, turn him loose, branded and bleeding, as an advertisement and a warning. In the seventies and early eighties there was great unrest among the Indians in New Mexico. The Apaches, the Utes and the Navajos, to name only three of the tribes, had grievances of importance, but believed that only by going on the warpath would the attention of the federal government be focused on them and their problems. With great mining booms in Nevada, Colorado, Montana, it was inevitable that hundreds of prospectors and miners would explore the hills and mountains of New Mexico, looking for gold, silver and other precious metals. Even Thomas A. Edison, convinced that gold in great quantities could be recovered in the placer diggings a few miles from Santa Fe, came to the Territory in the early nineties and spent many days supervising the erection of machinery designed to recover nuggets, an enterprise which finally failed dismally.[1]

The coming of the Santa Fe Railroad to New Mexico in 1879 marked the beginning of the end of the old-time colorful days in New Mexico. The promoters of the railroad had visualized a line that would pass through Cimarron, home place of Lucien B. Maxwell of Maxwell Land Grant fame, that would follow the old Santa Fe Trail into the capital of the Territory, and then parallel the Rio Grande into Albuquerque, with an extension from there to deep water at Guaymas, Sonora, Mexico.

Expensive grades and adverse conditions changed the original plans. The Santa Fe Railroad, when it did come to New Mexico, served only a comparatively small part of an immense territory. There

---

1. That Thomas A. Edison, the "Wizard of Menlo Park," was interested in mining in New Mexico in the nineties, has been confirmed by a document unearthed by Judge Clarence M. Botts, Dean of the Albuquerque Bar. In examining an abstract of title to a part of the Ortiz Grant in Santa Fe County, Judge Botts found an agreement dated February 9, 1898, between the Galisteo Company, a New Mexico corporation, of the one part, and Thomas A. Edison "of the County of Essex and State of New Jersey" of the other part. The agreement provided that inasmuch as the Galisteo Company owned rights in a mining property on the Ortiz Grant, it was agreed that "as soon as possible in view of his duties in the New Jersey Iron Mills," Edison was to work out plans and "devise a process for working auriferous mesa gravel upon said Grant, without the use of water, whereby mills of 10,000 tons capacity per day of 20 hours can be successfully operated." Edison agreed to supervise personally the construction of the first mill to be erected under the provisions of the contract. Net proceeds of the venture were to be divided one-third to Edison and two-thirds to the Galisteo company. The agreement referred to an underlying lease between the New Mexico Mining Company and James W. Perry of New York City.

remained for future development great spaces of open country, among them a vast area dominated by the Pecos River. That area, at one time almost entirely within the exterior boundaries of Lincoln County, beckoned to the man who had no fear of things to come. Men went to the Pecos River country following the cattle trails. Men went over the mountains from the Pecos Valley to Lincoln, to White Oaks, to Tularosa, to out-of-the-way places where sixty-day mail service was nothing to complain about. Southeast New Mexico attracted many men of outstanding courage and ability. Some of these men accomplished things of significance and importance in connection with the development of the Territory. A sincere effort has been made in this volume to tell some of the things about some of the men who helped to give life and color to New Mexico from 1870 to 1912. Southeast New Mexico, because it had no land grant problems, because it was really a new country when contrasted with other parts of New Mexico, offered a golden opportunity to men seeking a new horizon of life. Many men embraced the opportunity, made the most of it.

Worthy of attention, perhaps, is the fact that this volume deals almost exclusively with men who came to New Mexico from elsewhere. Native-born New Mexicans had but little to do with the development of southeast New Mexico, for the reasons suggested in the item "Frontier Land Problems."

WILLIAM A. KELEHER

Albuquerque, New Mexico
June 1, 1962

THE FABULOUS FRONTIER

PROLOGUE

SOON it will be one hundred sixteen years since Stephen Watts Kearny and his Missourians invaded that part of Mexico then and now known as New Mexico. It is now one hundred years since Carleton's California Column marched into New Mexico during Civil War days.[1] It is more than eighty years since New Mexico became identified with the outside world by means of rail communication. Proceeding intelligently with its policy of manifest destiny, the State Department had seen to it that things were made comparatively easy for Kearny's army of conquest. James Magoffin and associates had made arrangements which facilitated and expedited the Occupation.[2] Kearny and his soldiers traveled from the Missouri

---

1. The New Mexico Legislature of 1863 got into difficulties when it adopted a resolution praising the "rapid march of Brigadier General James H. Carleton with the California troops, across the Great Desert, as one of the most remarkable achievements of the age." The resolution recited that "during the late Texas invasion, while the rebel hordes threatened our Territory, the gallant soldiers of California, and our sister Territory Colorado, came to our assistance, and uniting with our patriotic and true hearted sons, drove the invaders from the land." Such high praise was given in the resolution to General Carleton and his Californians, that the Territory of Colorado entered a protest through its governor. This prompted the adoption by the Legislature of New Mexico on February 3, 1864, of a resolution designed to pacify the people of Colorado. The resolution of 1864 declared that it had not been the intention of the Territory of New Mexico "to do the least injustice to the bravery and sacrifices of our neighbor Territory of Colorado, nor to place their brave and patriotic soldiers second to none in the defense of this Territory." The resolution concluded: "That we have not remained insensible or indifferent to the blood that flowed in our defense . . . we . . . take pleasure in expressing our thanks and appreciation to the brave Colorado Volunteers, assuring them, on the part of our constituents, a reciprocal service in aid of our neighbor, when called upon, to the last of our resources."

2. Magoffin spent some thirty thousand dollars of his own funds in making the arrangements, was imprisoned in Mexico for his efforts and had great difficulty in

River to the Mora River in New Mexico, a distance of 775 miles, without having seen an inhabited house. The Missourians came into New Mexico through Raton Pass, following a trail that later became a stagecoach road, nearby the present line of the Atchison, Topeka & Santa Fe Railway. The invaders made their first camp in present New Mexico on the west side of Raton Mountain, on ground occupied in the seventies by the Red River House, noted for extending genuine Western hospitality to stagecoach travelers while in operation. Kearny issued an order of the day, just before entering New Mexico, prohibiting his men from disturbing a blade of grass, or taking an ear of corn from any man's property. Officers Swords, Weightman and Gilmer overtook Colonel Kearny soon after he had left the Raton pass and presented him with a commission as Brigadier General. Stephen Watts Kearny and his men traveled quickly from Raton Mountain to the beautiful Mora River country. The cavalrymen snipped the heads from wild flowers with their quirts as they rode along, impressed by high mountain ranges, tall pine trees and the abundance of grass and foliage. General Kearny read his carefully prepared manifesto to the people of New Mexico at Las Vegas on August 15, 1846. He promised them protection of life and property in exchange for loyalty to the American flag. He warned them against committing overt acts against the United States of America. Nearly twenty years after the Kearny march, R. S. Elliott, who had been a soldier in the army of invasion, wrote his recollections of the journey from Missouri to New Mexico.[3]

Referring particularly to Las Vegas, Elliott wrote:

At 8 o'clock, August 15, 1846, we took the town of Las Vegas, not with shooting of guns, but by quietly marching in. The General as-

obtaining reimbursement for his expenditures by the Congress of the United States. New Mexicans knew little or nothing of Magoffin's participation in intrigues at the instance of our State Department. That Magoffin had troubles of his own in New Mexico, after the American Occupation, is indicated by the fact that the Legislature passed a law on February 1, 1854, permitting free access to salt lakes in the southern part of the Territory. The preamble to the act recited that "James Magoffin, a citizen of Texas," had set up a fictitious claim to the salt lakes, prevented people from taking salt out of them, "attacked them with bodies of armed men, fired upon and wounded them, destroyed and carried off their property."

3. For a soldier's recollection of the journey into Raton Pass, the Mora country and Las Vegas, see Las Vegas *Gazette*, March 27, 1875; and article, "Kearny's March Into New Mexico," by R. S. Elliott, *Inland Magazine*, St. Louis, March, 1875,

cended the roof of one of the houses—one story—to swear in the
alcalde and make an American citizen of him, in the bright sunshine,
and in full view of all the people; while the unterrified soldiers sat
on their horses in the plaza, or public square, calmly looking on. The
reader, who has never seen war, may perhaps think it is a small matter to take a town in that way; but I can assure him it is a very comfortable way for both the takers and the taken; and the reduction of
Las Vegas was an important incident in the ceremonies indulged in.
The General made a speech and very well meant, but without fault
of his, it turned out in some important particulars to be somewhat
of a delusion, if not a snare. Las Vegas is not now the same town it
was in 1846. It has increased greatly in population, and does a large
business in the purchase of wool, hides and pelts, and other products
for export, as also in the importation and sale of merchandise. It has
many new buildings, some of large size, and has public schools, and
churches of several denominations. It has three newspapers, the
Gazette, Advertiser, and the *Revista Catolica,* the latter a church
paper. The daily coaches for Santa Fe, and the wagon trains for all
points south of Santa Fe—whether in the eastern border of the Territory, or in the valley of the Rio Grande, all pass through Las Vegas,
which is thus a sort of gateway to about three-fourths of the
Territory.

The invaders of 1846 were disappointed when the soldiers under
General Armijo failed to meet them in battle. Swords, Weightman
and Gilmer, who had hurried to New Mexico as much to get into the
fight as to deliver a certificate of promotion to Kearny, shared in the
disappointment.[4]

---

4. Brigadier General Stephen W. Kearny, in command of the Army of the West,
entered Santa Fe on August 18, 1846, and took possession of the city and of the
then Province of New Mexico in the name of the United States. A provisional
Territorial government was organized with Charles Bent as Governor. General Kearny's
column was composed of 800 regulars and the First Missouri Mounted Volunteers,
under the command of Col. Alexander W. Doniphan. A few weeks later the Second
regiment of Missouri Volunteers, under command of Colonel Sterling Price, arrived
at Santa Fe and marched on to join Fremont in California. Colonel Doniphan and
his regiment continued on their celebrated march to Chihuahua and thence across
Northern New Mexico to the Rio Grande. The treaty of peace with Mexico was signed
at Guadalupe, Hidalgo, on February 28, 1848, ratified by the United States on March
10, 1848, and ratified by Mexico May 24, 1848. By that treaty the United States
acquired territory embracing California, Nevada, Utah, New Mexico, most of present-
day Arizona and portions of present-day Colorado and Wyoming; and by the same
treaty Mexico relinquished all claims to the state of Texas.

The people of New Mexico were docile enough. They accepted the change in government from that of Mexico to the United States of America with outward indications of good will. Only the Taos Rebellion in 1847, culminating in the assassination of Governor Charles Bent, for which the conspirators paid dearly, reflected smouldering resentment and opposition in some places to the coming of the Americans.[5]

With a lone delegate in Congress, and a governor, with minor exceptions, always from the States, the Territory of New Mexico for decades was to all practical purposes forgotten and abandoned by the United States of America. A frontier country, without a railroad or a navigable river, communication with the outside world was maintanied by means of rumbling stagecoaches, caravans of freighters and emigrant trains and occasional spectacular dashes by a fast riding courier to the centers of civilization. True, the army was in New Mexico, in rather an important way, mostly cavalry, instructed to subdue the Indians. But the army, with all of its men and horses and rifles and rations, had for many years serious difficulties and encounters with the Utes, Apaches and Navajos, and seemed at times unable to cope with the situation. Of the red men, only the Pueblo Indians, with an individual culture, self-governed and disciplined, refused to be stampeded by the spectacular events that followed the American Occupation. With expert knowledge of farming and irrigation and of community life, the Pueblos accepted their new associates in New Mexico with dignity and composure.[6]

---

5. For some details of Bent's assassination and the difficulties in Taos, see *Senate Document No. 442*, 56th Congress, 1st Session, and *Senate Document No. 70*, 1st Session, 30th Congress, page 18.

6. Commenting on the manner in which the army sometimes chased the redmen, the Las Vegas *Gazette* of July 18, 1874, said: "It is really a melancholy, if not a shameful way in which the military go to work to protect the settlers on the frontier, especially so in time of actual danger. As soon as the news reaches a post that depredations by Indians have been, or are being committed, a troop of cavalry or even infantry, is called out, on the spur of the moment, who, reaching the scene of the disaster, either find the bird flown or if in the neighborhood, the supplies of rations which were taken along, will not justify the troops to follow on the trail, and home they go again. Why does not the army of the U.S. inaugurate the policy formerly so laudably carried out by the natives of New Mexico on similar occasions, of sending out parties as quick as possible, with one day's rations, and then let a well prepared pack train follow in their wake to enable them to hunt up the redskins, if need be, to their very home? This method alone will strike terror to their savage heart."

For many years after the American Occupation, New Mexico was faced with problems that were unique in America. No other state or territory had language or racial difficulties comparable to those with which New Mexico was obliged to contend. The sweep of Kearny's army through New Mexico dislocated business and property affairs. Severance from Mexico thrust upon the inhabitants of the Territory an alien tongue, new laws and customs, and created conditions which called for prompt and vigorous assistance from the federal government in the national capital. The assistance, however, was not readily forthcoming. For decades New Mexico was almost allowed to stew in its own juice.

By the year 1853 things had settled down sufficiently in the Territory to permit New Mexico leadership to assert itself and to enumerate the things believed to be essential for the conduct of a half way successful territorial government. Many things were required, according to a memorial to the Congress adopted by the Legislature of New Mexico in 1853, and strange to say, a penitentiary was near the top of the list. "A penitentiary in this Territory is one of the primary wants of the community, for the punishment and suppression of crime," the memorial recited. The memorialists begged leave to "represent to your honorable House and Senate that the various civil convulsions through which this country has passed during late years, and the presence of armies, has had the effect which is always produced by this state of things, namely, to sow the seeds of vice and immorality. . . . It is the conviction of your memorialists, that a well organized penitentiary would not only rid the community of a class of malefactors, who afflict the country at this time, but that it would also have a salutary influence in preventing the commission of crime; and it might even be the means of reforming some criminals." The Legislature asked the federal government for fifty thousand dollars for a penitentiary, but not for many years after 1853 did the Congress do anything about helping New Mexico to house its criminals adequately. The memorial of 1853 touched upon the educational situation, calling "to the attention of Congress the subject of the education of the rising generation, . . . merely bringing before Congress the undeniable fact that in no part of the United States are the means of education so deficient as in New Mexico." The memorialists of 1853 pleaded with Congress for roads and highways, calling attention "to the insular position of this Territory; to its immense Territorial area, to its limited and scattered population, to the danger to which our people are constantly exposed, from surrounding Indians, who greatly outnumber our population; and to the distances to be traversed; the deserts to be crossed; the appalling difficulties, especially in the winter, to be encountered in reaching this Territory, and in going hence to any of the States or Territories."

The legislative memorialists, acknowledging no hope for a railroad, pleaded for common roads to Missouri, Arkansas, Texas, California and Utah, "with station houses a day's ride apart on the road to Missouri." The importance of the road to Missouri was emphasized by the memorial in the statement: "The road to Missouri is the great business thoroughfare of the Territory, for this reason it is an object of peculiar interest not only to the people of this Territory, but to the whole United States." The memorial went into detail about the road to Missouri, asking that it be declared a public highway by act of Congress, "with a suitable width of land on each side of it to supply fuel and grass for travelers, and that a line of station houses may be established upon it from Fort Union in this Territory, to Council Grove or to the state line of Missouri. The distance from Fort Union to Independence is more than seven hundred miles, and on this long and dreary line of road there is, at this time, but a single military station, a single Indian trading post, and at these two places only can the traveler receive any assistance in his greatest needs.[7] These stations might be simple and inexpensive structures, containing quarters for four persons, to take care of them, and vacant rooms for travelers, with a yard for the protection of property, and a cattle shed, and each station should be obligated to supply shelter, fuel and water, gratis to all travelers. It is believed that 12 stations on this line would afford sufficient accommodations for the present and that the

---

7. The military post of Fort Union near Las Vegas, New Mexico, was established in 1851. At a cost of three hundred thousand dollars, the United States erected at Fort Union, supposedly on a government reservation, improvements consisting of buildings required for a four company post, for depot stores, and for a magazine. As originally established the post was to be eight miles square, with the fort as the central point. By an Act of Congress approved June 21, 1860, the Mora Land Grant was confirmed in its claimants. The government found out, as shown by a report by the Committee on Military affairs, 47th Congress, 1st Session, March 22, 1882, that when the Mora Grant was confirmed, the site of Fort Union was within the grant, and the United States had no title to the property. The conflict was finally adjusted by appropriate legislation.

sum of thirty thousand dollars would build and furnish them with everything necessary for them."

The memorialists of 1853 were rather serious about the station houses and their request that travelers be given free accommodations. They referred to the losses that occurred in human life and property on the Missouri road and outlined for the Congress the road and mail situation then existing in New Mexico:

> The limits of a Memorial, do not permit a detail of the yearly loss of human life and property upon the road to Missouri, your memorialists therefore refer your Honorable Bodies to the various sources from whence this information may be derived, the War Department, alone, can furnish an astonishing amount of losses in Horses and other Cattle nearly all of which might have been prevented had a line of Station Houses been established on the road, nor will your memorialists venture to enumerate all the manifold benefits which would result from a good common road with the proposed facilities upon it, they will however advert to the Mail and Stage Coach facilities, which would be presented to the public, at present we have a monthly Mail to Missouri and a Mail every two months to Texas, and it requires three months or more to receive an answer to a letter addressed to any place east of Independence or San Antonio. These Stations would present a ready means for a Mail every fortnight to Missouri; and if we had a monthly Mail to Arkansas and a monthly Mail to Texas, these might be so arranged with the Texas line as to give us a weekly line to the States, with all the benefits that would result from the facility of travelling to the State of Missouri in two weeks, and of receiving letters from the States and answering them every week. The roads in the Territory, are in a bad condition, and the great extent of these roads make the expense of a thorough repair of them altogether beyond the means of the people themselves. It is therefore desirable that a limited sum should be appropriated by Congress to make these repairs. Your memorialists also respectfully ask for an appropriation of Eight Thousand Dollars to create common wells on the Mail road across the Jornada del Muerto, a distance of 90 miles without water. The interior Mail facilities, of this Territory, also need extensions. At present we have monthly Mails, only, whereas, we ought to have weekly Mails. The location of Public Roads from this Territory to California and Utah is all that can be expected from Congress at the present time, unless a monthly Mail on each road should be added, a Mail to California

would be a great accommodation to the people of this Territory. These two important roads can be located at little expense to the United States by intelligent officers of the Topographical Corps, if assisted by citizens who possess a real knowledge of the Country through which the road may pass.

The Legislature was acutely aware of the Indian problem in New Mexico in the early days after the American Occupation. Mescalero Apaches swooped down on the people living in and about Galisteo in 1854, frightened the entire community and caused great damage to life and property. On December 28, 1854, the lawmakers adopted a memorial calling upon the Congress for assistance, referring to the "bloody incursions of the numerous roaming bands with which this country is infested, which consist of the Jicarilla Apaches, Utah, Cheyenes, Arapahoes, Kiowas, Comanches, Mescalero Apaches and Navajoes."[8]

---

8. The memorial of 1854 gives an interesting outline of the Indian troubles suffered by the people of New Mexico in the settlements up and down the Rio Grande. To quote a part of the memorial:

"In the month of November last one hundred and fifty head of horses and mules, and more than a dozen valuable lives, fell victim to the inroads of the Apaches and Cheyennes in the county of Taos alone; and such depredations have been almost daily occurring in the different parts of the Territory. Within a few miles of Santa Fe, and almost within sight of the Stars and Stripes that wave over the Capital of New Mexico, such outrages of murder and robbery have been committed within the last few months; and since the commencement of the present Legislature, though but fifteen days in session, authentic information has been received of the loss of two thousand head of sheep, most of which was brought from the state of Missouri, for the purpose of improving the stock of the country, and consequently of great value to their owners and the country. In addition to this, intelligence has just been received of the loss of five hundred head of cattle near Fort Union; and in the month of October, in the county of Valencia, Mariano Pino was wounded by the Indians, his two sons killed, two boys carried into captivity, and one hundred and eighty head of cattle and fifty mules taken by them. In the county of Bernalillo, in the same month, five thousand sheep, belonging to Mr. Perea, and fifty head of horses and mules belonging to the Pueblo of Isleta, were carried away by the same marauders. Innumerable smaller losses occur daily; and instead of growing in wealth and prosperity, our Territory is daily depopulated and impoverished by the forays of the neighboring tribes . . . the military force at present stationed in this Territory is altogether insufficient for the purpose of furnishing adequate protection to the lives and property of her people. . . . We have an immense frontier to defend, with a population of nearly seventy thousand . . . and we ask that you afford us, for the future, a security against those disasters which have in the past reduced our citizens to poverty, and plunged their families into grief. . . . Nothing can be done in the prosecution of any human plan of civilization toward the marauding savages until they become satisfied that we can pursue them into their hiding places

New Mexico was not free from livestock thievery in the early days subsequent to the American Occupation. The Legislature of 1851 looked into the problem and passed a law providing that any person who forged a bill of sale to livestock should be fined not less than one hundred dollars, or imprisoned at hard labor for not less than two years, or in the alternative, should receive not more than fifty nor less than thirty lashes, "well applied to the bare back." There were difficulties, too, in the very early days with clergymen and lawyers. Slander in the churches was a problem. The Legislature undertook to remedy the situation in 1856 by passing a law providing a fine of from twenty-five to fifty dollars "if in the future any minister of the gospel of any denomination whatsoever, shall slander any other person or persons, within any temple." The preamble to the law gave the key to the difficulty, reciting that "various ministers of the gospel are frequently committing grave slanders against particular persons in temples and chapels, losing sight of charity and evangelical meekness, and profaning those sacred places which are dedicated exclusively to the worship of the Supreme Being."

With the clergy reprimanded in 1856, it was not until 1864, just before the end of the Civil War, that the New Mexico lawmakers got around to curbing the activities of members of the bar. In that year the Legislature passed a stringent law aimed at attorneys. The act provided, among other things, that any attorneys or counselors at law, defender or defenders, in the courts of the Territory, "who maliciously reveal the secrets of their clients to the opposite party, or who, being charged with the defense of one party, and having informed himself of his cause and means of defense, shall desert him and defend the other, or who in any other way whatever, shall knowingly jeopardize his client in order to favor the opponent or derive some personal profit or because greater fees have been proffered him after having been retained by his client, upon conviction of such evil proceedings before any court whatsoever of this Territory, shall be fined in a sum double the amount he may have received for the defense of the cause."

Having touched on the educational situation in New Mexico by its memorial of 1853, the legislative session of 1854 pressed the at-

---

in the mountains and there visit upon them due punishment for the robberies and murders which they are daily perpetrating upon our people."

tention of the Congress of the United States to the problem. Among other things, the memorial recited that "the territory is entirely without schools, except in the capital, in which there are one or two, supported by private subscription. No part of the United States is so deficient in the means of education as our Territory, and although the general government has made what appears to be a liberal donation for school purposes, these donations in truth are of no value, as the 16th section can be of no value unless it is situated near some river from which water could be had for irrigation." The memorial informed the Congress that by the census of 1850, New Mexico had over 25,000 adults who did not know how to read or write, "which is seven-eights of the population." The memorialists asked that some provision be made to create and support public schools throughout the Territory by an annual appropriation of money, instead of by donations of land which could not produce revenue.[9]

Lack of mail facilities caused the Legislature in 1856 to memorialize the Hon. James Campbell, Postmaster General of the United States. The memorial recited that "the people of this Territory have suffered for many years for the want of a semi-monthly mail between this Territory and the United States. Our geographical position, being in the center of the American continent, without navigable rivers or means of communication by railroad, renders our situation as remote from the federal capital in communications through mail facilities as the Sandwich Islands. The least time in which a reply can be had to any communication from this Territory,

---

9. A discouraging report on conditions in New Mexico was made to his conference in 1870 by Rev. Thomas Harwood, a young Methodist minister who had served in the Twenty-fifth Wisconsin Volunteers as soldier and chaplain during the Civil War and who had come to New Mexico on October 1, 1869, settling first at Tiptonville, Mora County, and later establishing missions in Santa Fe, Albuquerque, Peralta, Socorro and Las Cruces. Accustomed to camp meetings and church conditions in peaceful, God-fearing communities of the middlewestern states, Missionary Harwood for a good many years could not become reconciled to life as he found it in New Mexico. In his 1870 report, he said that, "intellectually, morally and religiously, New Mexico is one of the darkest corners in Christendom," and blamed conditions on "want of Bibles, schools and proper instruction." "These wanting," the Harwood report continued, "there can be but little advancement or any material progress." In all his travels in 1870, the missionary told the conference, "not a public school could be found, hardly a Bible in one family in a thousand, and only a few other books; hardly a public road or a bridge only as they had been built by the government or the Protestant pioneer; hardly an American plow, wagon or buggy could be found." See Vol. 1, *History of New Mexico Missions, 1850-1884*, El Abogado Press, Albuquerque, 1908.

is three months, and only then by prompt attention being given to it, and we seldom get a reply from the Eastern cities under four months. By such a length of time between communications and replies, our public officers are often greatly embarrassed in relation to their most urgent duties. The commerce between the Territory and the States has increased within the last six years from one half million to two millions of dollars, and is still increasing. The whole of this amount has to be remitted in drafts, bills of exchange, vouchers and certificates, drawn by our civil and military officers, and any delays by accident, robbery of the mail or informality in the remittance made, notice thereof does not reach our people for three, and often four months, thus depriving them of the possibility to duplicate their drafts, to amend informal vouchers or receipts in less times, or receive advice and instructions from their correspondents relative thereto. We think we deserve, and know that we need, the boon asked for in this memorial."

During the Civil War years the people of New Mexico were obliged to contend with many problems, two of the most important being the Indian depredation difficulties and the fear of a second invasion by Texans. Depicting the Indian situation, the Legislature adopted a joint resolution on January 23, 1864, calling to the attention of the Congress of the United States the deplorable plight in which the people found themselves. The Legislature recited in the resolution that it was being adopted under extraordinary circumstances, the Legislature being "filled with the deepest feelings of grief, caused by the cries of the people of this Territory, heard every moment, who are to be found today in the most painful and miserable state at the hands of the Navajo tribe, murders and robberies from day to day, citizens of this Territory; owners of large herds of cattle and sheep, as owners of other livestock, suffer today their misfortunes, and those of their numerous families, well nigh reduced to beggary and poverty; fathers mourn the loss of their children slain or captive by Indians; children that of their fathers; wives mourn their husbands; and these their wives; friends their friends and these their countrymen; livestock of all kinds, from week to week, pass away to the Navajo country, and there only remains to their owners the hoof prints and paths where these red plunderers sweep rapidly with their great capture."

The memorial of 1864 went into details, informing Congress that the Territory was "on all sides infested by hostile Indians; that the Navajos are daily committing murders and robberies to such an extent that during the past fifteen months there has been reported ninety-nine killed, forty-seven wounded, eighteen taken captive by the Indians; and that the property taken included 821 horses, 4,809 cattle, 98,448 sheep, 641 mules, 3,437 goats and 83 donkeys." The Legislature reported that the value of the property stolen amounted to $448,638.92. The memorial concluded:

> Your memorialists would further represent that we, as a people, are loyal to the government of the United States, and are willing to peril our lives and property in the maintenance of the Constitution and the Union, and that in the struggle against the wicked rebellion we will, to the full extent of our ability, support the government that has adopted us; and if we can get rid of the savage enemies, our Territory can and will furnish gold and silver to aid in defraying the expenses of the government in putting down and punishing the rebels.[10]

Although isolated to a great extent from the furies of the Civil War, the Legislature of New Mexico, fearing a second invasion from Texas, adopted a resolution on January 29, 1863, urging Congress to strengthen the fortifications at Fort Union in the northeastern part of the Territory and Fort Craig[11] on the Rio Grande in the southeastern part, not far from historic Valverde. Reciting that "the revolution inaugurated by the insurgent states of the south against the legitimate government of the federal union and against the true spirit of the national constitution still exists, and the people of this Territory desire to remain ever faithful to the government and to constitutional law, and justly apprehending that a second invasion from Texas, one of the southern states, may reopen hostilities against the people of this Territory," the Resolution provided a plan for opening subscriptions for "voluntary and patriotic" contributions in money. The probate judge in each county was called upon to enroll volun-

---

10. As late as July 26, 1874, citizens of Santa Fe held a mass meeting to protest against attacks made by the Kiowa, Cheyenne and Arapahoe Indians on communities in San Miguel, Mora and Colfax Counties.

11. The remains of 140 soldiers interred at Fort Craig during the Civil War, were removed April 1, 1876, to Santa Fe, by the federal government, and buried there in a national cemetery.

teers to work at the forts, to receive subsistence out of the funds contributed. The Territory was divided into two sections; volunteer workers from Santa Ana, Bernalillo, Valencia and Socorro Counties were to report to the commanding officer at Fort Craig; and workers from Santa Fe, Rio Arriba, Taos, Mora and San Miguel were to report to the commanding officer at Fort Union.

A frank resume of conditions in New Mexico in the seventies, as he observed them from the editor's chair, was submitted by J. H. Koogler, publisher of the Las Vegas *Gazette*, in its issue of October 10, 1874. The railroad had not yet reached New Mexico, but had reached Kansas and Colorado points, enabling New Mexico overland transportation distances to be greatly reduced. Declaring that he could not deny that New Mexico then stood almost at the bottom of the list of "enterprising and civilized communities on this continent," Editor Koogler undertook to "explain in a few remarks the cause of her tardiness to keep apace in the march of progress with the rest of the world." To quote Koogler:

Look at our Territory, for instance, at the time of the annexation to the United States, or even later, just before the building of the Pacific railroad, and what do you find?

A province trodden in the dust by the despotic rulers of military governors of Old Mexico, in whose eyes it was a crime to be poor and who, in company with priests, tried to keep the people in ignorance, so as to be better able to make them subservient in all things. Poor people, as peons, were sold at public or private bargains everywhere. The nearest points of commercial relations were the settlements on the Missouri River, the interior of Mexico, or the Pacific Coast, wherefrom to bring goods it took a caravan or train nearly ten months. Hostile bands of Indians took their tribute by force in every direction, and lucky, indeed, was the party who returned from beyond the limits of the settlement without loss to life or property.

Immigration to New Mexico from the States, after annexation, caused a new impetus among the natives, but the real progress, the true change for the better did not commence until a few years ago, after the completion of the Pacific railroad.

Since then the forked sticks are making room for American plows and cultivators; scythes, reapers and mowing machines are taking the place of the old fashioned sickle, and all kinds of tools and improved machinery for mills, are daily brought among us. Sheep, which a few years ago were only raised for the value of their meat, the wool being of no commercial value, are now being improved with Merino and Cotswold bucks, for the sale of their fleeces, and in short, New Mexico is now improving and progressing fast.

One or two railroads within our borders, a company or two of enterprising capitalists and a lot of industrious immigrants, to commence with, would soon speed us along in our endeavors to place our Territory on an even footing with other localities. The means to enrich not only New Mexico, but the whole American nation, we have at our doors, and our mineral, agricultural and grazing facilities only await the arrival of capital and skilled labor to make our country the symbol of happiness and prosperity.

On the same day, October 10, 1874, the Las Vegas *Gazette* published an editorial on "Home Rule and Carpetbaggers." The *Gazette* strongly objected to the appointment of people from outside New Mexico to offices controlled by federal officers in Washington. In conclusion, the editorial said: "We have here in New Mexico, among our native and foreign population, as well bred, well educated and talented men as can be found anywhere. Why then import officers from the east? It certainly cannot be because they are more honest or able."

Statistics on the population of New Mexico and its commercial aspects were given in a memorial adopted by the Legislature of 1871 urging action on legislation then pending in the National Congress. The Resolution, in part, recited that:

As near as can be ascertained, the value of the various articles of commerce which passed across the state of Kansas and were transported from the end of the railroad into New Mexico during the year 1870, amounted to about $8,000,000, and the commerce from Old Mexico, $2,000,000 more, making an annual amount of $10,000,-000. . . . In 1860, the population of New Mexico was 93,516, which included 10,508 wild Indians, making a population of 83,008 persons, exclusive of Indians. Since that time a portion of the Territory of New Mexico was given to Colorado with about 18,000 of the population, and another portion was created into the Territory of Arizona, taking from New Mexico 7,000 more of the population, which left New Mexico with a population of only 58,008 persons. . . . The present population, by a census of 1870, gives the number of white citizens in New Mexico, 86,481, the number of citizens living on the

Pueblo lands, 5,543, miners and citizens on the wild Indian reservations, 218, the number of Pueblo Indians civilized and living in nineteen villages, 7,648, a total of 99,890. . . . It will thus be seen that within the last ten years the increase of the population of New Mexico has been 41,882 persons, and that without including the wild Indians, and after giving territory and population to Colorado and Arizona, the Territory of New Mexico now has a citizen population of 99,890 persons.

W. G. Ritch, Secretary of the Territory, on November 14, 1874, in a report to Hon. John Eaton, Commissioner of Education, summed up the situation in the Territory from the viewpoint of a newcomer:

It is well to bear in mind the entirely anomalous condition of the people and Territory, when compared with any other State or Territory in the Union, and that the power in all cases has not been vouchsafed to human wisdom to eradicate the abuses of years in a day. New Mexico, before its acquisition by the United States had been utterly neglected for generations by the government of Old Mexico, in all things pertaining to its material prosperity and social advancement; and the people were only cognizant of a superior power, as indicated by the presence of exacting revenue officers or the recruiting sergeants, incident to the chaotic and turbulent state of a government beset with revolutions and counter revolutions, which were, of course, paralyzing to productive industries, exhausting to accumulated resources, and which made even existence itself problematical. In those times self preservation, the first law of nature, became the chief thought in the family circle, and the main business of life with each family. There was no time, opportunity or impulse for social or intellectual improvement, nor had there been for generations. Such in brief, was the condition in which the government of the United States found the people at the time the Territory became a part of the Republic. They were, and likewise continued to be, for a long time, beset on all sides by hostile and nomadic Indian tribes, embodiments of all the villainies incident to unregenerate man, and also with not a few of the outlaws, a hair brained and graceless set, ever present on the frontier of an advancing American civilization. Scarce had the government, through civil and military authorities, made an impression toward bringing order out of chaos, when the Civil War followed, threatening the integrity

and the life of the nation, during which event, be it said to the credit
of the people of New Mexico, they remained true to the flag, and
cheerfully contributed their quota of patriotic citizens toward the
defense of her soil and the suppression of the rebellion. This event,
of course, still further kept education and progress in abeyance.

But for the army, and its many military forts in New Mexico and
the Southwest, it is doubtful if the Territory would have had much
in the way of stagecoach transportation in the seventies and eighties.
Transportation facilities were available largely because of the necessity of inter-communication of the military operations in New Mexico and Arizona. However, from time to time stagecoach operators
established new lines, believing that travel over the new routes would
justify their continuance. Jerens and Mitchel of Fort Smith, Arkansas, established a new tri-weekly mail route between Las Vegas
and Mesilla, "equipped with buckboards and coaches," according
to an announcement in the Las Vegas *Gazette* of April 11, 1874,
which would "go through the principal stock raising country of New
Mexico, along the valleys of the Pecos and Hondo Rivers, and bids
fair to become the succesful rival of the stage line along the Rio
Grande, via Santa Fe and Albuquerque." The establishment of the
new route from Las Vegas down the Pecos and across to Mesilla in
Doña Ana County prompted the operators of the Santa Fe to Mesilla
route to greater efforts. The stagecoach schedule from Santa Fe to
Mesilla, by the year 1878, had been reduced to the almost unheard
of running time of sixty hours. The mail route between Santa Fe
and Prescott, Arizona, was important, not only furnishing communication between the Territories of New Mexico and Arizona, but
affording communication with California. The New Mexico Legislature memorialized the Congress in 1880 to authorize a daily mail
between Santa Fe and Prescott, but the day of the stagecoach on that
route was about over. The memorial bravely recited, however, for
the information of the Postmaster General, that "mail route No.
40,101, between Santa Fe and Prescott, passed through a country
which is rapidly settling up with a thrifty and energetic people, and
touches the towns of La Bajada, Pena Blanca, San Isidro, Jemez,
San Mateo, Bacon Springs, Fort Wingate, Navajo Springs, St.
Joseph, Brigham City and Camp Verde." The settlements named in
the memorial, and others served on the route, were declared by the

memorial to be "prosperous business communities, and rapidly increasing in population and importance."

The need for railroad connections in New Mexico was expressed from time to time in the newspapers of the day. Writing from Silver City on May 4, 1873, to the editor of the Las Vegas *Gazette*, George W. Campbell, after telling of the mineral wealth in that part of the Territory and describing especially the copper mines at Santa Rita, urged the building of a railroad and emigration of settlers from New England as the two outstanding requirements of the Territory. Campbell said in part:

> Oh, for a railroad! What an immense amount of wealth lies exposed here. Oh, for an avalanche of Yankees from down east! That is what we want. Your go-ahead, clock peddling, horsetrading, butter making, bean growing, picayune loving, law abiding, mill making, school house building, nigger loving, sabbath keeping, punkin eating, house building, puritanical, psalm singing, hard working Yankee. Let us have a lot of them. We have enough gamblers, petifogging judges of whiskey and Indian agents, carpetbaggers, barkeepers, billiard sports and horse thieves already. New Mexico, with all these burdens of society, is still a good country. With all her superstition and ignorance, with all her childish trifling and useless wrangling over her little school funds, with all her thieving, murdering Indians, and speculating missionaries, New Mexico is still a good country for an industrious man who can support his family without running a dance hall or a whiskey mill.

There was unrest in many parts of New Mexico as the year 1879 came to an end and 1880 began. Chief Victorio, with about one hundred Apache warriors in war paint and fighting regalia, passed through Silver City on January 7, 1880, traveling in the direction of the Black Range, pursued by Major Morrow and five companies of cavalry. The Mescalero Apaches in Lincoln County were causing trouble. A correspondent of the *News and Press* of Cimarron, writing from Lincoln on January 6, 1880, commented on the situation as follows:

> It looks as if an Indian outbreak is imminent with all its attendant deviltry and horrors. At the present time this section of the country is full of miners, comparatively unarmed who would be at the Apaches' mercy should they go on the warpath. Ranches and herds

of stock in the same situation. A band of 50 armed Indians, only, in the present state of affairs could create a vacuum in the industries of this country that would take years to fill up. A few hundred could wipe us out so completely that tradition as to our existence would be considered skeptical in the future. . . . The Mescalero Agency from its inception has been a sink hole of rascality of which the most has been made of by the Agents thereon, and by an unmitigated set of scoundrels at Santa Fe. The government has been swindled out of thousands of dollars thereat, and it is safe to presume with the cognizance of the immaculate military authorities stationed at this post, and district headquarters in the past. A finer or safer base to depredate from into Texas or any other country than the Sacramento Mountains which forms the major part of the Mescalero reservation could not be imagined. And if the reports of the civil and military authorities of Texas be considered John Apache has not been slow to make the most of his advantage ground. . . . There is no question but that a few regiments of cavalry are needed in this part of the country very much, or at least desired by those individuals doing business here, who are in moribund condition financially. But as Santa Fe has its maws on all the dinero disbursed hereabouts the cantonment of the whole army with the German Empire thrown in as an adjunct at this place, would not ameliorate the condition of the people in general in the least.[12]

That the highway between Las Vegas and Santa Fe was "the poorest on earth for the amount of travel," was the complaint of the Las Vegas *Gazette* in its leading editorial on November 6, 1875. The *Gazette* said:

The seventy-five miles of road between Las Vegas and Santa Fe can safely be set down as the worst known to the modern traveler. The main range of mountains running south from the Raton pass to Cimarron and Mora are subdivided into many smaller ranges flung down between the two towns like branches of a tree. It is a bad tangle of hills and ravines. Around and over these separate ridges the road winds its way. The route is an old one. The greater portion of it has been a public thoroughfare for the last fifty years. The first trains from St. Louis, freighted with merchandise for Santa Fe and the then Mexican frontier, passed over it. The road was undoubtedly better then than it is now. . . . Constant travel does not

12. See *News and Press*, Cimarron, Jan. 15, 1880.

improve it. .... Floods have deepened and widened the arroyos. The succession of ruts and sunken places renders travel throughout the whole length disagreeable, and frightful chasms make it at many points precarious. It is the worst road in the United States over which there is a daily stage.

Further on in the editorial, the stagecoach people were taken to task by the *Gazette*:

It is scarcely to be wondered at that the Overland Mail and Express Company keep up their passenger rates to twenty cents a mile. The wear and tear on the vehicles and stock nearly justifies it. The company, however, takes its revenge out on the innocent traveler, first by charging him as long as they can hold their breath, and then churning him to death in short coaches, admirably built for the purpose.

That the stagecoach road was important in the mercantile field was indicated by the editorial:

Over this route millions of dollars worth of freight annually pass. Immense cargoes of goods for the large wholesale houses of Santa Fe, are taken across this rough thoroughfare at a wonderfully small cost, and the wool, hides and mineral products of the Territory in exchange, which comes by way of Santa Fe, are brought out at equally low rates. Ox and mule trains are constantly going and coming and there are few days in the year when less than fifty thousand dollars worth of freight passes any given point between Las Vegas and Santa Fe. That correspondents and strangers become disgusted with the country after being jolted in a stagecoach over these execrable roads is not at all astonishing. It would warp the judgment of a saint and embitter the fancy of the most equable person in the world.

Stagecoach and bull whacking days for large areas of New Mexico approached the end on Sunday, September 7, 1879, at 8:06 P.M. On that date the first Santa Fe passenger train from the East passed through Raton tunnel. The railroad tracks were laid not far from the stagecoach road, near by the trail over which General Kearny and his Missourians had passed into New Mexico thirty-three years before. For·many years, stagecoaches, oxen trains and freight caravans had gone up the eastern slope of Raton Mountain slowly and laboriously and traveled down the western slope even more slowly, with creaking brakes and wheels squeaking for axle grease. Railroad engineers had bored a tunnel through Raton Mountain, leaving Uncle Dick Wootton wondering about the future of his toll gate.[13] An entire year had been required to complete the tunnel. Work trains had shuttled up a switchback to a height of 317 feet, operating under the direction of Trainmaster G. A. Sands. Peter Mulvany of Fitz-

---

13. The Legislature of New Mexico, as early as 1872, undertook to put Virginia-born Richens Lacy Wootton out of business. Lucien B. Maxwell in the sixties carved a strip of land out of his fabulous "Maxwell Land Grant" and deeded it to Wootton. Wootton gave Maxwell a perpetual right to pass over the land and established a toll gate. Rifle in hand, Wootton collected his toll in money, merchandise or trinkets, which he traded off to the Indians. Annoyed by constant complaints about the toll road, the New Mexico legislators passed an act on February 1, 1872, providing "that any charter which may be held or owned by one Richard Wootton or any other person or persons under the general incorporation act of this Territory, over any portion of the Trinidad and Raton mountain road, running from Red River in this Territory, to the town of Trinidad in the Territory of Colorado, and passing by the house of said Richard Wootton, shall not be received as evidence of the existence nor as the charter of any corporation or company, and the said charter or so-called charter, is hereby declared void and of no effect, and the said road is hereby declared to be a public road of this Territory and subject to the statutes concerning Territorial or public roads."

Notwithstanding the action of the New Mexico Legislature, Wootton continued to collect tolls on his road almost up to the time of the coming of the railroad. That "Uncle Dick" was still battling as late as 1879 is revealed in a controversy he had with his son, R. L. Wootton, Jr. In a Trinidad paper on Sept. 11, 1879, R. L. Wootton, Sr., published a notice, addressed "To the Public," which read as follows: "I desire to say to the public that I fully exonerate Padre P. J. Monnecom from all connection with an affair as between R. L. Wootton, Jr., Sheriff of Las Animas County, and myself, and on the pretext of which said R. L. Wootton, Jr., this morning attacked and verbally assaulted Padre Monnecom on the public streets of Trinidad, and I hereby denounce the act of Dick Wootton, Jr., as an unwarranted and uncalled for proceeding, for which I hold him personally responsible to myself. I further denounce the act of striking an old man as unmanly and beneath one bearing my name, and I hereby declare that for shame of such conduct I shall petition the next Legislature to change my name to Richey Lacey Birm, my mother's maiden name, for myself and children from Richard Wootton down, in order that we may not bear the same name. I further declare that Dick Wootton, Jr., has used the name of Wootton to my disadvantage; that I have fostered and protected him, and in return he has abused the confidence reposed in him by me; and that he has opened my business letters, directed plainly to my private address, in order to pry into my private affairs." Richens Lacy Wootton died on August 22, 1893. He had lived in Virginia until he was seventeen, then moved to Christian County, Kentucky. Wootton was one of the first Anglo residents in New Mexico, coming to the Raton Mountains and Taos country some years before the American Occupation.

gerald, Malory and Flynn, the contractors on the tunnel job, made an informal talk to Conductor Turner and the men and women on the first passenger train to pass through the tunnel, saying:

> "On the part of the contractors and men who excavated and completed the tunnel through Raton Mountain, may I say to you that we heartily turn it over to you as the best piece of tunnel work done in the west. To the civil engineers, William Engle, and others, who had charge of the tunnel and switchback, the contractors owe everything for the success and speedy completion of the tunnel and invention of the switchback. So accurately did William Engle perform his duties as engineer that the tunnel headings came exactly in line although the work was done from both sides of the mountain."

The Santa Fe *New Mexican*, in its issue of January 31, 1880, published the valedictory of Santa Fe Trail stagecoach days, saying:

> On January 25, 1880, Barlow & Sanderson drew off their entire stock from the eastern branch of the famous Southern Overland Mail. Originally, the line was 850 miles in length. Kansas City was the nearest railroad point to Santa Fe. The trip from Kansas City to Santa Fe required about two weeks of constant traveling. The line was gradually shortened with the extension of the railroad westward until it reached the last station, Las Vegas, 70 miles away, previous to its discontinuance. It has carried mail, express and passengers with surprising regularity and safety, over roads which were at times almost impassable, at all times liable to attacks of road agents and sometimes of Indians. It has received its full share of round and emphatic abuse from suffering and irritated passengers, its patrons, worn out with fatigue and torture of a long journey, but they will all remember the line with more charity now that it is a thing of the past. The contract time had to be made and it usually was made. It is certain that all that good management and business energy could do was accomplished by the old S.O.M. Ex. Co.

The Las Vegas *Gazette* of January 29, 1880, struck a nostalgic note concerning the Santa Fe Trail, as the Santa Fe Railroad was about to reach the Territorial capital. After sketching the early history of the trail, the *Gazette* mentioned several New Mexicans who had been interested in its commerce, among them Elisha Stanley,

Dr. Samuel Hubbs and David Waldo, "father of Judge Waldo, our present Attorney General and formerly Chief Justice. David Waldo is now dead and was buried in Santa Fe." In conclusion, the *Gazette* said:

> The Santa Fe trade increased from year to year, until at the time of the American Occupation it had reached enormous proportions, supplying not only New Mexico, the most northern province, with goods, but likewise extending into the departments of Durango, Zacatecas and to points 1,500 miles south of Santa Fe. It was truly a vast commerce transacted on these boundless plains. The trail from Independence was almost a straight line and with few sinuosities. The whole distance was about 800 miles. It crossed the Arkansas above Caches, and crossed the Dry Cimarron and McNee's Creek, running to the north of Rabbit Ear Mountain, past the Point of Rocks, Rio Colorado, Ocate, Wagon Mound, Gallinas Crossing (now Las Vegas), San Miguel, Pecos and Santa Fe. The immense caravans which traversed this route have left a road worn deep in the surface of the prairies which will take many years of disuse to obliterate. But though the rains may wash it out and the grass of the prairies grow over it to a green sod, yet it will live in history. It was the line of an international commerce which has no counterpart in American history. Over it caravans of goods were transported, armies were marched, battles were fought and reputations made. It was the route for trappers and adventurers as well as for merchants. It gave rise to such scouts and pioneers as Kit Carson, Bent, Pfeifer, Aubrey, St. Vrain, Wootton, Maxwell and a host of others. Around it was thrown the glamour of romance and the coloring of the picturesque. It has been the prolific scene of fiction. Mayne Read, Captain Maryat, and a host of writers of lesser note, have followed the Santa Fe Trail and depicted the character and bravery of the scout, the frontiersman and hunter; and likewise the beauty and charms of the coy Mexican maiden of the Spanish frontier. It has been the source of profit, history and fiction, and the iron trail will not entirely obliterate it, or destroy its prestige. In the strides of modern civilization and advancement, the Santa Fe Railroad has become the legitimate successor of the Santa Fe Trail. It has followed it through Kansas, Colorado and New Mexico with but slight deviation. It will be the rapid and sufficient means of transportation for a growing state and an enlarged commerce. It has been demanded by modern advancement and is now a reality.

On February 9, 1880, just a few months after the Santa Fe had
tunneled through the Raton Mountains, the railroad reached Santa
Fe, the capital of the Territory, by means of a branch line from
Lamy. The welcome extended by Santa Fe to its namesake railroad
was sincere and enthusiastic. Santa Fe County had voted a bond
issue of $150,000 as a bonus to induce the railroad to build into the
capital. The proclamation urging voters to favor the bonds was
signed by many prominent citizens, with J. B. Lamy, Archbishop
of Santa Fe, heading the list. There was a procession from the plaza
to the railroad track, with the Ninth Cavalry band furnishing the
music. General Edward Hatch, commanding U. S. troops in New
Mexico, Governor Lew Wallace, Chief Justice L. Bradford Prince of
the Supreme Court, members of the Legislature, students of St.
Michael's College headed by a band, each student carrying a small
American flag, all took part in the procession. The last spike in the
rail line to Santa Fe was driven by General Hatch, assisted by Governor Wallace, Chief Justice Prince and County Commissioner A.
Staab.

With its ever ready facility for adopting memorials and resolutions,
the New Mexico Legislature took official notice of the coming of
the railroad to the Territorial capital. A Resolution was adopted
which, among other things, recited that:

> The Legislature of New Mexico observes with pleasure and satis-
> faction the completion of a line of railroad to the City of Santa Fe,
> the capital of the Territory, and the rapid extension of the same
> southward through the great valley of the Rio Grande. This event
> may well be regarded as the most important in the history of the
> Territory, and as the beginning of a new era, in which, through the
> development of its resources and the improvements which are cer-
> tain to follow the establishment of means of rapid communication
> with other parts of the country, New Mexico may be expected soon
> to take the position in the American Union to which she is justly
> entitled. In the celebration of the advent of the railroad to the
> capital, which took place on the 9th of February, 1880, participated
> in by the representatives not only of the City of Santa Fe, but of the
> whole Territory, this assembly recognizes an evidence of the good
> will and progressive tendency of the whole people with regard to
> the important improvements and changes which are now at hand.

The coming of the railroad to Raton, to Las Vegas, to Santa Fe, Albuquerque and other towns in northeastern and central New Mexico, of immense importance to those parts of the Territory, was of slight significance to southeastern New Mexico. Lincoln County alone embraced 27,000 square miles of territory, almost one-fourth of the entire area of New Mexico. Lincoln County, after the annexation of a part of Doña Ana County, under the provisions of Chapter 34 of the Laws of 1878, was nearly the size of the Texas Panhandle, slightly smaller than the State of New York, a trifle larger than the State of Massachusetts. Roughly, Lincoln County was two hundred fifty miles in length, one hundred sixty miles in width. Residents of Seven Rivers and Lookout traveled from one hundred twenty-five to one hundred fifty miles on horseback to get to the county seat in Lincoln town. Lincoln County's immensity attracted many men who longed for wide and wild open spaces. Because it was next door to Texas on two sides, many desperadoes and outlaws, driven out of that state, slipped into Lincoln County, assumed a new name, started to grow up with the country. Because of great distances, lack of roads and transportation facilities, the law enforcement of the country was inadequate.[14]

A great breeding ground for cattle, with millions of acres of public domain available to free use for grazing, Lincoln County attracted cattlemen and cowboys from many parts of the world. Mining booms in the White Oaks and Nogal districts lured men who hoped to strike it rich. Camp followers, saloonkeepers, gamblers, horse thieves, gunmen, inevitable in every new country, made for color and adventure. For twenty years, from 1870 to 1890, there was no like area

------

14. Talk in New Mexico in the seventies about "bad men" running into the Territory from Texas had considerable foundation in fact. The State of Texas officially issued in 1878 a book containing 226 pages, copies of which were sent to peace officers throughout the West, giving the name and alleged offense of 4,402 fugitives from Texas justice. According to the book, the list was not complete because "forty counties had not reported," among them some of the most populous in Texas. Rusk County wanted 282 men, Lamar, 167, Smith, 130, Panola, 128, Travis, 159. The average from 108 counties was forty. Rewards ranging from $50 to $1,000, in a total amount of $90,000, were offered for the return of 300 of the fugitives, most of them wanted for murder. Colorado, New Mexico and Mexico had been the places of refuge for most of the criminals. "The State of Texas is now rid of nearly every prominent desperado, and there are fifty per cent fewer fugitives in the State than there were two years ago," was the encouraging statement made in the preface to the book. (See Las Vegas *Gazette*, March 9, 1878.)

in the entire west which offered so much sure-fire action, in such a short time, as Lincoln County, New Mexico. Into southeastern New Mexico, made up of Lincoln County before it was dismembered and Doña Ana County before it was divided, in addition to riffraff and drifters, there came many men who were honest, able and fearless, who could think quickly, and shoot straight from the hip. These men went into southeastern New Mexico for serious purposes, invested their money and wanted to grow up with the country.

one

DOWN THE PECOS,
UP THE TULAROSA

LINCOLN COUNTY, NEW MEXICO, was named in memory of Abraham Lincoln, the Great Emancipator. Union men were in the saddle in the Territorial Legislature. New Mexico had been on the northern side in the Civil War. Historically, sentimentally, New Mexico had no ties with Abraham Lincoln. Judge Kirby Benedict of Santa Fe was one of the original "Lincoln County" men in the Territory and had a hand in drafting the bill that named the new subdivision after the martyred president. New Mexico had never been really concerned over the slavery question. Nevertheless two laws of significance and importance dealing with the question were passed by the Territorial Legislature, one in 1857 indicating that free Negroes were not welcome within the borders of New Mexico, the other, enacted in 1859, extended protection to slave ownership. Concerning free Negroes, the act of 1857 provided:

> That no free Negro nor mulatto of the African race, whether he, she or they were born free or were emancipated according to the laws now, or at any other time in force—in any State or Territory within the United States—or out of them, shall come to this Territory for the purpose of living and establishing themselves here, for a time exceeding thirty days; and if any person or persons of the aforesaid, shall attempt to establish themselves in this Territory, contrary to the provisions of this Act, such person or persons shall be the subject of indictment in the county in which he, she, or they may pretend to establish themselves, and on conviction, shall be fined in a sum of not less than fifty nor more than one hundred dollars, and moreover, shall be sentenced to hard labor in the peni-

tentiary for a term of not less than one year, nor more than two years, at the discretion of the court.

The law of 1859 provided among other things that any person convicted of unlawful killing of a slave should suffer the same penalties as if the party "upon whose person the offense was committed had been a free white person," prohibited stealing of slaves; prohibited assistance of slaves in escaping; prohibited furnishing of forged free papers, "or false evidence in print or writing of the freedom of such Negro"; prohibited the sale of fire arms, ammunition or any dagger or deadly weapon to a slave; prohibited playing cards or any game of chance or hazard with a slave; required sheriffs to pick up runaway slaves and advertise details of their detention in some public newspaper, with a provision that if the runaway should not be claimed within a period of seven months the sheriff could sell the slave at the "door of his jail or of the courthouse, to the highest bidder for cash, and shall execute to the purchaser a bill of sale for such slave, which shall vest in the purchaser a good and indefeasible title against all persons whatsoever."

Care was taken in the final paragraph of the Act to distinguish between slavery and peonage by the use of the words "this Act shall in no manner apply to relation between masters and contracted servants in this Territory, but the word 'slave' shall only apply to the African race." Belief on the part of some members of the Legislature that confusion might arise over the difference between slavery and peonage prompted the passage of an act on January 26, 1859, providing that "no court of this Territory shall have jurisdiction nor shall take any cognizance of any cause for the correction that masters may give their servants, for they are considered as domestic servants to their masters, and they should correct their neglect and faults; for as soldiers are punished by their chiefs, without the intervention of the civil authority, by reason of the salary they enjoy, an equal right should be granted those persons who pay their money to be served in the protection of their property, provided, that such correction shall not be inflicted in a cruel manner with clubs nor stripes." Under the same law, servants who ran away from their master were considered fugitives from justice, arrested and imprisoned; persons who contracted out as shepherds were obliged to serve out the time stipulated in the contract and abandonment of animals by sheepherders subjected them to liability to pay all damages suffered by the master. See Code of Laws, 1865, p. 550.[1]

---

1. The legislative acts of January 26, 1859, and February 3, 1859, dealing with slavery in New Mexico were nullified by the Congress of the United States on May 10, 1860. The Act of Congress carried the title: A BILL TO DISAPPROVE AND DECLARE NULL AND VOID ALL TERRITORIAL ACTS AND PARTS OF ACTS HERETOFORE PASSED BY THE LEGISLATIVE ASSEMBLY OF NEW MEXICO, WHICH ESTABLISH, PROTECT, OR LEGALIZE INVOLUNTARY SERVITUDE OR SLAVERY WITHIN SAID TERRITORY, EXCEPT AS PUNISHMENT FOR CRIME UPON DUE CONVICTION. The vote on the nullification was 97 for, and 90 against. All of the Republicans voted in favor of the Act with the exception of Thayer of Massachusetts, who joined with the Democrats and "South Americans" in voting against it. John A. Bingham of Ohio, of the Judiciary Committee, managed the passage of the nullification act, and made a report entitled: BILL AND REPORT OF JOHN A. BINGHAM, AND VOTE ON ITS PASSAGE, REPEALING THE TERRITORIAL NEW MEXICAN LAWS ESTABLISHING SLAVERY AND AUTHORIZING EMPLOYEES TO WHIP "WHITE PERSONS" AND OTHERS IN THEIR EMPLOYMENT, AND DENYING THEM REDRESS IN THE COURTS. Congress passed the nullifying act under authority of United States Statutes at Large, Vol. 9, p. 449, Sec. 7, providing for the organization of New Mexico by the act of September 9, 1850, which declared that "all the laws passed by the Legislative Assembly and Governor shall be submitted to the Congress of the United States, and if disapproved shall be null and void." In his report on the passage of the bill, Bingham commented that:

"Mr. Douglas made his boast in the Senate in his speech of the 16th of May, 1860, that the South had, by squatter sovereignty, gained territory to slavery in New Mexico."

The Bingham report contained an interesting sidelight on the methods used at Santa Fe to defend the slavery law, and to prevent its repeal by the Territorial Legislature. To quote Bingham:

"The following extract from a letter written by a resident of the Territory, to a member of the present House of Representatives, dated Barclay's Fort, New Mexico, April 10, 1860, will show the demon spirit of the slave driver and man stealer: 'At my solicitude, Judge Keithly (who was Speaker of the House of Representatives in the Legislature of New Mexico) introduced a bill for the repeal of the slavery law, but as he is a plain, honest, straight-forward old farmer, he took no steps to get backers amongst the other members of the Legislature, holding that the bill was certain to pass on its own merits. The introduction of the bill came like a thunder-clap on those corrupt office-holders who had procured the passage of this law, and a Santa Fean arose in his place, and moved that the bill (of repeal) be rejected at once. This motion found no favor in the House, and they proceeded to the discussion of the bill, Judge Keithly making a speech in its favor in which he was supported ably by the New Mexicans who advocated its passage. The opposition (to the repeal) having nothing to say, and dreading the result of a free discussion of the question on public opinions, the House adjourned. . . . What they despaired of effecting in the House, they determined to accomplish by outside pressure. Government officials kept open house that night. John Barleycorn did his work, and 'mint drops' were freely administered where other means failed. . . . One of the New Mexicans, who advocated the passage of the bill (for repeal) was brought over by the promise of the Speakership. The result was, that on

Lincoln County's northern boundary line was the south line of San Miguel County. Eastern boundary lines of Lincoln and Doña Ana Counties crowded up against the then Texas counties of Bailey, Cochran, Yoakum, Gaines and Andrews. The Pecos River was every-

---

entering the House the following morning, Judge Keithly was presented with a note by the Doorkeeper, informing him that the Speaker's chair was vacant, and the member above mentioned (the New Mexican) was at once installed in the chair. Judge Keithly entered a solemn protest against these summary proceedings, and defended his right to express his own opinions, and those of the people he was sent to represent, but could gain no hearing. He demanded that the proceedings in his case should be entered on the Journal of the House, but this was refused. He resigned his seat, and returned home, heartily disgusted with the leaders of the party with which he had previously acted. He now understands exactly what *National* Democracy means."

The Bingham report fastened upon Miguel Antonio Otero, Delegate in Congress from New Mexico, the responsibility for instigating the slavery laws in the first instance. Quoting Bingham:

"The following letter, from Hon. Miguel A. Otero, the Delegate in Congress of New Mexico, of date 16th December, 1858, to A. M. Jackson, shows that this slave code had its origin in Congressional, Southern, and Executive intervention:

HOUSE OF REPRESENTATIVES, D.C., *December 16, 1858.*
Hon. A. M. Jackson, Secretary of the Territory of New Mexico.

Sir: I have been requested by General R. Davis, of Mississippi, to write you a letter, requesting you to draw up an act for the protection of property in slaves in New Mexico, and cause the same to be passed by our Legislature. I know that the laws of the United States, the Constitution, and the decision of the Supreme Court in the Dred Scott case, establishes property in slaves in the Territories, but I think something should be done on the part of the Legislature to protect it. You will perceive at once the advantages that will result from the passage of such a law in our Territory, and I expect you will take good care to procure its passage. Immediately after its passage, you will dispatch copies to all the principal newspapers in the Southern States for publication, and also a copy to the New York Herald "very quick." Very respectfully, your obedient servant.

Mig. Ant'o Otero."

That the laws enacted by the Legislature had vicious provisions was contended by Bingham in the following words:

"The white slave code of New Mexico, it will be seen, subjects and authorizes all white laboring men and women to be whipped by their employers, and denies them any redress for such outrages in courts of justice. The black slave code allows any person to arrest any one whom he calls an absconding slave, by force, and without legal process from any court or magistrate, and to deliver such person so arrested to the sheriff of the county in which the arrest may be made, which sheriff shall imprison such person for six months (without a commitment), and advertise for a master, and if no master come, shall imprison six months longer, and advertise for sale; and at the end of twelve months imprisonment, the sheriff shall sell such person, at the door of the jail or courthouse, to the highest bidder, for cash, and his bill of sale 'shall vest in the purchaser a good and indefeasible title against all persons whatever,' not excepting the sold man's right to himself!"

thing to Lincoln County, but not of such great importance to Doña Ana County which had its Rio Grande, with many settlements along its course including Fort Selden, Robledo, Picacho, Doña Ana, Las Cruces, Mesilla, Fort Fillmore and Amoles. On territorial maps of the period the entire country east of the Pecos River in Lincoln and Doña Ana Counties was marked off as "Staked Plains."

Section 9 of the 1869 act creating Lincoln County provided that the town of Rio Bonito should be the county seat. On December 20, 1869, the Legislature passed and approved an act providing that "the name and style of the county seat of Lincoln County is hereby changed to Lincoln in place of Rio Bonito, which was heretofore established by law." The town of Rio Bonito, now Lincoln, was ten miles from Fort Stanton, an army post, burned and sacked in 1862 when Baylor was in New Mexico with his Texans.

From the Rio Grande country, travelers went into Lincoln County through San Augustin Pass if starting from Mesilla or Las Cruces; through Mockingbird Gap and Lava Gap if starting from country near Socorro. From Texas most of the travelers followed the Pecos River, up stream or down. An ordinary journey by horse and buggy from Santa Fe to Lincoln plaza required five days of traveling. As late as August 25, 1892, Judge Charles Blanchard made a trip in a single rig from Las Vegas to White Oaks, a distance of 182 miles, in fifty-six hours, establishing a record for fast travel.

In the seventies and early eighties, the town of Las Vegas in San Miguel County was the hub of all commerce and business for southeastern New Mexico. Beginning in the summer of 1874 a tri-weekly stagecoach, carrying mail, passengers and express, operated from Las Vegas into Lincoln town and return. Passengers spent nearly a week on the journey, but the trips were made safely and fairly comfortably, with stops every few hours to rest the passengers and change horses. From Las Vegas the coaches followed the Gallinas River down to its junction with the Pecos. The first stop was at the Hays Ranch at Apache Springs, another stop was at Anton Chico, an important village surrounded by farms and orchards. The valley between Anton Chico and Puerto de Luna was narrow and irrigation from the Pecos was difficult; consequently there was no great development of the land in that area. Puerto de Luna was one of the most attractive stops on the route. The village nestled in a pleasantly situated valley, which at times gave the illusion of a half moon.

From Puerto de Luna the stagecoach drivers cut across a rough country of rolling prairie intersected by several creeks, including the José de Dios, Cañon Colorado and Alamo Gordo. John Gerhardt's Ranch, with its pretty garden, orchard, and ample spring water, was a popular stop with the passengers. The stages always stopped for a meal at Milnor Rudolph's house at Sunnyside, and then at nearby Fort Sumner. Passengers saw a broad plain near Fort Sumner covered with grama grass in season, sloping gently away to the east from the Pecos River. Many buildings at Fort Sumner were still standing and in good condition in the seventies, a reminder of the attempts the federal government had made to subdue the Navajo Indians and their kinsmen. Above the old army post, for a distance of four miles, there were two rows of cottonwood trees, already in the seventies, of substantial size. There were evidences remaining of the attempts the army had made to teach the Indians to plow, plant and cultivate the soil. The remnants of the earthen dam, built by the Indians under supervision of the army to impound the waters of the Pecos at a place called Alamo Gordo, were plainly visible from the stagecoach.

From Fort Sumner to Bosque Grande, the early day traveler saw the Pecos Valley widen out until at times it reached three miles in width. The grama grass, in good years, attained a growth of three feet. Some miles out of Bosque Grande, the stagecoach horses forded Salt Creek, with headwaters in the Capitan Mountains, flowing directly into the Pecos. Good-sized lakes were soon encountered, covered in season with hundreds of water fowl. Roswell was the important stagecoach stop after leaving Fort Sumner. Here, for the first time the passengers got a glimpse of the Spring River country with water seemingly flowing from all directions. Passengers were told that the Hondo, North and South Antelopes, North and South Spring Rivers all flowed through the Hondo into the Pecos; that there were an estimated 160,000 acres of land, most of it public domain, open to homestead entry, in the Roswell area and that some day, irrigated by waters of the Pecos River, the land would be valuable. Passengers for the most part shook their heads, resumed their journeys to Lincoln, to White Oaks, to Fort Stanton, Tularosa and other more important places. If a directory of Roswell had been published in 1880 giving the names of the men who were settled in and around the country about the stage station, it would have contained the names, among others, of John S. Chisum, A. J. Ballard, Henry R.

Hudson, Captain Sansom, Mrs. Spencer, A. K. Dale, W. H. Miller,
Wm. L. Holloman, James Haptom, Harton Corn, S. A. Johnson,
A. B. Lyle, G. Lackey, M. A. Upson, B. Dickerson, C. C. Larimore,
Mrs. Henly, Judge E. S. Stone, O. Bell, P. F. Garrett and Captain
J. C. Lea.*

---

* Since the town was founded, Captain Joseph Calloway Lea has been recognized
as the "Father of Roswell" and the "founder" of the New Mexico Military Institute,
established in Roswell by Act of The Legislature on February 23, 1893. Born in Cleveland, Tennessee, November 8, 1841, the son of Dr. and Mrs. Pleasant J. G. Lea, Captain Lea died of pneumonia in Roswell, February 4, 1904. The Leas moved in 1849
from Tennessee to Lea's Summit, a place named in honor of Dr. Lea near Independence, Missouri. At the outbreak of the Civil War in 1861, Joseph C. Lea enlisted in
the Confederate Army and was assigned to the Sixth Missouri Regiment, in a part of
Shelby's Brigade. Entering the army as a farmer boy without any military training,
young Lea became a colonel in the third year of his service. He had made his reputation
as a Captain, however, and was known by that title throughout the rest of his life.
Lea was married to Miss Sally Wildey, daughter of Major W. W. Wildey of Satartia,
Mississippi, in 1875, and came to New Mexico with his bride in 1876, residing for a
year in Elizabethtown and other places in Colfax County and arriving in Roswell in
1877. Two children were born to Captain Lea and Sally Wildey Lea, a son, Harry
Wildey Lea, and a daughter, Ella, the first child of Anglo parentage born in what is now
the City of Roswell. Ella was married to Hiram M. Dow, a Roswell attorney, in 1913.
She died in 1962. Sally Wildey Lea's two brothers, Ernest and John Wildey, came to
New Mexico. Ernest settled in Roswell and John established a ranch in the Tularosa
Basin with headquarters at a place which became known as "Wildey's Well" where
the famous gunfight took place in 1898 between Oliver Lee and Jim Gililland on one
side and Pat Garrett and his deputies on the other.

Throughout the Lincoln County War Captain Lea maintained a position of strict
neutrality, although he held close friendships among leading participants of both sides.
Elected from Lincoln County, Captain Lea was a member of the Lower House in the
Territorial Legislature, Session of 1889. He was largely responsible for the enactment
of the law creating Chaves County by the 1889 Legislature and gave the new county
its name in honor of his close friend, Col. J. Francisco Chaves, who had fought on the
Union side in the Civil War and who was then Speaker of the Lower House of the
Legislature. Maj. W. H. H. Llewellyn of Dona Ana County, a member of the 1889
Legislature, became Speaker of the House of Representatives in 1917 and took an active
part in the creation of Lea County in order to honor Captain Lea by giving the new
County his name.

After the adjournment of the 1917 session of the Legislature, Major Llewellyn wrote
Mrs. Ella Lea Dow, Captain Lea's daughter, telling her that Sim Eaves and others from
Lovington had presented to the House a bill to create a new county with Lovington,
a small town at the time in Chaves County, as the county seat. The Eaves Bill provided
that "Llano" would be the name of the new county, after Llano Estacado, Spanish for
"Staked Plains." Llewellyn argued in a committee hearing on the bill that nobody
would be able to pronounce the name provided for the new county, much less spell
it correctly. By way of compromise Llewellyn promised to get the bill passed if its
sponsors would agree to name the county in honor of his old-time friend, the late
Capt. J. C. Lea. Major Llewellyn recalled that in the 1899 Legislature Captain Lea had

From Roswell to Lincoln Plaza, the stagecoaches followed along the Rio Hondo for almost the entire distance. The first stop was at the ranch of August Kline, a German farmer, forty-six miles from the nearest postoffice. The Rio Hondo forked ten miles east of Lincoln Plaza. The traveler could take his choice. The south fork went into the Ruidoso country. The north fork went into Lincoln. Old-timers called the south fork the "Rio Doso" and the north fork, "Rio Bonito."

The town of Lincoln, on the Bonito, was the county seat of Lincoln County. Originally the settlement had been called "Las Placitas," the Spanish diminutive of Plaza, or "Little Town." Later it was known as Rio Bonito, the Spanish for "Pretty River."

Lincoln County experienced a gold rush in the late seventies, which for some years threatened to overshadow the already important cattle industry in southeastern New Mexico. John J. Baxter, a happy-go-lucky prospector from Missouri, arrived in the county in 1878 with a couple of burros, a miner's pick, shovel, a few tin pans and a bit of acid for assaying. He made camp in a clump of white oak trees near a spring of water. Baxter used his pick and shovel so effectively that he discovered gold. The mountain in which the discovery had been made and the gulch leading up to it were soon known as Baxter's Mountain and Baxter's Gulch, and the camp quickly became White Oaks. Baxter was satisfied with a return of a few hundred dollars in gold, left the country, drifted down toward Silver City, where he was shot and wounded in an Indian raid on the Gila in 1885. He returned to White Oaks in the late eighties, found it a riproaring mining camp, the claim on which he had filed and then abandoned, an important property. Baxter's strike was the beginning of a trek of prospectors and miners to the White Oaks camp from all parts of the country. On August 14, 1879, Tom Wilson "struck it rich" in gold on the Homestake claim. Jack Winters, a Wilson partner, to celebrate the Homestake strike, bought a wagon load of whiskey, passed around tin cups, invited everybody to "help himself," and the whole town of White Oaks got drunk. "Uncle Jack" Winters did not live long to enjoy the thrill that came to him as co-owner

---

resisted all persuasion on the part of his friends to permit the naming of Chaves County in his honor. The Lovington people readily agreed. The Bill passed both houses of the Legislature and became law.

Captain Joseph C. Lea, founder of the City of Roswell and of
the New Mexico Military Institute, in whose honor Lea County
was named by the New Mexico Legislature of 1917.

of an important mining claim. He died in White Oaks on January 21, 1881, and his body was buried in the little burial ground about a mile south of the camp. Relatives in West Virginia learned that "Uncle Jack" had struck it rich in White Oaks. Soon after he had passed into eternity, they sorrowfully undertook to establish their heirship and ownership in the Homestake mine.

This afforded lawyers the opportunity to do prospecting on their own. Reluctantly they filed suits and asked for injunctions. Other lawyers were required for the defense, to oppose motions and argue demurrers. Lawsuit begot lawsuit in the little mining camp. For a time the future prospects of the gold mining ventures were so blighted by litigation and threats of litigation, that the miners and prospectors threatened to hang a few lawyers to the nearest tree. The litigation finally developed into two principal cases. One case, involving the validity of the claim to the Baxter property, was that of *Baxter Gold Mining Co. vs. Patterson*, 3 N.M. (Johnson) 179, 3 Pac. 741, decided on May 3, 1884. The Baxter Company lawyers were Beall, Chandler, Hough and W. T. Thornton; William Burr Childers was counsel for Patterson. Attorney Hough was Emerson Hough, later to forsake law for literature and to become a noted novelist. The other case was the famous case of *Brunswick v. Winters' Heirs*, 3 N.M. 241, 5 Pac. 706, involving ownership of seven hundred fifty feet of the Homestake gold mine, in which Harvey Butler Fergusson represented West Virginia heirs of "Uncle Jack" Winters and prevailed in the litigation.[2]

---

2. Harvey Butler Fergusson was born in Alabama, September 8, 1848, son of a wealthy plantation and slave owner, who served as a captain in the Confederate army during the Civil War. His fortune gone with the war, Captain Fergusson gave his son Harvey one hundred dollars in money, a gold watch and urged him to seek an education. Harvey Fergusson walked from Birmingham, Alabama, to Lexington, Virginia, enrolled in the Washington College, while General Robert E. Lee was president of that institution, later to become Washington & Lee University. Harvey Fergusson taught Greek to help pay his expenses, received degrees of Bachelor of Arts and of Law and Master of Arts. He practiced law in West Virginia, came to New Mexico in 1882 to represent the Winter heirs in the Homestake litigation at White Oaks. He remained a citizen of New Mexico until his death in Albuquerque, June 10, 1915. An outstanding lawyer, an orator of the William Jennings Bryan school, Fergusson was elected to the 55th, 62nd and 65th Congresses. He was a political leader in the Democratic party in New Mexico for decades. Serving his first term as congressman, Fergusson pushed through Congress legislation known as the Fergusson Act, which gave millions of acres of public domain to New Mexico for common school purposes. While waiting for the Winters case to come to trial in Lincoln County, Harvey B. Fergusson set up a checker-

The Baxter strike in Baxter Gulch and the Homestake strike were followed by the discovery of rich ore in the "Old Abe" at White Oaks, and the camp soon became nationally known. The "Old Abe" became a famous mine. Considerable money was spent developing it into a property and it paid fabulous dividends to its owners for many years. The gold rush to White Oaks produced speculation in real estate. A townsite was laid out; corner lots commanded fancy prices. First shacks, and then better buildings, housed the saloons

---

board in the postoffice, played checkers with all comers, got acquainted with men who later served on juries, made political friends and alliances. In the famous case of the *Territory of New Mexico vs. Oliver Lee*, which was tried in Sierra County in the late nineties, Harvey B. Fergusson was associated with Albert Bacon Fall and Harry M. Dougherty for the defense. Inheriting from their father Harvey B. Fergusson, a talent in the use of words and from their mother Clara Huning Fergusson (whose father, Franz Huning, came to New Mexico from Germany in 1849) traits of industry and application, Erna Fergusson, Harvey B. Fergusson, Jr., and Francis Fergusson, "the writing Fergussons," all born and reared in Albuquerque, have achieved eminence in literary work.

Erna Fergusson, presently working on a book for the University of New Mexico Press on the life and political career of the late Clyde Tingley, twice Governor of New Mexico, has written many books, among them *Dancing Gods*, 1931; *Fiesta in Mexico*, 1934; *Guatemala*, 1937; *Venezuela*, 1939; *Our Southwest*, 1940; *Our Hawaii*, 1942; *Chile*, 1943; *Cuba*, 1946; *Albuquerque*, 1947; *Murder and Mystery in New Mexico*, 1948, and *Mexico Revisited*, 1955.

Harvey Fergusson served his apprenticeship on the Washington political scene many years ago as writer and editor for the Haskin Syndicate and later worked in motion pictures in Hollywood. His best known books: *The Blood of the Conquerors*, 1921; *Capitol Hill*, 1923; *Women and Wives*, 1924; *Hot Saturday*, 1926; *Wolf Song*, 1927; *In Those Days*, 1928; *Footloose McGonigal*, 1930; *Rio Grande*, 1933; *Modern Man— His Belief and Behavior*, 1936; *The Life of Riley*, 1937; *Home in the West*, 1945; *Grant of Kingdom*, 1950, and *The Conquest of Don Pedro*, 1954.

Francis Fergusson, the youngest of the Fergusson family, is a noted literary critic and authority on the drama. Educated at Harvard and Oxford, Francis has taught drama and humanities at Bennington College, Princeton and Rutgers. Important among his books: *The Idea of a Theatre*, 1949; *Plays of Moliere, Critical Introduction*, 1950; *Dante's Dream of the Mind*, 1953, and *The Human Image*, 1957. In 1962 Francis Fergusson was elected to membership in the National Institute of Arts and Letters. Attainment of membership in the Institute, limited to 250, is generally conceded to be the highest honor to be achieved in arts and letters in the United States of America.

Mrs. Lina Fergusson Browne of Berkeley, California, will soon be aligned as an author with her sister, Erna, and brothers, Harvey and Francis. Mrs. Browne is presently preparing for publication a manuscript on the life of J. Ross Browne, author of *Adventures in the Apache Country* and many other books on the Southwest. Mrs. Browne's book will be based on diaries, notes and correspondence assembled and edited over the years by her late husband, C. Spencer Browne, grandson of J. Ross Browne.

and business establishments, offices of doctors and lawyers. The Pioneer saloon, on the ground in the early days of the camp, sold three different grades of whiskey at different prices out of the same barrel, depending on which brand the customer called for, and as he always called for the same brand, there never was any complaint. Soon, however, the Pioneer had a competitor in business when Henry J. Patterson started the "Star" saloon. "Starr's Opera House" was built and the miners declared a holiday when the "Mitchell Dramatic Troupe" offered the opening performance. The manager and leading actors played roulette after the play and lost, and the actors and actresses were stranded for want of funds to get them out of town.[3]

When Col. D. J. M. A. Jewett arrived in White Oaks on July 20, 1880, he discovered that everybody in town "was a millionaire, but nobody had any money." J. Howe Watts, who arrived in White Oaks in 1879, was named town surveyor. A. G. Lane started a drugstore. Hewitt and Watson opened a law office. During the summer of 1880, while the camp was still recovering from the effects of the gold strikes, someone started a "carborate" excitement on the Carrizozo flats. From end to end the plain was plastered with mining locations and prospect holes, with Ike Smith, William Rexford and Jones Talia-ferro in the vanguard of the prospectors. According to Col. Jewett, "the association of which Billy the Kid was the honored head" had several representatives in town, and fears of what Billy might do

---

3. The site of White Oaks, the new mining camp, was described in the Las Vegas *Gazette* of March 28, 1880:

"To begin with, no more beautiful place for the future county seat of Lincoln County (White Oaks City), could have been selected, even if we had all New Mexico to choose from. Imagine a valley level as a billiard table, containing about one thousand acres available for building purposes, surrounded on all sides by hills, "rock ribbed and ancient as the sun," covered with stately pines, and its more lively sister, the piñon, the plain itself entirely free from timber or undergrowth and then perhaps you can understand why we think ourselves so favored by mother nature, in that respect at least. On the west side of the valley, Baxter Mountain, in which is situated the Home-stake and other lodes destined to become equally as famous, rises abruptly to an altitude of some fifteen hundred feet, while in a more northerly direction, the Lone Mountain is seen, standing in isolated grandeur, as if impressed with a sense of its own importance, caused no doubt by a knowledge of the hidden treasures it holds within its grasp. On the south the Carrizozo Mountain, covered with its mantle of never failing green, looks down upon its lesser sisters, and take it all in all, a fairer picture would be hard to find. Already the cabins of the miners dot the plain, and soon, beyond a doubt, the village of White Oaks will become White Oaks City, in fact as well as in name."

White Oaks, once a thriving mining camp, now a ghost town, as it appeared in the 1890's.

tended to excite the citizens from time to time. Adna Lampson was the first postmaster at White Oaks. A daily mail route was secured from Socorro to Fort Stanton via White Oaks and the first trip was made on October 15, 1880. With a daily mail, White Oaks needed a newspaper and *The Golden Era* was established, with J. H. Wise as the first manager. The *Era's* first number was printed on December 18, 1880. During the gold rush in 1880, prices of commodities soared in White Oaks. Flour sold at six dollars a hundred; tea from a dollar to a dollar and a half a pound; sugar, twenty cents; butter, fifty cents a pound; canned corn and tomatoes, twenty cents a can; canned apricots and peaches, sixty cents a can. Drinking water sold for forty cents a barrel. Most of the supplies for the camp were hauled by mule team from Las Vegas.

By the time White Oaks was ten years old, it was a place of history and traditions. Major William Caffrey, publisher of the *Lincoln County Leader*, rounded up some of the old-timers and persuaded them to write their recollections of the early days of the camp. Jud Beard on November 16, 1889, wrote his recollections:

> I will now endeavor to fulfill my promise. What brought many others to Lincoln County also attracted me. I first landed at the Jicarillas in June 1877, with a team and wagon and three partners, expecting ere the snows of '77 would fall that I would have a wagon load of gold, and be on my homeward journey rejoicing. But my feet were tender and the snows of '89 have now fallen and my wagon is still unloaded and my partners, where are they? I went to the Jicarillas when the Ginn & Taylor dry washers were having their boom and many a poor devil came down from Colorado to soon leave in disgust, not with the country, but with the gold saving machine. I first gazed on the beauties of White Oaks July 4, 1877. From there I went to Stanton, and was at Nogal Gulch, White Mountain, Rio Bonito, and finally went to work in Baxter Gulch. We would carry water from the springs in our kegs on ponies to the Gulch and rock out 2, 3 and sometimes 4 dollars a day. Those were happy days for mountaineers—good feed for our ponies, deer, turkey and bear at our door, plenty of gold in our claims, lashens of flour, tobacco and whiskey at Stanton, plenty of gold dust to buy it with; and what more does a miner want? . . . Let us move along to '79, when the rich Homestakes were first discovered. At this time all hands had moved to Baxter Gulch and our little band had re-

cruited several. Jack Winters, Charley Starr, Dick McGinnis, George Gaines and George Gay. Lo, and behold, in a few days, the Homestake was discovered, Jack Winters bought out a lot of the interests of the others, and in a few months there was talk of a town. White Oaks Valley, like the center of gravity, began to attract from all sides, and in the spring of '80, here they came. Soon the valley was swarming with men looking for hidden treasure. '80 was a busy year in White Oaks, and a wilder, more harumscarum set of mortals never mingled together. What with the Indian scares and six shooters popping in the air of evenings, one would be led to imagine that the town was surrounded by Indians and scalps felt loose . . . where only ten years ago antelope grazed in what are now homeplaces of a busy people.

Charles Metcalf, then living in Las Cruces, writing under date of October 16, 1889, told his story as follows:

I came into the White Oaks and put in my tenderfoot days there because in Las Vegas I saw a few chunks of Homestake gold ore, which I was told was found in "any of the gulches around White Oaks." The stage coach which brought me down unloaded us at Whiteman's corral on June 11, 1880. The next morning our party started out for Tortolita Canyon, lured on by the "rich strikes," which are always in the next camp. Many weary days did I spend climbing over the rough mountains surrounding the Tortolita country. John George and Joe Stoneking were camped not far from us, and our nearest neighbors were occupying the old sheep ranch at the mouth of the canyon. They were a select party, engaged in various occupations, principally horse stealing. The most prominent member of the crowd was "Billy the Kid," while O'Falliard and Rudebaugh, Wilson, and nearly a dozen others were lesser lights, but none the less adept at "borrowing horses." . . . I am quite glad I saw the Homestake mines in their infancy; that I saw the first coal prospect, a hole not knee deep; that I set the first stick of type ever set in the great county of Lincoln in the office of THE GOLDEN ERA, and the old timers will always be pleasantly remembered by me."

On October 19, 1889, S. J. Woodland wrote:

You want me to give you some of White Oaks' first history. I will tell you some of it except dates. I came to what is known as White Oaks in the fall of 1879, in company with Wm. H. Hudgens and a bottle of whiskey. We found camped there James Allen, his son, Harry, and old Livingtone. We visited the now famous Baxter Gulch and found imbedded in the side of a hill Chas. Starr, Geo. Gaines, Geo. Gay, Tom Walters, Dick McGinness and Jack Winters, better known as "old blue skin." There was very little work done there at that time.

In the spring of '80, Mr. Hudgens and myself put up a saloon on the flat where White Oaks now stands. We stocked it with Dowlin and De Laney's tanglefoot and pure Havana cigars imported from Arkansas in the same box with the late Charley Ross, and I tell you we did a rushing trade. But the town commenced to grow and we concluded to build the old Pioneer saloon. Then came James, the merchant, Jim Sweet also came and played poker with the boys, and many more too trifling to talk about. About that time we made arrangements to have the mail forwarded from Lincoln and Stanton to the Pioneer saloon and there, if we were sober enough, people got their mail. . . . Now, old man, I've told you all I was concerned in, with the exception of a few killings.

Loyalty to White Oaks was a dominant characteristic among the people who had settled in that place when it was a struggling mining camp and who had remained there, through thick and thin, until hopes for the future of the town had grown dim and they were obliged to seek their futures elsewhere. A surprising number of White Oaks settlers remained in Lincoln County, however, and were still proud to be called former residents of the camp. As of 1900, of the pioneers who had settled in White Oaks in 1880, the following citizens of Lincoln County would have answered "here" to the roll call: J. B. Collier, E. T. Collier, M. G. Paden, A. Ridgeway, J. R. Brent, Wm. Watson, W. C. McDonald, Jas. Woodland, Wm. F. Blanchard, D. J. M. A. Jewett, Jerry Hockradle, Geo. E. Slight, Ed. B. Homan, Jones Taliaferro, B. F. Gumm, Chas. Bull, E. W. Parker, M. H. Bellomy, John Y. Hewitt, J. H. Rudiselle, U. Ozanne, A. G. Lane, Wm. Lane, Samuel Wells, J. P. C. Langston, Ed. S. Comery, Jake Miller, Mrs. Brothers, Mrs. Kestler, J. C. Klepinger, W. S. Ross, F. Spilcke, G. W. Prichard, Fred Mayer, P. Donovan, John Walters, J. O. Mabours, Mrs. Allen, Jay Allen, Harry Allen, Newt Allen, Wm. Henley, Thos. W. Henley, Jos. Stut, Samuel Beard, Gus Collier, T. Lalone, Mrs. Barber, J. H. Leighmor, A. M. Richardson, Mrs. Hudgins, Richard Cavanaugh.

Travelers from Las Cruces and Mesilla into Lincoln plaza in the seventies and eighties passed through the Tularosa and Mescalero country, beautiful, picturesque, attractive in every season of the year. Romance and adventure lurked in the high hills. The soil of the valleys, irrigated by waters from streams frequently subject to difficulty and litigation, produced fruit and vegetables that found a ready market throughout the whole country. Wayfarers from the lower Rio Grande came into the Tularosa country on horseback, in stage coaches, army ambulances, buckboards. Most of them passed through San Augustin Pass, flanked by projecting crags that gave the impression of the pipes of a gigantic organ.

P. Coghlan and Goldenberg Brothers were the principal merchants at Tularosa in the early days. They carried large stocks of merchandise and did a thriving business. A traveler leaving Tularosa for Lincoln followed a winding road for twenty miles up Tularosa Canyon, which divided the Sacramento and White Mountains. Cultivated fields greeted the eye for the entire distance. Col. W. L. Rynerson and John H. Riley owned a large cattle ranch above Tularosa. Further in the country there were pretentious places owned by Dave Easton, Andy Wilson, A. Loomis and others. Twelve miles from Tularosa wayfarers passed from Doña Ana County into Lincoln County and were soon close to the reservation where Mescalero and Jicarilla Apaches were confined.[4] A signboard warned all persons

---

4. The Mescaleros received their name from the extensive use of mescal, or century plant, for food and dwelt principally in the southeastern part of the Territory of New Mexico, west of the Pecos and east of the Rio Grande; and the Jicarillas, or little baskets, received their name from the small wicker vessels made by the women of the tribe. They were found generally in the mountains north of Taos, roamed over the Maxwell Land Grant and were closely affiliated with the southern Utes. The Mescalero and Jicarilla Indians were true Apaches, two tribes of the original nine Apache tribal divisions. The word mescal is a modernization of the Spanish word mezcal, used to identify a species of maguey or American agave, and also to describe an intoxicating liquor distilled from the plant. The Jicarilla Indians had commingled for a time with the Mescaleros on the reservation near Fort Stanton, but were finally removed to the northern part of New Mexico near present Dulce. The Jicarillas had been taken to the Mescalero reservation in 1884. The Mescalero reservation in 1895 contained in excess of 86,000 acres. In Lincoln County there were 56,160 acres of the reservation and in Dona Ana County, 30,000 acres. In the early eighties there were about twenty-five men of the old Victorio band living with the Mescaleros, with whom they intermarried. For years, the Apaches, whether identified as Chiricahuas, Gilenas, Mimbrenos, Mescaleros, Jicarillas, Pinalenes, Coyoteros, Mogollons, Tontos, or otherwise, kept the U.S. Army busy in New Mexico and Arizona.

of the penalties for trespassing. Just before reaching the Mescalero
Agency headquarters, the traveler on the Tularosa passed a collec-
tion of houses known as South Fork, or Blazer's Mills. For years
the grain of the surrounding country had been ground into flour at
Blazer's and an old time sawmill furnished the lumber wants of the
people for many miles around. It was here that the "Buckshot"
Roberts incident occurred during the Lincoln County War. Lew
Wallace, governor of the Territory, spent weeks at a time at the
Blazer homestead and wrote chapters of *Ben Hur*, while waiting his
turn to testify before a military court at Fort Stanton.

For many years the Mescaleros had been rather docile. Slowly the
federal government was converting their thoughts toward abandonment of the war club and rifle for the hoe, the scalping knife for the
branding iron. During the year 1885, the Mescalero reservation Indians had eight hundred acres of land in cultivation and had herds
of fat cattle grazing in the hills. Through the encouragement of their
then government agent, Maj. W. H. H. Llewellyn, the Mescaleros
had joined the Lincoln County Livestock Association and were beginning to acknowledge the benefits that accrued from mutual protective measures adopted by many cattlemen of the county. In place
of the scattered jacals[5] that had made up the reservation a few years
before, the government had a number of substantial dwellings for
the Mescaleros and the children were being taught to read and write
before being sent off to Albuquerque and to Carlisle, Pennsylvania,
for higher education.

Leaving the Mescalero Agency, the highway wound around the
foothills of the White Mountains for more than thirty miles, passing
through a well timbered country where pine and spruce predom-
inated. Blanco Peak, one of the highest mountains in the Territory
and a landmark in the region, was seldom free from snow. The
Ruidoso, Eagle and Bonito, whose waters came from the higher
regions of the mountains, were forded before the traveler reached
Lincoln. These streams offered trout fishing in the early days to
those who knew or cared about that pastime. These three streams
provided water for livestock and irrigation waters for many small
farms adjacent to their banks. At the crossing of the Ruidoso, there
was a place called Dowlin's Mills, a familiar name throughout the

---

5. A Spanish word for Indian hut or wigwam.

entire country. The name of the postoffice at Dowlin's Mills was Ruidoso.[6] Frank Lesnet was the postmaster there in 1885. Besides the mills at Dowlin's, there were a store and a blacksmith shop, but the postoffice was the magnet that drew people there from all parts of the surrounding country. Reaching the Rio Bonito, the traveler followed that idyllic stream for a dozen miles, passing Fort Stanton, beautifully situated, which in the eighties had five companies of cavalry. Below the military reservation, the valley was thickly settled with Spanish American families. A few miles from the Fort was Lincoln, the then county seat, pleasantly placed in a rather sleepy hollow, with one long straggling street containing all the business houses and nearly all the residences, offering little outward evidence of the fact that on occasion it received nationwide attention because it attracted men who were anything but pusilanimous.

Major William Henry Harrison Llewellyn, the Indian agent at Mescalero, who was later to move to Las Cruces and live a stormy political life, was no namby-pamby guardian of the affairs of his red-skin charges.[7] Fond of printer's ink, the Major had the good sense to drop into an editorial office from time to time and pass the time of day with the man who published the paper. Because of alleged political activities, it appeared in 1885 that Major Llewellyn might be relieved as Indian Agent. He was accused of taking sides in the Tularosa water rights squabbles and permitting some of the brethren friendly to his side to graze a few hundred head of cattle on the reservation from time to time without the formality of valuable consideration moving to the Indians. Major Llewellyn made a hurried trip to Albuquerque and the *Journal* of that town said in an editorial:

> Major Llewellyn has the reputation of being one of the most capable Indian agents in the west. He certainly exerts an extra-

---

6. *Ruidoso* is a Spanish word for noisy, clamorous, obstreperous.

7. William Henry Harrison Llewellyn was born in Minnesota, died at Beaumont Hospital in El Paso, Texas, on June 11, 1927. After serving as Indian agent on the Mescalero reservation, he practiced law at Las Cruces, New Mexico, and was repeatedly elected to the Legislature. He was Speaker of the House for one term and was a member of the Constitutional Convention in 1912. Llewellyn helped recruit Troop G of the Rough Riders and participated in the battle of San Juan Hill. During the Spanish-American War he formed a friendship with Theodore Roosevelt, which continued when Roosevelt became President of the United States and for years afterward.

ordinary influence over his savage warriors . . . he has many advantages over theorists . . . he is right on the ground . . . and has a solution of the Indian problem . . . it would draw the fangs of the Redmen without impairing his capacity for development in the right direction . . . that remedy is simply to disarm the savages and make it an
offense involving imprisonment for twenty-five years for anyone to
sell an Indian firearms or ammunition. . . . They cannot do harm
without ammunition. . . . Major Llewellyn certainly has earned a
prolongation of his office by his wise and timely suggestion.

Notwithstanding his efforts, Major Llewellyn was obliged to resign
the Mescalero Agency and was succeeded by Col. Hinman Rhodes,
father of Eugene Manlove Rhodes. The Kansas City *Journal* of August 20, 1885, expressed regret, saying among other things:

Agent W. H. H. Llewellyn, of the Mescalero Apaches, has resigned, or gotten out of the way as an offensive partisan. Just what
Mr. Llewellyn's Republicanism should have to do with his management of the Apaches, we cannot understand, but he has been a
marked man ever since the present administration came in. . . .
Llewellyn is a cool, determined and most courageous man, and has
had a remarkable career. For a long time he was employed in the
secret service of the United States, with headquarters at Omaha, and
while there won much renown for breaking up the Doc Middleton
gang of horse thieves who stole cattle through Western Nebraska,
Wyoming and adjoining states. The account of the extremity to
which Llewellyn went, jeopardizing and risking his life in his efforts
to break up this murderous gang of desperadoes is one of the most
thrilling stories ever written of frontier life.

Commenting on Llewellyn's resignation, the *Golden Era* of White
Oaks said that "it would be extremely hypocritical for the settlers
here to pretend sorrow over Llewellyn's departure."
Travelers to New Mexico from Mexico and Texas in colonial days
and for many years after the American Occupation followed the road
along the Rio Grande from near present El Paso to old Doña Ana.
Here casks were filled with water for man and beast and caravans
left the Rio Grande and struck out on a trail menaced by Apache
Indians and cursed by lack of water. The name of Jornada del Muerto, "Journey of the Dead," was given to this road as it drew away

from Doña Ana and extended over country adjacent to the San Diego, Caballo and Fra Cristobal Mountains. The dangers lurking on this road were widely known and greatly feared.

On February 3, 1854, only a few years after the American Occupation, the Legislature of New Mexico took official notice of the terrifying conditions that existed on the Jornada and a memorial was adopted on that date, addressed to the Congress of the United States, reciting:

> We would respectfully represent, that the Jornada between Fra Cristoval and Robledo, is ninety miles without water, and the only route of communication between the capital of this Territory and Texas or Mexico—that it is the mail route, and the only source of communication between the Headquarters of the 9th Military Department and the military in southern military posts, and has been the cause of great loss of human life, and stock, both to the inhabitants of the Territory and the government of the United States.
>
> We therefore ask that an appropriation may be made by your Honorable Body to establish at least three artesian wells on said Jornada del Muerto. We respectfully ask the attention of Congress to this subject.

Sixteen years after the Memorial of 1854, the water problem was on its way to a solution. Jack Martin, who had been a lieutenant in a California company at the post at Dead Man's Spring, Fort Mc-Rae, produced water on the Jornada. Martin started drilling for water at Aleman in 1868 and, after twenty-six months' work, found it at two hundred feet.[8] A part of the story was told in the Las Vegas *Gazette* on December 4, 1874, through correspondence from Mesilla dated November 28, 1874:

> Jornada del Muerto is the name given to a cheerless journey of ninety miles by the Spanish explorers. Formerly the distance across this plain from water to water was so great, that the unsuspecting emigrant, or unwary traveler, often suffered extreme torture, or perished from thirst on the journey, should he even escape the attacks of hostile Indians. The Jornada, however, is not a sandy, or

8. Las Vegas *Gazette*, April 19, 1873.

barren desert, but a high, rolling prairie, covered with an excellent growth of grama grass on which hundreds of tons of hay are cut each year. The plain is about 40 miles wide. Jack Martin, now styled Jornada Chief, dug a well near the center of this plain, finding abundant, good water. He went to bed one night with the pleasing reflection that all his money and credit had been sunk in a dry well 200 feet deep, and awoke next morning to find in it 100 feet of water, and his fortune assured. Two other wells are being dug, one twenty miles east of the first, by Mr. Martin, and the other by Mr. Lea. Both have reached the depth of between 150 and 200 feet. South of the Jornada is a wide and beautiful valley known as the Mesilla.

As a reward for Jack Martin's enterprise in development of water on the Jornada, the Legislature of New Mexico passed an act on February 3, 1869 (Chap. 15, "Local and Special Laws, New Mexico, 1884") providing "That John Martin is hereby exempted from the payment of any territorial or county tax for the carrying on of any business in the 'Aleman'[9] in the Jornada del Muerto, supposed to be in Socorro County, New Mexico." In Section 2 of the same act, the Legislature offered inducement to others who might want to try for water by providing that, "the provisions of the preceding section shall be applicable to any person whatsoever who shall discover a sufficient supply of good and pure water in said Jornada del Muerto, not nearer

---

9. *Aleman,* Spanish for "German," pronounced "ah-lay-mahn," at the time of the discovery of water by Jack Martin was the place of the Aleman Ranch, located about a half mile east of the present Santa Fe Railway station of Aleman. In the old days a part of the Butterfield Trail and stage route started from Fort Craig, opposite Valverde on the west side of the Rio Grande, then followed the river down to Paraje, then on to Fort McRae (now in the middle of Elephant Butte Lake), then on to Engle, and to Aleman Ranch, then on to the Point of Rocks and Fort Selden, back to the Rio Grande again, thence west by Mason Tanks and Massacre Mountain to Fort Cummins, at the foot of Cook's Peak. On June 5, 1885, Captain Thomas Branigan of the Mescalero Indian reservation police, while out on a scouting trip wrote to Major W. H. H. Llewellyn, the agent: "Fort McRae must have been quite a place in its day, but it is badly dilapidated now. The cemetery contains about thirty graves, the inmates of nearly all being killed by the Apaches. In the center of the graveyard is a neat and pretty monument, nine feet high, erected to the memory of the colored volunteers, by surviving comrades." Branigan had gone with Fort Stanton cavalry, under the command of Major Van Horn, with Officers Wallace, Stanton, Stotsenberg, Davies, Cruse and Paddock on the staff, to quell an Indian uprising in the San Mateo Mountain country. One day the cavalry had made fifty miles in eight hours, another day, 70 miles in ten hours.

than twenty miles to said 'Aleman' or in the Magdalena Cañon, or near the same, or on the road from Mesilla to Pinos Altos, provided the owners of the Jornada del Muerto shall not be taxed for the use of the water whenever they may need it." The 1869 Legislature also extended tax exemption to "Frederick Buckner and his associates at the place known as 'Point of Rocks,' on the Jornada del Muerto, in the County of Doña Ana," for anticipated water development projects.

With the Martin water development in mind, the Legislature of 1876 adopted a memorial to the Congress of the United States, reflecting the water situation at the time, reciting:

> Your memorialists, the legislative Assembly of New Mexico, would most respectfully represent: That there are in this Territory extensive tracts of land entirely destitute of water, that these lands are now practically worse than useless, being an actual obstruction and impediment to travel. That at one point upon the Jornada del Muerto experiment has proved that living water can be obtained by sinking a well, although at other points and at greater depths, no water has yet been reached. Now, therefore, for the benefit of travelers and government troops compelled to cross these plains, as well as to utilize these lands, Congress is respectfully asked to encourage the donation of lands, the sinking of wells, and to authorize then by law the Commissioner of the General Land Office, to designate points where persons may sink wells, and if successful in obtaining an abundant supply of living water, to grant free patents to as much land as in the wisdom of Congress would encourage such enterprises.
>
> Your memorialists, conversant with the difficulties and expenses and hazard of a failure of such work would respectfully suggest at least four adjoining sections be donated to each well, provided, that such wells shall be located at least ten miles from any living water.

Jack Martin's discovery well at Aleman, demonstrating that water could be developed on the Jornada, gave an impetus to the growth of the territory east and west of the Organs and adjacent to the San Andreas and other mountain ranges up and down the country between the Rio Grande and the Pecos River. By the year 1884 all springs and running water in Lincoln County had been occupied, many of them acquired by important cattle interests. There was no running water left for the little man. The Aleman well offered fresh hope to men crowded out of Texas and other states, looking for grass, pushing into the Tularosa Basin country, anxious to take up a homestead and get some range land together, anxious to own eventually a bunch of cattle and a cattle ranch.

Maj. W. H. H. Llewellyn, lately resigned as agent on the Mescalero reservation, became enthusiastic over the possibilities for water in Lincoln and Doña Ana County. He announced in the *Golden Era* of February 28, 1884, that he had organized a company that would drill wells, "expecting to go down 900 to 1,000 feet for water." Editorially, the *Golden Era* commented: "If Llewellyn is successful with his first well, he will have no trouble in finding all the work he and his associates can do. There are thousands of acres of splendid land in Lincoln County that would have been taken up years ago, only for the scarcity of water." Complaining again on December 11, 1884, that "all available springs and water courses in Lincoln County had been taken up," the *Golden Era* agitated the use of wells and windmills, saying: "If windmills are practicable in Illinois and Iowa in supplying stock and farms with water, there is no reason why they should not be used in redeeming the waste places in New Mexico."

Hardy pioneers took up the challenge in various parts of southeastern New Mexico and drilled for water. In no part of the Territory, however, was the task more formidable, or the results more discouraging, than in the Tularosa Basin.[10]

Nature contributed generously to the mountain country adjacent to the villages of Tularosa and Lincoln by providing streams, timber, irrigable lands and abundance of grass, but in striking contrast, in another part of early day Doña Ana and Lincoln Counties, nature had been niggardly, if not spiteful and vengeful, in forming a large area to the west in the direction of the Rio Grande. For want of a

---

10. In 1897 when the El Paso & Northeastern Railroad, later the El Paso & Southwestern, and still later a part of the Rock Island and Southern Pacific system, began construction of its rail line through the Tularosa Basin, development was retarded by water problems that stumped the ablest engineers. The operation of locomotives through that section of New Mexico proved a perpetual headache for operating officials until water was brought from the mountain tops to the railroad. On the map of New Mexico made by Lieut. J. W. Abert and Lieut. W. Peck, U. S. T. E., 1846-1847, published by order of the War Department, Jornada del Muerto had been marked on the map and labelled, "Table lands with grama grass, but no running water," and most of the land later to be known as Lincoln County was marked "Indians."

better name, geologists of late years have called it the "Tularosa Basin." In a part of this area, a happy hunting ground for scientists, the earth has been buckled by the heat of volcanoes, seared by lava, sorely afflicted by the violence of wind and water. Here nature calculatingly erected underground barriers, walling off the waters of the earth, accomplishing a project designed to thwart man's ambition of conquest.

Beginning roughly in the region of Gran Quivira, the Tularosa Basin extends south to the New Mexico border and on into a part of Texas and Mexico. Volcanoes distributed ribbons of lava over an area forty-four miles in length and from four to five miles in width, west of the present towns of Carrizozo, Oscuro and Three Rivers. Classified by scientists as "old" and "young" lava flows, the result was the same, serious damage to great potential plains country. To the south of the malpais, there is an area occupied by the White Sands, gypsum deposits, drifting at the rate of a mile every twenty years, covering in extent two hundred and seventy square miles; nearby there are quartz sand dunes, one hundred square miles in area. To the west and north of the White Sands there are the alkali flats, probably formed by wind erosion, occupying one hundred and sixty square miles of country.[11] The annual rainfall in the Tularosa Basin country is ten inches or less. With no living water in the country, or only occasional isolated springs or seeps, no country in New Mexico seemed to offer less to a homesteader or prospective rancher.

The *Lincoln County Leader*, of September 15, 1883, announced the new credo of the Lincoln country, saying:

> Lincoln County was, until a recent period, a terra incognita. Her inaccessibility obscured her resources, and the "Lincoln County War," rendered life and property insecure. Pat Garrett became Sheriff in 1880, on a square platform of law and order, as against anarchy and violence. He justified the confidence of the people, by exterminating "Billy the Kid" and his gang, and maintaining with a firm hand, the supremacy of the law during his term. His efficient deputy in that good work, John W. Poe, is the present sheriff, and no one can look at his burly figure, and square, honest face, without a feeling of greater security. He is a terror to evildoers. Let no one

---

11. See *Geology and Water Resources of Tularosa Basin*, by O. E. Meinzer and R. F. Hare, Government Printing Office, Washington, D.C., 1915.

remember then, against Lincoln County, her former bad record. She is now as law abiding, as any county in the west.

With the days of Billy the Kid behind her, southeastern New Mexico began a new era. With the land along the small rivers and streams in the high country owned by those who expected to retain them indefinitely, many newcomers decided to settle in the Tularosa Basin country, where water was the big problem, or in the Jornada country, where Jack Martin years before had shown the way.

On the west side, men filed on homesteads from Mockingbird Gap to San Augustin Pass, determined to match their wits against nature and the elements. With its lava flow and its sink holes, its alkali flats and its sand dunes, a land of little moisture, the Tularosa Basin country was settled up gradually by men who were rough and unyielding, reluctant to abandon an enterprise on which they had once set mind and heart. The country offered little to the man looking for farm land and the settlers coming into the Basin limited their efforts to livestock production. Water was obtained in the Tularosa Basin country only through hard work and great effort, and only occasionally in sufficient quantities for irrigation of crops. Fortunate indeed was the rancher who found water for his livestock at a shallow depth, doubly fortunate those who found water useful for both livestock and domestic purposes at any reasonable depth, or at any depth. Much of the water developed was heavily impregnated by alkali, sodium chloride, or other minerals, and was unfit for consumption by man or beast. In some locations with windmills and pumps on wells, an adequate supply of water could be made available for a considerable bunch of cows. At other places only a trickle of water could be developed, just enough for a few head. Ranches were known for their good or poor drinking water. A rancher with a good supply of water fit for human consumption soon found a road beaten to his place. Travelers from the Rio Grande to the Lincoln country, whether going through Mockingbird Gap, Lava Gap or San Augustin Pass, were careful to spot the waterholes before undertaking a journey.

In the late eighties and early nineties, a new country was opened up in the Tularosa Basin and the Jornada, in which a man could make a living for himself and family if he got up before daybreak and worked until after sundown. Wrangling horses, rounding up cattle, worrying about the water supply occupied most of his time. Early day settlers in that country included the J. A. Bairds, west of the alkali flats; James Cooper, southwest of Ancho; W. W. Cox, north of the Organ range, southeast of San Augustin Peak; J. B. French, between Ancho and Coyote; Walter George, at Lava Gap; Jim Gililland, a few miles from George's place; W. F. Gililland, a few miles from Jim Gililland's ranch; George Henderson, a few miles west of Salt Creek; Mark Hunter and William Hunter, James Lee, near the lava country; Oliver M. Lee, near the south end of the Sacramentos and in the valley at Wildey Well; W. H. McNew, near the edge of the White Sands and at a place called "Point of Sands."

In the development of the Tularosa Basin and Jornada country there was much trading and trafficking in range lands; there was quarreling over range rights and grazing privileges; there were notes and mortgages to think about; and always the talk about the price of calves and cows. There was the concern about the weather, with always an eye toward the sky, where sometimes clouds drifted about, giving occasional promise of rain, a promise seldom fulfilled. With skies that were generally clear, with air generally dry and rare, the days both in summer and winter were ordinarily pleasant. The nights in summertime were cool and in the winter were cold.

In that country, in its settlement, there developed a rugged type of New Mexico citizen, fully able to take care of himself and his property. Strong physically, accustomed to the hardships incident to a life on the frontier, with resources within himself to sustain himself and his family, all he asked was to be left unmolested. Little by little the Tularosa Basin and Jornada, inhabited mostly by men bred in the industry, became a worthwhile cattle country. Some of the settlers prospered and extended their ranches. Many of the people in that country were related by blood or marriage. Feuds and quarrels that mile-high mountains could not settle grew up in that region; men there, as elsewhere, had fights over range and cattle and personal affairs that at times were ended only by resort to six-shooter or rifle.

two

ABOUT JOHN S. CHISUM

FOR SOME YEARS in the seventies, Custer County, Montana Territory, with its 13,000,000 acres of land, boasted that it was the largest county in area within the confines of the United States of America. However, in the seventies and eighties, Lincoln County, New Mexico, with its 27,000 square miles of territory embracing 17,280,000 acres of land, easily held first place. Of a variable character, as was consistent with such a vast quantity of land embraced within its boundaries, Lincoln County territory had never been looked upon with any degree of hopefulness by pioneers of the Spanish or Mexican colonial periods. There were, first of all, the savage Indians to consider, with their war whoops and their tomahawks and later their rifles and bullets furnished to them by renegade traders, or stolen by the Indians in their pilgrimages of plundering. Then there was, perhaps more important, the scarcity of water. The Mescaleros and other Plains Indians made only occasional forays in the fifties, sixties, seventies and early eighties, into distant Lincoln County country. The Indians themselves experienced the same difficulties encountered by the white men, desert land, and waterless, except in a few isolated places. Time had been when the Indians, of what tribe no one can say with much authority, had been in the Lincoln County country, permanent settlers perhaps, as evidenced by the petroglyphs near Three Rivers and other nearby evidence of early habitation. From time to time the Mescaleros had claimed as their own the best parts of the country up and down the streams in the mountains. Further to the north in the Tularosa Basin country there had been long inhabited pueblos at Gran Quivira, Abo, Quarai and Manzano, probably abandoned in the eighteenth century because of the lack of water, with raids by enemy Indians from the plains country as a contributing factor.

No Spanish or Mexican colonist had ever been sufficiently interested in the "Staked Plains" country, as it was identified on the maps for many years, to petition for a grant of land there from the government of Spain or Mexico. In other parts of the Territory, notably up and down the Rio Grande and on the far Upper Pecos, there had been numerous grants of great tracts of lands. With no land grant problem involved, because there had been no grants, and with title to most of the land in Lincoln County vested in the United States of America, the entire area offered the possibilities inherent in a frontier country to the man who wished to undertake its difficulties and work out a salvation. The federal government from time to time surveyed the lands into townships and sections, but prior and subsequent to surveys most of the land had been open for settlement. Many homestead entries were made at Las Cruces by men who had served in the Civil War. A few homesteaders had seen service in the Mexican War of 1846; some had served in the famous California Column and many took up land who had grown to like the country after a hitch or two in the cavalry at Fort Stanton.

Next door to Texas, many a Texan came across the border into New Mexico, some leisurely bringing livestock and goods, others hurriedly, to escape the clutches of a Texas sheriff armed with a warrant of arrest. Men who had served in the army, accustomed to gunfire and the handling of guns accepted readily enough the rough and tumble of early Lincoln County days. The code of the country was: "Stand a heap of abuse before you kill a man," but at times there were killings, sometimes unavoidable because "he needed killing," and other times with small justification. Men serious in their ambitions to get along on their ranches and with their livestock holdings soon got to know the killers of the country; and at times gunmen were dispatched hurriedly into the other world. A preliminary hearing before a justice of the peace and coroner's jury in such cases ordinarily resulted in a verdict that "the deceased came to his death accidentally, after having given due provocation," and the grand jury of the county seldom, if ever, was called upon to review the findings.

It was inevitable that Lincoln County with its vast acreage would become an important livestock breeding country. Some men who came into Lincoln County in the early days were better businessmen and better cowmen than others, better supplied with money when they came, more resourceful to withstand the hardships and privations of the times. Before the close-feeding sheep came into the country in the middle eighties, Lincoln County was a cattle-raising kingdom without a rival in the Southwest. Looming large in the early days of the Lincoln County cattle industry was the figure of John S. Chisum, who had come into the country from Texas in 1865, endowed with ability, about ten thousand head of cattle and some money. A pioneer cattleman in the true sense of the word, the name of John S. Chisum has become legendary in New Mexico. He was born in Madison County, Tennessee, August 15, 1824, was just over forty years old when he came to the Territory, anxious to get in on the beef contracts for the Indians at Bosque Grande.

The first to become a "big business" cattleman in New Mexico, John S. Chisum had ranches at various places in Lincoln County, first on the Black River, then on the Pecos River near Bosque Grande, then over near Fort Stanton, and later, down at Three Rivers. The Fort Stanton ranch was reported to control sixteen hundred sections of land. For many years, John S. Chisum controlled many miles of country up and down the Pecos River. In 1873, Chisum removed his cattle from the Black River range to the Pecos River country. The new range extended fifty miles on either side of the river from what was known as the "Eighteen Mile Bend" below Fort Sumner to the mouth of Salt Creek, one mile above Lloyd's Ranch. Shortly before moving to the Fort Sumner range in 1873, Chisum bought the Wylie Brothers' herd and ran 30,000 head on that range. As early as 1874, after a New Mexico residence of about ten years, John S. Chisum was known as the "Pecos Valley cattle king." In that year he was the successful bidder for the Apache Indian beef contract with the government. His bid for Southern New Mexico was .0219¢ per lb., for Mescalero Apaches, .0198¢ per lb. By 1875, John Chisum had become so well known that he was called the "cow king" of New Mexico. In that year he employed one hundred cowboys on his ranges, ran eighty thousand head of cows and claimed that he could fill an order on short notice for forty thousand head of beef cattle. A writer in the Las Vegas *Gazette* of November 25, 1875, described the Chisum ranch of that day:

> The Chisum ranch is situated on the Pecos River, New Mexico. It extends south along the river from near Fort Sumner to Seven Rivers, a distance of one hundred fifty miles. This is the extent of

LINCOLN, NEW MEXICO, IN 1886, ALMOST IDENTICAL WITH THE LINCOLN OF THE LATE 1870'S AND EARLY 1880'S.

the range north and south. East and west, it reaches as far as a man can travel, on a good horse, during a summer; practically, as far as stock can range from the river without water. The country, on both sides of the river, is high rolling prairie, covered with a thickset, heavy growth of black grama, the most nutritious of grasses. The grass is knee high on every hill and mesa this year. The river is the second in size in the Territory, and is fed from the snows and springs of the mountains of the west. To the eastward extends the Staked Plains from which side there is not a single tributary to the Pecos. The plains fall gradually to the east and the water from the rains flows to the eastern border, giving rise to nearly all the rivers of Texas. Heavy snows and storms are unknown and the winter range can almost always be depended upon. The grass cures to natural hay on the ground. The home ranch is at Bosque Grande, fifty miles below Fort Sumner. At this point, a general store is kept, buildings and large corrals constructed. At convenient points up and down the river from the home ranch, are secondary stations, or cow camps, which the herders occupy as temporary homes. Not less than a hundred employes are constantly employed in taking care of the cattle. The expenses of Mr. Chisum for horses, during the last ten years, have been very heavy, due to losses from Indian raids. At one time, after an Indian foray, only ten head of horses were left on the ranch. The savages captured at that time three or four hundred head of horses. The men had to herd afoot until other stock could be purchased. The horses have been of a variable quantity, ranging from a dozen to a thousand head. This year, however, has been unusually quiet. The Indians have not committed a single depredation. The spring round up will take place next February.

In 1875, Chisum was the successful bidder with Ewing and Curtis of Tucson, who had the contract for furnishing beef to all the Indian agencies in the Territory of Arizona. In the summer of that year Chisum furnished 11,000 head to the Arizona contractors. Urged by his friends in Lincoln County in 1875 to run for the Legislature, John S. Chisum demonstrated that he was not much of a politician. When the votes were counted for the House of Representatives, the tally showed: John P. Risque, 163, John B. Patron[1] 114, John S. Chisum 93, John M. Ginn 63.

---

1. John B. Patron was murdered by Mitchell Manley at Puerto de Luna on April 1, 1884. Patron had been a prominent citizen of Lincoln County for many years, had served in the militia during the Lincoln County War, and had been Speaker in the House of Representatives in the New Mexico Legislature.

On January 12, 1876, John S. Chisum enjoyed the excitement of a stage robbery. Traveling with Thomas F. Conway, his long-time personal attorney, Chisum was riding in a stagecoach enroute from Silver City to Mesilla. As the stage was going up to the rocky hill at Cook's Canyon, three masked men, with handkerchiefs tied above their eyes and blankets below, stopped the conveyance and compelled Lancaster, the driver, and Fred Kaiser, the guard, to get down. The robbers then lined up the passengers. John Chisum had $1,000 in currency on his person when the robbers stopped the stage, but before they got to search him, he had shoved the money into a bootleg and handed over only a small sum. The robbers took silver bricks from the stage safe, of the value of $4,000, shipped from Silver City by H. M. Porter and J. F. Bennett, consigned to Kountze Brothers, New York City.

In the spring of 1876, when smallpox was the scourge of the Rio Abajo country, John Chisum became ill of the disease at his Bosque Grande ranch, but recovered. The pestilence was so severe in the Territory at the time that courts were adjourned in Los Lunas and Socorro for many months. Fort Union was isolated by army orders and deaths averaged two a day in the Rio Grande valley. In 1877 smallpox was a scourge in Las Vegas where there were eighty-two deaths from the disease in nine months, with many deaths also in Chaperito, Tecolote and Anton Chico.

On the way to fulfill a contract in Arizona, Chisum's herds passed Dowlin's mill in the Tularosa country on August 23, 1877. Here some of the cowboys got hold of whiskey. Cowboy Johnnie Evers shot himself in the leg and was taken to the hospital at Fort Stanton. Ramon Garcia, half Comanche Indian, shot and killed J. M. Franklin, one of Chisum's most reliable men. George Hogg, foreman on the drive for Chisum, had Garcia arrested and started for Fort Stanton, but on the way Garcia was killed by one of his guards "trying to escape." Hogg reached the Mesilla Valley with 2,300 head of cattle. Seventy head had been lost on the drive from Tularosa to the Rio Grande due to the scarcity of water on the road for the cattle and too much whiskey on the road for the cowboys.

Stealing cattle from John S. Chisum was a popular pastime. Many hides with Chisum's brand could be seen in out-of-the-way houses, up and down the Pecos River. The Las Vegas *Gazette* of June 19, 1884, said of the Chisum brand: "John S. Chisum needs no introduction, as he is known far and near. His brand, for both horse and cattle is U on the left shoulder. U will know John's brand wherever you see it and if U should happen to visit the lower country U will see it on about twenty to thirty thousand head." In the spring of 1878, Thomas B. Catron of Santa Fe had John S. Chisum arrested and put in jail in San Miguel County in connection with a suit on a debt. Catron alleged in court pleadings that "Chisum was about to depart" from New Mexico and asked for a writ of *ne exeat*. Chisum got out of jail on $25,000 bail and on June 8, 1878, Judge Samuel A. Parks handed down an opinion, sustaining the contention of Thomas F. Conway, attorney for Chisum, that there was no such remedy in New Mexico as a writ of *ne exeat*.[2]

John Chisum unwisely became associated with A. A. McSween, an attorney in Lincoln, and with R. D. Hunter of St. Louis in a banking enterprise known as the "Lincoln County Bank." The Las Vegas *Gazette* of August 4, 1877, said: "A. A. McSween, Esq., has built a new dwelling house in Lincoln, also a building for business purposes; in which he will have one of the nicest and best furnished law offices in the Territory, also a bank—the Lincoln County Bank—and store. The proprietors of the bank are Col. R. D. Hunter, St. Louis, John S. Chisum of Bosque Grande, and A. A. McSween of Lincoln. The safes and necessary paraphernalia are enroute." The Mesilla *Independent* of Sept. 8, 1877, said: "We received a check this week, drawn on the Lincoln County Bank. We had heard that something of the kind was contemplated, but this is the first intimation we have received that the bank was really in existence. We are informed that John S. Chisum and A. A. McSween are the principal managers." The McSween bank, a factor in the Lincoln County War, was short-lived. Chisum's identification with it and its affiliated enterprises drew the fire of men who had previously been indifferent to Chisum and his cattle interests.

While the most pretentious operator in New Mexico with the finest herd of cows, John S. Chisum did not have a monopoly on the livestock business in the Territory. On March 2, 1877, José Leandro Perea of Bernalillo, New Mexico, made a sale of 17,000

---

2. A writ used in early days in England to prevent a person from "departing from the Kingdom."

sheep to A. B. Matthews through Kingsberry & Holmsley at the Kansas City stockyards, the largest sale of sheep, up to that date, ever made at one time in that market by an individual grower. Captain J. G. Clancey, a retired sea captain, born and reared in Vermont, in August of 1877 drove 3,000 head of fine sheep overland from California to New Mexico, partly to escape the drouth then withering the grass in California, partly because he was looking for a new sheep-raising country. With fifty thousand dollars in gold, Captain Clancey traveled to New Mexico in a wagon drawn by a team of mules. The gold coins were cached in innocent looking metal containers. Settling on the Pecos River near Puerto de Luna, Clancey became a neighbor and friend of John S. Chisum. He placed his gold for safekeeping in a large iron safe in the store of Alexander Grzelachowski at Puerto de Luna. For a long time the Grzelachowski safe was the only one of its kind and size in the Territory. Grzelachowski, who had come to New Mexico in 1864, was well acquainted with William H. Bonney and gave orders to clerks in his store: "Always give Billy the Kid anything he wants; never argue." The Kid always had the same request, cartridges and bullets for his guns. As soon as the railroad reached Las Vegas, Captain Clancey had a carload of Rambouillet bucks shipped to him there from his old home in Vermont and drove them over to Puerto de Luna to improve his flocks.

Chisum's herd of cattle, believed to total 30,000 in 1884, was probably a low estimate. He had sold 25,000 head of cattle in 1881 to Hunter and Evans, who ranged on the Panhandle; and in 1883, the Chisum outfit branded 6,000 calves. John Chisum knew the value of improved stock. Bulls valued at from $100 to $1,000 roamed his range.

On Chisum's home ranch, located at the head of South Spring about six miles from Roswell, there was a combination adobe-frame structure, 148 feet long and 39 feet wide. About the center of the building there was a hallway which connected with a veranda to the rear, under which ran a stream of pure water. The house was enclosed with a painted picket fence, inside of which there were many ornamental trees and apple and peach orchards. The house was handsomely furnished, but John S. Chisum's bed was made up of three blankets spread out on the floor, the kind of bed on which he had slept for forty years, indoors and out in the weather.

In the Spring of 1883, "Uncle" John S. Chisum imported forty-two head of shorthorn Durhams from Missouri, reported at the time to be "as fine a bunch of animals as ever held down hoofs." The cattle cost Chisum from $150 to $1,500 each, were delivered on the railroad at Las Vegas and driven down the Pecos River to the Chisum ranches. John S. Chisum was greatly interested in agriculture, especially in feed for his livestock. From the South Spring River ranch on August 6, 1880, John S. Chisum wrote a letter to the editor of the Las Vegas *Gazette*, in which he said:

> You will find, in a box sent you, two heads of millet I raised on my ranch. I have been trying the different kinds of grasses and millet, to find which suits our climate and soil best. From all I have been able to learn, this I send you is the best. It grows from four to six feet high, producing a large quantity of fodder and making more feed to the acre than any other feed. I would request you to examine this, and if you know of any better millet, let me know what it is, so I can get the seed, and if what I send you proves to be the best I must be content.
>
> We have rain and grass in abundance; also plenty of newcomers from Kerr County, Texas. They are well pleased and are getting themselves homes as fast as possible.
>
> I remain, as ever, Yours,
>
> JOHN S. CHISUM

There was a note by Iowa-born J. H. Koogler, editor of the *Gazette*: "The heads of the millet are larger than ears of popcorn and are unusually well filled."

When the Lincoln County War started to get hot, Col. R. D. Hunter, with the 25,000 head of cattle he had acquired from John S. Chisum and his other herds, started to move every hoof of cattle he had in New Mexico along the Pecos River across the Staked Plains into the Panhandle of Texas, taking part of them later to Colorado and Wyoming. Gunfire frightened settlers out of Lincoln County as early as 1878. The Las Vegas *Gazette* of August 17, 1878, reported that:

> Six wagon loads of emigrants from North and South Spring in Lincoln County, passed through town Tuesday going north. They

were driven out by the lawless element of the section. They had tried hard to take no part in the contest and preferred to leave rather than to take either side. About twenty horses had been taken from them. A deputy sheriff rode up and demanded that they take up arms and go with them and fight. This they refused to do and loaded up and left the country. They left their houses, lands, standing crops, garden and everything pertaining to comfortable homes. They will seek employment on the railroad. No new country can well afford to lose so industrial and law abiding class of people."

It was estimated that there were 500,000 head of cattle in the Territory of New Mexico in the year 1881, yielding for market annually about 90,000 head. Of this number, it was estimated there were about 300,000 head of cattle in Lincoln County; and there were in the county in the same year about 15,000 horses, mules and burros, but only a few sheep. Prices in the Territory in that year, according to the annual report of Governor L. Bradford Prince, were as follows: Young cows and calves, $25.00; two-year-old heifers, $12.00; two-year-old steers, $12.00; yearling heifers, $7.00; yearling steers, $7.00; high grade bulls, $75.00; common ewes, $1.50; common wethers, $1.25; graded merino ewes, young, $2.00 to $3.00; graded wethers, $2.00 to $3.00. Lowest grade native wool in 1881 brought 15¢ per pound, the choicest, improved, unwashed, brought twenty-four cents. In the fall of 1884, the Holt Cattle Company imported 200 head of Durham bulls from the east for their ranges in the Seven Rivers area, where the outfit ran 8,000 head of cattle under the direction of Sam Collins. The Holt Company was sinking wells at remote points from the Pecos River in an effort to solve the problem of getting water to distant ranges.

After nearly twenty years of effort in the cattle industry in New Mexico and at a time when he had achieved the top place in the business of the Territory, "Uncle" John S. Chisum began to suffer from stomach troubles, which Kansas City surgeons diagnosed as cancer. He underwent a surgical operation there and, seriously ill, sometime later went to Eureka Springs, Arkansas. On December 20, 1884, John S. Chisum died at Eureka Springs. Bennett Howell, a longtime right-hand man on the range, took over management of the Chisum properties in New Mexico. Commenting on his death, the *Golden Era* of Lincoln, on January 1, 1885, said:

> Our readers will be pained to learn of the death at Eureka Springs, Ark., of John S. Chisum, which occurred at that place about two weeks ago. Mr. Chisum was one of the pioneers and frontiersmen of Lincoln County, having come here at a very early day, and had been identified with its history ever since. Eccentric in many ways, gruff in manner, yet he was always a warm friend, and no man ever looked closer after the pleasure and comfort of the men under his employ during his long experience as a cattleman.

three

PATRICK FLOYD GARRETT

MORE WIDELY KNOWN personally and more exten- sively publicized than any other New Mexican of his day, Patrick Floyd Garrett, frontier sheriff, slayer of "Billy the Kid," came to New Mexico at a time when the Territory was emerging from its long period of isolation from the outside world. Stagecoach days were about at an end; the coming of the railroad was assured to succeed the frontier oxen and wagon-train transportation. Bull- whackers were being forced into retirement.

Born on June 5, 1850, in Chambers County, Alabama, Pat Gar- rett's family took him as a child to Claiborne Parish, Louisiana, where he spent his boyhood days. Pat's long legs were cramped and he was uncomfortable trying to keep within the narrow confines of a desk. He left school while in the grades. Reared in the deep South in the years following the Civil War, young Garrett was anxious to go to a faraway country—to the West—land of romance and adven- ture of which he had heard and read so much. On January 25, 1869, when not nineteen years old, Patrick Floyd Garrett left the Louisiana home of his father, Col. John L. Garrett, and traveled toward the setting sun.

Garrett went first to Lancaster, Dallas County, Texas, where he worked as a cowhand, trailing cows as far north as Dennison. During the winters of 1875, 1876 and 1877, he worked as a buffalo hunter in the Texas Panhandle and finally drifted into Tascosa, Texas. The rumor tagged behind him that he had killed a man in the buffalo country. In Texas, Garrett had learned to rope skillfully, to ride well and to shoot accurately. He was six feet four inches tall in stocking feet. High-heeled boots and high-crowned sombrero accentuated his height and made him an imposing figure.

Fort Sumner, New Mexico, destination and place of downfall of many a good cowboy, was not a great ride from Tascosa and it was in Fort Sumner, on the Pecos River, that Garrett arrived in the Fall of 1878. Here Garrett first met William H. Bonney, known as Billy the Kid, a carefree youngster who was ugly on occasion and at times generous and of good heart. That acquaintance was Garrett's first step toward a relationship with William H. Bonney that continued intermittently through Garrett's life, whether Bonney was alive or dead. Up and down the Pecos River, Pat Garrett was occasionally employed as a cowboy and horse wrangler. The natives of Fort Sumner were somewhat aghast at his great height. Among themselves they called Garrett "Juan Largo" (long John).

When he arrived in Fort Sumner, Garrett knew enough Spanish to be courteous at the bailes when asking the señoritas for a dance. He danced, gracefully enough, to music of the violin, guitar and accordion on the rough boards of the dancehall floors of the village. Sometimes his head brushed against the coal oil lamps that blazed and sputtered from the ceiling vigas.

Garrett's name first appears in New Mexico documents on the records of the Roman Catholic Church at San Jose de Anton Chico, then in San Miguel County, where on January 14, 1880, Father A. Redin performed the marriage ceremony which united "Patricio Garrett to Polinaria Gutierrez, daughter of Dolores Gutierrez and M. Valdez Gutierrez of Fort Sumner, according to the rites of the Catholic church." The witnesses to the marriage were Manuel Abreu and Alejandra Segura. On the same day and at the same place, Father Redin married Barney Mason, a friend of Pat Garrett's and later to be his companion on many a law and order mission, to Juana Madril, daughter of Santos Madril and Anna Maria Gallegos of Fort Sumner. The witnesses to Garrett's marriage, Manuel Abreu and Alejandra Segura, served as witnesses for Barney Mason's marriage to Señorita Madril.

Back in Fort Sumner with his bride, there was much whispering among the people of the village, and many an old woman raised an eye toward heaven because, it was said, that Pat Garret had been married not so long before to Juanita of the same village and that Juanita Garrett had pined and worried because she had "not been married at the altar"; believed that her marriage was invalid in the eyes of the church. Juanita, they recalled, had died suddenly while attending a dance with Pat Garrett in Fort Sumner, remorseful to her dying moment that her marriage had been performed by a justice of the peace instead of "el padre."

Drifting down the Pecos River, Pat Garrett visited White Oaks, Lincoln and other places in the adjoining County of Lincoln. Political leaders in Lincoln County were looking for a man who would run for sheriff of that county on a hell-raising reform platform. Garrett modestly assured leading stockmen that he would make an ideal candidate; promised that he would go out and arrest livestock thieves and put a stop to the thieving and killing that had been going on in the country; that he would shoot it out with Dave Rudabaugh, with Billy the Kid, or any other horse thief.

Reflecting the situation that confronted the law abiding citizens of lower San Miguel County and of Lincoln County, the Las Vegas *Gazette* of November 30, 1880, published an article which said:

> As is well known, there has been a gang of horse thieves along the Pecos, who have run off stock from many ranches and who are believed to have committed other depredations. The headquarters of the gang are at Fort Sumner and their market for stolen stock at White Oaks. Last week, three of the crowd, Dave Rudabaugh, 'Billy the Kid' and Billy Wilson went to the Oaks to dispose of some of their surplus stock and while there Sheriff Kimball of Lincoln County, who learned of their where abouts, came with a posse expecting to corral them. They skipped out before the sheriff reached the camp and were met by the sheriff's party at Coyote Springs, seven miles away. They refused to surrender and showed resistance, a sharp fight following. The gang seemed to have the best of the fight and drove the attacking party into the Oaks, following them up all the way. In the struggle Rudabaugh and 'The Kid' both had their horses shot from under them.

The prominent citizens of Lincoln County were still resentful over a recent shooting episode in which Billy the Kid and his gang had murdered James Carlyle at the Greathouse and Kuch ranch during the winter of 1880. Joe Steck, who was an eyewitness to the murder of Carlyle, writing to Major Caffrey of the White Oaks *Lincoln County Leader* on December 7, 1889, not so many years after the Greathouse ranch battle, told the story of that fight in his own words. To quote Steck:

My dear Major: I left Silver Cliff, Colo., the day after the Presidential election in 1880, and started for White Oaks via Pueblo, La Junta and the A.T. & S.F R.R. to Las Vegas. About the 10th of November I left Las Vegas to come on to White Oaks. . . . After being out four days on the road, and having beautiful weather, we camped one night this side of Alkali Wells, in the timber. When we turned in, the weather was fine, sky clear, moon shone bright and everything was lovely and serene. Towards morning I woke up and found myself covered with snow, and it was still falling. . . . We decided to stop where we were, and we remained three nights and two days. On the third day we left and got as far as the Greathouse ranch, Greathouse and Kuch kept a store and camp house for travelers on the Vegas and White Oaks road. They wanted a man to drive their team and haul water . . . from the Abeel Lake for their ranch. Having heard that times were dull at White Oaks I accepted the situation.*

I found at the ranchhouse, besides Greathouse and Kuch, some six or seven cowboys. Things went on smoothly for a week or so. Travelers came and went. I attended to my business of hauling logs for a corral and water when needed. One day the cowboys went away, returning after three days. The next morning, after daylight, I got up, went out to where my team was picketed. When about 300 yards from the house somebody hollered, 'halt!' I turned around to see what was up, when to my great surprise, two men had their guns pointed at me. They ordered me to approach them, all the time keeping their guns pointed at me. I went like a little man. When I go to them, they got behind me and ordered me to march towards what I supposed was a bunch of fallen timber—and so it was, but there behind it were two bold, bad, ferocious looking men, with plenty of guns and ammunition. When I was among them one of my captors said: 'Captain, we got one of the sob's,' and I didn't resent it, even a little bit. They ordered me to lie down with them and I did so. They wanted to know if Billy the Kid, Wilson, or Dave Rudabaugh were in the house. I told them I did not know. They doubted my word and I didn't allow myself to get mad. They

---

* In an article entitled "Village of Corona," published in the *New Mexico Magazine*, November 1960, Beulah Meeks locates the Greathouse and Kuch or "Cook and Greathouse" ranch near Corona in present-day Lincoln County. To quote from the article: "In 1899 Corona began its development from an earlier settlement known as the Red Cloud Postoffice located on the Cook and Greathouse ranch, which was a few miles southwest of the present townsite. The post office was on the old stagecoach route from Las Vegas to the mining town of White Oaks."

gave me a description of the men they were after, and I told them there were three such looking men in the house. Then they told me they were a Sheriff's posse from White Oaks and wanted those men, dead or alive. After a consultation among themselves, more coming from different posts around the house, they decided that perhaps I was not so hard a citizen as I looked, and if I would give them my word of honor to come out again I could carry a dispatch into the house telling the boys to surrender, as a posse of thirteen men from White Oaks had come during the night, surrounded the house on all sides, and large parties from Lincoln were enroute with provisions and supplies and everything necessary for a siege, and they had better surrender at once as there was no chance for escape.

I took the note in and delivered it to the one I knew to be Billy the Kid. He read the paper to his compadres, who all laughed at the idea of surrender. They told me also, to rest easy and not be alarmed, as no harm would come to me from them. They sent me out with a note demanding to know who the leader of the party was, and invited him into the house to talk the matter over. Carlyle, the leader of the White Oaks party, at first objected, but Greathouse putting himself as a hostage for his safety while he was in there, he took off his arms and walked into the trap. In the meantime I was backward and forward between the two parties carrying dispatches.

Getting hungry about 11 o'clock I went into the house to rustle up a dinner. I found Carlyle getting under the influence of liquor and insisting on going out, while the others insisted on his staying. While I was getting dinner, Mr. Kuch, Greathouse's partner, carried dispatches between the camps. For some reason the White Oaks boys became suspicious; things were not as they should be with their leader, and they decided to storm the fort, therefore sent me word by Mr. Kuch to come out as war would commence in earnest. I stepped out of doors intending to go to some safe place and witness the conflict. After being out Kuch called me to stop a moment and he would go with me. I stopped and turned when, crash, a man came through a window, bang, bang, the man's dying yell, and poor Carlyle tumbled to the ground with three bullets in him, dead. I started to run away from the house, with Kuch behind me and towards a barricade of the White Oaks boys when they commenced to shoot at us, and so did all the other boys behind the different barricades. About 60 or 75 shots were fired at us, bullets flying from all directions, and I began to feel decidely uncomfortable. I jumped several feet in the air, threw my hands up over my head, and fell flat on my face and lay there. Kuch, behind me, thought it was a good scheme, so he imitated my example. After 3 or 4 more bullets came very close to my head, the firing suddenly stopped. We crawled out amongst the boys when they told us it was a mistake; they thought we were making a feint to cover the retreat of the desperadoes.

This is about all there is to the trouble at the Greathouse ranch. Kuch and myself went that night to Abeel's ranch, about three miles from there and returned the next morning. We found poor Carlyle frozen stiff where he fell, tied a blanket around him and made a hole a little toward the east from where he fell and buried him the best we could. He was afterwards taken up and put in a box by a sheriff's posse.

Pat Garrett was elected sheriff of Lincoln County in the Fall of 1880, after a spirited campaign on a law and order platform. Sheriff George Kimball was his opponent. Lousiana-born George Curry, who had seen all of the best known outlaws of the day in Dodge City, Kansas, and had known most of them personally, was running the Block cattle ranch in Lincoln County during the days of the Garrett-Kimball campaign. The ranch was owned by Dowlin and Delaney, Fort Stanton post traders, the nearest postoffice at Richardson, a village named after Andy Richardson, brother of Judge Granville A. Richardson of Lincoln and Roswell. During the campaign, a young man appeared one evening at the Block ranchhouse and asked George Curry for shelter for the night. The request was granted with genuine display of Southwestern hospitality. The young stranger told Curry he was on his way to a dance at a settlement a few miles distant and urged him to go along. Curry said he could not go; that he had been instructed by his bosses to go out and see some people about the election to be held the next day and get them to work in the interest of Pat Garrett who was running for sheriff. "Do you know Garrett?" questioned the stranger. "No, I don't, but from all I hear he is a splendid man," Curry replied. "Do you think he will be elected?" pursued the questioner. "I don't know," Curry said, "but I'm sure he will carry this precinct. I have a gallon of whiskey on hand, and I think that will help carry it." The stranger went to the dance, returned early in the morning and was up a daybreak. Curry, the perfect host, had flapjacks and hot coffee ready for breakfast. As he was about to leave, saying goodbye, thanking Curry for his hospitality, the young man said: "You are a good cook and a good fellow; but if you think Pat Garrett is going to carry this precinct for sheriff, you are a dam'd poor politician." Later in the day George Curry learned the name of his overnight guest. It was William H. Bonney. At the dance the night before, the Kid had campaigned against Garrett. The precinct went for Kimball in the election.

Elected sheriff of Lincoln County on a promise that he would break up cattle and horse thievery, that he would fight it out with Billy the Kid and his gang and kill the Kid if necessary, Pat Garrett had before him a program of action that called for courage and persistence. On July 14, 1881, at old Fort Sumner in a many-roomed house that had once been the residence of United States Army officers in the days of the Navajo Indian warfare, Patrick Floyd Garrett fired the shot that sent Billy the Kid to his grave. Peter Maxwell, eyewitness to the shooting, was a son of Lucien B. Maxwell, once owner of the vast Beaubien-Miranda land grant in Colfax County, New Mexico. According to gossip of the day, Pete Maxwell was not entirely opposed to a visitation of sudden death upon William H. Bonney. Reluctant to discuss the incident in after years, Pete Maxwell always summed up his recollection of the event with the remark: "The trouble with Billy that night was that he talked before he shot; always before that he shot first, and talked afterward."

They buried poor William H. Bonney, just a bit more than old enough to vote, dressed in a borrowed white shirt that was much too large for him, in a coffin of plain wood in the little cemetery of Fort Sumner, where his pal, Tom O'Folliard, had been laid away, where Lucien B. Maxwell years before had found eternal rest and where Juanita, Pat Garrett's bride of a few months, had found refuge from remorse of conscience.*

---

* On March 12, 1962, Judge E. T. Hensley, Jr., of the De Baca County district court, handed down a decision from the bench which was of far-reaching importance to the inhabitants of De Baca and Lincoln counties, and of interest to all followers of the life and career of the late William H. Bonney. Judge Hensley's decision stemmed from a petition filed in his court by Lois Telfer of New York City, who claimed to be Bonney's next of kin and only surviving relative, and who alleged that the present custodians had neglected to take care of Bonney's grave, and had permitted it to be over commercialized. In a deposition Miss Telfer submitted in evidence an interesting family tree, compiled from church records and faded tombstones in Connecticut, New York and Michigan, one entry tending to show that the Bonneys came to America in

Out of the talk that buzzed in his ears after the shooting, Pat
Garrett remembered quite vividly the expostulation of Deluvina
Maxwell, the Indian slave girl, who had rushed into the room where
the Kid was being laid out and shouted at the Kid's slayer: "You
piss pot you! You didn't have the nerve to kill him to his face." *

1643, as evidenced by carving on a tombstone in Cornwall, Connecticut. Miss Telfer
traced her kinship to Bonney through a branch of the Bonney family which settled in
Michigan.

At the trial of the case it was apparent from the pleadings and testimony that if the
court allowed Bonney's remains to be removed, the removal would in all probability
infringe on the rights of two outlaws of other days, the late Tom O'Folliard and the
late Charles Bowdre, both shot and killed in shooting affrays on or about Dec. 19, 1880,
and both buried in graves in close proximity to Bonney's grave. The Telfer petition,
simple enough in the beginning, became somewhat complicated by the alignment on
her side of the Board of County Commissioners of Lincoln County, and by opposition
expressed in appropriate pleadings filed by the Board of County Commissioners of De
Baca County. In order that full justice might be done, the court permitted Louis A.
Bowdre, employed by the postal service in Bartlesville, Oklahoma, to intervene in the
case, on assurance that he was Charles Bowdre's distant cousin. Louis Bowdre's testimony left no doubt but that the remnant of the Bowdre family which he represented
was definitely opposed to the removal of Bonney's remains, because such removal would
involve the disturbance of Bowdre's remains. Judge Hensley decided that the evidence
in the case demonstrated that the exact location of Bonney's grave was not known; that
in order to disinter Bonney's remains it would inevitably lead to disturbing the remains
of those buried in adjoining gravesites, and this should not be permitted.

* From all available information, Deluvina Maxwell was a colorful character. It was
Deluvina's belief that she was born of Navajo parentage in Cañon de Chelly, stolen by
Apaches and sold to Lucien B. Maxwell at his Cimarron home for ten head of horses.
"Tata Makey" was her name for Maxwell. Deluvina was fond of recalling the days of
glory at Maxwell's mansion in the Cimarron country. She remembered that bands of
roving Navajos, Utes and Apaches called on Maxwell from time to time and on such
occasions he invariably ordered a cow butchered, supervised the cooking of the meat
in huge iron kettles, then invited the Indians to help themselves. While living in
Cimarron, Deluvina was married to Juan Beaubien, also an Indian slave, the property
of Lucien Maxwell. The marriage lasted only a short time, but there was no divorce.
Before her marriage to Juan, Deluvina had a son whom she named Felipe Maxwell,
who was adopted by a family named Crosby and who died when a young man. After
the death of William H. Bonney, killed at Fort Sumner by Pat Garrett, Deluvina frequently told of how she "cussed out" the Kid's slayer, "grabbed a candle, and walked
into the room where he had been killed," not to help Garrett "who was asking for
someone to volunteer to go into the room because he was afraid to go in himself," but
"to help the Kid, for he might be only wounded and need help."

As the years crept upon Deluvina, she gained weight until at one time she weighed
more than 300 pounds. At times Deluvina imagined herself a glamor girl, insisted on
going in and out of Fort Sumner saloons, although there was a law prohibiting females
from entering places where liquor was sold. On one such occasion, with a drink or two
under her belt, Deluvina let down her long black hair, started doing an Indian dance
on the main street of the town, challenged cowboys lounging about a saloon entrance

Over at Anton Chico, when he learned of the Kid's death, Padre Redin commented: "Billy did not have a bad heart; most of his crimes were crimes of vengeance." No more around Fort Sumner did William H. Bonney, through protruding front teeth, sing and whistle bars of the song hit of the day "Silver Threads Among the Gold," a few words of which, because he knew only a few of them, he sang over and over again, even when on missions which he knew would end for someone in death or disaster.

With William H. Bonney out of the way, Pat Garrett's fame increased to substantial proportions. He was acclaimed as a hero by many people in Lincoln County, down in Doña Ana, over in San Miguel. Citizens of Las Vegas opened a subscription list and collected a purse of several hundred dollars for the slayer of the Kid. Pat Garrett traveled to Santa Fe to collect the $500 reward that he thought had been offered for the killing of the desperado by Governor Lew Wallace on behalf of the Territory of New Mexico. Politicians in Santa Fe pointed out that Lew Wallace had worded the offer of a reward "for the delivery" of Billy the Kid to the sheriff of Lincoln County, not for killing him.[1] Chagrined, Garrett spent nearly five hundred dollars buying drinks in Santa Fe for members of the 1882 Legislature, before they passed an act making it possible for him to draw down his reward from the Territorial Treasury.[2]

Words of praise for Sheriff Pat Garrett and his exploits were published in *The Claiborne Guardian* at Homer, Louisiana, and edited by a boyhood friend. The *Guardian* said:

> For some time we have noticed that Pat Garrett, a sheriff in New Mexico, has attained considerable celebrity as a gallant official whose

---

to a riding contest. When the cowpunchers declined to compete, Deluvina selected one of their mounts, managed to get hold of the bridle reins, then succeeded in getting a foot in a stirrup and in some way found herself catapulted onto the saddle. The startled horse objected to such unorthodox horsemanship and Deluvina soon found herself a casualty of an extraordinary bucking bronco performance. Blushing cowboys hurried to her rescue. Borrowing a blanket from a saloonkeeper, four cowboys managed to wrap Deluvina within its protective folds and carried her to Pete Maxwell's house for safekeeping.

1. The notice of Governor Wallace, as published in the Las Vegas *Gazette*, of December 24, 1880, read as follows: "$500 Reward. Notice is hereby given that five hundred dollars reward will be paid for the delivery of Bonney, alias, 'The Kid,' to the Sheriff of Lincoln County. Lew Wallace, Governor of New Mexico."

2. See Chap. 101 of 1882 New Mexico Session Laws.

name was a terror to the desperadoes who are so common in a new country. His last exploit was the killing of a young villain who rejoiced in the name of Billy the Kid. The lad, only 21 years old, boasted of having killed a man for every year of his age. In spite of his open defiance of the law, his fierce animal courage and recklessness, he met his fate at the hands of Sheriff Pat Garrett, who killed him in attempting to arrest him. The coroner's jury returned a verdict of justifiable homicide and added thereto the statement that Sheriff Pat Garrett deserved the thanks of all good people for having rid the Territory of such a villian. All these facts were seen in the Associated Press dispatches without ever dreaming that the Sheriff spoken of was an old schoolmate. We learn, however, that such is the case, Sheriff Garrett being the son of Col. John L. Garrett, deceased, at one time one of the most prominent citizens in this parish. Pat Garrett at school was quiet, most gentlemanly, much liked by his associates because of his quiet manners. We can understand how he could have the pluck to kill a desperado, and we do not suppose that he has any of the loud, blustering, big pistol talking manners some men think an accompaniment of pluck and resolution. It gives the editor real pleasure to know that his old schoolmate is so popular and seems to do so well. We wish him a continuation of the honorable position he holds as an officer and a man. Good luck and happiness wherever he goes, for no man deserves it more than Pat Garrett, unless he has changed greatly.

Along with rejoicing in the Territory over the slaying of Billy the Kid, there also was a strong undercurrent of criticism of Pat Garrett because of the methods used to do away with the young outlaw. There was much talk that Garrett had not shot it out with the Kid face to face; that he had not beaten him to the draw in accordance with the code of the West, but had killed him when the Kid didn't have a chance. The talk became so widespread that Garrett told his version of the killing in a book entitled, *The Authentic Life of Billy the Kid, the Noted Desperado of the Southwest*. Pat Garrett gave his name to the book and much of the information about the actual shooting of the Kid came from him, but Marshall Ashmun Upson wrote every word of it.

Pat Garrett was not renominated as a candidate for sheriff of Lincoln County at the election succeeding the slaying of Billy the Kid. Kentucky-born John W. Poe, who had been with Pat Garrett the night of the slaying of the Kid, was the choice of the party managers in Lincoln County and he became sheriff. Poe was radically different in character, temperament and disposition from Garrett and soon put the law enforcement machinery of Lincoln County on a business-like basis. With his red-wheeled top buggy and fast horse, Poe traveled from one end of the immense county to the other. He arrested criminals, collected taxes, as was the duty of the sheriff in New Mexico in those days and conducted himself as an efficient sheriff. Whenever there was a shooting or livestock thievery, Sheriff John Poe was soon on the trail; once on the trail, bulldog-like, he never let up until the culprit was in jail or across the Mexico line.

Out of office as sheriff of Lincoln County, Pat Garrett went into the cattle business, registered PAT as his cattlebrand. His postoffice address was Fort Stanton, New Mexico. Garrett had a good many friends and neighbors in the cattle business in the Lincoln County country. Among them were J. C. Lea of Roswell, R. C. Allison of Black River, W. W. Brazil and Emil Fritz of Ruidoso, Eddy Brothers at Seven Rivers. James A. Alcock owned the nearby Carrizo Ranch, with postoffice at White Oaks. Poe and Goodin ranged on the Salado, Rio Bonito, Little Creek and Eagle Creek, and, like Garrett, received their mail at Fort Stanton.

By 1884, Pat Garrett had built up a good sized herd of cattle. To run them he bought a well-watered ranch with a splendid range, located on Eagle Creek, from Ki Harrison for five thousand dollars. Ki Harrison never took the trouble to deny the story circulated in the cow country, that he was a British lord exiled in America. To stock his new range, Pat Garrett bought three hundred head of cattle from Boney Baca and branded them in his PAT brand. Although doing fairly well in the ranch business on Eagle Creek, Pat Garrett accepted an invitation from Sheriff East of Tascosa in 1885 to organize a company of rangers, under the authority of the Governor of Texas, to work for the protection of the stockmen on the Texas–New Mexico border line. The acceptance of the commission meant that Garrett would be obliged to neglect his cattle outfit. Unable to resist the apparent advantages of the opportunity, Garrett undertook the work. He was described at this period of his life in an article in the *Golden Era* of November 5, 1885, as follows:

> Pat Garrett is a man about 6 feet 5 inches tall, with mild blue eyes, and low pleasant voice, and gives the appearance of being too modest

[*Photograph, facing page*]

PAT GARRETT AND ASSOCIATES: THE PICK OF POLITICAL POWER AND PERSONAL
PRESTIGE IN SOUTHEAST NEW MEXICO MORE THAN FIFTY YEARS AGO.

George Curry of Tularosa, known all over southeastern New Mexico
in the early days, was catapulted into the governorship of the Territory
in 1907 by Colonel Theodore Roosevelt, Rough Rider President of the
United States, through friendship which had its inception during the
Spanish-American War. The Curry inaugural ceremonies were held in
Santa Fe on August 8, 1907. Old time friends of Governor Curry, regardless of political faith, journeyed to the Territorial Capital to observe the
amenities of the occasion. The most prominent men of the day in southeastern New Mexico went to the inaugural in the *Ahumada*, a private
car borrowed from the El Paso, Rio Grande & Sierra Madre Railway. The
Ahumada was hauled over the El Paso & Northeastern from El Paso to
Alamogordo and Carrizozo, thence to Torrance, where it was switched to
the New Mexico Central tracks and hauled through Willard, Estancia
and other stations in the Estancia Valley, thence to Kennedy and Santa
Fe. At Torrance Junction, on August 7, 1907, the men who were making
the trip on the *Ahumada* posed for a group photograph. Time and events
proved the photograph to be of rare historic interest. Reading from left
to right, the standing men in the photograph are: William Ashton
Hawkins, associate of J. J. Hagerman and C. B. Eddy in railroad construction and development of southeastern New Mexico; William C. McDonald of Carrizozo, first governor of the State of New Mexico in 1912; Pat
Garrett of Las Cruces, who shot and killed William H. Bonney ("Billy
the Kid") at Fort Sumner, on the Pecos River, on July 14, 1881, and in
turn was shot and killed near Las Cruces on the Rio Grande on February
29, 1908, presumably by Wayne Brazil; Andrew H. Hudspeth of White
Oaks, first U. S. Marshal for New Mexico after statehood, and subsequently elected a Justice of the Supreme Court of New Mexico, onetime
sole owner of the ghost town of White Oaks; John Gerald Griffin, of
White Oaks, a newspaper man, uncle of Marcus Griffin, newspaper publisher of Carlsbad; Charles V. Safford of Santa Fe, then Territorial Traveling Auditor, later private secretary to Senator Albert B. Fall; Charles F.
Hunt of El Paso, a vigilante in Raton in 1885, who moved to Albuquerque
and was elected Sheriff of Bernalillo County in 1894.

Reading from left to right, bottom row: William Riley of Roswell,
cousin of George Curry; Herbert B. Holt, for decades prominent attorney
of Las Cruces and southeastern New Mexico, who, with Albert Bacon
Fall as associate counsel, obtained a verdict of acquittal for Wayne Brazil
when he was tried in Doña Ana County for the killing of Pat Garrett;

and backward to fight even if imposed upon. There is nothing of the braggart about Garrett. Pat Garrett was induced to run for Sheriff in Lincoln County by friends who reminded him that he was a quick, dead shot, and that "Billy the Kid" and his gang were afraid of him. "You can clear them out," they said to him. "You might get killed, but if you can get away with them, you will make your reputation and fortune."

The article might have added that Pat Garrett had a mole on the underside of his left jaw and wore what was known in the old days as a "killer" mustache, two items of identification that he carried to the grave. In his early years in New Mexico, Pat Garrett was a Democrat. He was a delegate from Lincoln County to the Territorial Democratic Convention in Albuquerque on August 19, 1884. José Montano, G. R. Young, J. J. Dolan and Capt. J. C. Lea, along with Pat Garrett, were the delegates; and the alternates were B. J. Baca, Wm. R. Ellis, Geo. T. Beall, Jr., John P. Baker and Wil-

---

Felix Martinez of Las Vegas and El Paso, perhaps the ablest and most gifted Spanish-American to participate in New Mexico affairs in his time, prominent in development of Elephant Butte dam project, personal representative of President Woodrow Wilson in 1916 on important confidential missions to Mexico and other Latin-American countries; Albert Bacon Fall of Three Rivers, judge of the Territorial Supreme Court during Grover Cleveland's second term as president, twice Attorney-General of the Territory, elected by the Legislature to be one of New Mexico's two first United States senators after statehood, re-elected to the Senate by vote of the people, who resigned from the Senate to become Secretary of the Interior in the cabinet of President Warren G. Harding; Holm Olaf Bursum of Socorro, chairman of the Territorial Republican Central Committee, Fall's successor in the U. S. Senate by appointment of Gov. M. C. Mechem, upon Fall's resignation to enter the cabinet, and elected to the Senate by vote of the people upon expiration of his appointive term; Mark B. Thompson of Las Cruces, noted trial lawyer, District Attorney of the Third Judicial District, who prosecuted Wayne Brazil for the murder of Pat Garrett in 1908, close friend of Albert Bacon Fall. Thompson went to Washington, at Fall's request, when Fall became involved in the tempest over Teapot Dome oil reserves.

Photograph by H. G. Clunn, El Paso; courtesy of H. B. Holt, Las Cruces.

liam H. Hudgens. Garrett attended the Lincoln County Democratic convention at Lincoln on July 21, 1884, and served on the committee on permanent organization and was named on the executive committee. W. C. McDonald, later first state governor of New Mexico, was chairman of the county convention.

On January 1, 1885, Pat Garrett and his family left for Las Vegas, from which town Garrett planned to carry on the work entrusted to him by the Governor of Texas. One of the things that Garrett was expected to combat was the practice of some New Mexico cattle operators, who made a business of giving bills of sale to cowboys for mythical "remnants" of cattle in Texas. To a bill of sale, there would be attached a power of attorney authorizing the holder to pick up in Texas and return to New Mexico any cattle found running under specified brands. This game, a variation from ordinary cattle stealing, was worked quite frequently and successfully. See *Crabtree v. Segrist*, 3 N.M. (Johnson) 278, 6 Pac. 202. If the cattle once got into New Mexico, the cowboys running them into the Territory from Texas were assured of ample compensation; if caught by officers in Texas, they claimed that they had been imposed upon, exhibited bills of sale and the power of attorney from an employer.

Pat Garrett kept his commission from the Governor of Texas only a few months. During his rambling up and down the Pecos River, endeavoring to organize his company of rangers, he became acquainted with Capt. Brandon Kirby, described as "an English gentleman." Brandon Kirby was in the Southwest looking for cattle and cattle ranches. He had spent five months searching for suitable properties in the Northwest, but had found nothing to his liking in Montana, Idaho, further north. Engaging in chance conversation with Pat Garrett in Tascosa, Captain Kirby learned that Garrett was well acquainted in the cattle country in New Mexico. Brandon Kirby had substantial English capital to invest. Pat Garrett showed him the ranch country near the Mescalero Indian reservation and other places in Lincoln County. Within a few days Kirby agreed to buy Garrett's ranch and a number of other properties in that region. Capt. W. W. Brazil, on Eagle Creek, was one of the first men to sell out to the Englishman. Four hundred head of cows and bulls went with the Brazil ranch. S. J. Slane sold his cattle and range to Kirby for fourteen thousand dollars. John W. Poe and his partner, Goodin, sold a fine range and a good herd of cattle to Brandon Kirby for eighty thousand dollars, a substantial sum of money for the times. The Poe and Goodin, Garrett, Slane and Brazil ranches on the Rio Bonito, Eagle Creek and tributaries, not far from Fort Stanton, afforded summer and winter range and were choice properties.

John W. Poe resigned as sheriff of Lincoln County on December 31, 1885, and returned to Lincoln County on August 21, 1886, from a six months trip he had taken to South America. Poe took with him to South America a letter of credit for the money he received for his share of the Poe and Goodin ranch sale from Captain Kirby, expecting to invest there in the cattle business. On his return to Lincoln, Poe expressed in a newspaper interview the opinion that New Mexico was a more favorable place for the investment of capital in stock raising than the Argentine Republic or any other country he had visited; that he would now be quite content to settle down at home.

With the increase in population in the southern and eastern part of Lincoln County there was an increasing demand for creation of one or more new counties. The great distances to Lincoln, the county seat, was the unanswerable argument. The population factor was not of great significance. On September 1, 1885, a census disclosed the following figures: Lincoln precinct, population, 959; San Patricio, 285; Picacho, 307; Three Rivers, 175; Roswell, 475; Lookout, 350; Seven Rivers, 300. Agitation for more accessible county seats continued to gain momentum and the Territorial Legislature in 1889 enacted laws creating Chaves County, named after Col. J. Francisco Chaves,[3] and Eddy County, named after Charles B. Eddy.

---

3. A Spanish name was given to the newly created County of Chaves, embracing a part of the Territory that had not been particularly kind in early years to people of Castilian descent. The name of the new county was in tribute to a great citizen of New Mexico, who had worked for years to create and maintain a better understanding and friendship between the people of the old and new cultures. J. Francisco Chaves was born in Las Padillas, Bernalillo County, on June 27, 1833, educated at St. Louis University and other schools in the East, in which he studied medicine as well as the classics. In 1853 and 1854, he took some twenty-five thousand sheep from New Mexico to California markets, fought the Navajo Indians in 1860, was a Major in the United States Army during the Civil War, serving with Ceran St. Vrain and Kit Carson. Chaves was the military officer to escort the civil officers on December 31, 1863, from New Mexico to the newly created Territory of Arizona, conducting the formal exercises incident to the occasion at Navajo Springs; he was elected to the 39th, 40th and 41st Congress of the United States; studied law and was admitted to the Bar of New Mexico

\ Brandon Kirby invested three hundred thousand dollars in Lincoln County ranches within a short time, established headquarters of the outfit at Little Creek; announced a policy of selling off the steers he had purchased and running only a breeding ranch for fine stock. He brought fine Angus bulls from Scotland to Galveston seaport, shipped them into Lincoln County through Fort Worth, Texas. Cattle growers in the country had complained for years of the shortage of bulls. The tendency in the free range country to depend on a neighbor for bulls was deplored on many occasions. Brandon Kirby answered the complaint promptly by stocking his range by the importation of bulls from Scotland. George L. Brooks of Albuquerque sold Kirby and others high-priced land scrip, with priority rights on public domain. Through use of scrip, substantial areas of public domain were blocked out, extending the boundaries of ranches acquired through use of capital from England, Ireland and Scotland. The invasion of foreign money dislocated prices and conditions in Lincoln County to such an extent that the small cattle ranchers were placed at a great disadvantage. The choicest range land went to the big operators, and the little fellow was left to fight for the remnants. Problems incident to the use of the public domain had been the nightmare of thinking livestock men for many years.

In the fall of 1885 Pat Garrett resigned his commission as Captain of Texas Rangers, abandoned his plans to organize a company of rangers to guard the Texas-New Mexico border against livestock thieves and accepted a place as manager of the ranches and cattle acquired by Captain Brandon Kirby. Garrett had entire control over Kirby's outfit and rode frequently over the ranges along the Salado, Bonito, Little and Eagle Creeks and the Ruidoso. Soon after he took over the Brandon Kirby interests, Garrett issued an order prohibiting

---

and assumed a prominent place as District Attorney of the Second Judicial District, and in private practice. Colonel Chaves served with great ability in many sessions of the Legislature of New Mexico, including the one during which Chaves County was created, manifesting at all times an interest in educational affairs. He was assassinated at Pinos Wells, New Mexico, on November 26, 1904. The mystery of his death was never satisfactorily solved. It was believed by many that Colonel Chaves was sent to the holy land at the behest of highly-placed Republican party leaders because they considered him inimical to some of their intrigues. See *Historical Society of New Mexico*, No. 31, with eulogies by Paul A. F. Walter, Frank W. Clancy, and Miguel A. Otero.

any cowboy on his range from carrying any kind of a gun or pistol. Penalty for disobedience was immediate dismissal.[4]

In addition to the cattle bought originally in the Lincoln country, Brandon Kirby purchased 7,000 cattle on the Canadian River and 4,800 head from the Prairie Cattle Company of Texas, which were trailed to ranges along the Ruidoso. The entire outfit was of considerable importance and gave Pat Garrett an excellent opportunity to demonstrate his ability as a manager and producer.

The Texas fever hit Lincoln County cattle in the summer of 1885; the cowboys resented Garrett's order against carrying firearms; friction developed between Garrett and the ranch owners over the manner in which the business was being conducted. Garrett resigned as manager on April 24, 1886, and announced that he expected to devote his entire time to ranching near Roswell. Garrett was succeeded as manager of the Brandon Kirby outfit by John W. Poe, his former deputy sheriff. Garrett owned some property in the Roswell country and increased his holdings there when he acquired on January 6, 1886, from W. L. Holloman two hundred acres of land for $3,000 and a quarter-section of land from A. S. Lewis. Garrett had visions of promoting an important land and irrigation project along the Pecos River. He interested substantial outside capital in the venture and undertook to execute important parts of the work. His efforts did not achieve the hoped for results, but his ideas in some respects were carried forward years later by Charles B. Eddy, J. J. Hagerman and others in connection with the development of the Pecos Valley.

Not very happy about the results obtained in land development enterprises near Roswell, Pat Garrett was anxious in 1889 to become the first sheriff of newly organized Chaves County. No particular opposition to his candidacy was manifested until John W. Poe promoted another candidate for sheriff and elected him. Some years before Pat Garrett and John W. Poe had quarreled over money matters in connection with a land transaction in the Eagle Creek country. Poe claimed Garrett had not paid the entire amount due on a promissory note. The two men had been cool toward each other for a long time. Pat Garrett's pride was hurt when he discovered that John W. Poe's influence had prevented him from being the first elected

4. Garrett probably had a selfish motive in forbidding cowboys to carry guns on the range, fearing that a cowboy friend of "Billy the Kid" might shoot him.

sheriff of Chaves County. He believed that his usefulness in the community had ended.[5] Pat Garrett left Roswell for Uvalde, Texas, accompanied by Ash Upson, an ever-faithful friend. Upson died in Uvalde on October 6, 1894.

Always passionately fond of breeding quarter horses and racing them, Garrett in Uvalde made horse raising his principal business. John Nance Garner, later vice-president of the United States during the first and second Franklin D. Roosevelt terms, was a political power in Uvalde in the early nineties. Pat Garrett became acquainted with Garner and they became friends and companions. Then in his thirties, John Garner, like Garrett, was fond of horses and horse racing. Pat Garrett named two of his race horses after him.[*] Garrett dabbled in politics in Uvalde and was elected County Commissioner of Precinct No. 1 in a hard-fought campaign against D. W. Barnhill, a strong candidate.

Pat Garrett would probably have remained in Uvalde, Texas, indefinitely, if he had been able to resist siren calls of New Mexico politicians who started a letter writing campaign urging him to return and accept an appointment as sheriff of Doña Ana County. Numa Raymond, a businessman of Las Cruces, had been elected sheriff. He had neither time nor inclination for the office. Garrett's friends in Doña Ana County held out the possibilities for fame in

---

5. John W. Poe, early day character in Lincoln County, was born in Mason County, Kentucky, October 17, 1850, was a buffalo hunter in Texas, then Town Marshal, at Ft. Griffin, Texas, for one year. In 1879, Poe went to Ft. Elliott, Wheeler County, Texas, served as deputy sheriff and U.S. Deputy Marshal. He ran for sheriff of Wheeler County, lost the race by one vote. John W. Poe wrote his version of the killing of Billy the Kid, for E. A. Brininstool, Los Angeles, published in the *World Wide* magazine in December, 1919. The narrative was incorporated in the volume, *The Death of Billy the Kid*, published by Houghton Mifflin Co. 1933, with an introduction by Maurice Garland Fulton of Roswell.

* Quoting John N. Garner's letter to the author from Uvalde, Texas, April 5, 1943: "I knew Pat Garrett well and thought a lot of him. He named some of his race horses after me—one John Garner and another John Nance. I joined him in promoting a horse race once at Rocksprings, Edwards County, Texas, and my recollection is that our horse was named Minnie. We ran her against a horse named Gulliver. We had lots of fun. That was forty-five to forty-eight years ago. I don't know of anything else I can tell you about Pat Garrett other than he was the most devoted man to his family I have ever known, especially to one crippled child. He gave her everything to make her happy and I think finally made quite a musician of her." Mr. Garner undoubtedly referred to Elizabeth Garrett, blind daughter of Pat Garrett, composer of the state song, *Oh, Fair New Mexico*.

solving the mystery of the Fountain disappearance and the opportunity to win large rewards "for the arrest and conviction of the
murderers of A. J. Fountain." Possibly eager to recapture a bit of
the notoriety that had belonged to him in the Territory as the slayer
of Billy the Kid, Pat Garrett in 1897 returned to New Mexico. He
renounced his political affiliation as a Democrat, became a Republican and was chosen sheriff by the Commissioners of Doña Ana
County. Garrett served out the appointive term and was elected
sheriff in the campaign of 1898. Pat Garrett's immediate task as
sheriff was to arrest Oliver M. Lee, Jim Gililland and W. H. McNew,
in connection with the Fountain murder mystery.

After the acquittal of Oliver Lee and Jim Gililland at Hillsboro,
Pat Garrett lived quietly near Las Cruces as an ex-sheriff, doing a
bit of ranching, waiting for the turn of the wheel of fortune. The
post of Collector of the Customs at the Port of El Paso became
vacant. Garrett was anxious to obtain the appointment. Under a
Republican administration, the office of Collector of the Port, although Texas patronage, ordinarily went to a New Mexico appointee.
With the endorsement of many Republicans of New Mexico and the
help of his old friend, John Nance Garner of Uvalde, Texas, Pat
Garrett's name was sent to the Senate for confirmation by President
Theodore Roosevelt. Roosevelt had a weakness for appointing gunmen and western characters to important administrative positions.
He knew about Pat Garrett's brush with Billy the Kid and that
among his other qualifications, he was handy with a six-shooter. The
President was a bit disturbed by the flood of telegrams that reached
him, protesting against Garrett's appointment because he was a race
horse follower and a poker player. Confirmed as Collector of the
Customs in 1901, the people of El Paso gave a banquet in Pat Garrett's honor. Introducing Garrett, the toastmaster said: "Here is the
man that President Roosevelt was worried about, because he had the
reputation of being a poker player. Everybody in El Paso knows that
Pat Garrett isn't a poker player. He only *thinks* he's a poker player."

Collector of the Port of El Paso, only forty miles away from his
home town of Las Cruces, Pat Garrett was a flamboyant and picturesque figure. He entertained in the manner and style of the day,
wore rather flashy suits of clothes, usually stripes in the pattern, and
was one of the best-known men in El Paso and the Southwest. Garrett served four years as Collector of Customs and then returned

to his hobby, the raising of blooded horses on his little ranch a few miles from Las Cruces. With the money he had saved out of his position as Collector of the Port of El Paso, Garrett purchased a bunch of good mares and several good stallions and started to raise quarter horses.*

No longer occupying the important position of Collector of the Port, or sought after as a celebrity, Pat Garrett found time idling on his hands in and around Las Cruces. He attempted to "beat up" Jim Baird, a neighboring rancher, with a six-shooter, an incident which did him no good out in the range country. Garrett visited saloons in Las Cruces rather frequently and played poker with much younger men. Although he had not taken a drink of liquor for a year prior to his death, Garrett was sometimes mean and irritable. Poker players about Las Cruces feared him in his moods of irritation.

Raising blooded horses did not prove profitable and Garrett was in poor shape financially toward the end of his life. Only a few days before he was killed, Pat Garrett wrote to his old friend, George Curry, then Governor of the Territory of New Mexico, saying: "Dear Curry: I am in a hell of a fix. I have been trying to sell my ranch, but no luck. For God's sake, send me fifty dollars." With characteristic generosity, Governor Curry immediately sent Garrett his check for the amount requested. Some days later, when the Governor went to Las Cruces to investigate Garrett's death, the uncashed check was found on his person.

On February 29, 1908, Pat Garrett was shot and killed on the road from his ranch in the Organ Mountains to Las Cruces. Wayne Brazil, who had been at one time a cowboy on the adjoining W. W. Cox ranch, twenty miles from the town of Las Cruces, confessing that

---

* Garrett and his friends tried hard to get President Roosevelt to reappoint him as Collector of the Port. The El Paso *Herald* of December 31, 1905, reported: "President Roosevelt has emphatically declined to reappoint Pat Garrett Collector of Customs at El Paso. It is said Tom Powers, Proprietor of the Coney Island Saloon, who is in Washington with Garrett, has wired his friends to get all the endorsements possible and they are now at work."

The late Maury Kemp, prominent lawyer of El Paso and keen observer of men and events, wrote in 1945: "The reason Teddy Roosevelt fired Pat Garrett was because Pat and Tom Powers, owner of the Coney Island Saloon, went to a Rough Riders' convention in San Antonio and Pat got Tom into a picture along with the President. When Roosevelt learned that he had his picture taken with a saloonkeeper, and that Pat Garrett was responsible for the lese majeste, he was through with Garrett."

he had done the shooting, voluntarily surrendered to Sheriff Felipe
Lucero of Doña Ana County. Sheriff Lucero and Dr. W. C. Field left
Las Cruces at once for the scene of the killing. They found Pat Garrett's body as it had fallen, undisturbed, in a six-inch sand drift by
the side of the road. Garrett's shotgun was about four feet off to
one side. Garrett had a glove on his right hand, but none on the left
hand. According to the testimony of Dr. Field at the inquest, there
was a pathway in the center of the back of the head made by a .45
bullet, which had driven Garrett's long hair into the brain and torn
away the right eyebrow, unmistakable evidence, in his opinion, that
Garrett had been shot from behind. Another .45 bullet, later ex-
tracted by Dr. Field, had penetrated the body from the upper part
of the stomach to the upper part of the shoulders. Before the coroner's jury, Carl Adamson, an eyewitness, testified: "We stopped to
urinate. Wayne Brazil and Pat Garrett started to argue. Pat Garrett
was getting out of the buggy with a shotgun in his hand. Wayne
Brazil shot him. I didn't see how it all happened." Dr. Field, who had
made careful measurements of distances and closely investigated
conditions at the scene of the crime, declared unequivocally at the
inquest over the body that in his opinion the shooting of Pat Garrett was murder in cold blood, murder in the first degree.

Governor George Curry, long-time personal friend of Pat Garrett,
accompanied by James M. Hervey of Roswell, Attorney-General of
the Territory, and Fred Fornoff, Captain of the Territorial Mounted
Police, left for Las Cruces as soon as word of the shooting reached
Santa Fe. Both Curry and Hervey knew personally of the ramifications of the Doña Ana and Lincoln County feuds. George Curry had
spent many years of his young manhood in Lincoln County. Hervey
had spent his boyhood in Lincoln and later served there as court
reporter.

Governor Curry asked many questions in Las Cruces, seeking facts
in connection with Garrett's death; Attorney-General Hervey probed
at the inquest, asked searching questions directed to Wayne Brazil
and Carl Adamson. The case seemed plain enough. Many signs
pointed to murder. But why murder? Even if true, the story told by
Wayne Brazil did not seem to justify the taking of human life.

Subsequent to the shooting, James M. Hervey went to Chicago
and sought out his old-time friend, Emerson Hough, famous as a

writer, whom he had known many years before in Lincoln. Hough and Pat Garrett had been good friends in the old days; some years before his death Pat Garrett had taken Hough over the Lincoln country and had told him again how he happened to shoot Billy the Kid. Emerson Hough knew of the feuds on the ranges, of the hard feeling there was against Pat Garrett on the part of the Lees, the Cox families and others in the Organ Mountains and elsewhere in southeast New Mexico. After Hervey told him the details of the Pat Garrett shooting, Emerson Hough said to him: "Jimmy Hervey, I'm going to give you some good advice. Go back home and stay out of this Pat Garrett shooting. If you don't, you will be the next one to be killed." James M. Hervey followed Emerson Hough's advice, preferring a quiet life in the practice of law in Roswell and Albuquerque to a big funeral as one of the legatees of the Pat Garrett feud.

Death came to Patrick Floyd Garrett in his fifty-eighth year. He died with the proverbial boots on, as he had frequently predicted to Cesario Pedragon of Las Cruces and other friends. His six feet and four inches had bowed somewhat with age; his hair, worn long, had turned badger grey. Never a religious man, Pat Garrett at various times in his later years had expressed views that were in harmony with those of Robert Green Ingersoll, noted agnostic of his day. Although not a man who read much more than the daily newspapers, Pat Garrett had read one of Ingersoll's books, *Some Mistakes of Moses*, and had also committed to memory a favorite passage from Ingersoll's writings which, in the proper mood, he would recite for friends. The passage, a part of a Fourth of July oration, was as follows:

> These heroes are dead. They died for liberty, they died for us. They are at rest. They sleep in the land they made free, under the flag they rendered stainless, under the solemn pines, the sad hemlocks, the tearful willows, the embracing vines. They sleep beneath the shadows of the clouds, careless alike of sunshine or storm, each in the windowless palace of rest. Earth may run red with other wars —they are at peace. In the midst of battles, in the roar of conflict, they have found the serenity of death.

At Pat Garrett's brief and simple funeral service in Las Cruces, a friend read Robert Green Ingersoll's eulogy, delivered in 1879 at the grave of his brother, Ebon Clark Ingersoll. The reader, over Pat Garrett's body, finished, as Bob Ingersoll had done, with the words:

PAT GARRETT FAMILY GRAVE SITE, LAS CRUCES, NEW MEXICO.

Life is a narrow vale between the cold and barren peaks of two eternities. We strive in vain to look beyond the heights. We cry aloud—and the only answer is the echo of our wailing cry. From the voiceless lips of the unreplying dead there comes no word. But in the night of death Hope sees a star and listening Love can hear the rustling of a wing.

Another friend, long an admirer of William Jennings Bryan, opposed to the Bob Ingersoll atmosphere, read at Garrett's funeral a few words from a eulogy that William Jennings Bryan had delivered in the Fifty-third Congress at memorial services for a fellow congressman:

I shall not believe that even now his light is extinguished. If the Father designs to touch with divine power the cold and pulseless heart of the buried acorn, and make it burst forth from its walls, will he leave neglected in the world the soul of man, who was made in the image of the Creator? If he stoops to give to the rosebush, whose withered blossoms float upon the breeze, the sweet assurance of another springtime, will he withhold the words of hope from the sons of men when the frosts of winter come? If matter, mute and inanimate. though changed by the forces of nature into a multitude of forms, can never die, will the imperial spirit of men suffer annihilation after it has paid a brief visit, like a royal guest, to this tenement of clay? Rather let us believe that He who, in His apparent prodigality wastes not the raindrop, the blade of grass, the evening's sighing zephyr, but makes them all to carry out His eternal plan, has given immortality to the mortal, and gathered to himself the generous spirit of our friend.

Pat Garrett had found the end of the trail. His burial was in the family plot in Las Cruces.*

---

* With the exception of Elizabeth Garrett, who died on Oct. 16, 1947, and is buried in Roswell, all deceased members of the Patrick Floyd Garrett family are now buried in a family plot in the Masonic Cemetery in Las Cruces. The bodies were removed in 1959 from their former resting place in the abandoned Odd Fellows cemetery and reinterred in the Masonic Cemetery across the highway. In the center of the plot there is a large granite monument bearing the family name. There are individual granite markers, with the name, dates of birth and death of each decedent. The removal of the bodies was accomplished with the consent and under the supervision of Miss Pauline Garrett and Jarvis Powers Garrett, the only surviving children of Mr. and Mrs. Pat Garrett. The headstones: Ida Garrett, 1881-1896; Patrick Floyd Garrett,

The Doña Ana County grand jury returned a true bill against Wayne Brazil on April 13, 1908. Brazil was released at once on a $10,000 bond with W. W. Cox, Geo. W. Freeman, J. S. Quesenberry, F. H. Bascom, J. W. Taylor, J. D. Isaacs and J. H. May as sureties. The indictment against Wayne Brazil charged that "he, the said Wayne Brazil, did on the twenty-ninth day of February, 1908, in Doña Ana County, Territory of New Mexico, with force and arms in and upon one Patrick F. Garrett, there and then with a certain pistol, loaded with gunpowder and various leaden bullets, did kill and murder the said Patrick F. Garrett." The trial of Wayne Brazil for the murder of Pat Garrett, before a Doña Ana County jury, resulted on April 19, 1909, in a verdict of not guilty.

Through Mark B. Thompson, prosecuting attorney, the Territory had endeavored to uncover evidence of a conspiracy to kill Garrett. Subpoenaes were issued for telegrams sent over the Western Union Telegraph Company wires by and between Wayne Brazil, Carl Adamson, J. P. Miller, W. W. Cox and A. P. ("Print") Rhodes. The case was tried before Judge Frank W. Parker. Ten years before, Judge Parker had presided at the Oliver Lee trial in Hillsboro in which Pat Garrett had been one of the principal figures. Carl Adamson, eyewitness to the Garrett killing who had testified at the coroner's inquest, although available, was not called to testify at the trial of Wayne Brazil by either prosecution or defense.

There was before the jury the testimony of Wayne Brazil, which was in direct conflict with the physical situation on the ground described by Sheriff Lucero and Dr. Field as they recalled seeing it soon after the killing of Pat Garrett on February 29, 1908. Nobody was surprised when Brazil testified in support of the old reliable plea of self defense. According to Brazil's testimony, Pat Garrett had owned a ranch outside of Las Cruces which Brazil had leased from him. Some days before the killing, Garrett told Brazil that he was negotiating with J. P. Miller of Oklahoma and Carl Adamson to lease to Miller the range which Wayne Brazil occupied, if satisfactory arrangements could be made all around. Miller told Garrett, according to Brazil, that he had bought a thousand head of cattle in Mexico

---

1850-1908; Apolinaria Gutierrez Garrett, 1861-1936; Patrick Floyd Garrett, Jr., 1896-1927; Anna Garrett Montgomery, 1890-1922; Dudley Poe Garrett, 1882-1932; Oscar Lohmann Garrett, 1904-1951; Feliciana V. [Valdez] Gutierrez [mother of Apolinario Gutierrez Garrett] 1846-1919.

for delivery in El Paso on March 15. Miller explained to Garrett, so Brazil testified, that he did not want to ship the cattle to his Oklahoma ranch until fall, and wanted New Mexico grass in the meantime. Brazil testified that he had told Garrett he was willing to get off the ranch and surrender it to Miller, if Garrett could arrange for the sale of eighteen hundred goats which he, Brazil, owned and was pasturing on the range.

During the three-cornered negotiations between Pat Garrett, Carl Adamson and Jim Miller, it developed that Miller was willing, at Garrett's request, to undertake to find a buyer for the goats. Miller reported back to Garrett that he had found a purchaser who would buy 1,200 head of goats from Brazil, but that he had been unable to sell the others. Brazil told Garrett he would not leave the ranch until he could sell all the goats. Garrett and Adamson discussed the entire matter with Brazil at Garrett's ranch, decided there should be some way to close up the deal and all of them started for Las Cruces to interview Jim Miller. Garrett and Adamson rode in Garrett's buckboard. Wayne Brazil, on horseback, rode alongside. On the way to town, Brazil testified, Garrett suddenly got out of the buckboard, shotgun in hand and said to him: "Brazil, I want you to get them dam'd goats off that range; if you don't, I'll make you take them off." Brazil testified that, with Garrett's well-known character as a gunman, he feared for his life and had no alternative but to shoot. He recalled that after the first shot Carl Adamson had called out to him: "Don't shoot him again," but was too much agitated to stop from shooting a second time. Only a perfunctory effort was made by the prosecution to develop on cross-examination, that Garrett might have been shot in the back of the head, or that Garrett had been found dead with a glove on his trigger finger hand. With no evidence before it of a substantial nature to prove that Garrett had been murdered, in the manner and form charged in the indictment, the jury quickly returned a verdict of not guilty. Wayne Brazil was a free man.

Out on the W. W. Cox ranch in the Organ Mountains, there was a barbecue celebrating the acquittal of Wayne Brazil.* The celebration, attended by ranchers and cowboys from the range country for many miles around, soon turned into an occasion of rejoicing over the passing of Pat Garrett.

---

* For many years, before and after Brazil's acquittal, the W. W. Cox ranch in the Organ Mountains, known as the San Augustine Ranch, was one of the outstanding

Although not present at the Wayne Brazil trial in Las Cruces, eyewitness Carl Adamson had recently been in court on other business. He had been indicted in the Sixth Judicial District of the Territory in a case in which the United States of America was the complainant, charging that he had, on June 18, 1908, "unlawfully, feloniously, knowingly, wickedly, falsely, and corruptly, conspired, combined, confederated and agreed, to and with various and divers persons," to bring into the United States of America from the Republic of Mexico certain Chinese persons. Carl Adamson pleaded not guilty, but, on trial in Alamogordo, the jury found him guilty. He was sentenced on December 14, 1908, to serve a year and a half in prison. Through his attorneys, Adamson announced an appeal to the Supreme Court of the United States, but the appeal was never perfected.

When cowpuncher Allen Hightower, standing in front of the Little Casino Saloon in White Oaks, heard that Carl Adamson, whom he knew slightly, had been arrested in Alamogordo on a charge of smuggling a wagon load of Chinamen into the United

---

cattle ranches in New Mexico. It was here at San Augustine Springs that Major Isaac Lynde on July 27, 1861, while enroute from Fort Filmore to Fort Stanton, surrendered 700 Union troops to Col. John R. Baylor, in command of some 200 Texans. Lynde surrendered his command without unsheathing a sword or firing a shot, an incident which provoked much comment at the time. The circumstances surrounding the surrender, and possible justification for it, continued to be discussed for many years after the end of the Civil War. William Webb Cox, long time sole owner of the San Augustine Ranch, which eventually contained 105,000 acres of land, was born in De Witt County, Texas, on November 12, 1854. He died on December 23, 1923. W. W. Cox and Oliver M. Lee were brothers-in-law. Cox married Margaret Zerilda Rhode, Lee married her sister, Winnie P. Rhode.

W. W. Cox spent his boyhood years in an atmosphere of fighting and feuding in Texas. Coming to New Mexico in 1886, he brought with him vivid recollections of feuding in his native state. In 1873, his father, James Webb Cox, was shot and killed in a fight with the Taylor crowd and several men who had stood with him in the fight were wounded. When young Cox arrived at the scene of the shooting he found that his father's body had been riddled with fifty-eight bullet wounds, almost any one of which would have been fatal. Tradition has it that W. W. Cox blamed John Wesley Hardin personally for his father's death and vowed vengeance. For years thereafter young Bill Cox and Hardin were prepared to shoot each other on sight. On one occasion they exchanged shots, both men being wounded. In Hardin's book, *The Life of John Wesley Hardin, From the Original Manuscript, as Written by Himself*, published by Smith and Moore in Seguin, Texas, 1896, Hardin commented briefly on the Jim Cox fight: "A fight came off not long afterwards near Tomlinson Creek, in which Jim Cox, one of the leaders of the Vigilant Committee, and Jake Christman were killed. It was currently reported that I led the fight, but as I have never pleaded to

W. W. Cox

States from Mexico, he remarked: "Hell, I'd rather be caught trying to steal a wagon load of calves, than to get caught smuggling in a load of Chinese. It would be a damn sight more respectable."

With Pat Garrett in the grave and Wayne Brazil given a freedom which later turned into oblivion, the name of Jim Miller began to be mentioned frequently in conversations in connection with Pat Garrett's tragic death. People, who before the trial of Wayne Brazil had remained silent, reluctant to say anything that might involve them in any phase of the case, were now willing to tell what they knew and suspected.

Bit by bit the name of Jim Miller began to become more significant in connection with the Garrett shooting. It developed that Jim Miller had close ties in New Mexico, was related by marriage to Carl Adamson and was a brother-in-law of Constable Manning Clements of El Paso, subsequently shot and killed there in the Coney Island

---

that case, I will at this time have little to say, except to state that Jim Cox and Jake Christman met their death from the Taylor party about the 15th day of May, 1873."

Some twenty years after his father's death, Cox was enabled to let down his guard to some extent when he learned that John Wesley Hardin had been shot and killed by John Selman in El Paso, Texas, not many miles away from Cox's ranch, on August 19, 1895, Selman in turn being killed by George Scarborough in El Paso on April 5, 1896. Starting a cattle ranch in a modest way, in the 80's, in the San Andreas mountain country, living for a time in a dugout near Los Alamos Spring, W. W. Cox gradually extended his holdings. In 1893, when the country was in a financial panic, Cox had the courage to buy the San Augustine Ranch, rated as "the queen of them all." When he passed away in 1923 it seemed probable that the San Augustine ranch would continue to be a cattle producing unit for many years to come. However, in 1945 the federal government acquired 90 per cent of the total area of the ranch and converted it to military use. As a result of negotiations with the government, James Webb Cox, son of W. W. Cox, and grandson and namesake of James Webb Cox, managed to salvage a bit of the ranch for his own use, including the house in which he was born, on Feb. 7, 1895.

From Jim Cox's ranch home there may be seen the extraordinary, almost incredible changes that have come over the landscape during the last decade through the establishment of areas and facilities dedicated to development and testing of missiles, silent testimony to the fact that breeding and raising of cattle on an extensive scale are things of the past insofar as the San Augustine ranch may be concerned. The cowboy and horsewrangler, important figures on the San Augustine range in the colorful years of Eugene Manlove Rhodes, have been superseded by men of an entirely different era, most of them young, highly educated and skilled as scientists. Many of the newcomers belong to Phi Beta Kappa, a large number of them have Ph.D. degrees. Their minds focused on technical problems relating to launching sites, rockets and guided missiles, they have little time to consider the proclivities of bucking broncos, or peculiarities of yearling steers.

saloon. Jim Miller had been seen in White Oaks not so very long before the shooting of Pat Garrett. In White Oaks he attracted particular attention because he was dressed pretty much like a preacher, wearing, it was recalled, a Prince Albert coat and a black bow tie as part of his outfit. Miller had been seen at the Park Hotel and at one of the banks in Las Cruces on the day that Pat Garrett was killed; and he had been seen in and around El Paso for several days. People on the streets in Las Cruces said that Jim Miller had been the brains behind the shooting of Pat Garrett; that he was a hired gunman; that he had deceived Pat Garrett, fooled him; that Miller had no ranch in Oklahoma, had not purchased a thousand head of Mexican cattle for delivery in El Paso in the spring of 1908, never had any prospective purchaser for Wayne Brazil's goats. Miller, it was claimed, simply undertook negotiations with Pat Garrett as a pretext to involve him in a situation from which Garrett would be unable to extricate himself without losing his life. Pat Garrett died, in the opinion of many of the old-timers of southeast New Mexico, a victim of Jim Miller's machinations. Wayne Brazil may possibly have shot Pat Garrett, they said, because he admitted that he had killed him; but behind Wayne Brazil there was Jim Miller, with his brains and his ability as a planner and director.

Pat Garrett knew Jim Miller slightly and was fairly well acquainted with his background, but Pat Garrett was no match for a man of the character and ability of Jim Miller. When just a boy of eighteen, Jim Miller had been accused of killing John Coop, his brother-in-law, on July 30, 1884. John Coop was assassinated about 9 o'clock at night on that date while he was in bed at his home on Plumb Creek in Coryell County, eight miles northwest of Gatesville, Texas. Jim Miller was arrested for the crime, tried before a jury, convicted of first degree murder and sentenced to the penitentiary for life.

Miller's attorneys took the case to the Texas Court of Appeals, where it was reversed. A retrial was granted on the ground that the trial court had erred in refusing to grant Miller a requested continuance, in order to permit him to perfect an alibi, and in giving to the jury an instruction found to be contrary to law. Reported in *James Miller vs. State of Texas*, 18 Texas Court of Appeals, 232, the case had all the color, glamour and intrigue that later on characterized Miller's activities.

Following the shooting of John Coop, circumstances pointed strongly to young Jim Miller. When tried for the crime, Miller could account for all of his time on the night that John Coop was killed, except for a period of forty minutes. Jim Miller's testimony at the trial showed that he had attended a camp meeting with Miss Georgia Large at Camp Branch, three miles away from the Coop home. Miss Large testified that Miller had gone with her to the camp meeting; that they had gone "into the arbor together and sat side by side," that Jim Miller had remained at her side "until the preaching began" when he excused himself, and that he returned "when the regular service was over and the shouting had commenced." The jury decided that Jim Miller had enough time between the beginning of the preaching and the commencement of the shouting to ride three miles to the Coop place, kill him and then return to the side of his companion at the camp meeting. Testimony showed that Jim Miller rode a fast horse to the camp meeting place that night; that some days before the night of the killing, Jeff Coop, a brother of John Coop, had made a test ride to show how many minutes would elapse between the start of the Coop place, arrival at Camp Branch and return to the places of starting. Watches had been held on the rides at both ends. Evidence was before the jury that Jim Miller knew of the ride and knew almost to a second how long it would take him to ride to and from the camp meeting, place a load of buckshot into the body of his brother-in-law and return to the "preaching and the shouting." The camp meeting killing was the first of some twenty murders that had been chalked up against Jim Miller. He never denied that he had committed them. Miller's favorite method of destruction was with a shotgun, fired from ambush. A blast from a shotgun, escape on a horse, release on bond, a capable lawyer for defense if discovered, these were all part of Miller's technique.

Jim Miller had the reputation of being a professional killer for hire and those who knew him well said he made no bones of it. In appearance he was a mild-mannered man, but had a hard glint in his blue eyes. He did not drink, gamble, smoke or chew, and never used profanity.

For several years Jim Miller lived in and about Memphis, Texas, managed to get himself appointed on the Texas Rangers, bought a half interest in a saloon, discussed his killings casually with friends, sometimes predicted them. After leaving Memphis, Miller resided briefly in Gainesville and Monahans, Texas, and after service as a Texas Ranger, worked for a time as a United States deputy marshal.

Tom Coggin and Jenks Clark of San Saba County, Texas, were frequently Jim Miller's sureties on appearance bonds when he was in trouble. Among many others, Miller had killed former Sheriff Bud Fraser in Pecos, Texas; District Attorney Stanley of the Forty-sixth Texas Judicial District; two men near Midland; a man at Lawton, Oklahoma; and in 1904 shot and killed Frank Fore in Fort Worth, Texas. After he had been acquitted of the Fore shooting, a friend of Fore's took a shot at Miller. The bullet went through the crown of Miller's hat and he went on his way unconcernedly as if nothing had happened. Barney Riggs of Fort Stockton was the only man in Texas of whom Jim Miller was afraid, and the fear prompted Miller to wish Riggs out of the way. On one occasion Miller walked into a saloon at Fort Stockton, hoping to provoke Barney Riggs into a quarrel. He offered to buy a drink for Riggs, then a cigar. Riggs refused both invitations, watching minutely every move Jim Miller made.

Born in Van Buren, Arkansas, Jim Miller was taken by his parents to Robertson County, Texas, when one year old. Here both parents died and, when eighteen years old, Miller moved to Coryell County, Texas. For many years Jim Miller was a familiar figure around Fort Worth. He joined the church there and could be seen almost any evening in an armchair among the loungers in the Delaware Hotel.

Having dealt in death for many years, perhaps Jim Miller was not surprised when death overtook him. On March 31, 1909, James P. Miller was arrested on a farm near Hicks, Texas, a few miles west of Fort Worth, Texas, and brought to Ada, Oklahoma, where he was lodged in jail. Fond of jewelry, Miller was wearing a diamond ring and diamond shirt stud when arrested. On April 6, 1909, Jesse West and Joe Allen of Canadian City, Texas, were arrested in Oklahoma City and placed in the Ada jail along with Miller and B. B. Burwell of Dalhart, Texas, who had been arrested a few days before. Jim Miller, Jess West, Joe Allen and B. B. Burwell were accused of the murder of A. A. (Gus) Bobbitt, a prominent farmer and cattle grower of Ada, who had been shot and killed on February 26, 1909. Bobbitt had been a United States deputy marshal for the southern district of the old Indian Territory during the Grover Cleveland administration and had dealt vigorously with outlaws in that part of the present state of Oklahoma. On April 19, 1909, at 2 o'clock in the morning, the power was shut off at the electric light plant in Ada and the town was left in darkness. A mob went to the Pontotoc County jail, overpowered the jailer, escorted Miller, West, Allen and Burwell to the old Frisco barn, just a short distance away and hanged them by the neck until they were dead.[6]

Just as they were about to put a rope around Miller's neck he said: "Boys, if you're going to string me up, do it quick." He asked that his diamond ring and shirt stud be sent to his wife in Fort Worth, which was done.

The killing of Gus Bobbitt had occurred a year almost to the day after the date of the murder of Pat Garrett at Las Cruces, New Mexico. Bobbitt was on his way home about 7 o'clock in the evening, driving a team of horses hauling a load of cotton-seed meal. Several miles out in the country from Ada, an unidentified man on a horse rode close to Bobbitt and riddled his body with a blast from a double-barreled shotgun. Bobbitt lived an hour and a half. He managed to tell his wife that he could not identify his assailant, but gave her the names of two men who were his enemies and whom he thought responsible for the crime. Officers traced the hoofprints of the horse carrying the man who had shot Bobbitt from the place of the crime to the farm of a man named Williamson, near Francis, Oklahoma.

When they found that Williamson was a nephew of Jim Miller, the officers felt they were on the right trail. Williamson implicated Oscar Peeler, who, on April 19, 1909, made a statement telling the entire story. Jim Miller had told Peeler that he had a cattle and land deal in the vicinity and wanted to stay at his house. Jesse West had given money to Peeler to pay for Miller's keep and in that way West was involved and soon Allen and Burwell were implicated. Jesse West and Joe Allen had large sums of money on deposit in the State National Bank of Shawnee at the time they were hanged at Ada. They had resided in and about Ada and that part of the old Indian Territory for many years before. Jim Miller, with much grey in the hair of his head, had reached the end of his professional career. His body was shipped to Fort Worth for burial.

6. See the *Evening News*, Ada, Oklahoma, April 19, 1909.

Both Jim Miller and Pat Garrett, representatives of the two extremes in Southwestern gunmanship, had passed to their respective rewards.*

---

* On March 2, 1908, the El Paso *Times* published an editorial under the caption "The Real Pat Garrett," which at the time appeared to be a just and accurate appraisal and evaluation of Garrett's character and personality. The passage of the years has served to substantiate and confirm the tenor of the editorial, which was as follows:

"The man who lives by the sword shall die by the sword" is a misquoted proverb that was repeated by many lips yesterday when the tragic death of Patrick Garrett of New Mexico was announced in this City. And yet Pat Garrett was anything but a violent man. But because, while in the discharge of his duty as an officer of the law, he, years ago, killed 'Billy the Kid,' a noted Western outlaw, Mr. Garrett was listed as a 'bad man'—a man who placed small value on human life, and was ever ready to draw his gun and risk his life in a fight.

"In truth, Pat Garrett deplored the reputation that followed him because of his killing of 'Billy the Kid.' He did not like to hear it discussed. There was nothing of the swaggering bully about Pat Garrett. He was as modest as a girl and shunned every appearance at dangerousness. He has been known to endure bullying from a boy in order to avoid a quarrel. He was an indifferent marksman for the reason that he did not want to be known as a dead shot. While he lived in El Paso nearly five years and has been in and out of town constantly for the past ten and fifteen years, no person ever heard of him seeking a quarrel. He loved peace and always managed to evade trouble. He was uncompromisingly loyal to his friends and his generosity to them kept him in debt.

"Pat Garrett was the victim of a reputation he did not seek and for which he was not responsible, simply because he was placed in the category of dangerous men."

four

FRONTIER LAND PROBLEMS

TULAROSA RIVER and its valley, between the sixties and eighties, held an important place in the affairs of southeastern New Mexico. The Mescalero Apaches had an idea that they owned the entire country between the Rio Grande and the Pecos. Perhaps in equity their claim was well founded. However, the legal title to the land was vested in the United States of America. The federal government stationed soldiers at Fort Stanton to see that the Indians behaved themselves. There were frequent clashes in the Mescalero country between and among Indians, settlers and soldiers. Most of the fights in the vicinity of Tularosa grew out of difficulties over water rights in the Tularosa River. No doubt but that the Indians were entitled to priority in the use of water, but the scheme of things in those days did not support such a contention.

Complications developed in 1862, when a number of Spanish-American citizens settled in the Tularosa country. They moved to Tularosa from Doña Ana County. The settlers from the Rio Grande used water for irrigation and occupied lands on the Tularosa formerly used by the Indians.

The name of the Tularosa settlement of 1862 came from a place in the nearby mountains called "Ojo del Tularosa." The difficulties between the settlers and the Indians prompted the Legislature of 1866 to pass a law which undertook to establish and confirm existing claims to water rights in the Tularosa valley. The act of 1866 recited "that a small number of men of Doña Ana County, whose property was destroyed by the terrible floods of the Rio del Norte, in 1862, and who in consequence of their destitute condition, resolved to settle in the Tularosa," where "said inhabitants had to suffer great obstacles, thrown in their way by the Mescalero Apaches, who at said time were in open hostility with the inhabitants of the Territory of New Mexico." The law provided that inasmuch as "said settlers have had possession of said valley and rivers with which the lands thereof are irrigated up to this time and having chosen the most eligible place for their settlement," their rights to land and water should be protected against the Indians and all other persons in accordance with the provisions of the Statute.[1] The Mescalero Apaches, theoretically on a reservation, frequently complained that they had no knowledge of boundaries and did not know when they were on or off the reservation. As of July 1, 1873, the military authorities, on instructions from Washington, established the reservation, containing roughly 575,000 acres, with lines as follows:

> Commencing at the southwest corner of the Fort Stanton reduced military reservation, and running thence due south to a point on the hills, near the north bank of the Ruidoso, thence along said hills to a point above the settlements, thence across said river to a point on the opposite hills, and thence to the same line upon which we start from Fort Stanton, and thence due south to the 33d degree of north latitude; thence to the top of the Sacramento mountains and along the top of said mountains, to the top of White Mountains; thence along the top of said mountains to the head of the waters of the Rio Nogal, thence to a point opposite the starting point, and thence to the starting point.

The Indians, however, were not the only offenders. Tularosa settlers themselves became involved in a water rights fight in the spring of 1873. Troops from Fort Stanton interfered. A complaint to the grand jury at Las Cruces resulted in a report prepared by Foreman Daniel Frize, submitted to the court on July 1, 1873, censuring the "interference of Capt. McKibbon of Fort Stanton, in the recent dispute between the settlers of the town and the canyon of Tularosa," saying that it was "unwarrantable and tyrannical conduct, which caused the murder of citizens." Soldiers under the command of Capt. Chilson went on a drunk, resulting in a fight on July 28, 1873, at Lura Springs near Fort Tularosa between the soldiers and Mescalero

---

1. The Act of 1866 used the spelling "Tuleroso" instead of "Tularosa." Tuleroso was possibly a combination of "tule," a word used to describe a type of bamboo-like sticks used in parts of New Mexico to weave baskets, and "roso," the Spanish for red, rosy.

Apaches in which a squaw was killed. Six hundred Indians, resenting the action of the soldiers, went on the warpath. Some of them went as far as the Pecos River mail station in Texas, where they killed Juan Chivari, the caretaker, stole thirteen mules and one horse. The Pecos trouble caused the El Paso *Sentinel* to comment on July 25, 1875:

> These raids have come to be of so common an occurrence as to scarcely excite comment, and as long as the government maintains, under the name of Indian reservations, places of refuge for thieves and murderers, just so long will American citizens be murdered and plundered. These reservations have come to be nothing less than nests of villainy, where savage Indians are armed and rationed, and sent out to depredate on peaceable citizens, and where they find a ready market for their plunder and immunity from punishment for their crimes.[2]

From Tularosa, people of Spanish and Mexican ancestry extended their settlements up and down the Pecos River and its tributaries, some of them building homes near the Texas border. They were later deprived of much of the land upon which they settled, through chicanery, imposition and rough treatment by Texans, through their ignorance of the requirements of the homestead law and by the indifference and neglect of both federal and territorial authorities. These authorities had apparently forgotten about the promises of General Kearny, made in Las Vegas on August 15, 1846, on the occasion of the grand entrada into New Mexico: ". . . From the Mexican government you have never received protection," Kearny told the Mexican citizens of New Mexico: "The Apaches and Navajos come down from the mountains and carry off your sheep and even your women whenever they please. The American government will correct all this. It will protect you in your persons and your property, and I repeat again, will protect you in your religion." Kearny must have spoken of protection of property rights in a prospective sense, as well as with reference to existing property rights.

For nearly forty years after Kearny's conquest, the government of the United States, although spending millions of dollars in fighting the Indians, never afforded adequate protection to the people of New

---

2. Fort Tularosa was far to the west of the present town of Tularosa. Maps of 1879 show an "Old Fort Tularosa" and "Fort Tularosa."

Mexico against the Apaches or Navajos, Comanches or other tribes of marauding Indians.

The Alcalde on the roof top in Las Vegas must have grinned broadly as General Kearny spoke of protecting the people against the Indians and protecting them in their property rights. The fine promises Kearny made at Las Vegas were for the most part repudiated in Washington. Ignorance, stupidity, traditional red tape, an occasional bit of fraud, all had a place in federal government dealings with New Mexico. More than forty years passed after 1846 before hostile Indians were forced to remain on the reservations. The fault was not to any great extent with the Indians, but with the methods and policies employed in handling them and their affairs. General Kearny had promised the people of New Mexico security in their property; and the treaty of Guadalupe-Hidalgo, signed in 1848, promised the same thing. The government of the United States, however, failed to adequately execute that treaty, particularly in regard to that provision which contemplated assurance that Mexican citizens who remained in the ceded country should have their possessions secured to them. A reasonable interpretation of that provision would have been that Mexican citizens should continue to hold their property undisturbed; and that their interests acquired in the future would be safeguarded. The belief prevailed at the time of the signing of the Treaty of Guadalupe-Hidalgo that if the government of the United States should claim any part of the Territory as public domain, it would at its own cost and expense, find out what it might be entitled to and, in doing this, necessarily ascertain the boundaries of private estates, whether called land grants or small homesteads.[3]

The Congress of the United States required all claimants of lands under Spanish or Mexican grants to pay for their own surveys, to undertake and carry forward long, burdensome and expensive procedures and litigation to perfect their titles. Litigation required the services of lawyers and lawyers were quick to learn that they could exact important interests in land grants for professional work. Government officials, at times, in the office of the Surveyor General of

---

3. For details of the treaty of Guadalupe-Hidalgo, see the message from James K. Polk, July 6, 1848, entitled "Message from the President of the United States Communicating a Copy of the Treaty with the Mexican Republic, of Feb. 2, 1848, and of the Correspondence in Relation Thereto, and Recommending Measures for Carrying the Same into Effect," 30th Congress, 1st Session, Senate Doc. Executive No. 60.

New Mexico, in the Commissioner of the General Land Office in Washington, were not adverse to whittling down acreage, to throwing out entirely genuine land grants, on the pretext that they were fictitious and fraudulent. Mexican citizens soon found their estates in jeopardy. Many of them lost their landed interests entirely, became pauperized as the result of the failure of the promises made by Kearny, or the failure of the United States of America to back up in good faith the assurances extended in the Treaty of Guadalupe-Hidalgo. Families which had been in undisputed possession of small tracts of land for one and two centuries found themselves on the defensive. Land grant owners found their property an attractive prize to scheming Anglos. The conquered people had no assurance they could continue to hold even an acre of their properties, great or small, that they had been led to believe were to be protected by the new order of things under American rule.

The loss of their homesteads by the citizens of Spanish and Mexican descent in Lincoln County and other counties of the Territory, through ignorance of the homestead law and toleration by the territorial authorities of a condition by which homesteads could be lost, could all well be charged back to a failure on the part of the government in Washington to comply with the wording and the spirit of Kearny's proclamation in 1846, of the Treaty of Guadalupe-Hidalgo in 1848. The promises to protect the future citizens in their persons and property had not been kept.[4]

There were only two land offices in the early days of the Territory, one at Santa Fe, the other in Las Cruces. From distant places in Doña Ana County, or from far places in Lincoln County, to Las Cruces was a hazardous journey, undertaken only by men of exceptional enterprise and initiative. Bad men from Texas and other states and territories, greedy for the lands settled up by the native people, took advantage of Spanish-American settlers in some parts of southeast New Mexico, whipped them out of their holdings, threatened not only to drive them out of the country, but to take the lives of the menfolk and the lives of their wives and children as well.

There were in use in the eighties in New Mexico two vicious forms

---

4. For an interesting discussion on the right of Mexican nationals, after the American occupation, to become citizens of the United States or remain citizens of Mexico, see opinion written by Judge Kirby Benedict in *Carter v. Territory*, July 1859, reported in 1 N.M. 317.

of land acquisition. There was the right of preemption, a privilege given by the federal land laws to citizens of claiming and buying under certain specified conditions, a quarter of a section, 160 acres, of public land. This preemption law was repealed on March 3, 1891. There was also the right to use scrip, a formal certificate of right and authority, generally issued in lieu of payment for bounties and bonuses for service in various wars and other purposes. Under Acts of Congress of 1874 and 1879 scrip became a high-powered method of obtaining title to surveyed or unsurveyed land belonging to the federal government.

A plan of saving for the native people the lands, which in the best of faith they had taken up and occupied for many years, was laid before the General Land Office in Washington on August 3, 1885, by W. S. Burke,[5] newspaper editor of Albuquerque and father of the public school system in Bernalillo County. In addition to its present boundaries, Bernalillo County in that period embraced what are now known as McKinley and Sandoval Counties and a portion of Torrance County. Mr. Burke protested to Washington that the rights of Spanish-American citizens were being violated in various parts of the Territory; that scheming men, by superior knowledge of the federal land laws and by threats of actual violence, were driving native-born citizens from their homes. Burke suggested a ruling by the General Land Office that mere filing upon public land did not give the right to possession where the land was claimed by others, until the question of title had been properly determined. William

---

5. William Smith Burke was born in Brownsville, Pennsylvania, Nov. 2, 1835. He never attended school. He learned the printer's trade in the *Intelligence* office in Wheeling, West Virginia, served in the Seventeenth Iowa Infantry during the Civil War, owned newspapers in Leavenworth, Kansas, after the war in association with D. R. Anthony. Coming to Albuquerque in 1880, Burke bought an interest in the *Albuquerque Daily Journal* in 1881 and from that time until his death in 1910 was almost continuously editor of that paper. Fond of politics, interested in education, Burke became the first Superintendent of Public Instruction in Bernalillo County. He was instrumental in having Edmund Gilbert Ross emigrate to New Mexico from Kansas after a stormy career in the United States Senate before and during the time of the trial of President Andrew Johnson on articles of impeachment. Burke promoted the name of Ross for Governor of the Territory of New Mexico, and succeeded in getting enough support from old Kansas friends to have Grover Cleveland appoint him to the place. A Republican in politics, Burke was quite independent and frequently clashed with the leaders and policies of his own party. Frail physically, Burke was frequently escorted to his home early in the morning, after his paper had gone to press, by an armed bodyguard.

Walker, Acting Commissioner of the General Land Office, replied to Burke's protest, but indicated his lack of understanding and appreciation of the entire situation in its fundamental aspects. Walker wrote:

X   "The reason given for your request is that the native inhabitants who have long been in possession are now ousted from their homes by persons who are permitted by the local land officers to make filings for the land occupied by them, thus causing much trouble and frequently crime and bloodshed. You state that the matter is a fruitful source of mischief in the Territory; that the class of holdings spoken of as being infringed upon are those of Mexicans which have been occupied by undisputed possession for generations; that of being required to fence their holdings or otherwise mark their boundaries and cultivating but portions of the land, leaving the remainder for grazing purposes. You say that it is often the case that intruders have filed upon those portions kept for grazing, sometimes even upon the entire farm, knowing it to be occupied, but expecting to hold it against the actual occupancy simply because through ignorance of our system of land titles, that occupant has failed to have his claim recorded in the district land office. You are informed that I have no power to make the order requested. The only way that inhabitants of land can be protected is by making their claims known to the U.S. Land Office. Intruders will not be permitted to make entries of land against the rights of actual inhabitants, if such habitancy is known. But it cannot be known unless the occupants of the lands themselves assert their claims in the manner provided by the laws of the United States. When this is done, their entries secure their possessory rights and prevent other entries from being made of the same lands. I respectfully suggest that the executive of New Mexico might, by some proper proclamation or other official manner, advise the inhabitants of their rights under the laws of the United States and the necessity of filing their claims in the United States Land Office."

Charles B. Eddy, who had come to Lincoln County in 1880 and purchased a herd of cattle with ranches and improvements in the vicinity of Seven Rivers, had a contest several years later with the federal authorities over alleged land frauds. Cattle sold in the Seven Rivers country in 1884 at $22.50 all around, a price which made the livestock business profitable, and there was a demand throughout

Lincoln County, which meant most of southeastern New Mexico, for ranches and lands. Eddy gave his views on livestock production in the county and the Territory in an interview published in the *Golden Era* on December 24, 1885, in which he said:

> It is the want of water that makes New Mexico the worst place on the face of the earth for small settlers to go to. The cattle raising industry in Lincoln County has about reached its growth under present conditions of things. The county is just about as full of stock as it can be, and there would be no money in increasing the stock unless water can be found in the very large section of the country which is now perfectly dry, though it is a magnificent grazing country.[6] The search for water though is almost hopeless, very many and costly efforts to locate artesian wells having failed utterly.

Charles B. Eddy was accused in 1885 by the government investi gating agencies of acquiring lands from settlers, especially Spanish-American homesteaders, through coercion. Many Spanish-Americans in the early days had taken up land along the Pecos River and other streams and occupied waterholes and springs in the Lincoln County country. Through ignorance of the land laws, they were in many instances technically in default in paper perfection of their titles. The charges against Eddy were quickly denied not only by Eddy, but by Ash Upson, a long-time resident of Lincoln County, and others. Upson maintained in affidavits filed with the government authorities that Eddy had befriended the settlers of Spanish and Mexican descent and had only acquired their lands as a favor to them after they had been driven from their homes and locations by bad men, mostly from Texas, who claimed that the "Mexicans" had no rights in the country and had to "get out." In addition to being a defense of Eddy's land activities, Ash Upson's affidavit threw light on the attitude of some of the early settlers in the vicinity of present-day Chaves and Eddy Counties toward the native people.[7] Upson admitted that Charles B. Eddy had acquired lands from them, but explained:

---

6. Artesian wells subsequently developed in the Pecos Valley near Roswell attracted nationwide attention, helped to establish one of the great agricultural and livestock areas of the west.

7. *Golden Era*, Dec. 17, 1885.

that a great part of this land was originally bought by him from the original Mexican settlers who preempted the same; that a very strong class feeling exists between the less intelligent Americans and the Mexicans along the Rio Pecos in this section of the country for a distance of nearly one hundred miles above the Texas line; that for several years past, but few Mexicans have been allowed to live within these limits peaceably and without any molestation, for any considerable length of time; that many Mexicans have been killed outright, without provocation, several have been wounded, and many more driven away from their homes by intimidation and threats of shooting assassination and mob violence. . . . That M. J. Denman, who pretends to be a land agent, is the recognized leader of a gang, composed of outlaws from Texas and fugitives from justice. That the Denman gang in September, 1885, did by threats and intimidation drive some four or five industrious Mexicans from their homes on the Rio Pecos; that in the month of November of the same year, Denman did procure the arrest on a frivolous charge, of nine or ten other Mexicans on Black River, while they were peaceably at work, making an irrigation ditch, and had them all illegally taken before a justice of the peace, with the avowed object of driving them away from their lands and homes; that the said Mexicans, upon being released upon their own recognizance, almost immediately disappeared, leaving many of their effects behind, and have not since been seen in their homes.

Upson's affidavit cited other instances in which he claimed that Denman and others had driven the native people from their homesteads in the vicinity of Seven Rivers. In his affidavit, Upson declared that Denman was "a liar, a thief and a perjurer." Charles H. Slaughter in a similarly worded affidavit exonerated Charles B. Eddy from wrongdoing in connection with his land transactions and recited instances where Denman had incited attacks against the native settlers. Slaughter's affidavit concluded: "That the said Denman and his followers will not allow a Mexican to be employed upon any of the ranches in this part of the county where by threats of violence he can prevent it; and that they will go to all lengths and stop at nothing in the shape of perjury or misrepresentation to invalidate, or upset, the titles which any citizen may have acquired, however honestly from a Mexican."[8]

---

8. The land title matters referred to in this chapter have nothing whatever to do with the so-called "land frauds" in New Mexico which became a red hot issue in

The difficulty over land matters was not confined to citizens of Spanish and Mexican descent. The public land situation was becoming increasingly serious. On several occasions governors of the Territory had spoken out on conditions which were becoming more and more aggravating. Quarrels over range rights and division of public domain were becoming more frequent. Murder, arson and other crimes were traced to range disputes. Governor L. Bradford Prince, who had a good grasp of the entire situation, in his 1881 message to the Secretary of the Interior, concisely stated the proposition, saying among other things:

> The laws of the United States, relating to the disposition of public lands are well adapted in a country like New Mexico to place in the hands of a few men a monopoly in stock raising. The Territory suffers most from a want of permanent water. There are in many places small streams and springs which supply water to large numbers of stock. These are located under the homestead laws, or otherwise obtained, and the lands for miles around are valueless to others. The owners of the water have the benefit of the pasturage of large tracts, which belong to the government, without cost. If the policy were so changed that larger bodies of land, which include water, could be disposed of, the government might derive some revenue, and a monopoly of mammoth proportions would be prevented. The existing laws thwart their own purpose (which is to distribute lands among the people to the fullest extent possible) in all this dry and mountainous region. Their practical operation is to reinstate the Spanish and Mexican land grant system—those manorial estates which have excluded the poor from the possession of landed property, and cursed so many countries.

Governor Lionel A. Sheldon, in his report to the Secretary of the Interior in 1883, touching on the public land question, said:

1882, 1883 and 1884. See *Title to Land in New Mexico*, Ex. Doc. No. 106, 48th Congress, 2nd Session, wherein are published many letters and reports on investigation into methods used to defraud the federal government of lands opened for homestead entry. Max Frost of Santa Fe, Register of the U.S. Land Office, prominent Republican politician, was under fire for many months because of claims made that he had conspired with cattle and sheepmen to build up ranches in Colfax County, and in the American Valley in Socorro County by use of dummy entrymen. Frost was accused among other things, "of doing a great deal of secret and private business, going in and out of the Land Office frequently, and holding low-toned sidewalk conversations with persons."

The homestead and preemption laws were designed to distribute lands among the people, and to prevent land monopoly. In those localities where the great body of the land is productive of the necessaries of life, the intended result has been experienced. In this dry and mountainous country, the contrary effect has been produced, and under the operation of the homestead and preemption laws the greatest land monopoly exists and of the most objectionable character. Locations are made which embrace springs, and the surrounding lands are valueless to any but the locators of the water. Hence the man who obtains 160 acres controls the usufruct of a vast tract without cost, and without paying any taxes to support the local government. A cattle company, or individual, may, by owning a few acres, have the occupancy of a tract as large as some of the states of the union. If existing practices are permitted to continue, it will not be long before the cattle business will be in the hands of a few, the government furnishing the land gratuitously. The government recognizes equal rights of usufruct to all citizens upon the public domain which is adapted to pasturage; and consequently there is no boundary established by right or by law between ranchmen. The courts cannot prescribe or define the limits of occupancy, and therefore. when differences exist they must be arranged between the parties by an agreement among themselves, or by price. Disorders not infrequently arise, and crimes result from these disputes, and as ranches become more numerous, these evils will be increased. Ranchmen, as a rule, are sensible and good men. Yet, in accordance with the grasping spirit of human nature, they are disposed to absorb as much as possible.

Governor Edmund Gilbert Ross, thinking in terms of his years of experience in the Middlewestern states, contended in his annual report to the Secretary of the Interior for 1885 that twenty acres of grass was required to prepare a steer for market and foresaw the coming of the day of diminished grazing lands. Ross urged better breeds of stock, smaller herds, better grasses, "leaving the ranchman as rich in a hundred head of cattle as he is now in many times that number." Ross concluded on this phase of his report with the statement that "other things being equal, it is a thousand times better for New Mexico, that a hundred thousand head of cattle be owned by a thousand men than by one man."

Discussing the same problem, Governor Ross said in 1886 in his message to the Secretary of the Interior in Washington:

It is notorious that possession of large quantities of the public lands has been obtained under the form of preemption laws through the boldest perjury, forgery and false pretense, and that in some instances, this has been done, if not with the connivance, at least through the inadvertence and carelessness of public officials. If these lands had been obtained for actual occupation and cultivation, the results would not be so disastrous to the Territory, but in many cases they have been thus absorbed into great cattle ranches, merely for the purpose of getting control of water courses and springs, and to thus keep out settlers and small herds; and in others, the lands have been thus stolen for purely speculative purposes.

There was so much squabbling over public domain that Governor W. T. Thornton, in his report to the Secretary of the Interior in 1895, was prompted to say:

The open range cattle business in New Mexico is a failure, because no man will improve his ground by opening water holes, storing water, or any other way, if his shiftless neighbor has the right to run his herd at will over the same ground. The interloper would destroy in a week the labor of months. Some method should be devised whereby the public grazing lands in New Mexico can be utilized; a good system of leases, not too long, at a fair rental, seems to be the most feasible plan.

The problem confronting Lincoln County particularly in regard to overcrowding on the range was discussed editorially by the *Golden Era* of October 23, 1884, in which it was said:

Overstocked ranges, and a way to prevent the threatened evil, is a problem whose solution is now disturbing stockmen in this country more than the spread of the cattle plague. How to adjust this matter without hardship or injustice requires calm, dispassionate judgment and a fair share of the milk of human kindness. Complaints come from different parts of the county of parties who secure a small seepage of water, either by purchase or location, only calculated to accommodate a few head of cattle under the most favorable circumstances, and turn loose thereon from one to three hundred head of cattle, and this to within the lines or contiguous to other ranges already overstocked, allowing them to roam at will until the round ups occur, thereby consuming the grass and water of their neighbors at will. This soon works great injustice to those who were first comers and tells with damaging effect, as shown by the thinness of the flesh and low spirit of all the stock on the range. On the other hand, a man's right to his portion of the public domain should not be questioned and a small owner has the same rights under the law as he who assumes to occupy a thousand hills, and so long as one acre of public domain is yet vacant, he has the same right to pasture his few cows on that vacant ground as his richer neighbors have to appropriate it all to themselves.

Disputes over rights on the public domain became intensified as foreign capital was invested in Lincoln County and sheepmen began to invade territory long considered exclusively a cattle country. J. A. Alcock in 1882 acquired, for $225,000 of capital from Ireland, the ranch of Thomas B. Catron and E .A. Walz, his brother-in-law. The headquarters ranch was eleven miles from White Oaks, originally owned by Maj. L. G. Murphy of Lincoln.[9] The property controlled a large area of public domain through its six well located springs and was well stocked with cattle and bulls. Concerning this sale the Las Vegas *Gazette* of November 11, 1882, said:

> The Carrizozo cattle ranch, near White Oaks in Lincoln County, formerly the property of T. B. Catron, of Santa Fe, has been sold to a young Englishman. The round up took place a few days ago. Over 1,400 calves were branded this year. This is an excellent ranch and is well watered by living springs. The winters are always mild and pleasant and the grass is exceptionally good.

---

9. Maj. Lawrence Gustave Murphy, forty-seven years old, died in Santa Fe on October 19, 1878, after a long illness. Murphy was born in Wexford County, Ireland, and graduated from Maynooth College, where young men studied for the Roman Catholic priesthood. He emigrated to America and drifted to New Mexico at an early day soon after the "Mormon War." He enlisted July 17, 1861, as First Lieutenant and Regimental Quartermaster, 1st New Mexico Volunteers, and was assigned to Fort Union by Col. C. St. Vrain. Murphy served in Kit Carson's regiment during the Rebellion and came out of the Army a major. When his regiment was disbanded in 1866, Major Murphy went to Lincoln County and for a long time served as probate judge. He was a post trader at Fort Stanton while serving as probate judge. Murphy was a member of Montezuma Lodge No. 1, A. F. & A. M. and Santa Fe Commandery No. 1, K. T. Col. Emil Fritz, who had been a partner of Murphy in Lincoln County enterprises, died in Stuttgart, Germany, on June 26, 1874. Major Murphy was well known throughout the Territory. A squabble over the Fritz estate in Lincoln County was one of the incidents that precipitated a chapter in the Lincoln County War.

The Carrizo Company, as Alcock's concern was called, acquired a dozen other springs in the Lincoln country and controlled thousands of sections of public domain. The Alcock outfit ran cattle only and tried to keep out the sheepmen. In order to get the sheep of Dionisio Chavez out of his country near Three Rivers, James A. Alcock in 1883 purchased the Chavez permanent water and grazing rights for $3,200. Alcock discovered some time later that Chavez had other water in the same country. On June 10, 1884, seven hundred sheep were killed in the night on the Carrizozo range, while being grazed by Arcadio Sais on a partido contract from Dionisio Chavez. Alcock was arrested for killing the sheep. Arrested with him were Rock Grumbless, Thomas C. Jacobs, Jeff Grumbless and James Wilson. It was claimed that Alcock and his cowboys had stampeded the sheep after they had bedded down for the night and had run through them with blazing six-shooters, killing them one by one, like wild animals, until they had all been killed. The suspects were arraigned before Justice of the Peace Collier, on August 31, 1885. The actual trial was continued from time to time and Alcock and his cowboys were finally released by the justice on October 30, 1885.

Taking notice of the trouble on the range between the cattlemen and sheep growers, the *Golden Era* of June 18, 1885, commented:

> As the ERA has said before, sheep and cattle were not made to run together. It is an indisputable fact that sheepmen have a lawful right to go on government land in the center of vast cattle ranges, and take up a small piece of land, and turn loose thousands of sheep if they can find sufficient water. We say they would have a legal right, but would it be right between men? It always has the appearance of blackmail. Let the sheepmen put themselves in the places of the cattlemen. Would they like it? That's the idea exactly. It's bound to make trouble every time. Let the cattlemen get to themselves and let the sheepmen get to themselves. Each industry needs the protection of our meagre property laws. Property is too expensive to be slaughtered off and let to rot on the range. Too many human lives have been sacrificed over difficulties more trifling than this and cattlemen should try to do right and sheepmen should also avoid trouble.

John W. Poe, sheriff of Lincoln County, had personal difficulties over rights on the range. According to the *Lincoln County Leader* of June 6, 1885, shortly before Poe sold his ranch property to Brandon

Kirby, Breece and Sons brought 750 sheep from the River Feliz to their ranch on Little Creek. The Breece ranch occupied a small portion of land along the creek between Pat Garrett's ranch and the Poe and Goodin ranch. John Poe sent his foreman, Noah Ellis, to talk with the Breeces and to deliver a request to remove the sheep from the range. The Breeces refused to get their sheep out of the country. Several days later, one of the Breece sheepherders was fired upon. The Breeces swore out a warrant before Squire Taylor of Bonito against John W. Poe, his partner, Goodin, Gray, Noah Ellis and Buchanan, ranch employees. They were arrested, charged with the shooting or responsibility for it. The trial before the Justice of the Peace lasted two days. A jury returned a verdict of not guilty for Poe, Gray and Ellis. The justice dismissed the cases against Goodin and Buchanan. The Breeces continued to graze the sheep in their own country.

The *Lincoln County Leader* of August 1, 1885, took a hand in the range war, claiming that E. A. Walz, brother-in-law of Tom Catron, had sold the Carrizo Ranch to J. A. Alcock and associates "a few years before, for an enormous price," and that a short time later "Walz had started to run a large band of sheep near the ranch he had sold." The *Leader* inquired: "Who is Walz?" and answered the question by saying: "A brother-in-law of Tom Catron, who is unfavorably known in this Territory in various ways and especially as the greatest land monopolist in New Mexico. Catron and Walz in a new role— with talk about being the 'friend of the poor man' and preaching 'down with the monopolies.' It is calculated to make a steer laugh to realize the situation."

five

THOMAS BENTON CATRON

THE ONE MAN who, more than any other, dominated New Mexico political and business affairs for fifty years, Thomas Benton Catron, died in Santa Fe on May 15, 1921. Able, resourceful and strong in mind and body, the name of Tom Catron for many years spelled power and influence in the Territory. That power and that influence were sufficient, when New Mexico became a state, to enable Thomas Benton Catron to cause himself to be selected one of the two first United States senators at the first legislative session after statehood. No man ever crossed swords with Tom Catron in New Mexico in a lawsuit, in a political row, or in a business transaction, who was not willing to admit that Catron was an expert swordsman, an aggressive and powerful adversary. Even in his final days when the shadow of many years burdened him, Thomas Benton Catron was looking forward to public service. In the eightieth year of his life, with the vigor and intelligence that always guided his efforts, Tom Catron was in communication with the State Department, anxious to procure an appointment as American minister to Chile. And it may be said that because of his profound knowledge of things South American, of his scholarship in the Spanish language and its literature and of his bent for intrigue and diplomacy, he would have been a credit to his country in any Latin American republic.

Tom Catron's arrival in New Mexico was just twenty years after the American Occupation. The Territory was still in the twilight zone of things that followed the invasion and conquest of New Mexico by the United States of America and Catron himself had just emerged from the bloody fratricidal struggle of the Civil War.[1]

---

1. Thomas Benton Catron was born on a farm four miles from Lexington, Missouri, on October 6, 1840. He attended the crossroads school of his neighborhood and on July 4, 1860, received a B.A. degree from the University of Missouri. He studied law

Within a few days after his arrival in the territorial capital in the summer of 1866, Tom Catron found employement as a scrivener with Kirby Benedict, a famous character of the day who had served for thirteen years, from 1853 to 1866, as a judge on the combination district and supreme court of New Mexico. Crippled from a bowie knife wound in the right hand, Judge Benedict wrote only with difficulty and was obliged to rely on others to write for him. Benedict, a native of Connecticut, was fifty-seven years old in 1866. He had been appointed to the territorial bench by President Franklin K. Pierce and before coming to New Mexico had practiced law in Illinois, where he was a friend of both Abraham Lincoln and Stephen Douglas. For some years after he came to the Territory, Kirby Benedict carried on correspondence of a personal and friendly nature with Abraham Lincoln, proudly exhibiting letters to Santa Fe friends written to him by Lincoln after he had been elected President of the United States. Although he had not traveled to New Mexico to be a scrivener, Tom Catron was glad to be associated with Kirby Benedict, because from him he learned much of the tradition and background of New Mexico and its people and learned about the decisions of the Supreme Court of New Mexico from the man who had written many of them during New Mexico's formative period.[2]

---

in a lawyer's office in Lexington, as was the custom of the times. The Civil War interrupted his studies. Catron, like so many Missourians, looked toward the South, enlisted in the Confederate army, was soon a lieutenant in Bledsoe's battery. He participated in the battles of Carthage, Wilson's Creek, Dry Wood, Lexington, Pea Ridge, Farmington, Iuka, Corinth, Port Gibson, Champion Hill, Black River Bridge, was in the battle of Lookout Mountain, fought at Mission Ridge, surrendered as commander of the Third Missouri light battery at Meridian, Mississippi. Back in Missouri after the war, Catron resumed the study of law, but recognized he would have difficulty in being admitted to practice because of a statute requiring an oath that the applicant had never borne arms against the federal government. Influenced by Stephen Benton Elkins, a classmate of his University days, Tom Catron decided to emigrate to New Mexico. He left Independence, Missouri, in May 1866, arrived in Santa Fe July 27, 1866. Enroute he studied a Spanish grammar and later perfected himself in the language by residing for several months in Alcalde, Rio Arriba County, New Mexico, where he spoke nothing but Spanish with the natives. He considered daily a menu dominated by chili. Briefly employed by Judge Kirby Benedict in Santa Fe, Catron, through Elkins' influence, he was appointed on February 22, 1867, District Attorney of the Third Judicial District with residence at Mesilla, Doña Ana County. Catron was formally admitted to the bar of the Territory on June 15, 1867. He was elected to the Territorial Legislature in 1868, relinquishing his place as District Attorney to accept appointment as Attorney General of the Territory on January 1, 1869. See Santa Fe *New Mexican*, May 16, 1921.

2. In later years, Judge Kirby Benedict, brilliant, at times erratic, became involved in

Even before he left Missouri, Tom Catron was aware that the Republican party was dominant in New Mexico and would likely continue to control indefinitely its political affairs. Soon after coming to the Territory, Catron abandoned the ideals of the Democratic party of his Missouri days and identified himself with the Republican party. Ever after, during a long lifetime. Thomas Benton Catron never swerved from loyalty to that political organization. His philosophy in relation to political preference was expressed in a conversation with Thomas O. Boggs, a Virginia-born Democrat, then a resident of Colfax County, New Mexico.[3] Boggs had soldiered with Catron during the Civil War and had known him only as a staunch Democrat. Visiting Santa Fe during a session of the Territorial Legis-

---

difficulties with the Supreme Court of the Territory and was suspended from practice. On January 16, 1874, the court appointed Attorneys Sydney A. Hubbell, Joab Houghton and William Breeden to investigate Benedict's petition for restoration to practice. The order of the court directed the committee to inquire into "the general character of Kirby Benedict for the three years last past, whether good or bad . . . ascertain and report as to the conduct and deportment of said Benedict during that period towards the justices of this court . . . to make full investigation from the files of the Santa Fe *Post* to ascertain what articles, if any, reflected upon the official or personal conduct of the judges of the court, published in said paper, were communicated to or published by Benedict," and also to "investigate into Benedict's connection with the Santa Fe *Union*, and to determine what articles he may have inspired to be published in that paper against the judges of the court; and to ascertain and report what connection Benedict had, if any, with the effort made in the Legislature of 1871 and 1872 to procure the enactment of a law compelling the courts of the Territory to permit Benedict to practice law . . ." and "to ascertain particularly his habits, including the excessive use of intoxicating drinks." Benedict apparently did not fare well during the investigation and he filed a petition with the court pathetically asking for restoration to the bar. "I present this petition to your honors in the spirit of confession, respect, obedience and supplication," the petition read. "I confess to have committed against this court, its dignity and judges, disorders, improprieties and contempts . . . for which I should be punished, but the punishment has now continued through suspension for over three years. I now come as a supplicant and sincerely crave the pardon and forgiveness of your honors. . . . Accumulating age, want and desolation press upon me, and I desire to be at peace and maintain just and honorable relations with the courts, the judges and others, in such remaining days as may be allotted to me, in such usefulness as I may be to my family and others in the practice of the profession of my life." See Record No. 375, Supreme Court, New Mexico, January 19, 1874. Benedict waited, but no order came restoring him to practice. Tired and discouraged, Benedict died in Santa Fe on February 27, 1874. The funeral was held on March 2, 1874, with W. W. Griffin of Montezuma Lodge reading the funeral service, and the 8th Cavalry band, "in new and flashy uniforms, leading the procession, playing funeral dirges to the grave." See Santa Fe *New Mexican*, March 2, 1874.

3. Thomas O. Boggs, known all over the Southwest as "Uncle Tom" Boggs, died in Clayton, New Mexico, at an advanced age on Oct. 1, 1894. He had been a life-long

lature in 1884, Tom Boggs was shocked to see Catron sitting as a Republican member of the Council, voting with the Republicans and active in their conferences. Boggs approached Catron during a recess of the Council and expressed astonishment that Catron had become a Republican. Catron explained to Boggs: "Tom, when I came to New Mexico, the Republicans were in power. It seemed to me they were likely to remain in power for a good many years. The only thing left for me to do was to join them and run them the way I think they ought to be run and that's what I'm doing."

Gunfire and bloodshed in New Mexico in the seventies and eighties were not things that disturbed Tom Catron. Four years and more of service in the Civil War had reconciled him to death and devastation. Sudden death from shot and shell had been an everyday affair with him. He had seen men die by the hundreds in battle. Reports of an occasional murder in New Mexico, killings now and then in the Lincoln County War, happenings that might shock some people, were of no great significance or importance in the every day life of Tom Catron.

Steve Elkins, who prevailed upon Catron to come to New Mexico, was admitted to the Bar at Mesilla, Doña Ana County, on Monday, June 6, 1864, and it was at Mesilla, on motion of Elkins, that Thomas Benton Catron was admitted to the Territorial bar on June 15, 1867. Tom Catron remained in Mesilla for a time, serving as district attorney, absorbing the atmosphere of a picturesque New Mexico town, occasionally handling a case sent his way by Elkins. After a brief residence in Mesilla, Catron realized that the political and legal machinery of New Mexico was manipulated in the Territorial capital and he moved to Santa Fe after serving in the Legislature of 1868. Upon recommendation of Stephen B. Elkins, he was appointed Attorney General of the Territory in 1869 by Governor Robert Byington Mitchell.[4]

---

friend of Kit Carson and it was at the Boggs ranch near Fort Lyon, Colorado, Kit Carson and his wife died. Boggs buried the Carsons near the banks of the Arkansas River in Colorado, but later supervised the removal of their remains to Taos, New Mexico, where they were both buried in the same grave in accordance with Kit Carson's request. Tom Boggs took the Carson children into his home and reared them as if they had been his own.

4. Born in Richland County, Ohio, April 4, 1823, Robert Mitchell died in Washington, D.C., on January 26, 1882, while serving as a member of Congress from Kansas. Mitchell served in the Mexican War, became a "free stater" in Kansas, enlisted in the

Catron's initiation into political affairs in New Mexico during the Mitchell administration proved of great educational value. By 1869, nearly a quarter of a century after the American Occupation, political intrigue had become an art in the Territorial capital. Conspiracy, espionage and counterespionage were highly developed. Tom Catron observed with interest the work of the masters in the political world of the Territory and was profoundly impressed by its possibilities.

It was during the turmoil of the Mitchell administration of affairs in New Mexico that Tom Catron learned his early lessons in political maneuvering. "Bob" Mitchell taught Catron to carry on an incessant fight with the political enemy; to apply tactics he had learned as a soldier in the war. Ambush and sudden attack were the weapons in offensive maneuvers. When no other course was possible or desirable, there was always the possibility of a skilfully executed retreat.

After three and one-half years of residence in Santa Fe, Catron was appointed United States Attorney for New Mexico by President U. S. Grant. Tom Catron smiled happily upon receiving the certificate of appointment as United States Attorney, because it bore the signature of the man who had been commanding general of the Federal army— an army that Catron had fought against in the field for years and which had locked him up as a prisoner of war. Catron served six

---

Union Army during the Civil War, became a Brigadier-General. Appointed Governor of the Territory of New Mexico on August 1, 1866, by President Andrew Johnson, "Bob'" Mitchell was one of the most colorful of many adventuresome New Mexico chief executives. He resigned as Governor in 1869. Even before the Legislature of 1866-1867 convened, his Excellency left for Washington and remained there during the entire legislative session. In his absence, the Secretary of the Territory as Acting Governor appointed the territorial officers, as he was empowered to do. Upon his return, with court martial-like orders and aided by a violent temper, Governor Mitchell removed the adjutant-general, auditor, librarian, and other officials who were appointed by the acting governor; assumed legislative power by designating new precincts in various counties of the Territory; issued a certificate of election to a candidate for the Fortieth Congress of the United States, when it was the duty of the Secretary of the Territory to issue such certificate; refused to sign a memorial to Congress passed by the Legislature condemning him; and otherwise usurped the rights of the Legislature and of the people of New Mexico. There was transmitted to Hon. Schuyler Colfax, then Speaker of the National House of Representatives, on February 24, 1868, by H. H. Heath, Secretary of the Territory of New Mexico, a copy of the resolution adopted by the Legislature, but which the Governor had refused to sign, setting forth its grievances against Governor Mitchell and demanding his immediate removal.

"No patriotic man," the resolution recited, "no man who is not cursed with a spirit of oppression or executive tyranny, can desire such powers as are demanded by Governor Robert B. Mitchell. No man who respects the people of whom he is an executive

years as United States Attorney for New Mexico. The federal grand jury was a most important institution. Grand juries indicted or failed to indict largely in the discretion of the District Attorney. The office was one which commanded respect, inspired fear. Tom Catron made a capable official and was soon recognized as a power in the Territory. The office was a stepping stone in Catron's climb to prominence in affairs in New Mexico.

Catron and Stephen B. Elkins formed a law partnership in Santa Fe. Together they invested in the stock of the First National Bank of Santa Fe and soon controlled it. They dealt in land grants and became identified with many important New Mexico enterprises. Active in Territorial politics, Stephen Benton Elkins was elected a Delegate in Congress from New Mexico. He met in Washington and married there a daughter of Henry Gassaway Davis of West Virginia. Elkins became a powerful figure in West Virginia and in the nation. Catron and Elkins remained lifelong friends. Their careers throughout life had many remarkable similarities. Almost the same age, they were graduated from the University of Missouri in the same class. Elkins served in the Union Army, Catron in the Confederate. Elkins[5] came to New Mexico; induced Catron to come. Elkins saw to it that Catron followed in his footsteps politically and in office-holding in the Territory. Both men became wealthy; both men achieved a seat in the United States Senate.

----

would desire such power; wherefore, we have come to the conclusion that he who desires not to wield this power is fit, and he who does desire to exercise it is neither fit nor capable to govern a free people. Your committee has, therefore, decidedly come to the following conclusion: That the official course of Robert B. Mitchell has been so gross and illegal, in many of its parts, as to render him an object almost of aversion to the masses of our people, instead of their true friend, and that the time has arrived when his power to do good among our people has entirely passed, when the occupation of the executive chair can but be considered by us an imposition upon our people, who are ignorant of having committed any crime wherefore they should be so punished."

5. Stephen Benton Elkins resided in New Mexico for nearly thirteen years. He was born in Perry County, Ohio, on September 26, 1841, graduated in the same class with Thomas Benton Catron at the University of Missouri in 1860 with a B.A. degree and received an M.A. degree from the same institution in 1868. Coming to New Mexico in 1864, Elkins was admitted to the Bar of the Territory in that year, served in the Territorial Legislature of 1864 and 1865, became a district attorney and attorney-general in 1868 and part of 1869, U.S. District Attorney in 1870 and 1872; elected to the 43rd the 44th Congress as a delegate from New Mexico, serving from 1873 to 1877. Elkins married Hallie Davis, daughter of the United States Senator Henry Gassaway Davis of West Virginia, and moved to that state in 1877. He became chairman of the Repub-

↶ During the days when A. A. McSween, John H. Tunstall and John S. Chisum were fighting battles against the Murphy-Dolan combine in Lincoln County, Thomas Benton Catron knew much about the inner workings of the feuds and murders of retaliation and vengeance. Although it has been repeatedly contended that Thomas B. Catron was a silent partner in Murphy, Dolan & Co., of Lincoln, it is certain that he was not in Lincoln County on April 3, 1878. For on the evening or night of April 3, 1878, Tom Catron's leather trunk was lost from the stagecoach somewhere between Cimarron and Las Vegas in the northern part of the Territory. Tradition has it that Catron's trunk contained valuable papers and documents pertaining to the Mora Grant. For many years after, whenever Catron offered in court to prove the contents of a lost instrument, he respectfully submitted to the judge that the document in question was among those in the trunk in 1878. Although he had little use for newspapers or newspapermen, Catron was so anxious to recover the trunk that he resorted to advertising. A sample advertisement, appearing in the Las Vegas *Gazette* of April 13, 1878, is as follows:

$150 REWARD
Lost

On the evening or night of April 3d, a small sole leather trunk, covered with white canvas. Said trunk was lost off the stage going to Santa Fe, somewhere between Cimarron and Las Vegas. It was full when lost, principally of papers only of importance to me and my clients, containing among them a number of deeds of conveyance, notes, drafts, etc. The trunk with its contents would weigh 70 or 80 pounds. It is either 28 or 32 inches long, about 1 foot wide, and a foot

---

lican National Committee and managed the campaign of Benjamin Harrison for the presidency for which he was rewarded by appointment as Secretary of War, which place he occupied from 1891 to 1893. Stephen Benton Elkins was twice elected to the United States Senate from West Virginia, serving in that body from 1895 to the time of his death. In early day New Mexico Steve Elkins became a specialist in land grants and made substantial sums of money in acquiring and disposing of interests in them. Possessing great ability to make money, Elkins accumulated wealth in New Mexico in a day when money was hard to get in the Territory. When Elkins married into the wealthy Davis family, large sums of money became available for projects in which he became interested in West Virginia. Elkins and associates invested heavily and profited handsomely, in coal, timber and railroad enterprises in West Virginia, founded the town of Elkins. The Elkins made their home for many years in Washington, D.C., and were socially, politically and financially prominent in the national capitol for decades.

or more high, had the words "Santa Fe, N.M." on one end, and immediately above it a small piece of canvas about 2 inches by 8 inches
sewed on to the other canvas, which piece covers my name, "T. B.
Catron." I will gladly give the above reward for the recovery of said
trunk and the papers which were in the same when lost, or for such
information as will lead to the recovery thereof. I do not presume
it has been stolen and will consequently take no steps to prosecute
the finder or possessor.

April 5th, 1878. T. B. Catron.

Not only was Catron financially interested in cattle and ranches
in Lincoln County in the early days, but he had been attorney for
Maj. N. A. M. Dudley in a court martial at Fort Union. Soon after
the Fort Union court martial, in which he was acquitted of all
charges, Major Dudley was transferred to be commanding officer at
Fort Stanton. He arrived at his new command just in time to be
entangled and enmeshed in the intricacies of the Lincoln County
War. Even today it is not possible to catalogue and classify Dudley's
activities in connection with the Lincoln County troubles. There is
little doubt, however, but that Major Dudley, grateful to Tom Catron for extricating him from the court-martial troubles at Fort Union,
followed Catron's advice as to how to proceed in handling military
developments in Lincoln County.

Serving in the New Mexico Legislature during the 26th, 29th, 33rd
and 36th sessions, Thomas Benton Catron helped write much of the
fundamental law of the Territory. Influenced by his early legal training, Catron prevailed on the Legislature to incorporate many Missouri statutes in the basic laws of New Mexico.

After a spirited campaign Tom Catron was elected as New Mexico's delegate in Congress for the term 1895-1897. While in Congress,
with his eyes on a seat in the United States Senate, Catron at once
became active in the fight for statehood for the Territory. At the time
of his nomination for Delegate in Congress in 1895, the Durango,
Colorado *Democrat* published an editorial paragraph which said:
"Tom Catron has been nominated for Congress by the Republicans
of New Mexico. Tom has a record that would stink a Ute out of his
tepee."

New Mexico finally was admitted to statehood and after much
voting and maneuvering, Thomas Benton Catron was elected to the

United States Senate by the State Legislature on March 27, 1912. He served in the Senate until March 4, 1917. At the time of his election to the Senate, Tom Catron was seventy-two years old. His election to an office which had been the goal of his ambition for many a year was a magnificent achievement and a tribute to his ability, personality and tenacity. For forty-five years Catron had held to the thought that some day he would sit in the United States Senate. Catron's colleague in the Senate, elected at the same time by the same Legislature, was Albert Bacon Fall. In the years of his affiliation with the Democratic party, Fall had energetically fought Tom Catron and his so-called "Ring" year in and year out at the polls, in court and whenever and wherever fighting seemed appropriate.[6]

Although courteous to each other in the United States Senate, Tom Catron and Albert Fall had very little in common. Much younger than Catron, Senator Fall had acquaintances and avenues of approach to places of power and influence in the national capital not readily available to Catron. Neither Catron nor Fall was inclined to look back or to discuss things that belonged to ancient history in their lives. Both of them, in their fight for the election to the United States Senate by the Legislature of New Mexico, had edged out William H. Andrews, a Pennsylvania politician of the old school who had planted himself in Territorial New Mexico a few years earlier—with frankly stated designs on a seat in the United States Senate. Catron, friendly with W. H. Andrews, wanted him in the Senate, but Fall was anxious to have "Bull" Andrews "shanghaied" to some distant place so he would be free of the threat that, through a coalition between Catron and Andrews, the astute Andrews would succeed Fall in the Senate.[7]

6. The original "Santa Fe Ring" was composed of T. B. Catron, Robert H. Longwill, H. L. Waldo, Frank W. Springer and A. Staab.

7. William H. Andrews was one of the most astute politicians in the long list of men who came to New Mexico from other states with a view to obtaining election to the United States Senate. Born in Youngsville, Pennsylvania, Jan. 14, 1842, Andrews came to New Mexico in 1902. Sixty years old when coming to the Territory, Andrews had been a political figure of importance for many years in Pennsylvania. He was recognized as an important ally of Matthew Quay. Andrews was State Chairman of the Republican State Central Committee in Pennsylvania in 1889. He served in the Pennsylvania State Senate 1895 to 1898 and in the House in that state for several years. His last service in the Pennsylvania Legislature was in 1902, the year in which he came to Sierra County, New Mexico. In 1903, in New Mexico just long enough to be a voter, Andrews was elected to the New Mexico Territorial Council. By 1905 Andrews

While serving in the United States Senate in the national capital, Tom Catron could look back on nearly a half century of activity in New Mexico of a range and scope unequalled by any man subsequent to the American Occupation. During his fifty and more years in New Mexico, Thomas Benton Catron figuratively painted on a big canvas with a large brush, using plenty of paint and many colors. Fearless, able and resourceful, when he attached himself to a cause for a client, Tom Catron's loyalty and devotion knew no limits. When a client's life or property happened to be at stake, Catron became reckless at times in his disregard for his own professional safety and name. Catron's legal ability was widely known. He had a prodigious memory and could carry in his mind for years the exact reference to citations of important law cases by the style of the case, the book and page of the published reports. In connection with contemplated litigation of importance, a New Mexico man went to St. Louis, Missouri, and sought to employ the famous Ben Butler. Butler declined the employment, advising: "Go back to New Mexico and employ Tom Catron. He is as good, if not a better lawyer than I am."

In the famous Borrego murder cases, classic in New Mexico, Tom Catron, as an attorney for the defendants, became involved in such legal and political entanglements that he was brought face to face with the possibility of disbarment from the legal profession. When the disbarment fight reached a point where it got really serious, Tom Catron swallowed his pride and wrote a letter to Albert Bacon Fall at Las Cruces and asked him for help, which was immediately given.

---

had such a grasp on New Mexico politics that he made a combination with Gov. Miguel A. Otero and pitched Otero headlong into a fight with Frank A. Hubbell, Republican Territorial chairman. When the smoke of the Territorial Convention in Albuquerque cleared away, it was found that Andrews had defeated Bernard S. Rodey for renomination for Delegate in Congress. Andrews was elected to Congress from New Mexico in 1905 and re-elected twice, serving in the 59th, 60th and 61st Congress, his terms of service extending over the years 1905 to 1911. Unquestionably Andrews had great influence in obtaining statehood for New Mexico and he fully expected to be rewarded by election as United States Senator from New Mexico. Friends of Thomas Benton Catron and Albert Bacon Fall, alarmed by the strength demonstrated by Andrews in early polls and fearing that both Catron and Fall would be defeated, decided to pool their political resources, and their election was the result. Andrews died in Pennsylvania on January 16, 1919, almost penniless, after having spent a fortune in politics, always hopeful that he would get a seat in the United States Senate. Imperturbable in political life, Andrews to the last held to his philosophy: "Never be discouraged by a political defeat. Another election is bound to come along. Don't forget that the precinct chairman is the man who wins the elections."

Thomas Benton Catron.
From a portrait by Paul Forrere, courtesy of C. C. Catron.
Photograph by H. De Castro.

Disliking each other personally, Catron and Fall nevertheless respected each other for ability, courage and resourcefulness. Catron escaped disbarment through the vote of Judge Humphrey B. Hamilton of Socorro, sitting on the Supreme Court of the Territory. See *In re Catron*, 8 N.M. 253. Catron fought the Borrego cases through to the Supreme Court of the United States and lost there. See *In re Borrego*, 8 N.M. 655, 46 Pac. 211, affirmed 164 U.S. 612, 41 L. ed. 572, 17 Sup. Ct. 182.[8]

The Borregos were hanged only after a legal battle without precedent in the Territory of New Mexico. Thomas Hughes, editor of the Albuquerque *Daily Citizen*, was obliged to spend two months in the Bernalillo County jail as one of the sequels to the trial. See "In the Matter of Contempt vs. Thomas Hughes and W. T. McCreight, Respondents," 8. N.M. 225. On October 17, 1895, a three-column article was printed on the editorial page of the Albuquerque *Daily Citizen*, reflecting, so it was contended later, on Chief Justice

---

8. The so-called Borrego murder cases, which resulted in the hanging of four men, had widespread political reverberations in Santa Fe and throughout the Territory. Francisco Chavez, ex-official, and prominent citizen of Santa Fe, was shot and killed in the night time on May 29, 1892, near the west end of the Guadalupe bridge. The perpetrators of the crime were arrested a year later. Their arrest came about through the confession of one Juan Gallegos, who told officers that he had originally agreed to participate in the assassination, but on reflection thought better of it and sent a written warning to Francisco Chavez. As a result of the Gallegos confession, four well-known Santa Fe men were arrested, charged with murder by lying in wait. They were Francisco Gonzales y Borrego, Antonio Gonzales y Borrego, Lauriano (Chino) Alarid and Patricio Valencia. A fifth accomplice, Hipolito Vigil, resisted arrest and was shot and killed by a sheriff's posse. The murder trial started on April 23, 1895, and continued until May 29, 1895. The two Borregos, Alarid and Valencia were found guilty by the jury as charged in the indictment. The crime grew out of political quarrels. Francisco Chavez was identified with the Democratic party; his assassins were affiliated with the Republican party. The trial produced sensation after sensation and was perhaps the most celebrated criminal case in New Mexico between the murder trials following the Taos rebellion and the year 1895. Giving an outline of the history of the Borrego case, Judge Laughlin, in a fifty-three page dissenting opinion, said, *In re Catron*, 8 N. M. 275: "Chavez, the murdered man, by reason of his personal presence, his goodness of heart, and his kind and generous disposition, had attached many followers, not only of his political faith, but of the opposite faith as well, so that at the time of his assassination, and for a number of years prior, he was the acknowledged leader of his party, and much the strongest man politically in the county, and it was well known that he could elect or defeat any man he desired in local politics; and the testimony given at the preliminary hearing and on the trial in the indictment, tended strongly to show that the primary motive for his assassination was political jealousy, a fear of his popularity and power, and an inordinate desire to remove him from the road of political preferment."

Thomas Smith of the New Mexico Supreme Court. Among other things, the article said that Judge Smith had gone to Albuquerque from Santa Fe and conferred for hours with William Burr Childers of the Albuquerque bar at his residence, regarding a plan to institute disbarment charges against T. B. Catron. The article charged that Smith, as a member of the Supreme Court of New Mexico, proposed to appoint a hand-picked committee of lawyers to press the charges against Catron and then sit in the case as a judge when it came on for trial before the court.

Tom Hughes permitted the article to be printed in the *Citizen*, although he was told it was "hot," by William Smith Burke, veteran newspaper editorial writer, who had been asked for an opinion. An attachment was issued for Hughes soon after the article was published, but Hughes had quietly left for the neighboring Territory of Arizona. According to the Supreme Court's opinion written by Judge Napoleon Bonaparte Laughlin, "Hughes fled to Arizona and was returned to New Mexico by a United States deputy marshal." Editor Hughes claimed at the hearing that he had returned to New Mexico voluntarily, that he was ignorant of the authorship of the article and only placed "takes" of it on the hook because there was a shortage of copy and the printers were calling "copy" so insistently that he took the first thing that came to hand to satisfy their demands. The Supreme Court found against Hughes and he went to jail in Old Albuquerque. From his prison, Tom Hughes continued each day to write editorials for his paper. With a style acquired only after years of effort, Hughes had the gift of expressing his thoughts and views in a few concise sentences. He had no patience with editorial writers who used high sounding words and long, involved construction. While in jail, Tom Hughes was careful not to make any reference in his editorial writing to courts or judges, but he could not resist the temptation to instruct the make-up man on the *Citizen* to insert a numeral at the masthead each day, beginning with 1 and ending with 60, symbolic of his day by day approach to final freedom.

Tom Hughes served sixty days in jail and thus purged himself of contempt. He rather regretted that the judge had not sentenced him to a longer term. In his prison sanctuary he had found peace and quiet. Kind friends and ambitious politicians had furnished him with a plentiful supply of good cigars, which he smoked at leisure. The cares and worries of running a newspaper and job printing plant had

been transferred by events beyond his control to the shoulders of
William T. McCreight, his partner in the publishing business.
Hughes was requested by the Republican leaders to remain in jail
until nightfall on the sixtieth day of his prison term. As darkness
descended in Old Albuquerque on the evening of the sixtieth day,
a procession left the county jail for the new town of Albuquerque.
The First Regimental Band headed the procession, followed by many
men carrying flares and torches. Riding in state in a hack, drawn by
two white horses, Tom Hughes puffed contentedly at a cigar, waved
to the crowd of well-wishers who joined in the procession.[9]

Always a student of history, Thomas Benton Catron read much on
the life of Napoleon Bonaparte, but thought that Cortes, conqueror
of Mexico, was a greater soldier than Bonaparte. Tom Catron never
recognized, however, that he had made history, or had lived history
in New Mexico. He always declined to write his memoirs and was reluctant to write on any subject pertaining to his life or early day
incidents in New Mexico. Catron had better opportunity than any
one subsequent to the American Occupation to know the inside history of New Mexico land grants. He acquired total or partial interests
in many a grant and at one time was believed to own more land indi-
vidually than any other person in the United States. Besides owning
a minor fractional interest in thirty-one land grants in the Territory,
Thomas Benton Catron in 1896 owned outright the following interests in grants: An undivided one-half interest in the San Cristobal
Grant of 91,032 acres; the Tierra Amarilla Grant of 584,515 acres;
the north 240,000 acres of the Mora Grant of 827,621 acres;
the Espiritu Santo Grant of 113,141 acres; Cañon del Agua, 3,501
acres; Mesita de Juan Lopez, 42,022 acres; Alamitos, 2,500 acres. In
dealing with land grant matters, Tom Catron very rarely sold any of
his holdings. He preferred to hold what he owned and to acquire
additional interests in grants. On one occasion Catron gave a verbal
option to Marion L. Fox, then editor of the Albuquerque *Morning
Journal*, to buy a hundred thousand acres of the Tierra Amarilla
Grant for a Holland syndicate at $2 per acre. Fox called at Catron's
office in Santa Fe to notify him that the syndicate had decided to buy
the land and that the option was being exercised at $2 an acre, "Who

---

9. The writer in 1937 asked William T. McCreight the question: "Mr. Mac, who
wrote that article for the *Citizen* about the Borrego case that got Tom Hughes in jail?"
McCreight answered promptly: "Tom Catron."

in the hell said $2 an acre?" demanded Catron. "I never said any such thing. All I said was 'about $2 an acre,' and when I said 'about $2 an acre,' I meant $3." The deal fell through. At one time in the early nineteen hundreds, Tom Catron was paying six per cent on a million dollars which he had borrowed to finance his land grant speculations.

In no sense a presiding elder in the use of money in elections, Catron had always adhered to his code of ethics in such matters. During a hot fight between Democrats and Republicans for candidates for the Santa Fe Board of Education, an excited politico hurried to Catron's office and told the Senator that the day had been lost; that the Democrats were going to carry the election unless a certain amount of money could be obtained immediately to turn the tide. Catron cursed and stormed, declared that he was not interested in school board elections, that they were beneath his dignity. Suddenly he turned and said: "Pancho, how much did you say you would require to get results in this election?" "Five hundred dollars, señor," was the reply. Catron called a clerk in his law office, sent him to the bank with a check for $500 with instructions to bring back the money immediately in one dollar bills. Then calling the clerk to witness, Catron shouted: "Pancho, here is the five hundred dollars, but I want you to understand distinctly that under no circumstances must this money or any part of it be used to influence an election. Do you understand that?" Pancho, who had been permitted to experience such interviews on former occasions, replied affirmatively. "Well," bellowed Catron, "get the hell out of here."

Lacking a sense of humor, inclined to be grim and permanently pessimistic, Tom Catron seldom laughed at anybody or with anybody. He was never known to try to laugh himself out of a difficult situation. At the outbreak of the Spanish-American War in 1898, Tom Catron hurried over to the office of Territorial Governor Miguel Otero in Santa Fe to recommend to his Excellency the appointment of officers of the military companies, then being hastily organized in the Territory for service in the national army. When Catron reached the executive offices, he saw George Curry of Lincoln County and W. H. H. Llewellyn of Doña Ana County sitting in the Governor's waiting room. Catron brushed by Curry and Llewellyn, walked into Otero's office without ceremony or announcement, and said to the Governor in a voice that could be heard by Curry and Llewellyn:

"Gillie, I understand you have two vacancies for captain and I want one of them for my son, John." Otero replied: "Mr. Catron, I am thinking of appointing Llewellyn and George Curry." "Dam'd good appointments!" boomed Catron, "Curry will take it and get killed. It will be a good riddance. I am only afraid Llewellyn won't go and won't be killed." Catron walked out of the office. Otero gave the appointments to Curry and Llewellyn. Neither one got killed in the war as Catron had hoped. On another occasion Tom Catron walked into Governor Otero's office and began to talk politics to the governor. The conversation became rather heated. Finally Catron stopped talking altogether and glared fiercely at the Governor. "Gillie" Otero snapped out: "Mr. Catron, you can't intimidate me by looking at me that way." Catron made no reply, picked up his hat and walked out.

Although Catron thought little of calling people all the hard names he could think of and on occasion treated people quite roughly, he never believed that anyone could harbor any ill will or ill feeling toward him, or resent anything that he had said to or about another person. Rough, tough, bluff, and at times discourteous, Catron had qualities in the opposite direction, which at times manifested themselves to the great benefit of clients and acquaintances. In the role of lawyer and adviser, Catron would listen patiently and painstakingly, like a father confessor, to problems submitted by people in inferior walks of life, or by those in desperate or necessitous circumstances. At the conclusion of the conference, Tom Catron would give them such advice and encouragement as he thought adequate and proper. Invariably as the interview ended, the question would be asked: "Mr. Catron, how much do I owe you?" Then as if coming out of a reverie, Catron would nearly always say explosively: "Not a damn cent! Not a cent! Now, get out of here."

Catron's views of people were ordinarily broad and charitable. One day in 1913, after he had been elected to the United States Senate, Catron told his secretary, William A. Bayer, that he, Catron, would have been better off if the Lord had only given him enough sense to have remained home in Santa Fe instead of getting himself elected to the United States Senate, obliged to live in Washington and put up with a lot of nonsense and protocol. Secretary Bayer was aware of what was passing through Senator Catron's mind. On the plaza in Santa Fe, every man, woman and child in that town and in almost every other town in New Mexico, knew and accepted Tom Catron for what he was. No one in New Mexico cared if Tom Catron preferred to wear a slouch hat, baggy, unpressed trousers, black bow tie of ancient origin; no one would think to remark that his old style stiff-bosomed white shirt might be a trifle soiled, or that his red bandana handkerchief might not be particularly appropriate for use on social occasions. Suddenly there was an interruption in the conversation between Senator Catron and Secretary Bayer as to the respective advantages and disadvantages of life in Washington and Santa Fe by the unannounced entrance of a stranger into the Senator's private office. The visitor was a tall gangling man, with bearing and appearance indicating that in former days he had been a man of power and ability. The stranger's jaw had been partly eaten away, probably by a cancerous growth. He was, altogether, a forlorn looking individual. Senator Catron stared, but finally recognized the wraithlike stranger as the famous James Addison Peralta Reavis, one-time citizen of Henry County, Missouri, long-time resident of New Mexico. More than a decade before Peralta Reavis had almost wrested a vast acreage of land from the federal government. In the course of the fight for the land, the government unearthed the most gigantic land fraud in the history of the United States of America. For twenty-five years, Peralta Reavis had been the moving spirit in a plot to obtain approval of the United States Government to a claim for a strip of territory twelve miles in width, extending from Phoenix, Arizona, to Silver City, New Mexico. Displaying tenacity, perseverance, monumental industry, technical knowledge and great resourcefulness, Peralta Reavis, in the late nineties, had almost persuaded the New Mexico Court of Private Land Claims to validate his claim of title. Not long before the trial, an apparently insignificant and unimportant document in the chain of title was discovered to be a forgery, as the result of which government experts proved the entire claim to be an attempted swindle of vast magnitude. Peralta Reavis was convicted on a charge of fraud and served a comparatively short term in the New Mexico penitentiary. Released from prison, he became a wanderer on the face of the earth. Tom Catron had been his attorney in a last minute attempt to keep Peralta Reavis from prison, but had not been his counsel in the land grant case.[10]

Recognizing Peralta Reavis in his Washington office, Senator

---

10. See Peralta Reavis case, 8 N. M. Sup. Ct. Rep., p. 27.

Catron said: "Hell, Reavis, I thought you were dead long ago."
Reavis demonstrated by a ghostlike handshake with Catron, that he
was still living. Closing the door of his inner office, Senator Catron
and Reavis conferred for a long time. Secretary Bayer speculated on
the subject of the conference, but knew how it would end. Catron
finally called out to Bayer: "Billy, bring me my check book." Peralta
Reavis left the Senate Office Building and apparently left Washington the same day. Catron watched Reavis walking slowly down a cor-
ridor of the Senate Office Building and then said to Bayer: "Billy,
that man is a dam'd scoundrel." Bayer inquired: "Why, Senator
Catron?" For many years private secretary to William H. ("Bull")
Andrews, Secretary Bayer had been privy to many a secret of political
skullduggery affecting Pennsylvania and New Mexico. Bayer expected that Catron would disclose some long-time hidden information about the gigantic land fraud with which Peralta Reavis had
been identified. Senator Catron muttered: "Billy, that Jim Addison,
who calls himself Reavis, was a soldier in my command during the
Civil War. He deserted. He's no dam'd good."

Tom Catron had a streak of curiosity, which revealed itself occasionally in regard to political things with which he had been connected. While Catron and Fall were talking one day in 1914 in the
United States Senate cloakroom, Senator Catron turned the conversation abruptly and said to Senator Fall: "Fall, now that it is all over
and we are both here in Washington, I would like to have you tell
me the truth about who it was that tried to kill me that time in Santa
Fe when they shot J. A. Ancheta." Catron was referring to an
attempt to assassinate him that had occurred during a session of the
New Mexico Legislature in 1891, in which Catron had been a member of the Council from Santa Fe County. Ancheta, known as "Toro
de Oro," had been a member of the Council from Doña Ana, Grant
and Sierra Counties. Fall, then a Democrat, had been a member of
the lower house from Doña Ana, Grant and Sierra Counties.

Now, many years after, Catron was anxious to find out from Fall
the identity of the would-be assassin. Senator Fall replied: "Catron,
the man who inspired that shot was Jacob H. Crist." Catron shook
his head and mumbled: "Fall, I don't believe it, I don't believe it;
Crist wouldn't have had me shot."

On the night of February 5, 1891, Catron was in conference in his
office with four members of the Territorial Council, Elias S. Stover of

Albuquerque, T. B. Mills of Las Vegas, Pedro Perea of Bernalillo and Joseph A. Ancheta[11] of Silver City. A charge of buckshot broke a pane of glass in the window of the room in which the conference was held. Nine buckshot entered the back of Ancheta's neck and shoulder. Ancheta sprang to his feet immediately after being hit by the buckshot. A bullet from a rifle or revolver whizzed close to his ear. Ancheta nearly died from the wounds. Surgeons wanted to perform an operation on his head, proposing to remove a portion of the skull and insert a silver plate. Ancheta refused to consent and finally recovered.

It was soon known throughout Santa Fe that the shots that wounded Ancheta had been intended for Tom Catron and were meant to kill him. A few seconds before the shotgun had been discharged, Tom Catron arose from the chair in which he had been seated for the conference and walked across the room. Ancheta, who had been standing, immediately went and sat in the chair that Catron had just vacated. The shooting followed almost instantly. For years after the unsuccessful attempt to assassinate him, Tom Catron was careful not to stand or sit near a door or window of his home in the night time.

Following the shooting of Ancheta, the Legislature of New Mexico promptly adopted a joint resolution condemning the "most dastardly outrage" that had been perpetrated in the "attempted assassination of J. A. Ancheta and other members of the 29th Legislative Assembly," and proposed a reward of twenty thousand dollars for the capture and punishment of the guilty persons. Charles A. Siringo, a nationally known detective, was employed in the case and soon developed important clews. When the trail got too close to the powers that managed the Democratic party, Detective Siringo was taken off the case. The law offering a reward was repealed by the 1893 Legislature.

---

11. Joseph Arthur Ancheta was born at Mesilla, Doña Ana County, on July 21, 1865. Ancheta's father, Nepomuceno Ancheta, a refugee from a revolution in Old Mexico, discovered valuable gold mines in Grant County, New Mexico, sold some of them for large sums and was called "Golden Bull." The son, Joseph Arthur Ancheta, inherited the name and was called "Toro del Oro" by Spanish-speaking people. Acquaintances claimed that the Anchetas, father and son, had a gold mine in Grant County which they visited secretly as they required money, mined enough ore for their needs, smelted it in a crude smelter, took the gold to the mint and exchanged it for gold coins. J. A. Ancheta was educated at Notre Dame University and admitted to the New Mexico bar in 1886.

Who shot Ancheta, why Catron had been marked for assassination and who had planned and managed the conspiracy, were questions that were never satisfactorily answered. Fall blamed Crist, but Fall and Crist were not too friendly.

Prominent for many years in Democratic politics, for a time District Attorney of the First Judicial District, Jake Crist was a leader in political maneuvering, a never-ending source of trouble and apprehensiveness to Republicans and Democrats alike. On more than one occasion Fall and Crist engaged in personalities. During the 1911 New Mexico Constitutional Convention, Fall and Crist had an acrimonious dispute over the provisions of a proposed article. Never a man to permit opposition without a show of temper, Albert Bacon Fall was always prepared for a fight and indifferent as to choice of weapons. A fist fight, a fight with a cane, or a gun, were all equally agreeable to Fall. Crist, himself a fighter and fire-eater, was not afraid of Fall. However, on the occasion of their argument in the Constitutional Convention, Crist was forced to retreat. Fall, unusually angry and threatening bodily harm, drove Crist out of the Constitutional Convention for the day.[12]

Thomas Benton Catron made several important speeches in the United States Senate. Undoubtedly the most significant and scholarly speech was on the subject, "Mexico, Its People and Their Customs," delivered soon after the Pancho Villa raid into Columbus, New Mexico. Some time after delivering the speech Senator Catron went to Juarez, Mexico, at the request of the State Department and interviewed Pancho Villa, explaining to Villa the viewpoint and attitude of the United States in its relations with Mexico. On another occasion he spoke on some phases of Schedule K. of the tariff bill then under consideration. The speech had been well prepared and was delivered with much of Catron's old-time fire and ability. The subject was not timely and the speech was addressed mostly to empty Senate benches.[13]

---

12. J. H. Crist was born April 3, 1865, in Louisville, Pennsylvania, came to New Mexico in 1884, operated coal mines several years, edited a Democratic newspaper in Santa Fe for four years. Admitted to practice law in New Mexico, Crist was district attorney in the First Judicial District for five years, during which time he prosecuted the Borrego murder case defended by Tom Catron. He served eight years as chairman of the Territorial Democratic Central Committee, was a Delegate to the New Mexico Constitutional Convention, but refused to sign the document before adjournment.

13. The Pancho Villa raid was one of the most exciting and dramatic incidents in

If Thomas Benton Catron had been socially inclined he could have achieved prominence in Washington society during his years of service in the Senate, not only because of his own personality, but through the assistance of Mrs. Elkins, wealthy widow of Stephen B. Elkins, his companion of early days in New Mexico. Mrs. Elkins was prominent for a generation in Washington society. Both her father, Henry Gassaway Davis, and her husband had served for many years in the United States Senate from West Virginia. Anxious to extend to him every social courtesy, Mrs. Elkins on many occasions invited Tom Catron to dinner and to social functions. The Elkins home at 1626 K Street was a magnificent establishment, staffed by many servants and furnished with everything that great wealth made possible. Catron refused most of the invitations extended by Mrs. Elkins, but finally, with some hesitation, he accepted a dinner invitation. "What shall I wear if I come?" Catron inquired cautiously over the telephone, within hearing distance of Secretary Billy Bayer. "Tom, wear anything; come just as you like," was Mrs. Elkin's reply. Tom Catron took Mrs. Elkins at her word. He went to the dinner party at the Elkins mansion in his street clothes, baggy unpressed trousers, long black coat, old time hard-boiled shirt and collar, with black cravat of

---

the history of New Mexico. On March 9, 1916, a few minutes after 4 o'clock in the afternoon, Villa, the Mexican bandit, the only man in uniform, attacked Columbus, Luna County, New Mexico, leading 1,000 Mexican bandits. Nineteen Americans were killed and many more were wounded. The attack turned out to be a massacre. Villa and his bandits entered Columbus from the southwest. The bandits attacked remnants of the four troops of the Thirteenth U. S. Cavalry stationed just outside of Columbus. Lieut. Castleman, officer of the day, rushed to town with fifty cavalrymen and saved it from being wiped out by the bandits. Burning, looting and pillaging, the Mexicans killed J. T. Dean, groceryman; C. C. Miller, druggist; W. T. Ritchie; J. J. Moore, merchant; Mrs. Milton Jones; Dr. H. M. Hart of El Paso; C. De Witt Miller of Tularosa; W. A. Davidson, El Paso; N. R. Walker, a guest at the Commercial Hotel, and eight United States soldiers. Columbus became known throughout the nation. Newspaper correspondents poured into the town and sent out lurid stories of the raid. Maj. Gen. Frederick Funston in San Antonio instructed Brig. Gen. John J. Pershing, in command of American troops, to take charge of the telegraph office and police all automobile roads leading from Columbus which might carry dispatches to the outside world. Funston declared that newspaper reports from the border had been revealing every movement of troops and the style and quality of their equipment. (See Columbus Courier, March 12, 1916, May 26, 1916.) A soldier writing to the Santa Fe New Mexican, after New Mexico National Guard troops reached Columbus, described the town as follows: "The town is a typical frontier town, reminding you of the kind you see in the movies. Deputy sheriffs with their guns strapped to their hips, soldiers in uniform at every turn, motor trucks wheezing as they pass in and out daily, newspaper

the school of Henry Clay, old-fashioned Congress gaiter shoes. The next day, Senator Catron complained to Secretary Bayer: "I was the only dam'd fool at the Elkins dinner last night who didn't wear a dress suit."

It may be certain, however, that Tom Catron held his own conversationally at the Elkins home at the dinner party or on any other occasion. From an early day, he had been an omnivorous reader. He had a very retentive memory and when interested in a person or in a subject spoke easily and brilliantly. His law library was the largest and most important in New Mexico and his private collection of Mexicana and New Mexicana was of great value. After his death the library was loaned to the University of New Mexico at Albuquerque by Senator Catron's four sons, John W. Catron and Charles C. Catron, (both now deceased), Thomas B. Catron II, and Fletcher A. Catron. In the Catron library were many rare volumes, including those purchased in Mexico by Adolph Bandelier, who went to Mexico in 1891 for the express purpose of purchasing for Catron the library of the famous Father Fisher, the Confessor of the ill-fated Emperor Maximilian. The Fisher library was acquired by Bandelier and shipped from the Augustinian Monastery in Guadalajara, Mexico, to Santa Fe. Writing on June 13, 1891, from Santa Fe, to Thomas Janvier, Bandelier urged Janvier to send through him a few lines to Catron thanking him for arrangements Bandelier had made with Catron for the loan of a rare book to Janvier. "Anything will please him, for he is a Bibliomane and has put it into his big head (he has a remarkably large cranium) to collect the largest library in the United States. He is in a fair way of doing it, too. . . . Now, as soon

---

correspondents and moving picture men in riding breeches and outing coats, vaudeville shows and picture shows, but unlike western towns of the movies, there are no saloons." Although there were no saloons in Columbus, there were any number of "clubs" that catered to the liquor traffic. Among the clubs were the Benovelent Order of Bees, The Loyal Order of Moose, Fraternal Order of Grizzly Bears, Camp Furlong, Punitive Expedition Social Club, N.C.O. Social Club, San Juan Social Club. Commenting on the "club" situation, the Columbus *Courier* of May 26, 1916, said: "No one club would sell a man booze enough to intoxicate him, but when a man belonged to three or four of them and tried to make them all in a single night, he was very apt to get loaded before he got to the last one." "Black Jack" Pershing pursued Pancho Villa into Mexico. Finally, in obedience to orders from his superiors, he abandoned the chase. Washington was impressed because of the possibilities for American involvement in the European War and did not want American troops in any number on Mexican soil. Pershing later became supreme commander of American troops in World War I.

as you can, send me the note for my friend, Catron. Please do it. Address him: Hon. T. B. Catron, and enclose the note to me. You will get the book forthwith."[14]

When Tom Catron appeared as chief counsel for the prosecution in the case of *Territory of New Mexico versus Oliver M. Lee and James Gililland* at Hillsboro, Sierra County, in 1899, he was at the peak of his ability as a lawyer. On the opposite side of the counsel table sat Albert Bacon Fall.

In his last will and testament, executed shortly before his death, as is customary with lawyers, Catron expressed his love for the Masonic order in which he had long been a devoted member and requested a funeral according to the rites of that organization.

Honored on many occasions with high office, including a seat in the United States Senate, Thomas Benton Catron had paid for those honors. Although a rock-ribbed Republican, by lending money he had involuntarily participated in a "share the wealth" program. Land grants that Catron had acquired in his lifetime were eventually sold for large sums of money. In lieu of ready cash, when Catron died he left a stack of outlawed and uncollectible promissory notes with a face value of a quarter of a million dollars, in amounts ranging from $1 to $5,000. The evidence of so many outstanding loans indicated Catron's method of doing business and furnished a key to the source of at least some of his political power and prestige. Regardless of the size of the loan, Catron took a note and mortgage from a borrower, indifferent as to whether the security was a horse, a wagon, or a small tract of land. He always went through the same routine with borrowers, first gruffly refusing to make a loan, cussing out everything and everybody; then reluctantly consenting to lend the money; then quibbling about the rate of interest and the time of maturity. The borrower always signed a mortgage and note, admonished by Catron of the strict obligation to pay on the due date, under penalty of foreclosure. Catron was frequently obliged to borrow money at a bank to finance loans he made to other people.

All of Catron's notes and mortgages went into a large iron safe. He seldom filed a mortgage deed for record; none was ever foreclosed. Few notes were ever paid by the borrowers. In making loans and

---

14. See *Unpublished Letters of Adolph F. Bandelier* by Paul Radin, Carl Hertzog, El Paso, Texas, 1942.

accepting notes there was in Catron's mind a desire to help out friends and acquaintances, but at the same time he wished to control the borrower politically. Among other assets listed in the inventory of the Catron estate were worthless railroad bonds, stocks in mining companies and other enterprises long since abandoned in which some two hundred fifty thousand dollars had been invested either in money or legal services.

When Tom Catron passed to the great hereafter on May 21, 1921, the Santa Fe *New Mexican*, through E. Dana Johnson, its brilliant and scholarly editor, commented editorially as follows:

> Thomas Catron was a powerful leader of his time; blunt, outspoken, uncompromising, at times he ruled with a rod of iron in the days of his greatest political ascendancy. He was, frankly, a "practical politician." The appellation, "boss," complimented instead of offending him; political power was meat and drink to him and those who went to the political mat with "Uncle Tom" always knew they had been in a fight. The NEW MEXICAN can testify to this whole heartedly. Nor would Mr. Catron himself expect this paper to bestow effusive economiums on a political record which so often and so honestly it attacked. Politics aside, we shall miss him, his occasional visits to the office, miss his personality on the streets and at political gatherings. The all round calibre of the citizen is shown by the gap he leaves in his home town; and Senator Catron, needless to say, leaves a big one.

six

WRITING MEN

IN THE SEVENTIES AND EIGHTIES, a number of men were attracted to New Mexico, curious to see for themselves people and things in which they were interested from the scientific standpoint, caring little or nothing for the romance and adventure of the day. Their principal tasks were in fields other than writing, but their written words are the signposts of students of New Mexicana of today.

Among the earliest modern day visitors to New Mexico was Washington Matthews, who came as a physician and surgeon with the United States Army, but remained to write important works on the Navajo Indians. Born in Dublin, Ireland, July 17, 1843, Washington Matthews resided for a time in Wisconsin and later in Iowa. He graduated in medicine from the University of Iowa in 1864 and died in Washington, D.C., in 1905. While stationed at Fort Wingate and other places in New Mexico, Dr. Matthews made notable investigations in ethnology and philology of the Navajo Indians. Among other books, he wrote *Navajo Silversmiths*, 1883; *Navajo Weavers*, 1884; *The Mountain Chant, a Navajo Ceremony*, 1887; *The Night Chant, a Navajo Ceremony*, 1902. Dr. Matthews had no flair for showmanship, used the technique of the scalpel in probing into Navajo ceremonies and wrote his reports in the style of a physician compiling a case history. During some of the years that Dr. Matthews was at Fort Wingate, he had a rival scientist in the field, Frank Hamilton Cushing, who was fond of dramatizing himself and his work. Born in Pennsylvania on July 22, 1857, Cushing died in Washington, D.C., on April 10, 1900. Cushing lived on a farm in Barre, New York, studied for a time at Cornell, then was employed by the Smithsonian Institution and sent with the Powell-Stevenson Expedition to

Zuñi Indian village in New Mexico. He lived for several years in the Zuñi pueblo, wore an Indian costume and followed their manner of life as nearly as possible. His story of life at Zuñi was published in the December, 1882, and February, 1883, issues of *Century* magazine and reprinted by E. De Golyer of Dallas, Texas, in the volume *My Adventures in Zuñi*, published in 1941. Cushing learned the Zuñi language and Zuñi rites, claimed to have been adopted into the tribe and ordained into their mysterious priesthoods. The Zuñis went on the warpath when they learned that Cushing's residence among them was for the purpose of learning their secrets and then publishing them to the world. Among Cushing's most important publications were *Zuñi Fetiches*, 2nd Annual Report, Bureau of Ethnology, 1882; *A Study of Pueblo Pottery, as Illustrative of Zuñi Culture Growth*, 4th Annual Report, Bureau of Ethnology, and *Zuñi Creation Myths*, 13th Annual Report, Bureau of Ethnology.

Hubert Howe Bancroft, prolific writer and compiler of Southwestern History, came to New Mexico in 1885 and by personal interviews and examination and study of documents obtained at first hand much of the material for the very valuable volume *Arizona and New Mexico*, published in 1889. Born in Granville, Ohio, May 5, 1832, Bancroft moved to San Francisco where he died March 2, 1918, with the satisfaction of knowing that he had published more books on Central America, Mexico, the Pacific States and the West and Southwest generally than any other man before him.

In August, 1880, soon after the coming of the railroad to New Mexico, a man at that time little known, came to the Territory—Adolph Francis Alphonse Bandelier. He was curious to confirm theories that he had long held and discussed by mail with Lewis H. Morgan, a noted scholar. Bandelier resided in Santa Fe off and on for several years. During his residence in New Mexico, Bandelier visited many Indian villages, made exhaustive studies, proved a prolific writer, gained national and then international fame as a student and authority in the fields of archaeology and ethnology. Born at Berne, Switzerland, August 6, 1840, Bandelier died March 19, 1914, the author of many books, countless reports, papers and pamphlets. Among the more important works on New Mexico subjects, Bandelier wrote *A Report on the Ruins of the Pueblo of Pecos*, 1881; *Historical Introduction to Studies Among the Sedentary Indians of New*

Mexico, 1884; *The Delight Makers*, a novel; *The Gilded Man*, and the monumental *Final Report of Investigation Among the Indians of the Southwest*, 1880-1885, Parts 1 and 2.

Charles Fletcher Lummis walked through New Mexico in 1884, liked the looks of the Territory and returned to live for five years at Isleta pueblo, thirteen miles south of Albuquerque, where he learned the language and customs of the people. Out of Lummis's experience in Isleta and other parts of the Territory grew several books about New Mexico subjects including *A New Mexico David*, published in 1891; *The Land of Poco Tiempo*, 1893; *Mesa Cañon and Pueblo*, 1925. Eccentric, energetic, tireless, Charles Fletcher Lummis preached the gospel of the Southwest and its attractions for nearly fifty years. Born in Lynn, Massachusetts, March 1, 1859, Lummis died in Los Angeles, California, on November 25, 1928.

No man of the type of Washington Matthews, Cushing, Bancroft, Bandelier or Lummis lived in the southeastern part of New Mexico in the early days. Perhaps Lincoln County was too tough for them; in all probability they had no interest in cattle or cowboys, sheriffs or six-shooters, outlaws or desperadoes, gold mines, faro bank, chuck-a-luck, roulette, or any other game of chance. It was left to men of an entirely different type of mind to write about things pertaining to the southeastern part of the Territory. There was but little to offer archaeologist or ethnologist in the way of ruins of Indian villages or traces of primitive man, but much to attract men who could write and who were interested in every day life.[1] In a country where live-stock and land, mines and minerals, were the predominant topics of conversation, men had little time for the liberal arts. Newspapers were published in the seventies and eighties in Mesilla, Fort Stanton, Lincoln and White Oaks, but times were difficult and all of them led a precarious existence, depending for the most part on political support for continuance of publication. The press itself was at times a severe critic of the Fourth Estate. The Las Cruces *Democrat* of

---

1. The El Paso, Texas, Archaeological Society excavated a ruin at Three Rivers, New Mexico, a few years ago declared to be "an adobe structure of typical pueblo form." See *American Archaeology*, No. 1, summary of archaeological work in the Americas in 1925, Pan American Union, 1925, where of the Three Rivers excavation it was said: "This is the most southeasterly site so far investigated, and the material recovered shows a very interesting and significant blending of pottery styles."

September 8, 1895, said editorially: "We can count upon the fingers of one hand the papers in this Territory edited by men whose education fits them for anything higher than herding pigs in a swamp."

Among the writing men who left their imprint on things in southeastern New Mexico may be mentioned Marshall Ashmun Upson, Emerson Hough, Major William Caffrey, Eugene Manlove Rhodes, Nathan Howard Thorp, John Wallace Crawford and Charles Siringo.

Marshall Ashmun Upson, itinerant journalist afflicted with, or gifted by, insatiable wanderlust, came to the Territory of New Mexico during Civil War days, why or whence he never disclosed even to close friends. Born in Wolcott, Connecticut, on November 23, 1828, Ash Upson went to New York City when a young man, and worked for James Gordon Bennett as a reporter on the New York *Herald.* Drifting west, he worked in 1864 as a printer on the *Register* in Central City, Colorado, and came to New Mexico in the latter part of that year. For a time he was employed as a purser on New Mexico stagecoaches. He established the Albuquerque *Press* in Albuquerque in 1867 and published it for two years. In 1870 he established and edited the Las Vegas *Mail,* which later became the Las Vegas *Gazette.* While in Las Vegas, Ash Upson became acquainted with Jesus Maria Baca,[2] a frequent visitor to Upson's shop, and on occasion Baca set a few sticks of type for the paper. Jesus Maria Baca wrote the copy in Spanish and set the type for *Estefeta de Las Vegas,* a Spanish weekly published by Upson as a companion paper to the Las Vegas *Mail.* Besides establishing papers in Albuquerque and Las Vegas, Upson worked on papers in Elizabethtown, Fort Stanton, Mesilla and other places. On June 1, 1875, Upson "assumed the tripod" of *Eco del Rio Grande* in Mesilla, and there made the acquaintance of Ira M. Bond, editor of the Mesilla *News,* who went to

---

2. Jesus Maria Baca, the oldest native printer in New Mexico, died in Las Vegas on May 1, 1876, aged 65. He learned his trade in Durango, Mexico, returned to New Mexico with Padre Martinez and, under the latter, established the first printing office in New Mexico at Taos about 1835; probably the first printing office west of the Mississippi Valley. He remained in the Taos office until 1847 when the plant was purchased and removed to Santa Fe by Hovey & Davies, who published the first newspaper of general circulation established and printed in the Territory. Baca remained in the Santa Fe printing office until 1857 at which time failing eyesight forced his retirement. He was related to the Pino and Delgado families. See Las Vegas *Gazette,* May 6, 1876.

Washington some years later to work for statehood for New Mexico. Bond was present on the occasion when President William Howard Taft signed the bill granting statehood to the Territory. From Mesilla on the Rio Grande, Ash Upson traveled eastward to the Pecos River and became an early day postmaster in the hamlet of Roswell. Commissioned a notary public and with some knowledge of land surveying, Upson became a noted character in the Seven Rivers country and beyond, over into the Staked Plains country in Texas. In the year 1869, during the administration of Governor Robert B. Mitchell, a somewhat kindred spirit, Ash Upson served for a brief period as acting Adjutant-General of New Mexico. Pressed to pay off a number of ancient Military Department obligations, Upson assumed authority to issue militia warrants to creditors. The Territorial Auditor promptly refused to honor the warrants and they were purchased by speculators at twenty cents on the dollar. Although importuned to do so at every session, more than twenty years passed before the Legislature of the Territory enacted a law validating the warrants. When the militia warrants caused him trouble in Santa Fe, Ash Upson, retired from the political field and went back to the printer's case. In the Pecos Valley country, Ash Upson was acquainted with every cowpuncher from Toyah, Texas, to Tascosa, and was familiar with all the gossip and scandal of the day from Mesilla on the Rio Grande to Roswell on the Pecos. As postmaster at Roswell, Ash Upson delivered mail to outlaws and good citizens alike. As a justice of the peace in a precinct covering hundreds of square miles, Upson settled quarrels and disputes that had not yet reached the six-shooter stage. With Lincoln County seat half a hundred miles away by horseback, Upson's justice of the peace court was, for many people of the area, a court of last resort.

The Las Vegas Gazette of September 13, 1879, commenting on the immensity of Upson's jurisdiction, said: "Ash Upson is justice of the peace at Roswell. His jurisdiction extends down to Seven Rivers and anywhere out on the Staked Plains of Texas. He has more country within his jurisdiction than half the district judges of the states."

Before coming to New Mexico, Ash Upson had been married and divorced. Only on rare occasions did he consent as a justice of the peace to perform marriage ceremonies. He was always doubtful of the final outcome of the procedure. In the late seventies, Justice Upson married a cowboy to a lady of his choice and carefully wrote out a certificate in testimony of the ceremony. He placed the certificate among papers in his desk in the Roswell postoffice. The cowboy rode up to the postoffice some weeks later and complained to Upson, in his capacity as justice of the peace, that the marriage had not turned out as he expected; that the bride insisted on remaining in bed each morning until after sunup, would not cook the kind of grub he liked, refused to help him break horses and round up cattle. The cowboy asked Upson to advise him on the procedure for divorce. "You don't need a divorce," said Ash Upson. "I kind of sized up that woman the day I was marrying you two people. I never sent the marriage certificate to Lincoln to be recorded." Thereupon, Justice Upson produced the certificate from a drawer in his desk, went outside, tore it into small pieces and threw them to the four winds. He told the astonished cowboy: "You are now a free man again; go back to the ranch and take the saddle and bridle off that woman, and turn her back to grass in Texas where she came from."

After Pat Garrett retired as sheriff of Lincoln County and moved to Roswell, Garrett and Upson developed a friendship which continued until Upson's death in Uvalde, Texas, October 6, 1894. Garrett and Upson had gone to Uvalde a few years earlier. Smarting under attacks that he had shot "Billy the Kid" unfairly, Pat Garrett decided a few months after the killing to get out a book telling his side of the controversy. Ash Upson wrote the story for Garrett at the Garrett ranch near Roswell. The book was entitled *The Authentic Life of Billy the Kid, the Noted Desperado of the Southwest, Whose Deeds of Daring Have Made His Name a Terror in New Mexico, Arizona and Northern Mexico.* Purporting to be "a faithful and interesting narrative," the book contained 137 pages. No question but that Ash Upson had a most favorable opportunity to know and understand the facts in connection with Pat Garrett's part in the killing of William H. Bonney. Upson claimed to have boarded with Mrs. Antrim, Bonney's mother, when she, as he claimed, conducted boarding houses in Santa Fe and Silver City. Nearly all books published on the life of Billy the Kid subsequent to 1882 have been built around the Pat Garrett volume. Ash Upson makes many statements in the Garrett version in regard to the Kid's early years which have not received corroboration from any other source. Dependent on Pat Garrett at the time he was writing the book, it may be assumed that Upson gave Garrett all the best of the controversy between the sheriff and the outlaw. In order to do this, Upson was obliged to paint the Kid in the darkest hues. Upson drew heavily on poetry to embroider his points and his descriptions are in conformity with the lurid and extravagant style of the eighties. The volume was published by the Santa Fe New Mexican in 1882. Writing to a relative soon after the book had been finished, Ash Upson said:

> The book, "Life of Billy the Kid," will be a success. It has been bungled in the publication. The Santa Fe publishers took five months to do a month's job, and then made a poor one. Pat F. Garrett, Sheriff of the County, who killed the "Kid" and whose name appears as author of the work (though I wrote every word of it) as it would make it sell, insisted on taking it to Santa Fe, and was swindled badly in his contract. I live with Garrett, and have, since last August. His contract said they were to settle on the book every sixty days. One week from today the first 60 expires. It is 220 miles to Santa Fe (no R.R.). The publisher does not know how to put the book on the market.

Before taking over the work of getting out the book for Pat Garrett, Ash Upson had clerked in the store of Capt. J. C. Lea. In a letter from Roswell to his sister, dated September 25, 1878, Upson makes reference to the arrangement:

> Capt. Lea, who owns the buildings comprising Roswell, will put in a stock of goods in a very fine storeroom, next to my office in a few weeks—soon as he is sure the bandetti are effectually dispersed, and I am to take charge of the store, as Capt. nor any of his people talk Spanish, and if they did, would not have time to attend to it, and would not anyhow. This will pay board, if no more. The Post-office pays very little but it is not much trouble. Several from here have gone back to Mississippi to harvest their cotton. They come from Satartia, Yazoo County and Warrenton.

While clerking in the store, Ash Upson had a misunderstanding with Lea and resigned from his position in a huff. A lady customer called for a bottle of "Hostetter's Bitters," a popular remedy of the day, with a generous alcoholic content. Captain Lea, who happened to be in the store at the time, observed that Upson could not locate a bottle of the patent medicine for the lady; Lea was certain that a considerable stock of the item had been on the shelves. Ash Upson was finally obliged to confess that he had personally consumed all of the bitters in the place. His excuse: "How in hell was I to know that some dam'd fool woman would come in here, wanting a bottle of bitters."

On occasion Ash Upson served as a correspondent for Territorial newspapers. In the *Lincoln County Leader* of November 20, 1886, he began his article from Roswell with the sentence: "The scintillating effervescence of genius hath succumbed to the practical life betwixt millstones of soup and pie, and once again I throw myself into the breach of common intercourse and condescend to mingle with the common herd."

Ash Upson went to Lincoln, the county seat, from time to time, visited around the courthouse and about town. During one term of court, Upson listened to the testimony of witnesses in a murder case being tried by a jury before Judge Warren Bristol. Upson heard the arguments and wrangling of the lawyers over instructions proposed to be given to the jurors. Well acquainted with Judge Bristol, Ash Upson approached the bench during an intermission and told His Honor that the lawyers were making too much of a to-do about the instructions. He informed the Court that he had heard the testimony, had sized up the case, and could write out an instruction in a few words that would clearly inform the jury on the law of the case. "Go ahead, write out the instruction, and let me see it," commanded Judge Bristol. Ash Upson quickly wrote out a proposed instruction to the jury and handed it to the court. The instruction proposed by Upson was as follows:

> In making your decision, gentlemen, please bear in mind that the deceased was reaching for his hip pocket when the defendant blazed away at him. The Territorial statutes, you understand, gentlemen, allow one man, when he sees another make this motion, to produce his gun and commence the bombardment. To be sure, it has been proved in this case that the deceased was reaching for his handkerchief, but that, gentlemen, does not make any difference; the law does not recognize any such movements. The very fact that he was carrying a handkerchief while in New Mexico, shows that he was an unfit member for our Territorial society. Please carefully weigh all of these important facts before bringing in your verdict.

Requested to submit his early day recollections of the country by
Maj. Wm. Caffrey of the *Lincoln County Leader*, Ash Upson wrote
for the issue of October 12, 1889, the following article:

> Do you think there would be any consanguinity between the re-
> sults of putting old tales in new dress and putting old wine in new
> bottles? What can I relate of twenty-five years ago in Lincoln
> County that has not been printed by more eloquent pens? More
> than twenty-five years ago I traversed this country from north to
> south and from east to west. The civilized inhabitants were lately
> citizens of Mexico, with here and there a "galvanized" American,
> and two companies of troops at Fort Stanton. The principal settle-
> ment was the Placita, now Lincoln, which was composed of a few
> families living in adobe houses, scattered in irregular fashion along
> the canyon. The savage population predominated, and consisted of
> the Mescalero Apaches, their comperes the Comanche renegades,
> Chirihuhua Apacjes [Chiricahua Apaches], Lopwas [Kiowas], Locka-
> poos [Kickapoos], et al, coyotes, prairie dogs, antelope, on the plains
> and in the valleys, and bear, wolves, mountain lions, panthers, deer
> and elk in the mountains. He was a brave man who took up an abode
> outside the protection of the Fort or a settlement, or who rode alone
> along the trails now converted into mail routes and county roads.
> Many a mutilated corpse this writer has seen (murdered and scalped
> by the "noble red man") buried by the wayside, or conveyed by
> friends to the Fort or within the settlements.
>
> The slow (extremely slow) march of civilization has so changed
> the very face of nature, that one looking back 25 years, can scarce
> conceive this to be the same vicinity where a man would wait for
> a week or a month for companionship on a journey of ten or twenty
> miles, and provide himself with arms and provisions for the round
> trip.
>
> Time and space forbid exhaustive detail of cause and effect. In
> 1877, and 8 and 9, I was postmaster at Roswell. Much of that time I
> was literally alone except on mail days, when settlers rode up in
> squads of 6 or 8, with rifles across their saddles, pistols in belt and
> belts of cartridges about their bodies and across their shoulders.
> This was during the bloody Lincoln County War. There was but
> one house within sight of the two buildings comprising Roswell, and
> the denizens of that isolated shanty made their stay very short. What
> with outlaws and assassins on one hand, and thieving Indians on the
> other, the roads and trails leading to my hermitage were deserted by
> "lone horsemen," and "mover's" equipage.

Ten years have passed. Trails have become county roads; the prairies are dotted with prosperous farms; where there was no sign of tree or shrub, snug farmhouses peep out from green groves of shade and fruit trees. Roswell is alive with busy toilers. Four hotels, four mercantile houses, three blacksmith shops, two drug stores, two shoemakers, five saloons, one bakery, one laundry, one saddle and harness shop, two barber shops, one newspaper, five carpenters, two masons, one brickyard, one lumber yard, one painter, three lawyers, three doctors, a Masonic hall, two livery stables and one tinner. . . . The affairs of political and social life are conducted in a dignified "United States" fashion. The crude manners of the wild and woolly west are superseded by the improved styles of the east. Bridegrooms no longer promise to cherish and protect with revolvers on belt and spurs on heel. Not now do the cowboys mount the jocund cayuse and run down and rope the coy bride to get her stockings on before the ceremony. "Where late was barrenness and waste, the perfumed blossom, bud and blade, sweet, bashful pledges of approaching harvest, give cheerful promise to the hope of industry."

For more than a quarter of a century Ash Upson kept pretty well in touch with the New Mexico newspapers. He wrote letters and articles for them which revealed a sense of humor and considerable ability. Under date of January 30, 1878, Upson wrote a letter from Roswell giving warning of a traveler of those days. Displaying Upson's inclination to have a bit of fun out of life, the letter to the editor of the Las Vegas *Gazette*, published on February 2, 1878, is as follows:

Your vicinity will, no doubt, be inflicted soon with the presence of one George Fisher, a German. He is not only a "dead beat," one could stand that; but he is a petty larceny thief. We were warned against him by John H. Tunstall and D. P. Shield of Lincoln; by Richard Brunner and John Newcomb, of Rio Ruidosa, but coveted verdure triumphed; we wanted greens and the golden-haired Teuton "got away with our baggage." He is a drunken, lying, thieving vagabond, who will doubtless use the names of parties whom he has victimized here, as a passport to the confidence of some other d----d fool! There would be no use in describing him. He has no shame. Will not deny his name, and will boast of friendship with gentlemen who have expelled him from their houses for theft. I will give $10.00 to the man who will warm up the basement of my pantaloons with my belt. Fisher stole them both. The following named gentlemen authorize me to say that they endorse every word of the above eulogy: Marion Turner, Heiskell Jones, John A. Jones, Jas. P. Jones, William Jones. Perhaps it would be well to warn the public &c., although Fisher is dangerous only in the country.

While serving as Land Surveyor in the Three Rivers country, Ash Upson, along with other early-day settlers, became involved in land fraud charges. Talking about the charges to George Ulrich in White Oaks, Upson said:

> I am waiting for a United States Deputy Marshall to come and arrest me on a land fraud charge. I will probably be taken to Santa Fe. That means nothing to me. I have owned the city of Santa Fe for a week at a time. I have reached the point in life where I can tell the fates with impunity to go straight to hell.

On another occasion, while Ulrich and Ash Upson were having a drink in a White Oaks saloon in 1882, Ash confided to him that he had recently received a letter from his father inquiring about his health and condition in life. Upson said that he had written to his father in reply that he "was getting kind of stoop-shouldered trying to carry around all the brains of the Upson family."[3]

Perhaps Ash Upson was justified in taking a snifter occasionally, for things were tough in the Lincoln County of his day. On June 1, 1881, L. S. ("Bladder") Allen interfered in a quarrel between C. H. Keys and George Ulrich in the Pioneer saloon at White Oaks. Before many seconds elapsed, "Bladder" Allen whipped out a knife, stuck the blade into Key's backbone, twisted it around and carefully put the knife back in his pocket. Allen then called on a few bystanders to help him throw Keys bodily out of the saloon into the street. Under Allen's direction, four men did the job, one man to each arm, one man to each leg. Left to suffer out in the road for hours, Keys finally received medical aid. Suffering great pain,

---

3. George Ulrich, old-time Lincoln County character, who had been surveyor, cattle owner and banker, died in Santa Fe, Sept. 17, 1944. Born in Louisiana, Ulrich learned to speak French when a child, later lived for some years in France. Lincoln County cowpunchers could never fully grasp how a fellow cowman could, of all things, speak French and read books printed in that language. In his last years Ulrich served as custodian of the Supreme Court building in Santa Fe.

he died seventeen days later. A post-mortem examination of the body disclosed that an inch of Allen's knife blade still remained in the spinal column. For that incident, "Bladder" Allen received from Judge Warren Bristol on May 22, 1884, a sentence of one year in jail. Before the year was up, "Bladder" Allen got out of jail, went into the Will Ellis billiard hall in Lincoln on May 5, 1885, and "accidentally" shot and killed Sam Anderson, the bartender. For that crime Judge Bristol sentenced him to serve five years in prison.[4]

On August 2, 1875, Robert Casey was shot and killed by William Wilson in Lincoln with a bullet fired from a Winchester rifle. Wilson was tried, convicted by a jury and sentenced to be hanged. On December 10, 1875, the appointed day, a large crowd gathered in the Lincoln jail yard to witness the hanging. Ash Upson was present as a representative of the press, but left shortly after the trap was sprung, probably to get a drink. After being suspended by a rope for nine and one-half minutes by the Sheriff's watch, Wilson's body was taken down from the scaffold and placed in the coffin. Spectators nudged the Sheriff and told him that Wilson was not yet dead. Red-faced and embarrassed the Sheriff and several helpers lifted William Wilson from his wooden coffin, escorted him once more to the scaffold. The rope was again tied around the condemned man's neck and he was suspended for an additional twenty minutes, at the end of which time there was not much doubt that the demands of the law had been satisfied.[5] Father Antonio Lamy, twenty-eight years old, a native of France, a nephew of Archbishop John B. Lamy of Santa Fe, had been a reluctant witness to the hanging. His parish area covered hundreds of square miles, with pastoral residence in Manzano. Padre Lamy had been in Lincoln on a missionary tour. He called at the jail to offer spiritual consolation to William Wilson, soon to be hanged. Wilson prepared himself for death under Father Lamy's direction and accepted his offer of company to the scaffold. The hanging and rehanging of Wilson proved too much for the frail young man of God. Rather desperately ill, suffering from chills and high temperature, the Padre insisted on returning on horseback to Manzano a few days after William Wilson had been hanged. Arriving in Manzano, Father Lamy's condition rapidly became worse.

---

4. *Golden Era*, May 31, 1884; *Lincoln County Leader*, May 13, 1885.
5. *Las Vegas Gazette*, Dec. 25, 1875.

He died there on February 6, 1876. The remains of the priest were buried under the floor of the parish church at Manzano. The story of Padre Lamy's death has for many years been kept alive in the Manzano community. His grave in the church has long been a silent sermon in opposition to the brutality of capital punishment.

Alongside Father Lamy's sepulchre in the church at Manzano, there is interred the body of Father Robert Garrassu. Born in France on February 3, 1844, he died in Manzano on June 2, 1897. Before he studied for the priesthood, Robert Garrassu served in the French army. Ordained a priest, Father Garrassu came to America and was given the parish of Mora, New Mexico. To Mora, one day, there came to visit Padre Garrassu no less a personage than the distinguished Archbishop John B. Lamy. The churchman was traveling in that part of the Territory, seeking funds to permit continuation of construction work on the cathedral in Santa Fe. Archbishop Lamy told Father Garrassu that the stonemasons and other artisans had not been paid for many weeks, that he owed accounts for material and feared he would soon be obliged to suspend the entire enterprise. His Excellency explained to the parish priest that he was not seeking gifts or donations, but wanted to borrow money and was willing to pay high interest rates to those who would lend on his promissory note. Padre Garrassu informed the Archbishop that things were bad in Mora County; that cattle and sheep were in desperate condition because of a long continued drouth; that the spirits of the people were greatly depressed. There was small possibility, the priest told the Archbishop, that any person in the parish might make either a donation or a loan of money in any substantial amount. Observing the gloom that overcast his superior's countenance, Father Garrassu finally asked: "Archbishop Lamy, how much money must you have?" The Archbishop replied: "I must have at least two thousand dollars." The parish priest asked: "How much money do you have with you?" The Archbishop replied: "I have only a few dollars." Father Garrassu then said: "Let me have that money, Archbishop, make yourself at home, take care of my parish for a few days." Padre Garrassu knelt and kissed the prelate's ring, left the house, saddled and bridled his horse, waved adieu and was off. Several days later Father Garrassu returned, greeted the Archbishop, handed him a bag of gold coins, saying: "Here is your two thousand dollars." "My son, my son," exclaimed his Excellency, "where did you get the money, and to whom shall I make the notes payable?" "The people from whom I got the money would prefer that their names be undisclosed," replied Father Garrassu. "Under the circumstances they would not, I am sure, agree to accept a note."

Some years later, still curious as to the source of the money, Archbishop Lamy, then retired, inquired of Father Garrassu as to how he had obtained it. Farther Garrassu smiled and said: "If your Excellency will promise not to scold me, I don't mind telling you now. But on the day I gave the money to you, I was terribly afraid. Archbishop, I won that two thousand dollars playing poker with the army officers at Fort Union. Many times previously they had insisted that I play cards with them. Always I had refused. When you assumed such a doleful appearance that day in Mora, when you were so worried about your cathedral, I decided that I would go to the Fort and accept the standing invitation of the officers. In my youth, in the army in France, I had learned about cards. I had a certain ability with them, not common to many men, what they call in America 'card sense.' With the few dollars you advanced to me in Mora, I won handsomely. I was embarrassed to quit the poker game so much ahead. But I knew I would be more embarrassed if I had to return to Mora and disappoint you by telling you that I had failed to raise the funds. So I excused myself to the gentlemen at Fort Union, hurried back to Mora as fast as my horse would carry me and now, Archbishop, you know everything. On my honor, Archbishop, as a priest of the Archdiocese and as a former soldier of France, I have never played in a game of cards from that day to this."

With the money received from Father Garrassu at Mora, Archbishop Lamy returned to his home in Santa Fe, paid past due wages of working men and other pressing obligations. Then the churchman hurried to the office of Abraham Staab, merchant prince of Santa Fe, to ask for an extension of time on promissory notes given in exchange for funds borrowed for the cathedral project. Friends of long standing, the ranking Roman Catholic prelate of the Southwest and the leading member of the Jewish faith in New Mexico exchanged the formalities of the day. Mr. Staab had already made substantial gifts to the cathedral construction fund. When money had become scarce in the hard times then prevailing, the merchant had become banker and loaned large sums to the Archbishop to prevent stoppage of the work. "How is the work on the cathedral progressing?" inquired Staab. "Times are hard," answered the Archbishop, "but the cathedral will be finished. All I ask is an extension of time on my notes." Staab went to a large iron safe, took out all the notes that the Archbishop had signed and said to him: "Archbishop, let me have a say in the building of that cathedral and I will tear up all of these notes." Cautiously, the man of God measured the eyes of the man of Commerce and Business and inquired: "To what extent, how, Mr. Staab?" Staab replied: "Let me put one word above the entrance of the Cathedral, chiselled in stone." "And what is that word?" parried the Archbishop. "You must trust me, Archbishop," replied Staab. Archbishop Lamy agreed to Abraham Staab's proposal.* Staab tore up the notes in the presence of the Archbishop, tossed the fragments of paper into a fire in the stove in the office. When the cathedral was finished, there for all the world to see, was the part that Staab had taken in its building, the Hebraic initials J V H, symbolic of the word "God" of the Christian faith, "Jehovah" of the faith of Israel.[6]

Lured to New Mexico by stories of "Billy the Kid" and the wild tales of the Lincoln County country, Major William Caffrey, a restless newspaper publisher of exceptional ability, came to White

---

* The story concerning Abraham Staab's participation in the building of the cathedral in Santa Fe, published in the first and second printings of this book, had many reverberations. Several scholars, expert in the Hebrew language, went to Santa Fe to see and study the inscription. In 1961, Texas Western College Press published *The Triangle and the Tetragrammaton, a Note on the Cathedral at Santa Fe*, by Floyd S. Fierman, Ph.D., Lecturer in Philosophy, Texas Western College, and Rabbi, Temple Mount Sinai in El Paso, Texas. The article contains also an extensive note on Abraham Staab, a list of donors to the Cathedral Building Fund, and other interesting information concerning the Cathedral and church liturgy. Somewhat mystified by the story as told in *The Fabulous Frontier*, Rabbi Fierman, in his monograph, expresses some doubt as to its authenticity. The author's source was Louis Ilfeld who married Anna Staab, daughter of Abraham Staab. Mr. Ilfeld told the writer that he had heard Mr. Staab tell the story about his part in building the Cathedral on many occasions and believed it to be accurate.

6. Abraham Staab was born in Westphalia, Germany, on Feb. 27, 1839, died in Pasadena, California, on Jan. 13, 1913. He emigrated to America in 1858 and came to Santa Fe in 1859, seven years after the arrival of John B. Lamy. Staab became a successful merchant, extending his business to all parts of the Territory and into Mexico, even in the days before the railroad. Abraham Staab became chairman of the Board of County Commissioners. He and Archbishop Lamy worked together to get Santa Fe County to vote a bond issue as a bonus for the construction of the Santa Fe Railroad into Santa Fe. Later Staab served under Governor W. T. Thornton on the Commission to Rebuild the Capitol Building.

Oaks in 1883. He brought along a printing outfit, including a press, type, forms and fonts, some of which are still in use in the office of the *Lincoln County Leader*, now published in Carrizozo. On his arrival in White Oaks, Major Caffrey claimed that he had published more newspapers than any man in the United States of America. To prove his assertion he brought with him to Lincoln County the bound volumes of the papers he had published elsewhere. Major Caffrey acquired ownership of the *Lincoln County Leader*, then published at White Oaks by Adna Lampson, Lee H. Rudisille, Paul Wagner and Ben Henry. The paper was moved years later to Lincoln and then to Carrizozo. Before coming to New Mexico, Caffrey had published the *Republican and Gazette* at Sterling, Illinois, the *Cairo Times* at Cairo, Illinois, the *Ohio Reveille* at Newark, Ohio, the *Southwestern Tribune* at Stockton, Missouri, papers at Fort Scott, Kansas, and Brownsville, Nebraska, and in 1877 was the publisher of the *Kansas Pilot* at Wyandotte, now Kansas City, Missouri. Writing of the early days in White Oaks in the *Leader* of October, 6, 1888, Major Caffrey said:

> January 13, 1883, when we arrived here, White Oaks presented a far different view from its present. Then it was verily, a "camp," its population largely being adventurers without capital or ambition; its houses were of the rudest, built but for a month or a year at the most; all of our mines which had been at all developed were locked up by litigation, and the prospect seemed uninviting as the day of judgment to an incorruptible sinner. Hope flitted upon the faces and lit up the hearts of the clear headed and sober minded, and while the fickle and unstable left, hied out in search of greener pastures, the former class took a firmer grip, resolved, like the immortal Adams, to "live or die, sink or swim, survive or perish," by White Oaks.
>
> Since then, the shakedown houses have fallen or been pulled down; poorly laid adobe and knotty frame structures have been razed, and in their stead have arisen fine brick structures and other sightly buildings . . . litigation locks upon our mines have been broken . . . and a railroad is reaching out its iron hands seeking an embrace. . . . White Oaks has increased from a scant 500 bodies to a plus 1,000 souls . . . and we challenge contradiction when we aver that no other 25,000 square miles of populated territory sends to heaven or earthly ears fewer wails of distress, or where the people

enjoy the bounty of Providence more than Lincoln County, New Mexico. . . . We will conclude in the language of the Episcopal service, "As it was in the beginning, is now, and ever shall be, world without end. Amen."

Major Caffrey died in Lincoln on December 7, 1893. For several years before his death he had urged old timers to contribute their recollections to the columns of his paper. He succeeded in inducing several of them to tell their stories of the old days. These the Major published in the *Leader*. They are of importance to the history of Southeast New Mexico.

Steeped in the history of the Civil War in which he had been a soldier, believing that the Republican party had been selected by destiny to save the nation. Major Caffrey was a hard-hitting editorial writer of the old school, with no quarter asked or given. Fellow editors of his day claimed that occasional bouts with John Barleycorn had always proved a burden he could not overcome and hastened his death.

Lincoln County, New Mexico, was the kindergarten for a young writer who eventually achieved a national reputation as a novelist. On June 1, 1883, Emerson Hough of Newton, Iowa, a graduate of the law department of the University of Iowa, formed a partnership to practice law in White Oaks with Eli H. Chandler. Chandler and Hough never had much of a law business. They docketed in the Territorial Supreme Court only one important case, that of *Patterson v. Baxter Gold Mining Co.*, reported in 3 N.M. (Johnson) 179.

With little or no legal business requiring his attention, Emerson Hough spent most of his spare time in the office of the *Golden Era*, a weekly newspaper published in White Oaks. Hough sought out the characters in Lincoln County and talked to them about the doings of the back country. On February 6, 1884, he wrote a notice for the *Golden Era* telling of the death of James Wicks. The notice said: "Died. At 1 a.m. of the morning of the 6th inst., of pneumonia, James Wicks, of White Oaks. Mr. Wicks' face was a familiar one to our people. He has gone over the range, to the miner's better country."

A few days later Emerson Hough returned to Iowa, called there by the serious illness of his mother. It was many years before he returned to New Mexico. However, he had absorbed enough color in

the Territory to last him for many years. A brief trial of the law in
New Mexico convinced Hough that he had no genuine love for the
profession. Back home in Iowa, Emerson Hough worked for a time
as business manager of the Des Moines *Times*, but in November,
1884, became associate editor of the *Register* at Sandusky, Ohio.
Working on newspapers in the Middlewest, Hough could not get
"Stumpy" Wicks out of his mind, nor could he forget a forlorn
looking, well educated man in White Oaks who had confessed to him
one day, with a wistful, homesick smile on his lips and a faraway
look in his eyes: "I used to be a preacher back east, and a dam'd good
preacher, too." So Emerson Hough wrote for *Peck's Sun* of April 1,
1884, published by George W. Peck at Milwaukee, Wisconsin, a
story about "Stumpy" Wicks and the former minister of the gospel,
entitled "Over the Range." The story was one of Emerson Hough's
first attempts to capitalize the local color of the Lincoln County
country. Later in his career Hough wrote "Heart's Desire," with
scenes laid in White Oaks, and drew generously in subsequent novels
and books on his knowledge of New Mexico of the days of his life
in the Territory. The "Stumpy" Wicks story is deserving of a place
in the history of Emerson Hough's early literary efforts and his
identification with early day New Mexico. The story follows:

Stumpy Wicks was dead. The mountain fever had killed him a
few days after he had started off into the hills, telling the boys that
he would find them something rich, or never go out again. He did
not find anything rich; and he never went out again. The fever laid
its grip upon him, and in three days he was dead. He had "gone over
the range," the boys said.

It became necessary to bury Stumpy Wicks. And how was he to
be buried? By his relatives? He had no relatives. By the town? There
was no town. By his pard? He had no pard. Forty years ago Stumpy
Wicks had left his home—no one knew where—and his people—no
one knew whom—to wander alone in the west. His wife, his mother,
his sister, if he had one, will never know where he died, or what
hands laid him in his grave.

It was the boys. They got together and made a coffin out of a box
or two and covered it with black cloth. They put Stumpy into it,
with a clean floursack over his poor, dead face. They chipped in and
hired an ex-parson, who for some years had abandoned his profes-

sion, to "give Stumpy a send off." They dug a grave to a good and honest depth in the tough, red earth. They went out and found a flat rock for a headstone, and on it, with an engineer's graver, they scratched the brief epitaph, "Stumpy Wicks." Then they followed the coffin-wagon to the grave, walking through the mud and rain.

There were forty men in that funeral procession and not one woman. Almost no one was drunk, and nearly all had taken off their six shooters. There were forty men who stood around the open grave, and not one woman to drop a tear, as the ex-parson offered a short prayer for the safe journey of Stumpy's soul over the range. There was no history of Stumpy's life. No one knew that history. It was doubtless a sad enough one, full of slips and stumbles; full of hope, perhaps, before he finally "lost his grip." They found a woman's picture, very old, and quite worn out indeed, in Stumpy's pocket, and this was buried with him. This was probably his history.

There was not a tear shed at Stumpy's funeral. Not a sob was heard. But neither were there any oaths or laughter. When the time came to fill up the grave, ready hearts assisted ready hands, and the experienced miners quickly did the work. They rounded up the mound, and fitted in the headstone. When the ex-parson stepped back from the grave he stumbled over the headstone of Billy Robbins, the gambler, whom Antonio Sanchez had knifed. There were a good many of the boys resting there. The bullet, the knife and the mountain fever had finished them, except those whom the committee assisted. It was the committee who put Antonio Sanchez at the foot of Billy Robbins' grave.

There was no green thing in this graveyard, no living plants, no little flowers. It lay, red and bare, upon a red and bare hillside. There were no white stones to mark the homes of the sleepers; those used were of the rough red granite.

The boys were quiet. They were thinking perhaps. They looked up at the sky, which, strangely enough for a sky in New Mexico, had in it no tinge of blue, and the sky, in pity that no tear was shed, wept some upon them.

As the funeral procession broke up and moved back to the saloons, one was heard to say that it was the "d---dest mournfullest plantin' he ever had a hand in." In fact, the camp did not get back to its normal condition until the next day. There was something too sad even for those rough souls in the lonely, broken life, the lonely unwept death of Stumpy Wicks. It made them think, and I wonder if some of them did not reach out their arms from their blankets that

night, and hold them up and call softly, "Oh, Stumpy, Stumpy—
What is it you see over the range? After a wretched, broken life,
what is there for a man over the range?"[7]

Although born in Nebraska, Eugene Manlove Rhodes is claimed
by New Mexico as its very own. The body of 'Gene Rhodes sleeps
in New Mexico soil. Despite long years of exile in Apalachin, New
York, until the day of his death at Pacific Beach, California, on
June 27, 1934, he held a deep and abiding affection for New Mexico
and its people. Born in Tecumseh, Nebraska, on January 19, 1869,
Eugene Manlove Rhodes accompanied his parents, Colonel and
Mrs. Hinman Rhodes, to New Mexico in 1882. Colonel Rhodes, a
retired Army officer, acquired a ranch property not far from Engle,
in the heart of the Jornada country. For a time he was associated in
the cattle business with W. G. Ritch, for many years Secretary, and
for a brief time acting Governor, of New Mexico.[8] All that remains
of the Rhodes ranch house today is a remnant of the stone foundation. When the name of Col. Hinman Rhodes, father of 'Gene
Rhodes, was being considered for the appointment of Agent for the

---

7. Emerson Hough was born in Newton, Iowa, June 28, 1857, died April 30, 1923.
Hough made his home for many years in Chicago. Some of his best known books
include *The Story of the Cowboy*, *The Way of the West*, *Heart's Desire* (written in
1905, with scenes laid in White Oaks), *Fifty-Four Forty or Fight*, *The Story of the
Outlaw*, *North of 36*. In order to get first hand information for some of the material in
The Story of the Outlaw, Emerson Hough returned to New Mexico in 1904 and
traveled with Pat Garrett all over the Lincoln county that he had known and loved
more than twenty years earlier.

8. W. G. Ritch, old-timer of New Mexico, died September 15, 1904, after a very
active political life in the days of the Territory. Ritch was a prolific writer for publication and carried on a correspondence with many people about Territorial affairs.
Frequently at odds with the Santa Fe *New Mexican*, Ritch had established a habit of
posting on bulletin boards in several saloons in Santa Fe, about drinking time at 5
o'clock, his version of any particular controversy then the subject of discussion in the
papers. The politically-minded read the bulletins and kept posted on Ritch's views.
An example of Ritch's technique in posting the news was contained in a bulletin tacked
up near the free lunch counter in a saloon, reading as follows: "Executive Office, Territory of New Mexico, Santa Fe, N. M. 5/21/1880. To the People of New Mexico:
The following letter to the editor of the Daily N.M., having been tendered to him
this day for publication, and publication thereof having been refused, it is, for manifest
reasons, and in the absence of another daily newspaper in the capital, posted in this
form for prompt and general information. W. G. Ritch—Acting Governor." Ritch
came to New Mexico June 30, 1873, to relieve W. F. M. Arny, appointed agent for the
Navajos at Fort Defiance.

nearby Mescalero Indians, the *Lincoln County Leader* of April 20, 1889, said of him:

> Col. Hinman Rhodes, of Engle, N.M., is a candidate for the Mescalero Indian Agency. The Colonel served in the war with Mexico and the Civil War. He enlisted Nov. 28, 1862, was made Major of the 28th Illinois Infantry, and on Sept. 15, 1865, he was promoted to Colonel. He participated in all the engagements throughout the war, in which his regiment was famous. He served a term in the Nebraska Legislature, is a respected citizen of the Territory of New Mexico, residing here seven years.

Colonel Rhodes apparently made a satisfactory Indian Agent, for the *Lincoln County Leader* of July 28, 1892, said:

> The superintendence of the Mescalero Agency has cost the G.O.P. ring of Las Cruces and Santa Fe no end of trouble and vexation of spirit since Col. Hinman Rhodes was appointed, and installed correct business principles in the management of the reservation. All sorts of corrupt means have been used by the ring to displace Rhodes because he was antagonistic to the idea of allowing the reservation to be used for the private emolument of certain cattle barons.

After his service on the Mescalero reservation, Colonel Rhodes engaged in mining ventures in the San Andres and Caballo mountains. Eugene Manlove Rhodes was brought up in the Jornado country with its cattle ranches and cowboys, its range quarrels, its sheriffs and their work in running down men who had changed cattle brands, stolen livestock, murdered people. Young 'Gene Rhodes had learned about Indians and their troubles on the nearby Mescalero Indian reservation. He talked to the Mescalero scouts and the old men there who had ridden with Geronimo, Victorio and Nana. With a most favorable opportunity to literally absorb the color of a fast-fading real West, it was inevitable that 'Gene Rhodes would eventually attempt to write about the things he saw and heard on range and reservation. When sixteen years old, 'Gene Rhodes packed a gun himself. His father, Colonel Rhodes, had a squabble out on the range with W. G. Ritch over their cattle business. Governor Ritch had a son, Watson L. Ritch, who was about the same age as 'Gene. According to the code of the range, the sons adopted the quarrel of their fathers and carried it on for some months, with a "shoot on sight" ultimatum out for each other. Older men learned of the difficulties 'Gene Rhodes and Watson Ritch were having over something that was not of their making and prevailed upon them to shake hands and patch up their boyish quarrel.

Colonel Rhodes and W. G. Ritch eventually settled their differences and frequently talked over old times in Engle, where Ritch served as postmaster in the latter years of his life.

'Gene Rhodes attended grade school at Eagle Creek in Lincoln County, and later taught the school there, living at the A. J. Gilmore ranch. Fond of wrestling, boxing and other sports, Rhodes was always eager to engage in a contest calling for physical endurance, stamina and combativeness. On many occasions, on the range and elsewhere, Rhodes engaged in physical combat for the sheer love of the contest. He never became angry during these contests of strength and endurance and accepted the result, win or lose, in a detached way. He could never understand why men could not slug it out, toe to toe, in a boxing contest, or wrestle to an exhausted finish and still remain friends. One day, while teaching school at Eagle Creek, 'Gene Rhodes jumped on a horse and rode to Roswell, ninety miles away, to see a baseball game. After his grade school days at Eagle Creek, 'Gene Rhodes had a bit more schooling at Mesilla. During one winter he attended a course of lectures on English literature at the nearby New Mexico College of Agriculture and Mechanic Arts. For a brief time he was a student at the Pacific College in California.

Back to New Mexico, to the heart of the country he loved, 'Gene Rhodes served an apprenticeship on the Bar Cross Range on the Jornada and various ranches as a cowboy and horse wrangler. Rhodes talked to cowboys and listened to their stories of roundup time, of branding, of chuck wagon days. If for no other reason, 'Gene Rhodes was known from one end of the Jornada and Tularosa Basin country to the other because of a speech impediment. He could not pronounce the letter "g" and had difficulty with his "r's." Apparently a handicap, the speech impediment was a factor that contributed to make 'Gene Rhodes famous. If he had been able to converse without difficulty, Rhodes might never have written a line. On one occasion, 'Gene Rhodes and his brother Clarence went to break horses on the Jack Cravens ranch. A Negro ranchhand accosted Rhodes at the Cravens windmill and inquired who he was and what he was going to do. "My name is Deen Dodes and I came down here to bake some boncs," replied 'Gene Rhodes. The Negro could not make out what Rhodes was talking about. Exasperated, 'Gene Rhodes turned to brother Clarence and said: "Tell this —— —— fool my name."

After working on several ranches in the country round about Engle, 'Gene Rhodes accepted steady employment from the H. G. Grahams on the HG Ranch. Here Eugene Manlove Rhodes made his first serious attempts at writing. He found a sympathetic listener and a frank critic in Mrs. Graham, not a formally educated woman, but a shrewd observer of people and of things. Cowboy and horse wrangler by day, 'Gene Rhodes did his writing at night. On a number of occasions, at midnight and later, Rhodes called out to Mrs. Graham, awakening her from a sound sleep, asking her to listen to something he had written, begging her opinion of the writing. "Gene was a good boy, but irresponsible as a cowhand," Mrs. Graham said, when asked for her recollections, "He wore me out so, while he was writing those stories, that I never did want to read them after they were printed." Mr. Graham's appraisal: "Gene Rhodes was never really qualified as a cowboy; at most he was a horse wrangler, a fair hand at watching and rounding up horses for the cowboys to use on the roundups. He was too absent-minded. One day, 'Gene started to sharpen a butcher knife on a grinding stone. The first thing I knew, I saw him get on a horse, with the butcher knife in one hand, and an open book in the other. A few minutes later, I rode by him. Still absorbed in reading the book, he had absent-mindedly jabbed the point of the butcher knife into the horse's flanks. He had entirely forgotten what he was about." *

---

* May D. Rhodes, widow of 'Gene Rhodes, challenged the accuracy of Mr. Graham's recollection about 'Gene absent-mindedly prodding his mount with the point of a butcher knife. In a letter written to the author from Apalachin, New York, on June 26, 1946, Mrs. Rhodes said: "It was with mingled feelings of pleasure and regret that I listened to your account of Eugene Manlove Rhodes in your *Fabulous Frontier*. 'The Hour and The Man,' was his first story. He wrote this while digging a well for Charlie Graham. He worked days and wrote nights. I am loath to believe that 'he wakened Mrs. Graham from a sound sleep.' He was always very considerate of sleeping people. He sent this story to me at my home in Apalachin, New York, where I was living and I hired a typewriter and typed it for him. He was a superb horseman. He could ride horses that no one else could stick on. I know, for 'I was there.' He only wrangled horses as a little lad. And when he started writing stories, he didn't 'approach the matter timidly.' He had it all written out in his mind. Words came fluently to his pen. He was, to some extent, absent-minded, as many great men are.

While on the HG ranch, 'Gene Rhodes had time to make the acquaintance and form a friendship with Oliver M. Lee who, with Jim Gililland, was on the "dodge" for several months, with Sheriff Pat Garrett of Las Cruces in pursuit.

After writing and rewriting short stories while on the HG ranch, 'Gene Rhodes submitted several of them to Charles Fletcher Lummis of Los Angeles. In *Out West*, formerly *The Land of Sunshine*, for February, 1902, there was published one of the first stories written by Eugene Manlove Rhodes. Although writing about a country he knew so well and of the people whom he knew intimately, Rhodes nevertheless approached the plot with timidity and had groped searchingly for words to express himself. "Lubly G-Ge and Gruff-grin," was the title of the story, which was about a five-year-old boy, lost in the Tularosa country, found by John Brady, an outlaw, and restored to his mother.

Rhodes depicted the dramatic meeting between the Sheriff of the county and the bad man; there was a courtroom scene at Alamogordo, the county seat, with Brady, the outlaw, pleading guilty; there was the sentence by the judge on the bench. Then the Governor of the Territory dramatically took over the entire situation in person and granted Brady a pardon on the spot. Charles Fletcher Lummis encouraged Rhodes to try again and there was published in the *Out West—Land of Sunshine* for February, 1903, a year after the publication of the first story, a more pretentious effort, "Loved I Not Honor More." The story was built around the mission of a British army officer, purchasing horses in southeast New Mexico for use in Africa during the Boer war. In this story, still indicating lack of technical skill that he later acquired, Rhodes nevertheless approached the pattern of the style that characterized the many stories and books that were later to come from his pen. In "Loved I Not Honor More," 'Gene Rhodes was more at home with his subject and better orientated. He gave to most of his characters the actual names of men he knew personally and who were widely known in southeast New

---

But he was also, a great lover of horses, and I couldn't possibly imagine him sticking a sharpened knife into the flank of a horse, and even having time to draw another breath before the horse threw him. For horses in those days were live wires, and didn't allow any liberties taken with them. This man is dead. He died twelve years ago tomorrow. He is not here to defend himself from this calumny as I am sure he would do. Even if you have absolute proof of these statements, it seems it would have been kinder to have omitted them. For what you said in his praise, I thank you."

Mexico, among them Pat Garrett, Emil James and W. H. McNew. Rhodes projected himself into the story, undoubtedly, as "Wildcat," a character who objected to the sale of range horses to the British for use in fighting the Boers. Rhodes reduced the war to the everyday talk of the range. Drawing a picture in cowboy language of the fight between the British and the Boers, the Wildcat delivered his argument:

> Supposing I had a big farm and was raisin' mighty fine crops on it. S'pose me and my brother had cattle on it once and quarreled and jawed and lawed and fought about them, 'til we most give out—and most broke, too. Then we makes it up and goes ahead and build fences around our land to keep out any of our neighbors' cattle, and put our own in the poorest fields, and wish to God we could get rid of 'em somehow. Then if I was to go 'way off somewheres, and buy a lot more cattle, range delivery . . . and s'pose you had just oodles of cattle—fancy stock, and Herefords and Polled Angus, and Durhams and Chihuahuas and old long horns—all kinds of cattle—more cattle than anybody—and a little old Dutchman was trying to be raising a little bunch of pan milk cows; and you was to crowd him, and eat out his grass and steal his calves and make him move. S'pose you made him move twice, and you got his ranch and improvements both times. And he went 'way out in the desert and you was to follow him up again.

The story ended with a description of a fist fight and wrestling match between "Wildcat" and the British officer. Undoubtedly, Rhodes was dramatizing himself. His early adventures in writing, under the guidance of Charles Fletcher Lummis, always a New Mexican at heart, were the forerunners of great success for Eugene Manlove Rhodes. He seldom deviated from his rule of writing of persons, places and things he knew personally. Encouraged by George Horace Lorimer, editor of the *Saturday Evening Post* and lover of western life, Eugene Manlove Rhodes found in that publication a home for his stories of life on the range in New Mexico. Reluctant to get right down and work, Eugene Manlove Rhodes seldom wrote on his own initiative. Some deadline was necessary—an insistent demand from the *Saturday Evening Post* for another serial, pressing financial obligations, or the urge to get out of his mind and on paper a plot that had long bothered him. Besides some fifty-five stories that appeared in the *Post* of George Horace Lorimer's time, there appeared over the years several books that gained the enthusiastic approval of many literary critics and a nationwide popularity. Indelibly marked with the characteristics and background of the New Mexico of his day and time, Eugene Manlove Rhodes left monuments of those days in such books as *Good Men and True*, 1910; *Bransford in Arcadia*, 1914; *The Desire of the Moth*, 1916; *West Is West*, 1917; *Stepsons of Light*, 1921; *Say Now Shiboleth*, 1921; *Copper Streak Trail*, 1922; *Once in the Saddle*, 1927. *West Is West* contained a brilliantly written fourth chapter entitled "Barnaby Bright," which was printed under the title "Penalosa" by the Writers Editions at Santa Fe in 1934, with a foreword by Alice Corbin Henderson. Regardless of its historical accuracy, "Barnaby Bright" or "Penalosa" was one of the few ventures made by 'Gene Rhodes outside the field of fiction. "A Ballad of Wild Bees" in three stanzas, published in *The Land of Sunshine* for March, 1902, was one of his first offerings in poetry.*

Some of the finest of Rhodes' writing is in "Paso Por Aqui," praised by many critics as his best short story. The scene is near the ranch of Poet Scout Jack Crawford, with Mockingbird Gap not far away, and Ross McEwen, through 'Gene Rhodes' eyes, is looking about him for a way of escape:

> He could see distinctly and in one eye flight, every feature of a country larger than all England. He could look north to beyond Albuquerque, pass the long range of Manzano, Montoso, Sandia, Oscuro; southward between his horse's ears, the northern end of the San Andres was high and startling before him, blue black with cedar brake and piñon, except for the granite gold top of Salinas Peak. Westward was the great valley of the Jornada del Muerto, its width the fifty miles which lay between the San Andres and the Rio Grande. And beyond the river was a bright enormous expanse, bounded only by the crust of the dozen ranges that made the crest of the Continental Divide—Datil, Magdalena, San Mateo, the Black Range, the Mimbres, Florida.

---

* W. H. Hutchinson of Cohasset Stage, Chico, California, has worked indefatigably over the years to assemble and classify the widely scattered literary work of Eugene Manlove Rhodes. In 1956 the University of Oklahoma Press published Hutchinson's *A Bar Cross Man*, a major contribution to the ever-expanding bookshelf about New Mexico's most famous writer.

The fugitive McEwen, forced to choose a way of flight, looked in the direction he must travel and 'Gene Rhodes paints the picture:

> Knuckled ridges led away from Salinas like fingers on a hand. The eastern flat was some large fraction of a mile nearer to sea level than the high plain west of the mountain, and these ridges were massive and steep accordingly. He made his way down one of them. The plain was dark and cold below him; the mountains took shape and grew, the front range of the Rockies—Capitan, Carizo, Sierra Blanca, Sacramento, with Guadalupe low and dim in the south; the White Sands were dull and lifeless in the midway plain. Bird twitter was in the air. Rabbits scurried through the brush, a quail whirred by and sent back a startled cry; crimson streaks shot up the sky, and day grew broad across the silent levels. The cut banks of salt creek appeared, wandering away southeast toward the marshes. Low and far against the black base of the Sacramento, white feathers lifted and fluffed the smoke of the first fires at Tularosa, fifty miles away. Flame tipped the far off crests, the sun leaped up from behind the mountain well, the level light struck on the White Sands, glanced from those burnished bevels and splashed on the western cliffs; the desert day blazed over this new half world.[9]

'Gene Rhodes explained the geography of the Jornada country where he had spent so many years of his young life in the opening paragraph of the second chapter in *Stepsons of Light*, saying:

> The Jornada is a high desert of table land, east of the Rio Grande. In design it is strikingly like a billiard table; forty five miles by ninety, with mountain ranges for rail at east and west, broken highlands on the south, a lava bed on the north. At the middle of each rail and at each corner, four pockets, there is a mountain passway and water; there are peaks and landmarks for each diamond on the rail; for the center and for each spot there is a railroad station and water—Lava, Engle and Upham. Roughly speaking there is a road or trail from each spot, each pocket to every other pocket. In the center, where you put the pin at pin pool, stands Engle.

---

9. The "Choza" or hut described in "Paso Por Aqui", in which Ross McEwen the hero of the story, stopped to nurse diphtheria patients, was an actual place, located about eight miles south of the White Sands not far from Alamogordo. The choza has been long since reduced to ruins.

Eugene Manlove Rhodes cherished for years a copy of "Rosy *Light of Dawn,*" a short story written by Kennett Harris, and published in the *Saturday Evening Post* of January 26, 1916. If the story had not carried the name of Kennett Harris as its author, critics familiar with Rhodes' style would have contended it was the work of Eugene Manlove Rhodes. "Rosy *Light of Dawn*" had the Rhodes technique, a plot that was somewhat askew and ended, as so many of the Rhodes stories, with an unexpected twist. Two days before he died Kennett Harris sent a copy of the story to 'Gene Rhodes and Rhodes always refused to part with it, as he wrote to a friend, J. V. Taylor of Carrizozo and Albuquerque, "for love or money."

Many times in his early days as a cowboy on the range, Rhodes had used Engle Ferry to cross over the Rio Grande. The ford and ferry, located near long-since-abandoned Fort McRae, once served a country over one hundred miles square, but are now submerged in the waters of Elephant Butte, a lake forty miles long up and down the Rio Grande covering a great stretch of territory once given over to the livestock industry. Rhodes remembered the ferry in a poem published in the *Saturday Evening Post* of August 10, 1929, "the ferry is narrow and deep . . . the current is strong and the banks are steep . . . a winding road up either hand, between black lava and yellow sand, between red water and close blue sky . . . angry echoes from hill to hill mutter and clamor and threaten still . . . Engle ferry is gone . . . never again shall moon or star kiss the hill where their campfires are . . . the passionless waters are deep and still on golden mesas and dreaming hill." *

---

* On September 22, 1945, Robert Martin of Hot Springs (now Truth or Consequences) wrote the author as follows:

"It was good to get your letter about Gene Rhodes. It brought to mind many cherished associations with him—from 1892 to about 1905, when he left these parts and I did not see him for some 20 years—then we got within 70 or 80 miles of each other in California and we saw each other quite often the last few years of his life. I probably knew Gene as intimately as any man—though I have no letters of his at this time—as little correspondence passed between us at any time—though I did hear from him once in a while—when he wanted the words of a Mexican song—the size of some certain corral, the name of certain rocks, etc.—and all of my recollections of him are from personal contact.

"The keystone of Gene's character was his love of justice and fairplay and for these he would fight any time—he was a medium sized man—140 to 150—about 5 feet 7, full of nervous energy, restless, busy at all times—loved to do hard work—a tireless reader—coffee drinker thru the day and night—smoked cigarettes constantly—poker playing fiend—always broke, drank no liquor of any kind—while I drank whiskey

Eugene Manlove Rhodes and E. Dana Johnson of the Santa Fe *New Mexican* exchanged friendly gossipy letters for a number of years. Rhodes had a habit of omitting from his letters the year in which he was writing, giving only the date and name of the month. In 1924, mentioning a book about New Mexico old-timers on which he was working, Rhodes commented: "I grind away on that book But it is hard work and comes slowly. The miners have a story of their own, the freighters, the railroaders, the sheepmen, the soldiers; the farmers have their own tragedy. The story of the surveyors; the forest service; a hundred others. The Butterfield stage line alone would need a better book than I can write. Or Eddy's adventures in railroad building. Do you know, my mind is of such a low and grovelling order that this same Eddy seems to me as romantic a figure as any of the old Spanish explorers? Or Kit Carson. To build a rail-road—two of 'em—from no place to nowhere, where nobody lived and the principal products were nothing—and to build them with no money, or in one case with no water? Some adventure; and he made it stick. . . . Did I say Eddy? I retract. The most interesting figure I have found in New Mexico is Calhoun, first Civil Governor of New Mexico. If ever a man was sent to make ropes of sand, Calhoun was the man."

Writing from Pacific Beach, California, on January 20, 1933, 'Gene Rhodes told Johnson that he was 64 years old the day before, "and not a lick of sense yet." Writing critically of certain novels published in 1933, Rhodes commented: "For my part I am also interested in the wandering foot, the empty belly, the shaping hand, the generous heart and the vague and fumbling mind." About Puritans, Rhodes wrote Johnson: "I have always disliked the Puritans, just because none of them had enough presence of mind, at the witch hanging time, to load up a blunderbuss with scrap iron and declare a referendum. That was the time to shoot the moon. One page of thoroughly dead magistrates would have stopped that foolishness. And it would have been the brightest page of history. Still and all, when it comes to a choice between the ethics of Plymouth Rock and those of a Rhode Island Red, I string along with the Puritans."

---

and chewed tobacco—for years we were much together in camp on the range—and I knew him as few men did. I can recount many amusing and interesting episodes in his life that never found their way into print—and I often wonder how he lived as long as he did."

New York book reviewers came in for a scolding when 'Gene wrote to Dana: "Are there no opinions about books, opinions wise or foolish, well based or prejudiced—other than those furnished by New York? Furnished by six or seven New Yorkers, copycatted by everybody else? Are we to send our thinking out to be done for us as we do with our laundry? Are we never to do our own thinking? Even if it is badly done?" New Mexico people are not book lovers, according to an opinion Rhodes expressed to Johnson in a letter written July 4, 1932. "The plain facts are that comparatively few New Mexicans care very much about ANY books; and of these few the greater number read entirely upon advice from New York." In the same letter, referring to a contemplated project for the publication of an edition of all of his books, Rhodes commented: "I am just a little proud of being associated in an attempt to do something in these days when so many have crawled under the bed. And if disaster, failure and defeat attend the venture—well, all of these things have long been circumstances familiar to me—and I never observed that they had any perceptible effect upon me. Certainly defeat has never made me either unhappy or bitter, and has not kept me from years crowded with joy and laughter."

From Pacific Beach, February 27, 1931: "Most remarkable Book, *The Great Plains*, by Walter Prescott Webb. Because he is quite lyrical in praise of myself, I am effectively debarred from reviewing it. But I wish somebody would. Ruth Laughlin Barker's *Caballeros* is remarkable for sustained charm and ease. It is like two friends chatting by an oak fire, over the walnuts and wood alcohol. Sir—this is a charming place. But it does not satisfy the soul. I could have endured the cold of Santa Fe—or the cotton from the alamos of Alamogordo—would have been delighted to have ended my days in either place. Santa Fe is the most charming town (and people) I have ever known—and Alamogordo is my own dear country."

'Gene Rhodes was greatly interested in the Albert Bacon Fall case. Writing to Johnson after Fall had been convicted and sentenced to prison in Santa Fe, Rhodes said: "For God's sake—can't you confer with yourself—and start a petition—to have Judge Fall paroled on the first possible day? It should not be left to chance—and it should be signed by New Mexico en bloc. All night I laid awake— a'wording that petition. I am not the man for the job. Not diplomatic. Would defeat my own purpose. . . . Honest, I do believe there are a thousand men who would have offered to serve Judge Fall's term—gladly—joyously. . . . The whole thing has crushed me more than any troubles of my own." Rhodes referred repeatedly to Fall's case in his letters to Dana Johnson. About the then possibilities for a parole, Rhodes said: "In the matter of a parole for Judge Fall—I have cudgelled my brains and I cannot see what better could be done for him than by means of the newspaper men. . . . If the New Mexico newspaper men would act unanimously—would be the voice of a state—and worth heeding. No individual could speak with such authority. . . . He has borne up under his bitter trouble wonderfully—without complaining. I have never seen anything so brave. I wish he might get home to die."

From Three Rivers, Rhodes wrote to Johnson about "the curious fortunes of the Panhandle of Socorro County" and referred to his serial story, "No Mean City," published in 1919: "Hue is the Mean City. I have a curious affection for that yarn. Pres Lewis was my earliest hero. Pres had a fine face. He looked like Jove. He was 45 when I was 13. I was a boy who climbed all the mountains within a radius—and found Ben Teagardner's notices. A. B. Fall knew Teagardner well." Rhodes had great affection for Clem Hightower, an old-time cowboy friend, who died some months before Rhodes passed away. From Three Rivers 'Gene Rhodes wrote to Dana Johnson, praising an article Hightower had written for the Santa Fe New Mexican. "His article was absolutely right," Rhodes wrote. "Neither over literary like my own stuff—nor the other extreme like Siringo's. He ought to quit everything and write a marvelous book. As you know I wanted to write a book in collaboration with him. We were both too ill—and also too poverty stricken—to get together. It was a great disappointment to me. I do believe that it would have been a better book than either one of us could have done separately. I also believe, and there is not one jot or tittle of mock modesty about it—I do believe Clem can write a more satisfactory book about old-timers than I can. He has seen more than I have and remembers it better—and in everything except the laboriously acquired literary training, he has the better mind." Rhodes was against the liquor traffic. In a letter to Johnson, discussing wets and drys, Rhodes said: "I was never a Prohibitionist. They are too mild for me. I want to abolish the damn stuff. To forbid it does no good. I want to have it stopped and forgotten—put away with cannibalism." Rhodes wrote critically to Dana Johnson following the publication of an article by Mary Austin in which she urged the hope that there might be developed a "point of contact by which the richer cultural possibilities of Mexico could be moderated to the American understanding." "Mary Austin has written much, in the past," commented 'Gene Rhodes, "which was very fine, but this article, and others, smacks too much of those who, for 365 days a year blush for their country eight hours a day, with time and half for over time. It is things like these—and the broadcasting that plain people are not worthy or welcome to look at Sangre de Cristo or Jemez hill—that make the words 'artist' and 'culture' abhorrent. Myself, after some study of the Pueblo ruins and guesses as to their history, it becomes plain and proven to my plebian mind that the major arts are lying, agriculture, transportation and cookery."

The body of Eugene Manlove Rhodes is buried on the summit of the San Andres Mountains in New Mexico at a spot in a shady glen by the side of the road eighteen miles from Engle, through Rhodes Canyon toward Tularosa. The grave is in a place surrounded by pine trees and scrub oaks in the heart of a country that 'Gene Rhodes loved and, to quote him, "filled with the mystery and the magic of distance, the mountains and the long leagues of the sun." E. Dana Johnson, editor of the Santa Fe *New Mexican*, long time personal friend and companion of Eugene Manlove Rhodes, wrote an editorial, "Good Man and True," at the time of his passing, saying that the place of "the clean winds, the purple distances, the color and shimmering sunshine, the storms and rigors, the black lava and the blue peaks of the land he loved," was where 'Gene Rhodes wanted to be buried.[10] A few old-timers, George Curry and others, met the train bearing his body at Alamogordo and accompanied it

---

10. E. Dana Johnson was easily the most brilliant working newspaperman in the history of New Mexico journalism. Born June 15, 1879 at Parkersburg, West Virginia, Dana Johnson died in Pasadena, California, on December 10, 1937. He graduated magna cum laude from Marietta College, where he made Phi Beta Kappa. Coming to New Mexico in 1902, Johnson was employed on the Albuquerque *Journal*, Albuquerque *Herald* and Santa Fe *New Mexican* for nearly thirty-five years. He went to Santa Fe in 1913 to become editor of the *New Mexican* and remained with that paper for nearly a quarter of a century, becoming an institution in that city of the same rank and importance as the governor of the state, the Archbishop of Santa Fe, or the United States District Judge. E. Dana Johnson had no rival for first honors in the newspaper field of New Mexico. A strong friendship existed between 'Gene Rhodes and Dana Johnson, broken only by death.

to the place of burial. It is now marked by an appropriate monument, the loving remembrance of artists and writers of Santa Fe, erected on May 19, 1941, in cooperation with the New Mexico College of Agriculture and Mechanic Arts, which institution also dedicated to his memory a beautiful building on its campus.*

From the top of San Andres Mountain 'Gene Rhodes had often gazed toward Tularosa, the Sacramentos, the eternal hills of that country; so had he also many times looked off to the far away San Mateos to the west. Here was the spot of 'Gene Rhodes' heart's desire. In life his heart had loved it; in death his heart was buried there.

Thousands of miles from New Mexico, in the South Seas, there is the burial shrine of a great literary craftsman, Robert Louis Stevenson, whose work 'Gene Rhodes admired greatly, and his last resting place and the epitaph above it are in harmony with the life he led and the places he loved most. So too, Eugene Manlove Rhodes has for his last resting place, at his own request and in harmony with his life, a bit of ground taken from the countless thousands of acres of mountain and pasture land of the New Mexico he had loved. *Paso Por Aqui* is the epitaph on his tombstone, by his own request, but Eugene Manlove Rhodes himself, perhaps pondering over things to come, not so long before his death scribbled a few lines which at some future day might appropriately be added to his tombstone: "Now hushed at last the murmur of his mirth . . . Here he lies quiet in the quiet earth." [11]

Nathan Howard ("Jack") Thorp spent many years of his life in southeast New Mexico. There he absorbed much of the color and feel of the country which made possible the authenticity of his songs and stories of the range. Jack Thorp and 'Gene Rhodes, almost the

---

* George Curry told the author that the following persons were present on the occasion when the body of 'Gene Rhodes was buried on top of the San Andreas range of mountains: George Curry, Frank Werden, Robert Martin, Hiram Yost and Mrs. May D. Rhodes, the widow. The place of burial is some eighteen miles from Engle. In accordance with 'Gene's request, there was no eulogy at the grave. As of the present time the place of burial is entirely surrounded by land controlled by the Atomic Energy Commission. Once a year, however, officials cooperate in arranging for a program, which includes a pilgrimage from Alamogordo to the gravesite and appropriate eulogies. New Mexico State University, Las Cruces, is official custodian of the Rhodes grave, under authority of the New Mexico Legislature.

11. See "Passed by Here, a Memorial to Gene Rhodes," by Eddy Orcutt in *Saturday Evening Post*, August 20, 1938.

same age, became acquainted in the late nineties where they both worked on the Bar W ranch in Lincoln County. They became close friends in the ranch country and wrote to each other frequently after Rhodes went to New York state to make his home. Thorp was an Easterner born and reared, lived in the west all his adult life. Rhodes was a westerner, born and reared, but fate obliged him to live out the best years of his adult life in the east. Jack Thorp's comment on Eugene Manlove Rhodes in the years of maturity after Rhodes had become famous as a writer: " 'Gene Rhodes was the best broncho buster I ever saw, either in New Mexico or Texas."

Nathan Howard Thorp was born on East 22nd Street in New York City on June 10, 1867, the son of Albert Gallatin Thorp, a prominent and successful lawyer of New York, and Mary Leland Thorp of Philadelphia. Nathan Howard Thorp was introduced at an early age into the highest society of the eastern seaboard. His boyhood days were spent at St. Paul's, an exclusive school for sons of the wealthy, his summers at Newport where his family owned a residence, sold in later years to a Belmont. Prep school days over, Jack Thorp went to Princeton University where he studied civil engineering for three years.* Thorp was bored by studies in engineering and he abandoned prospects for receiving a degree from Princeton upon receipt of an invitation to come west from his cousin, Frank Underwood, owner and operator of the Enterprise mine at Kingston, New Mexico. In 1886, when nineteen years old, Jack Thorp went to Kingston and for three years helped cousin Under-

---

* After publication of *The Fabulous Frontier*, several Princeton men were quick to challenge the statement that "Jack Thorp went to Princeton University where he studied civil engineering for three years." On Oct. 12, 1945, Annette L. Thorp, Jack Thorp's widow, wrote the author as follows: "Your letter asking about my husband's school has just been received. Yes, I remember telling you that Jack went to Princeton for a term of over two years. And I am sure he would not have said so, had he not gone. His brother, the late Charles Thorp, also told me Jack had gone to Princeton. Jack used to mention some of the young men in his classes, but as I did not know them, I was not interested and cannot remember their names." Recognizing the credit and prestige that Princeton would gain if Jack Thorp could be officially declared a Princeton man, Dr. George W. Arms, for many years a member of the English Department staff at the University of New Mexico, a Princeton man, kindly carried on an extensive correspondence with the Registrar's office in Princeton concerning Thorp's record there, if any existed. Alas, to Princeton's regret, perhaps chagrin, the verdict was handed down: Careful search had been made; Jack Thorp's name did not appear on the rolls as a student during the 80's. Thus was Princeton deprived of the fame and glory that might have belonged to it if it could only have lawfully claimed Jack Thorp, composer of "Little Joe, the Wrangler," as a onetime Princeton man.

wood develop his mining property. Underwood sold the Enterprise mine and Thorp left Kingston for Mexico, where he spent three years buying polo ponies for shipment to New York. He then went East, played on the Meadowbrook polo team with Theodore Roosevelt and other prominent young men of the day. Finished with polo playing, Jack Thorp, his brother Charles, and Marshall Field II of Chicago, bought a ranch on the Platte River in Nebraska, where they remained two years. Jack Thorp went from Nebraska to Texas, worked for a time on one of the Charles Goodnight ranches, then drifted from one Texas ranch to another, working as a cowboy and fence rider. He crossed the line into New Mexico in the early nineties and started to work for W. C. McDonald on the Bar W ranch, on which he became foreman. He left the Bar W's for the nearby Block ranch, where he worked for several years. Anxious to get away from a cattle ranch for a time, Thorp decided to make a try at his old profession of engineering. W. C. McDonald recommended him for a position with the engineering corps drilling for water on the El Paso & Northeastern Railroad between Santa Rosa and Alamogordo. Through his engineering work, Thorp became acquainted with John Hesch, who had a sheep ranch at Palma, New Mexico. John Hesch's daughter, Annette Hesch, and Jack Thorp were married on December 22, 1903. The Thorps homesteaded a place nearby the Hesch ranch, leased land from the New Mexico Public Land Office, ran from 1,200 to 1,500 head of cattle.

While Thorp was living at Palma, settlers started a rush for the Estancia Valley. P. A. Speckman, a surveyor in the valley, started the Estancia News, got acquainted with Thorp, discovered he was a civil engineer. Speckman prevailed on Thorp to do surveying for settlers and he went all over the valley, surveying land, locating people on homesteads. Speckman noticed that Thorp sang cowboy songs as he worked, learned that he had composed some of them. Speckman encouraged Thorp to write down the songs he sang, and in 1908 published a book for him called Songs of the Cowboy, now a rare collector's item, which contained a number of original songs of Thorp's composition, among them "Little Joe, the Wrangler." "Little Joe" became a song hit in all parts of the nation. Thorp copyrighted the book of songs, but did not protect his rights against phonograph and radio use. As a result he lost a fortune in royalties.

In 1914 Thorp published a second book of cowboy songs, some with original words and music, others that he had picked up in cow camps. Thorp published *Tales of the Chuck Wagon*, 1926, and wrote a number of stories and articles during the next few years about cow ranches and the west generally. In 1928, Jack Thorp went to Socorro, where he bought a bunch of cattle, turned them loose on the old Elmendorf ranch, now a federal bird and game refuge. When grazing was poor on the Elmendorf, Thorp leased some land in the Oscura Mountains from H. O. Bursum.

Jack Thorp lost everything he owned in money and property in the depression of 1932. Jack and Annette Thorp moved to Albuquerque, built a little adobe house near Alameda on the Albuquerque–Santa Fe road. Here Jack Thorp lived until his death on June 4, 1940. Until the day he died Thorp was interested in cowboys and their songs. Several months before his death, Jack Thorp wrote "Banjo in the Cowcamps," for the *Atlantic Monthly*, which told in detail how he happened to compose "Little Joe, the Wrangler," and other songs. The article was published in the *Atlantic Monthly* for August 1940. Thorp was anxious to see the article in print, but he died before it was published. In "Banjo in the Cow Camps," Thorp reminisced about his days and nights on the Pecos River, of his ranch life in Estancia Valley, of singing "Little Joe" for the first time in public in Uncle Johnny Martin's store and saloon at Weed, New Mexico.

Jack Thorp, to his regret, never learned to write on the typewriter. His wife, Annette Thorp, did the typing, corrected proofs, carried on the correspondence. He wrote his songs and stories in longhand. It was his habit to sleep until two o'clock in the morning and then begin to write. Thorp was a natural singer, played the banjo, was never happier than when singing songs of the range, many of them about the old days in southeast New Mexico.

John Wallace Crawford, known as "Jack" Crawford, the poet-scout, made his home near San Marcial, Socorro County, New Mexico, off and on for more than thirty years. The Crawford home place was located on a hill near the old Fort Craig stage station, overlooking the Rio Grande, six miles south of San Marcial. With his long hair reaching below his shoulders, mustache and goatee, buckskin coat, Crawford was a typical "Buffalo Bill" character, given to showmanship and exhibitionism.

Born in Donegal County, Ireland, on March 4, 1847, Crawford died in New York City on February 17, 1917. He came to America as a child, enlisted in the Union Army at the age of 14 and was wounded while fighting with the 48th Pennsylvania Volunteers during the Civil War. While recuperating in a hospital in Philadelphia, Crawford was taught to read and write by a Sister of Charity and began to scribble verses and poems, showing a talent for literature displayed throughout the rest of his life. At the close of the Civil War, Crawford drifted West and became acquainted with many noted characters of the day in the Black Hills country, including "Wild Bill" Hickox, General Custer and William F. Cody. Crawford claimed to have been one of the founders of Deadwood, Custer, Crook, Gayville and Spearfish.

Crawford participated in the Sitting Bull campaign of 1876, serving as second in command in General Crook's scouts. When William F. Cody ("Buffalo Bill") resigned as Chief of Scouts on August 24, 1876, Crawford succeeded him. In July, 1876, Crawford rode on horseback, carrying dispatches from Medicine Bow, on the Union Pacific from Rosebud, to Little Horn, through Indian country, a distance of nearly four hundred miles. Following the battle of Slim Buttes, Crawford carried the dispatches written on the field by the *New York Herald* correspondent to the telegraph office at Fort Laramie, a distance of 350 miles, in less than three days, for which feat the *Herald* sent him a check for $750. Crawford came to New Mexico in 1880 and participated in the Apache campaign in New Mexico and Arizona. On September 15, 1880, General Buell assigned to Capt. Crawford a mission of going to Chihuahua to locate Chief Victorio for the purpose of attempting to persuade him to return to the reservation in New Mexico. Crawford got within sign language distance of Victorio, but was unable, with all his eloquence, to convince the Chief that he should return to New Mexico or any other place.

During his years in the Dakotas, Crawford had written many poems. Discharged from the army in 1886, Crawford took up his residence near Fort Craig, New Mexico, acquired ranches at Grapevine Springs and at Dripping Spring in the Lava Gap country, over toward Lincoln County. He spent the summers on his New Mexico ranch writing verses, practicing for "a two gun man quick on the draw" act which he put on in connection with lectures delivered throughout the country in the winter months. Crawford's productions as a poet and verse maker would not stand careful scrutiny today, but many years ago the type of poem he produced was in popular favor throughout the country and his books had large sales. In 1881, Crawford published a book of song and story entitled The *Poet Scout* and two years later he published *Camp Fire Sparks*. *Tat*, a drama in three acts, written by Crawford, was produced at the Alta Theatre in San Francisco in October, 1900. He wrote *Whar the Hand o' God is Seen* and other poems published in 1913 and the *Broncho Book* in 1915, published and sponsored by Elbert Hubbard. Crawford left New Mexico temporarily in the gold rush in 1898, went to the Klondike, remained in Alaska two winters, lecturing, looking for gold, and gathering material for future verses. Crawford wrote his verses without any effort. The ordinary "poem" was written in some 15 to 30 minutes. With a little more education Crawford would have been a Robert Service. With a little more luck he would have been an Eddie Guest.

Charles A. Siringo, self-styled cowboy detective, author of a number of books, in some of which New Mexico characters are portrayed, was born in Matagordo County, Texas, in 1855, died in Hollywood, California, in 1928 while employed as an adviser in picture production on authenticity of character, make-up and equipment in western pictures. Siringo was in and out of west Texas and eastern New Mexico many times in 1881 and 1882 on the trail of cattle rustlers; was personally acquainted with Billy the Kid and other desperadoes. Siringo was employed in the nineties by the William A. Pinkerton Detective Agency and spent many years on assignments for that organization.

In 1885, he wrote *A Texas Cowboy*, which sold nearly a million copies in fifty years, most of them published in pirated editions. Out of his experiences of twenty-two years as a Pinkerton detective Siringo wrote his autobiography, *A Cowboy Detective*, published in 1912. In the original manuscript Siringo disclosed the name of the Pinkertons as his employers, made statements in regard to investigations on cases that were claimed by the Pinkertons to be dangerous to their clients and damaging to their business. Following threats made by the Pinkertons of a suit for damages and a request for an injunction prohibiting publication, Siringo made a number of changes in the manuscript. *A Cowboy Detective* is dedicated to Alois

B. Renehan, a prominent attorney of Santa Fe. On July 30, 1912, shortly after the publication of *A Cowboy Detective*, Siringo told the writer that he loved the danger and excitement incident to life as a detective, but detested one part he was obliged to play in his efforts to break up cattle stealing. He would work for weeks, Siringo said, and sometimes for months on cattle ranges, associating with cowboys, worming his way into their confidence and learning their secret plans for cattle rustling. After procuring sufficient evidence against the cowboys to convict them, Siringo would quit his job and disappear. The next time his cowboy friends would see him would be before judge and jury in a case in which they would be defendants. To quote Siringo: "I would be sworn in as a prosecution witness, and obliged to tell of all the snooping I had done. Facing these cowboys, who had been good to me on the range, and testifying against them, was the hardest thing I ever had to do as a detective."

In 1927 Siringo wrote *Riata and Spurs*. His greatest friend in New Mexico was Alois B. Renehan, who published a book of poems, *Songs From the Black Mesa*, in 1900. A classical scholar and brilliant lawyer, Renehan befriended Siringo on many occasions. Renehan's poem, "Retrospective", published in *Songs From the Black Mesa*, is an autobiography of Renehan's spiritual life. After retiring from service with the Pinkertons, Charlie Siringo lived near Santa Fe, in Roswell and other places in New Mexico, and was a familiar figure to many people in various parts of the state.

180

seven

JAMES JOHN HAGERMAN

S UBTERRANEAN WATERS emerge from their hiding places. Springs fed by the perpetual snow of mountain tops bubble from their depths. Here in northeast New Mexico, more than thirteen thousand feet above sea level, is the place of the headwaters of the Pecos River. From the heights of the Truchas, from Jicarilla and Penitente Peaks, from Pecos Baldy, Round Mountain and many another peak, streams empty their waters into the Pecos.[1] From early fall until late spring, the headwaters country of the Pecos is cold and at times quite bleak. The snowfall is heavy and in the winter time the higher peaks are inaccessible. In the summer time, below timber line in the mountains, the Pecos River country is one of matchless beauty. There are countless grassy meadows, bright with the color of wild roses, columbine, Indian paint brush, Shasta daisies, blue-bells and black-eyed Susans. In the upper regions, the Pecos River is guarded by towering white and yellow pine trees, stately blue spruce. Tall and graceful aspens nod and sway in the slightest breeze. The magic of the Santa Fe Mountains hovers over the spirit of the Pecos River for more than forty miles from its source. Witnesses to the magic are the golden glow of eastern skies at daybreak and purple haze that tells of the setting sun just before twilight.

---

1. Truchas Peak contributes its share of waters to the Pecos through Rito Azul and Rito de los Chimayosos. From the north and west Rito del Padre, Rito Sabadiosis, Azul and Chimayosos merge near Beatty's cabin and empty into the Pecos. From Pecos Baldy flows Jack's Creek, which enters the Pecos near Seven Pines. Horsethief Creek, the Panchuela and Rito Perro flow near Mystery Ridge and converge into one stream and join the Pecos near the Seven Pines ranger station. Lake Katherine and Stewart Lake contribute their waters to Winsor Creek, which joins the Pecos at Cowles. Spirit Lake contributes its waters to the Holy Ghost, which empties into the Pecos below Tererro. From the east, in the Upper Pecos country, the Lower Mora, Willow Creek, Bear Creek and Cow Creek and other streams, empty into the Pecos between Cowles and Pecos.

In the higher altitudes of the Pecos River country there are elk, deer and grouse. Ever expectant that hope will triumph over experience, fishermen whip the waters of the upper Pecos and its tributaries, a mission happily undertaken, joyfully endured, seeking the elusive trout in the quiet of shady nooks and rocky pools.

Before the coming of the white man, the Pecos and Picuris Indians called the Pecos country their own. Within the memory of men now living, the Penitentes trudged to secret places in the high mountain country for Good Friday devotions.[2]

Passing through a country unsurpassed for primitive beauty, the Pecos River, in its home mountains, falls from heights over stone worn by the waters of the ages, flows through canyons and gorges, swiftly and surely cuts its way to lower altitudes. For many miles from the headwaters, the Pecos is a sparkling mountain stream, its waters clear and its way free from the interference of man-made structures. Only occasionally on the way down from the mountain tops are the waters of the stream diverted. Here and there, the stream is tapped to furnish irrigation waters for the garden of a descendant of an early-day Spanish-American settler, or to furnish a bit of water for a trapper or a summer resident. At Pecos town in San Miguel County, New Mexico, forty miles from its source, at an elevation of seven thousand feet, the Pecos River begins to doubt its destiny and to lose its identity as a mountain stream and to assume the color and characteristics of the ordinary New Mexico river of the flats and valleys. Leaving Pecos town and following a channel cut in the red and brown earth of the lower altitude country, the Pecos River really begins its long journey to southeast New Mexico, to Texas and to the sea.[3] Soon the river passes a mile away from the now abandoned

---

2. Jicarilla Peak is rounded, like an inverted basket, and was the sacred mountain of the Picuris Indians. Until recent years they had a shrine on the summit. Lake Peak was the sacred mountain of the Tewas. Prayer plumes have been found on the summit within comparatively recent years. For place names in the Pecos headwaters country, see 29th Annual Report of the Bureau of American Ethnology, 1906-1907, pp. 338-350. The United States Geological Survey has established the elevations of the peaks in the Pecos headwaters country as follows: Truchas, 13,275 feet; Jicarilla, 12,944; Pecos Baldy, 12,623; Lake Peak, 12,380. Penitente Peak received its name as the result of visits made there in Holy Week each year by members of the Penitentes in the surrounding country. Brothers of Light, by Alice Corbin Henderson, is an understanding and sympathetic book on the interesting religious society of the Penitentes, still active and flourishing in some parts of New Mexico.

3. Espejo descended the Pecos River in 1583 from Pecos Pueblo to present northeast

ruins of the once important Pecos Indian pueblo, recollecting, if New Mexico rivers can recollect, days gone forever, when the Pecos priests, in secret places high in the nearby mountains, knelt at sacred shrines, scattered corn meal and attached eagle feathers to objects of prayer in ceremonials that began at dawn and ended at twilight.[4]

Touching places of historic interest at almost every bend, the Pecos River flows silently along to picturesque San Jose and then turns south to San Miguel, once a village of prestige and importance, but now chiefly remembered because it was the place of the capture of the poorly advised and ill-fated members of the Texas–Santa Fe Expedition in 1841.[5] Its flow strengthened by the waters of the Gallinas and other neighboring streams, the Pecos passes on to Puertocito then to Villa Nueva, formerly La Questa, an unspoiled Spanish-American village located on top of a stony hill, and then goes to San Jose de Anton Chico, an important stop in stagecoach times, but now a sleepy community basking in the glory of departed days. By the time the Pecos has reached Anton Chico, its waters have lost all the clarity they possessed in the upper mountain country beyond Pecos town. Now the river is burdened with the silt of mountain sides and its waters have been muddied to such an extent that in color the waters of the Pecos and the lower Rio Grande are identical. Passing through three important grants, the Anton Chico, Pres-

Texas, in the opinion of Bandelier. See *Final Report*, Bandelier, part 2, p. 123. The same authority gives "Tshi-quit-e" as the Indian name for the Pecos.

4. Pecos Indian Pueblo, about thirty miles from Santa Fe, was perhaps at one time the largest and most populous of the pueblos of New Mexico in historic times. In prehistoric times the Pecos were scattered up and down the Pecos River from about the site of the present Pecos pueblo ruins to Anton Chico, some forty miles away. Coronado is believed to have visited the Pecos people in 1540, at which time Pecos Pueblo had a population of 2,000 to 2,500. Hernando de Alvarado was the first Spanish officer to visit the pueblo at the time of Coronado's arrival. Coronado left two Franciscan friars behind him to convert the Indians of Pecos, but they were both probably killed in short order. The Pecos Indians undoubtedly irrigated their crops with waters of the Pecos. See A. F. Bandelier, in *Arch. Inst. Papers*, 1, part II, 1881, Frederick Webb Hodge, Oct. 1896 *Ann. Anthrop.*, and Hodge, *Handbook of American Indians*, Vol. 2, p. 220. For a history of Pecos Pueblo and report on scientific excavations there, see *An Introduction to Southwestern Archaeology* by Alfred Vincent Kidder, published by Yale University Press, 1924.

5. For an account of the capture of the Texans at San Miguel, see Chapters 13 and 14, Vol. 1, *Narrative of the Texas—Santa Fe Expedition*, by Geo. Wilkins Kendall, Harper & Bros., New York 1844.

ton Beck and the Perea, the Pecos River follows its course to Santa Rosa, on to Puerto de Luna and Fort Sumner.

Before Lincoln County was dismembered its northern tip touched the southern border of San Miguel County and the Pecos River entered Lincoln County at places then known on the map as Alamos Mochas, flowing on then to Navajo Crossing, Bosque and Lloyd's Crossing. Before Doña Ana County was dismembered, the Pecos River entered that county at Good Bend Crossing, flowed on to Gilbert's Ranch and Beckwith's place, where it said a final farewell to the land of its source and origin; and at nearby Captain Pope's Wells, the river reluctantly and regretfully entered the State of Texas.[6]

Even in the old days, after leaving Pecos town, the energy of the Pecos River was harnessed to serve the needs of man. Its waters were diverted to irrigate farms near San Jose, San Miguel, Villa Nueva,

---

6. The total length of the Pecos River, from its headwaters in the Sangre de Cristo Mountain range, northeast of Santa Fe, New Mexico, to its confluence with the Rio Grande near Comstock, Texas, is 755 miles, of which 435 miles are in New Mexico and 320 miles in Texas. The tributary drainage area comprises some 35,000 square miles, of which 20,000 are in New Mexico and 15,000 in Texas. For some 160 miles from Pecos, New Mexico, the river, with its principal headwaters tributaries, flows through typical mountain stream gorges and narrow valleys. Irrigation from the Pecos River was carried on by the Pecos Indians from time immemorial and by the Spanish colonizers for centuries, by means of community ditches. The Pecos River country in the middle and lower basins was all cattle country until the late eighties, when men began to think in terms of irrigable lands instead of livestock production. Technically, the Pecos River area is divided into three groups, the upper basin comprising the headwaters and tributary areas above the Alamogordo reservoir near Fort Sumner; the middle basin embracing the drainage between the Alamogordo reservoir and the New Mexico–Texas state line at the upper end of the Red Bluff reservoir; and the lower basin, which comprises the drainage in Texas extending from the Red Bluff reservoir to the mouth of the river. Below Fort Sumner valley, the river flows through a wide rolling plains country for some seventy miles to a point near Roswell. The area of the Roswell artesian basin, mostly on the west side of the Pecos, extends south from Roswell sixty miles to the river narrows several miles below McMillan reservoir. The Carlsbad project, United States Bureau of Reclamation, occupies the river valley from Avalon reservoir to near Malaga, some twenty miles. The river enters the narrows below Malaga and flows for about fifteen miles before reaching the New Mexico–Texas line. The Alamogordo, McMillan and Avalon reservoirs serve the Carlsbad project. For an excellent study of the status of the Pecos River problems and their proposed solution, see *Regional Planning*, Part X, National Resources Planning Board, and *The Pecos River Joint Investigation*, National Resources Planning Board, Government Printing Office, June 1942.

Cerrito, San Jose de Anton Chico, Santa Rosa, Puerto de Luna and old Fort Sumner.[7]

In the seventies and eighties thousands of cattle grazed up and down the many miles of its banks from Puerto de Luna to the Texas line. South and east in New Mexico beyond Fort Sumner, the Pecos assumed in the early days great importance and significance in the life of the country. Vast grazing grounds, once the home lands of the buffalo and antelope, were given over to the cattle industry. Men from Texas numbered their herds by the thousands. Six-shooters frequently handed down the final opinion in disputes and controversies over control of rights to the waters of the Pecos and appurtenant grazing land.

From Fort Sumner southward, the flow of the Pecos River is increased by waters from many streams. Salt Creek empties into the Pecos thirteen miles north of Roswell. The Hondo, formed by the confluence of the Bonito and Ruidoso, together with the Felix and Penasco, empty into the Pecos in the Roswell area. Seven Rivers, the Black and Delaware flow into the Pecos in the Carlsbad area. The lower Pecos River country, from north to south, is walled off from the western part of southeast New Mexico by the Jicarilla, Capitan, White, Sacramento and Guadalupe Mountains. Flash floods along the Pecos and its tributaries have done much damage from time to time in the Roswell area.

The life of the Pecos River in the early days had been simple enough in the mountain country of its source, but when southeastern New Mexico began to grow and develop, men sought for its waters, fought for them. Pat Garrett, late sheriff of Lincoln County, slayer of Billy the Kid, ranching in Lincoln County not far from Roswell, had visions in the early eighties of being an empire builder. Garrett had served his time as a buffalo hunter in neighboring Texas and knew that the day of the buffalo was over; he had seen the best and the worst of men up and down the Pecos River from San Miguel to the Texas line and beyond. He knew enough of history to realize that the Plains Indians, with their small but fleet ponies, had been forced back from the Pecos by stronger men, mostly from Texas, who rode stronger horses and carried six-shooters. Pat Garrett knew

---

7. At present seventeen rock and brush diversion dams are located along the river in the distance of one hundred miles from Pecos town to Puerto de Luna, 15 miles above Alamogordo reservoir.

that the days were numbered for such a man as John S. Chisum, with his immense herds of cattle ranging up and down the Pecos River, fattening his animals on grama grass, and growing wealthy on government contracts. Pat had learned enough from the clashes between the federal government and the Navajos and Apaches at old Fort Sumner to know why the army had failed in that project of imprisonment and attempted civilization. He knew that the Indians hated their shackles and detested their captors and did not want to live in a country where they were not happy.

Pat Garrett knew of the government-sponsored Alamo Gordo irrigation project on the Pecos for the Indians and believed that the project failed simply because the Indians themselves did not want to have anything to do with it. Visualizing great irrigation enterprises up and down the Pecos River, Garrett began to think in terms of men who might be anxious to live on land under an irrigation project, working from dawn until dusk to produce a crop of cotton, or milo maize or kaffir corn, the kind of crops he had seen produced in his boyhood days in Alabama, Louisiana and Texas. Shedding his six-shooter like a worn-out garment, Pat Garrett told to Charles B. Eddy, a pioneer cattleman of southeast Eddy County, his dream of harnessing the waters of the Pecos River country, of building reservoirs and irrigation canals. Gunman Garrett and Cattleman Eddy neglected their ranches, became enthusiastic promoters, turned their energies into grandiose schemes for development of the Pecos River valley in the vicinity of Roswell and present day Carlsbad. Garrett's effort at promotion, a career for which he was poorly equipped through lack of inherent ability, education or experience in life, is best told in an early day summary of the adventure written by Ash Upson, his boon companion.

Under a Roswell date line of November 23, 1888, and published in the *Lincoln County Leader* of December 8, 1888, Upson told of Pat Garrett's scheme to irrigate Pecos Valley land and at the same time gave an interesting picture of early-day Roswell:

> Roswell is now taking on a boom, thus exemplifying the old adage, "all things come around to those who wait." I will here say to those who are non-believers in the Darwinian theory of evolution that a review of the history of this place and the Pecos Valley will at least stagger their skepticism, if not overwhelm it altogether. Commencing with that stereotyped period, "but a few years ago,"

when this country was a part of the howling wilderness, the transi-
tion was short, to the era when the white outlaws supplanted the
red savage, and the peaceable settler was no longer robbed of his
horse by the barbarous Apache, but in the more courteous and
civilized style of "Billy the Kid." The incoming of the cattleman
rooted out the outlaws and the granger and the railroads are now
threatening the cattle.

Immigration is now setting in this way. Roswell is growing.
Several new buildings recently finished, several now in course of
construction and the construction of several others contracted for.

Roswell is to have a newspaper shortly. The editor of the paper
arrived a few days ago, bringing his type with him, and so soon as
he could get a building went to work and set up his forms, ready to
be struck off as soon as the press reaches here, which is on the road.
A new doctor has arrived and his drugstore will soon follow—that
is the drugs will follow—the store will be erected here and will not
follow. The stores, mechanics and laborers seem to have as much
as they can attend to, while the knights of the green cloth are busy
night and day, giving glad countenances to those who successfully
coppered the tray, and woebegone expressions to those who lost
on the ace.

The cause of this sudden prosperity is almost entirely due to the
energy and enterprise of Lincoln County's old "stand" familiarly
known as Pat Garrett. The irrigation ditch or canal upon which he
is now engaged is certainly a gigantic undertaking, and what is as
fully important, it wears every aspect of successful completion, as
large capital (about the figure 6 and five o's) has been subscribed
by the stockholders.

The survey of the canal commences close to Garrett's house on
the Hondo River, and then southward in an irregular line, according
to grade to the South Spring River, the waters of which stream it
will take up, thus insuring the volume of water in the canal. The line
will then continue in a southerly direction, but bearing away from
the Pecos to the Feliz, which is about 25 miles south of Roswell.
. . . The lands intended to be irrigated are the vacant lands lying
off to the south of the Chisum ranch. . . . It is the intention of the
stockholders to embrace 40,000 acres of land within the scope of the
canal's irrigation, and it is intended to flume the Feliz and make the
terminus of the canal somewhere about Tourlake. . . . The canal
is to be 30 feet wide at the bottom, and 5 feet deep. . . . The company
will give liberal terms to colonists who will settle along the ditch.

. . . They intend to make an avenue, lined with shade trees along the entire length of the canal, which when completed, will become as famous as the New Orleans shell road, and as dear to young lovers of New Mexico as the trysting places of Saratoga are to the elite of New York society. . . . As to the agricultural qualities . . . in the region lying east of Roswell is a large area of farming region which was once called "Pankinrow," but has now been advanced into the more respectable title, "among the farms." The yield of crops this year has been simply astonishing . . . alfalfa grass has yielded four cuttings this season . . . watermelons average from 30 to 40 pounds, while some have reached 75 pounds. I saw four sweet potatoes which weigh 23 pounds, and these were the average of the lot, while selected specimens of the same lot tilted the scales at 13, 15 and 16 pounds each. . . . This has been the first season that the fruit trees have been old enough to show their productiveness, and the abundance and quality of the crop will compare favorably with any other part of New Mexico. . . . In the construction of this canal two machines have been imported which are curiosities to most people. Imagine a large wagon frame, with a tread of eight feet, enormous wheels, with tires six inches wide. Underneath and at one side, is a large plow, of the kind known as a "prairie breaker." An endless band of gum elastic about three feet wide, revolving over rollers, extends from the plow at right angles with the furrows. A cog wheel attachment to the wagon wheel gives motion to this endless band. Now, when the machine is in motion the plow turns the sod or ground just like an ordinary plow, the dirt so turned over falls on the band, which in motion, carries it off to one side and deposits it a distance of 22 feet from the furrow. The machine in an up and down trip will excavate two furrows and deposit the dirt 44 feet apart. . . . Fourteen horses and three men work the machine, doing the work of thirty men and horses with ordinary plows and scrapers.

The origin of the irrigation enterprise is both curious and interesting. . . . It seems that all great discoveries are matters of accident, in the initiative, requiring great genius and thinking powers to utilize the incident. . . . Sir Isaac Newton . . . The search for a route to India caused Christopher Columbus to stumble upon a new continent, and the smile of a pretty Texas widow has caused Capt. Lea to discover some pathos in the ballad called Shamus O'Brien, especially those lines that say:

I'll smile when you smile,
I'll weep when you weep,
I'll give you a kiss for a kiss.

In the same manner that all these discoveries were made, even so it may be said that the idea of a great irrigation ditch was suggested to its originator by an accident.

To those who are not acquainted with Pat Garrett, it will be necessary to explain that in addition to being long headed, he is likewise long legged, his full height being somewhat under ten feet —I have forgotten the exact measurements. He had been for sometime past thinking how to get water on some of his river land, and as the water to the Hondo was in the bottom of a deep and steep chasm, it would be expensive to raise it to the level of the land. The Berenda comes in on the north side of the Hondo and is about on a level with the surrounding country. If he could only get it across the Hondo, then the irrigation problem would be settled. While wandering around looking at the situation, and studying over this question, he accidentally stepped across the Hondo where it was not more than twenty feet wide. From this circumstance arose the great train of thought which has culminated in the greatest enterprise the Pecos Valley has yet witnessed.

It required but a slight stretching of the legs to cross the Hondo, in person, it required but as light exertion of the intellect to flume it, another step to dam it, and so on. But all this would require capital. A trip to Chicago secured the necessary funds and now the work goes bravely on. Thus it will be seen how a great enterprise originated from two insignificant items, first, the Hondo River, second, a pair of long legs.

If Pat Garrett was not a natural born promoter, he had interested a man later conceded to be a genius in that particular field of human endeavor. Garrett's associate, Charles Bishop Eddy, born and reared in New York state, was gifted with the ability to paint word-pictures that prompted action; able, tireless, energetic, resourceful, and at times difficult and troublesome. Thinking along the same lines as Pat Garrett, but with an imagination that Garrett could not equal, Charles B. Eddy boldly enlarged on Garrett's scheme of things. He enlisted the services of Charles W. Greene, a promoter of considerable ability and well known throughout the Territory, perhaps too well known in Las Vegas, Santa Fe and other places in which he had displayed his professional talents.

In the eighties there was a newspaper feud on between R. A. Kistler, editor of the Las Vegas *Optic*, and Charles W. Greene, editor for a time of the Santa Fe *New Mexican*. On July 15, 1881, when perhaps the *Optic* should have published an editorial mourning the death of Billy the Kid, who had been killed the day before over at Fort Sumner, Editor Kistler had the following to say about his fellow editor, Greene:

> Greene of the New Mexican on each visit here, borrowed twenty-five dollars of the editor of this paper, to pay his hotel and whiskey bills, and, the last time he kept us out of our money for a full month. Subsequent developments assure us that we were more fortunate than many others in getting their money back at all. He's a stinker, and six months will conclude his residence in the Territory. . . . Greene draws a weekly salary of forty dollars on the New Mexican and gives employment on the paper to several members of his family. But the arrangement will not last.

Still angry the next day, Editor Kistler in the *Optic* of July 16, 1881, commented editorially:

> "Granny" Greene, of the New Mexican, so-called because of his feebleness of mind, his fickleness of purpose and his fondness for faultfinding—characterless Wanderer Greene, a booby in intellect; a thieving liar from choice; a grinning, dwarfish delver in deviltry; a coarse minded, foulmouthed bankrupt who is in arrears to the men in Kansas who fed his family a number of years for charity's sake; a depraved, lurking villian at heart, who is a catspaw in the hands of designing men, can't get the notice at our hands this evening, that we would like to give him owning to paucity of space.[8]

---

8. Charles W. Greene was born in Providence, Rhode Island, March 14, 1839, taught school in Pennsylvania, served in Company "B" Twelfth Connecticut Infantry in the Civil War, had charge of railway troop transportation in the Gulf Department. Drifting west, Greene worked on the Wichita *Herald* at Wichita in 1878, published the Anthony, Kansas, *Journal* in 1880. Coming to New Mexico in 1881, he was manager of the Santa Fe *New Mexican*, then owned by the Santa Fe Railroad. He resigned in 1882, started the Lake Valley *Herald* at Lake Valley, then the Kingston *Tribune* at Kingston during the mining boom, then established the *Tribune* at Deming; then managed the "Tertio Millenial" exposition at Santa Fe in 1882; established the *Evening Tribune* in El Paso, Texas. Newspaper publishing not being successful, Greene returned to the *New Mexican* in 1888 as a hired hand under Captain Max Frost, then helped Pat Garrett and C. B. Eddy in promoting the Pecos Irrigation and Investment Com-

Cattleman Charles B. Eddy, now turned promoter, joined by Promoter Charles W. Greene, adopting some of the ideas and visions of the tall, ungainly and ever-optimistic Pat Garrett, organized the Pecos Irrigation and Investment Company. They had engineers draw plans and specifications for irrigation projects up and down the Pecos River from Roswell to the Texas line, requiring expenditures of large sums of money. In their search for capital they made the acquaintance of Robert Weems Tansill, a resident of Colorado Springs, who had made a fortune in Chicago manufacturing "Punch" cigars. A direct descendant of "Parson Weems," credited with an early life of George Washington, Robert Weems Tansill was born in Prince William County, Virginia, on August 20, 1844, and died in Carlsbad, New Mexico, on December 29, 1902. Tansill invested in the promotion sponsored by Eddy, Greene and Garrett and later moved to Carlsbad to be near the projects and contributed time, money and energy to their eventual success. The capital produced for their enterprise by Promoters Eddy and Greene through the sale of stocks and bonds was totally inadequate. Their technical advisers, in some instances, had under-estimated the cost of construction and the promoters themselves had over-estimated their ability to find ready money. With some of the projects under way and desperate for funds, Charles B. Eddy in 1889 went to Colorado Springs, interviewed Robert Weems Tansill and urged him to invest additional capital. Tansill did better. He introduced Eddy to James John Hagerman, a retired capitalist, then residing in Colorado Springs. The handclasp between the two men proved to be historic. The casual introduction resulted in the development of the entire Pecos River country in New Mexico east and southeast from Fort Sumner, but marked the opening chapter in a series of incidents in the life of James John Hagerman which brought him great personal worry and distress and to the verge of financial ruin; it also involved him in numerous difficulties and bitter quarrels not of his making.

The meeting between Hagerman and Eddy in Colorado Springs was the beginning of an epic story in the life of southeastern New

pany up to the time when it was taken over by J. J. Hagerman. In 1891 Greene went to Chicago and New York on promotion schemes which took him to Europe. Greene's propensity for going from one scheme to another interfered with his success. He was a Republican in politics. R. A. Kistler founded the Las Vegas *Optic* November 4, 1879, and was its publisher until August 30, 1897.

Mexico. No man ever did more for New Mexico, alone and single-handed, than James John Hagerman.[9]

When Hagerman and Charles B. Eddy were introduced to each other in Colorado Springs, there was no doubt in Eddy's mind as to his objective. He was in search of a man with money, plenty of money, and a man who could be tempted to undertake leadership in a job of empire building. There never was a more plausible, enthusiastic or magnetic promoter than Charles B. Eddy. Hagerman was fifty years old in 1889 when he promised Charles B. Eddy that he would go to New Mexico and look over the country which both Eddy and Tansill praised so highly.

True to his promise, for Hagerman never made a promise that, if within the range of human possibility, he did not keep, James John Hagerman went to Toyah, Texas, in the autumn of 1889. As the train came to a stop in Toyah, Texas, not far from the New Mexico line, Hagerman was greeted by Charles B. Eddy, Robert Weems Tansill and other prominent men of the Pecos River country. Hagerman rode up the Pecos River from Pecos to Eddy with Charles B.

---

9. Before James John Hagerman ever set foot on New Mexico soil, he was a prominent man and, if he had never invested a dollar in New Mexico, or built a mile of railroad in the Territory, or encouraged the tilling of a single acre of land, he would have achieved much, according to the standards of accomplishment of his own day and in the light of subsequent events. Born on a farm near Port Hope, Ontario, Canada, on March 23, 1839, James John Hagerman died in Milan, Italy, on September 15, 1909. With him when death came was his wife, Anna Osborne Hagerman, whom he had married in 1867 and who had been his constant companion through years of elation over success, and of discouragement over defeat and failure. Of the marriage between James John Hagerman and Anna Osborne Hagerman there were born two sons. Percy Hagerman of Colorado Springs, who rowed on the varsity crew at Cornell, made Phi Beta Kappa, and was closely associated for many years in the Hagerman enterprises, and Herbert J. Hagerman, governor of the Territory of New Mexico in 1906-1907 and who later served in important capacities for the Navajo Indians as a representative of the federal government. The early life of James John Hagerman was a proving ground for the difficulties that were ahead. His father, James Parrott Hagerman, a powerful, restless, energetic man, became involved in speculation, left Canada and became a citizen of the United States, settling in Newport, now Marine City, on the St. Clair River in Michigan. Newport at the time was almost a wilderness. There was no railroad west of Buffalo, New York, and the states of Illinois, Wisconsin and Indiana were just being settled by hordes of immigrants from Europe. Travel from Buffalo west was by steamer on the Great Lakes. The child, James John Hagerman, was fascinated by the visible signs of the westward tide of immigration, the crowded steamers and sailboats traveling up the St. Clair River, passing close to his father's home. There was born in him at the time an ambition to run away, to become a sailor, and eventually a captain of a lake steamer. Until he was nineteen, Hagerman lived

Eddy in a top buggy, drawn by a team of spanking horses.[10] As the
Pecos River came into view and the valley widened, Charles B. Eddy
began a carefully prepared recitation of the possibilities of the country
and showed Hagerman partly finished irrigation and development
projects, pointing out from time to time with a buggy whip the immense tracts of land, which Eddy said could be sub-divided into
farms and irrigated by waters taken from the Pecos River. Eddy
pointed out the proposed location of the dam sites where the waters
of the river could be impounded; he told of the necessity of a line of
railway from Pecos, Texas, to Eddy and to Roswell, which would
help to settle quickly and populate the country with people from
all parts of America and even from Europe.[11]

On his first trip into the Pecos River country, Hagerman was profoundly impressed by the possibilities for development, more so than

---

in his father's house in Newport, a hard life and not entirely happy, because the parent,
intensely religious and inclined to obey the exhortations of the Bible literally, was a
hard taskmaster, obliging him to work long hours in the carpenter shop, flour mill
and on the farm. As a youth, Hagerman was fortunate in coming under the influence
of older men, who loaned him books by Robert Burns, Walter Scott, Charles Dickens.
An old French soldier, who had fought in the battle of Waterloo, fired his imagination
over the life of Napoleon Bonaparte and made Hagerman in later years a profound
student of the Napoleonic era. Ambitious for higher education, Hagerman went to the
University of Michigan in 1857, worked seven months of each year in order to pay
his way through school for five months, finally graduated from the University with the
class of 1861, the first year of the Civil War. The University of Michigan in the years
of Hagerman's attendance was a small institution, pioneering in a frontier country.
Among Hagerman's teachers at Michigan was Andrew D. White, a recent graduate
of Yale, who later became one of the founders and the first president of Cornell University. The teacher-student tie formed at Michigan resulted in a close, personal, lifelong friendship between the two men.

    10. The name of Eddy, a town named for Charles B. Eddy, was later changed to
Carlsbad. When the name of Carlsbad was substituted for that of Eddy, it was believed that mineral springs near the town would prove to be a most valuable asset in
years to come. Discovery of the world-famous Carlsbad Caverns, of vast deposits of
potash and of oil in the vicinity of the town demonstrated that the men who urged
the substitution of Carlsbad for Eddy, were, to say the least, not gifted with prophetic
vision.

    11. In 1890, Henri Gaullieur, a prominent official of Switzerland, was sent to the
United States on a mission to inspect projects throughout the west, with instructions
to select and recommend the one that indicated the greatest promise, with a view to
Swiss emigration. Gaullieur traveled to various parts of the country, examined into the
prospects of the more important irrigation projects and finally made a report to his
government, recommending the Pecos Valley project as the one that offered the greatest
opportunity for settlers of means. Based on the Gaullieur report, a number of people
came to the Pecos Valley from Switzerland and substantial sums of money were in-

JAMES JOHN HAGERMAN AT CHISUM RANCH.

he was willing to disclose or indicate to Charles B. Eddy. He sensed a personal challenge in the projects already undertaken and in those that were contemplated. Eddy drove back to Pecos, Texas, where Hagerman took the train on his return journey to Colorado Springs. Before leaving Pecos, Texas, Hagerman agreed to make a small investment in the enterprises. Within a few days he sent Eddy his check for forty thousand dollars. Confident that Hagerman would eventually be persuaded by the challenge of the development possibilities to invest large sums of money, Eddy wrote to Hagerman regularly, kept him advised of the progress that was being made, and of the plans for the future.

Back in Colorado Springs, Hagerman's thoughts invariably drifted back to the Pecos River country. He studied the blueprints and specifications of the projects that Eddy had sent to him. Sometimes, in his sleep, Hagerman dreamed of Pecos River waters, flowing along, impregnated with silt and mud, guided into canyonlike reservoirs and impounded there, to be released at the will of man. He dreamed that he could see the smile on the faces of farmers raising great crops on fertile lands, grown by waters obtained from the mains and laterals of an immense irrigation system. In his daytime thinking, Hagerman could almost hear the noise and visualize the smoke of locomotives pulling long freight trains over a railroad line that reached from Pecos, Texas, to Roswell, New Mexico.

Mrs. Anna Osborne Hagerman, a woman of great strength of character and many attainments, was decidedly opposed to her husband's participation in the Pecos River projects. Prompted by woman's intuition, she warned him against having anything to do with them. From the beginning, she feared that Charles B. Eddy might influence her husband against his better judgment, to commit himself to substantial financial assistance. From past experience, she was aware that once identified with a project, it was not his nature or disposition to let go easily. Mrs. Hagerman recognized the signs by which her husband was veering toward a commitment to participate with Eddy in his schemes of development of the Pecos Valley. "John, your friend Mr. Eddy may be a fine man," Mrs. Hagerman told her hus-

---

vested in farms and improvements. The Swiss colonists had their successes and their failures. For the most part, an alien tongue, new conditions, the hardships incident to a new country and other adverse factors, prevented the colonization from becoming an outstanding success.

band on one occasion "but somehow he reminds me of Svengali."[12]
There were but few men who called Hagerman by his first name.
Mrs. Hagerman always called him "John," his middle name, in preference to James, his first name. To nearly all of his friends and
acquaintances, he was "Mr. Hagerman," and no man ever presumed
to slap him on the back. He was that kind of man. One of the few
who called him "Jim," was Mark Hanna of Ohio, sponsor of William
McKinley in national politics. Friends as young men, Hagerman and
Hanna maintained a close friendship throughout life.

Before reaching a decision on the Pecos River proposition, Hagerman reviewed his entire life. He recalled a boyhood that had called
for hard, laborious work; of his struggle for a college education; of
his early business successes in the iron and steel industry; of his
achievements in the Menominee iron range in northern Michigan,
recalling with pride the discovery and development of the Chapin
mine, of the fortune that he made in those enterprises; he recollected
that he had succeeded in silver and gold mining in Colorado, when
many had said he would fail; that he had made a success of his leadership in the construction of the Colorado Midland Railroad to Leadville and Aspen; that he had been fortunate in his venture and risk in
the Molly Gibson mine. True, his health was not good, but neither
was it too bad; he had plenty of money, but he wanted to experience
again the joy of achievement, to be a creator of projects from blue-
print stage to final completion. He decided that he would go into the
Pecos River venture with Charles B. Eddy and help the people of
southeastern New Mexico found an empire.[13]

---

12. A hypnotic character in *Trilby*, a novel by George du Maurier. Svengali's influence, through the use of hypnosis, dominates the story.

13. After graduating from the University of Michigan in 1861, James John Hagerman went to work for Captain E. B. Ward, shipbuilder and owner, whose sister, Emily
Ward, had encouraged Hagerman to seek a college education. Employed as a clerk
and purser on Ward's ships on the Great Lakes, Hagerman's diligence and capacity
for hard work impressed themselves on Ward to such an extent that when Ward
decided to expand into timber and iron ore, he made Hagerman secretary and manager
of a company he organized for that purpose. In 1867 Hagerman operated an iron rail
mill in Chicago, later built a Bessemer plant at Wyandotte, near Detroit, where the
first steel ingots made in America were turned out. Believing that the days of lake
steamers were over and that the railroad would be the thing of the future, Ward
acquired thousands of acres of timber lands and great areas of what later proved to
be the Menominee iron deposits in northern Michigan. Ward took Hagerman along
with him in the enterprises and, from Ward, Hagerman learned much about various
types of business. The panic of 1873 and Ward's death in 1875, apparently disasters

Primarily, James John Hagerman looked upon the Pecos River venture as a great opportunity for the agricultural development of the Pecos Valley. He became infatuated with the idea. The infatuation and the refusal to heed his wife's warning cost him two and a half millions in money, almost twenty years of hard work and endless worry, disappointment in men and discouragement over many things. But before he died, Hagerman had the satisfaction of knowing that he had achieved greatly. The fame that came to him and that belongs to him, in the work incident to the development of the Pecos Valley in New Mexico, will outlast the credit that went to him because of his development work in iron ore fields of Northern Michigan, the construction of the Colorado Midland, or the sensational strike of silver in the Molly Gibson mine.[14]

Soon after Hagerman's active identification with the Pecos River projects, the Pecos Irrigation and Investment Company which Charles B. Eddy and his associates had organized and under which they had operated, was succeeded by Pecos Irrigation and Improve-

---

for Hagerman, proved to his eventual benefit. Hagerman and associates acquired long time leases on iron ore deposits on the Menominee range, organized the Menominee Mining Company, did business with Andrew Carnegie, Henry Phipps and Mark Hanna, all of whom remained close friends of Hagerman throughout life. In 1879 with the discovery of the famous Chapin mine, a producer of the present time, Hagerman and those who had ventured with him, made substantial fortunes. Forty-four years old, Hagerman had plenty of money, but poor health, and he and his family went to Europe and spent two years there. With time for study, Hagerman read many books on history, literature and art, pursued studies of Napoleon Bonaparte in Paris, walked over battlefields in northern Italy and Austria. Forbidden by physicians to continue to live in Milwaukee, Wisconsin, where he had made his home and had been successful in directing iron, steel and mining ventures, Hagerman's choice of a new place of residence was Colorado Springs.

14. When James John Hagerman became actively identified with the development of Pecos Valley enterprises, he was confronted with the principal part in financing the construction of the following projects: The Hondo reservoir southeast of Roswell; the Northern Canal starting near Roswell and running south, some distance beyond Hagerman; the Eddy (Avalon) dam and reservoir; the Southwestern Canal starting at the Eddy dam and running a long distance south on the west side of the Pecos River; the Southeastern Canal starting at the Eddy dam and running down the east side of the Pecos; the Hagerman Canal on the east side of the river about twelve miles below Eddy; the Pecos Land and Water Company Canal, designed to take water from the Pecos River near the New Mexico–Texas line and irrigate a large acreage in New Mexico and Texas; the construction of a railroad from Pecos, Texas, to Roswell, New Mexico. The McMillan dam and reservoir were not included in the earliest plans. It was first believed that the natural flow of the Pecos River, together with the small amount of storage at Lake Avalon, would meet requirements.

ment Company, which took over the assets and liabilities of the original company and through stock and bond issues obtained substantial amounts of money. The Pecos Valley Railway finished building its track into Eddy in December, 1890. The Northern Canal, the Eddy dam, and a large part of the canal leading from it, were completed in 1890 and 1891 and some work was done on the Texas Canal and the Hondo reservoir. The McMillan dam was finished in 1893 and the railroad was extended to Roswell in 1894. The dreams of Charles B. Eddy, James John Hagerman and their associates were beginning to come true. Great numbers of land hungry settlers came into the Pecos Valley, ambitious to establish farms. They exercised their desert land and homestead entry rights on public domain and soon demonstrated that the land, watered by irrigation, could produce bountiful crops. Impressed by the Pecos River projects and their possibilities for revenue, English capitalists became potential purchasers. Only the financial failures of 1893 prevented the sale to them of the railroad and development enterprises at a price that would have brought more than par for the stock.

Friction began to develop, as time went on, between the employees in the railroad department and the irrigation department of the Pecos Irrigation and Improvement Company. It was found necessary to divorce the operation of the railroad property from the irrigation projects and to organize subsidiary corporations for land development. Conflicts of a personal nature developed between Charles B. Eddy and James John Hagerman over policy and methods of management of the enterprises. Eddy had demonstrated that he was a promoter of the first magnitude, but a failure as an administrator. With some of his associates, Eddy had formed the Pecos Valley Town Company which owned townsites up and down the Pecos River. There were frequent clashes and squabbles between Hagerman and Eddy over matters relating to these enterprises and, in 1895, a feud blazed up between them which had repercussions throughout southeastern New Mexico. The difficulties between Eddy and Hagerman were to some extent the outgrowth of troublesome times that came to the Pecos River projects in 1893. The repeal of the Sherman law in that year was disastrous to Hagerman's silver mining investments in Colorado and Eddy's private enterprises were in a slump.[15]

---

15. In the early eighties almost all of Colorado was a mining camp. With ample money at his command, Hagerman listened to stories of mines and mining ventures in

The entire nation, in 1893, was experiencing a panic of unprecedented proportions. The Pecos Valley in New Mexico suffered along with the rest of the country. Millions had already been spent on the Pecos Valley irrigation projects, on the railroad and in other development work. More millions were necessary to finish the program. It was soon obvious that raising money in the east or abroad, for the New Mexico enterprises, was an absolute impossibility. Bankers refused to put another dollar into any kind of railroad or irrigation scheme. In October of 1893, when things looked pitch dark anyway for the entire scheme of things in the Pecos Valley, the waters of the Pecos and its tributaries rose to disaster stages. Floods washed out the Eddy dam, irrigation canals were without water, farmers were ruined. The railroad line was washed out in many places. The entire country in the Eddy dam area was in the doldrums. With vigor and determination characteristic of him throughout life, Hagerman plunged boldly into the center of the turmoil that followed the destruction of the dam. He quickly notified the farmers living under the irrigation project that the dam would be rebuilt, that water charges would be cancelled pending reconstruction and

----

Colorado until he could no longer resist the temptation to risk some of his capital. His first ventures in Colorado mining were in Aspen and Leadville. Aspen, on the western slope, was a camp of great promise, about fifty miles west of Leadville, over the Continental Divide. Hagerman became identified with a group of men who proposed to build a railroad from Colorado Springs through Leadville to Aspen, and other places on the western slope. Ultimately the plan was to build to the Pacific Coast by way of Salt Lake. With characteristic energy, Hagerman soon assumed an important place in the leadership of the construction of the railway from Colorado Springs to Aspen. Built at great expense and under great difficulties, the road was completed into Aspen in 1889. The financing had been done through New York and London, largely through Hagerman's efforts. The Colorado Midland, as the road was called, followed a route directly west from Colorado Springs and was the first broad gauge railroad in Colorado to be projected over the Continental Divide. The place of crossing over the Divide, in honor of Hagerman, was named Hagerman Pass. When the road was finished, the books of account showed that James John Hagerman was the largest stockholder in the Colorado Midland. Throughout his life, Hagerman made it a rule never to ask another man to invest money in an enterprise in which he himself was not already a heavy investor. Apparently a money-maker, with bright prospects for great earnings and possible expansion to the west, the Colorado Midland was sold to the Atchison, Topeka & Santa Fe Railroad in 1890. Hagerman personally negotiated the sale and the price was sufficient to get every stockholder out at a substantial profit. The Santa Fe, because of changed and changing conditions, abandoned the Colorado Midland in 1920 and most of its track was torn up. Booming as a result of railroad construction, the mining camp of Aspen skyrocketed to fame in the early nineties. Lucky at iron mining in northern Michigan more than ten years before, James John

that their rights would be protected in every way. Hagerman's quick action prevented an exodus. Many a farmer, packed up and ready to leave the country, was prevailed upon to remain. Hagerman dug deeply into his own pocket in order to help provide the $150,000 required to construct and repair the dam and canals, work which was promptly undertaken and completed by February, 1894. The breaking of the Eddy dam, however, was a deadly blow to the community and to all of the Pecos River enterprises with which Hagerman was identified.

For five years, from 1893 to 1898, the Pecos Irrigation and Improvement Company barely kept out of a receivership, largely through personal advances made by Hagerman and by Charles A. Otis, steel manufacturer of Cleveland, Ohio, a long time personal friend. Hopefully, the company built a sugar factory at Carlsbad in 1894. Operated for two seasons with only fair success, it was destroyed by fire and not rebuilt, ending an experiment that held great promise. Various crops were planted in the valley. Long staple cotton growing experiments were considered, but unkind fate, by way of disaster and panic general to the nation, had taken its toll of the

---

Hagerman struck it rich again at Aspen with the group of claims that had been brought together as the Molly Gibson mine. Hagerman agreed with associates in the enterprise to furnish fifty thousand dollars to overcome underground water difficulties and develop the property. For the fifty thousand dollars Hagerman received almost a one-third interest in the operating company. Almost the last dollar of the Hagerman money had been expended when, in March, 1891, there was great excitement in the saloons and on the streets of Aspen. Great pockets of silver ore had been struck in the Molly Gibson and every stock owner in the mining company became rich. Within a year all debts had been paid and stockholders had received a million dollars in dividends. The silver strike at the Molly Gibson was the sensation of the times. The average silver content of all shipments in the first year of operation following the strike proved to be four hundred fifty ounces to the ton. Silver sold at $1.29 an ounce. Probably the richest silver ore ever shipped in such quantities from any one mine in the history of America came from the Molly Gibson and, after paying an even million dollars in dividends in 1891, the mine paid a million seven hundred thousand in 1892, a million two hundred thirty thousand in 1893. With the repeal of the Sherman law in 1893 and the demonitization of silver, the silver mining industry in Colorado reeled and staggered. But not so with gold mining. For strange to say, as silver slipped at Aspen, important gold discoveries were made at not far off Cripple Creek. James John Hagerman organized and was the largest stockholder in the Isabella Gold Mining Company, one of the first large scale gold operations in the Cripple Creek area. The Isabella proved a very profitable enterprise. Crowded financially in Pecos River enterprises, lucky at mining, but unlucky at empire building, Hagerman was obliged to sell his Cripple Creek holdings in 1898 at a sacrifice.

Pecos Irrigation and Improvement Company. James John Hagerman had reached the point where he could no longer advance funds
from his personal account, or otherwise finance the enterprises. In
July, 1898, Robert Weems Tansill was appointed receiver for the
corporation. Largely through the efforts of Francis G. Tracy, the
Eddy dam-Carlsbad project was taken over by the United States Reclamation Service at a great discount from cost. With unlimited
capital available, experienced engineers and the ability to remould
the entire enterprise to suit conditions, the federal government undertook and carried forward a program of rehabilitation and construction that brought eventual outstanding success.

The railroad from Pecos, Texas, to Carlsbad and to Roswell, was a
line of communication and an accommodation to the public, but
"began nowhere and ended nowhere" and was not a financial success. After the railroad had been in operation for several years, Hagerman realized that it would be necessary to extend the line. His judgment was that people and commodities wanted to move north and
east, instead of south. When he began to think of a railroad extension
to the north and east, the headquarters of the Pecos Valley Railroad
were in Carlsbad. All the country north of Carlsbad, with a few exceptions, was undeveloped. A few thousand acres at Roswell had
been developed from what was then called the Spring Rivers, three
in number, all of artesian water source; and the old Chisum ranch at
South Spring, on the South Spring River near Roswell, contained
several hundred acres of highly developed land. Pat Garrett, C. D.
Bonney and others had promoted the Northern Canal which collected the waste waters from the Spring River and the Hondo River
at a point just east of Roswell and carried them down to lands near
Dexter and from there to Lake Arthur. This project, in its early days,
was a failure.

With Charles B. Eddy eliminated from the development enterprises, James John Hagerman undertook the role of promoter, determined to have a line of railroad built from Roswell to Amarillo. He
began active promotion of the railroad extension in 1895 and went
to New York to begin the financing. At the start, Hagerman believed
that he could easily persuade either the Santa Fe or the Rock Island
to assist in providing the money for the enterprise. But times were
hard. Bankers frowned on railroad extensions of any kind, at any
place, and particularly so on any contemplated railroad project in the

Territory of New Mexico. Hagerman spent month after month in New York, interviewing capitalists and bankers, railroad presidents and directors, many of them his personal friends. In the course of his rounds promoting his contemplated railroad, Hagerman was surprised to learn that his old friend, Charles B. Eddy, who had induced him to become interested in the Pecos River projects, was also in New York, attempting to interest the Chicago, Rock Island and Pacific Railroad Company to extend its railway line from Liberal, Kansas, to Santa Rosa, New Mexico, and to help him finance the building of a railroad from El Paso, Texas, to White Oaks, New Mexico. Former friends, now promoting rival railroad projects, Hagerman and Eddy became bitter enemies. Hagerman believed that because he had been the first to try and interest the Rock Island people in his project that it was unfair and unethical for Eddy to promote a rival enterprise through the same source.

In the middle nineties, Hagerman was at times even pinched for pocket money. He had sustained serious losses in the Pecos River projects. His silver mining investments were greatly reduced in value. His cash resources were lower than they had been since he had been a young man just starting out in life. On more than one occasion, while stopping at a hotel in New York City, promoting his Roswell to Amarillo railroad project, Hagerman found himself without enough money to pay his bill. It was the custom of the hotel not to present his bill until he was checking out. Hagerman was obliged, at times, to remain at the hotel for several weeks longer than he had intended, too much embarrassed to ask the hotel for credit, or his friends for a loan. It was during one of these visits to New York that Hagerman spoke his mind in writing a letter to Charles B. Eddy. After reciting the things that Eddy had been doing and the things that in Hagerman's opinion he should not have done, Hagerman ended his letter to Eddy with the words: "Now, we should have peace between us, until this promotion is ended. Our attitude is hurting New Mexico and I make you this proposition. If you will quit lying about me, I will quit telling the truth about you.[16]

---

16. Charles B. Eddy was successful in promoting his railroad projects. With C. D. Simpson and other associates, Eddy began in 1897 construction of the El Paso and Northeastern Railroad from El Paso. Eventually the line was extended through Alamogordo and Carrizozo to Santa Rosa. On December 25, 1901, the Chicago, Rock Island and Pacific Railroad finished a line to Santa Rosa from Liberal, Kansas, crossing

Hagerman's task in undertaking the promotion of the Roswell to Amarillo railroad was the hardest and most humiliating that he had ever faced. He dragged himself with a heavy heart from one possible source of financial help for his project to another, always feeling that there would be only discouragement and refusal at the end of the interview. On January 3, 1898, just when he had almost reached the conclusion that no financial institution would back his project, Hagerman, who was in New York, received the joyful news that $2,000,-000 would be made available for his venture. Hagerman at once notified John W. Poe in Roswell that the financing had been completed.

The Pecos Valley Railway Company, with its line from Pecos, Texas, to Roswell, was reorganized and the Pecos Valley and Northeastern Railway Company was incorporated, designed to own and operate the entire line from Pecos to Amarillo, a distance of 372 miles. Hundreds of men and teams were put to work. Hagerman was happy again. The construction work was started in May, 1898, and the road was finished into Amarillo in February, 1899. The Pecos Valley country boomed. Hundreds of homeseekers fought for land and established farms. The Pecos Valley became the garden spot of New Mexico.

James John Hagerman sold his home in Colorado Springs and took up his residence in Roswell, New Mexico, in 1900. He acquired the John S. Chisum ranch property of some 6,000 acres, built a handsome home not far from the old Chisum headquarters ranch house and planted an apple orchard of more than six hundred acres. He purchased land script at $1.25 per acre and placed it upon over 200,000 acres of land lying east of Roswell, extending to a point about due east of Elkins, New Mexico, and south to a point east of Hager-

over the Pecos River at Santa Rosa, to make a junction with the Eddy line from El Paso. Charles B. Eddy had, through master salesmanship, induced the Rock Island people to accept his railroad plan as against the plan of James John Hagerman. The Rock Island spent approximately twelve million dollars on the Eddy proposal. The Santa Fe Railroad acquired the railway line from Pecos, Texas, to Amarillo in 1900, through negotiations conducted by Hagerman. The contention of Charles B. Eddy that the Pecos to Amarillo road would not pay its way was sustained during many years of its operation. For some months in each year, its gross earnings did not exceed $25,000, not sufficient to pay operating expenses. Time and events were on Hagerman's side, however, because since the discovery of oil and potash near Carlsbad, the Pecos to Amarillo line is the best paying branch on the entire Santa Fe system.

man. After moving to Roswell, and with the Pecos and Amarillo railroad completed, Hagerman felt that the time had come when he should get out of the railroad business. More than ten years before he had sold the Colorado Midland Railroad to the Atchison, Topeka & Santa Fe. He began negotiations with the officials of that company looking to the sale of the line through the Pecos Valley and on into Amarillo. After months of negotiating, the Santa Fe agreed to buy the road, gave the stockholders a fair price for their holdings and assumed the bonded debt. Hagerman was now free to devote his time and attention to the work of salvaging from the wreck of his own personal fortune such items as he could, represented by equities in various Pecos Valley projects. When the Pecos Irrigation and Improvement Company was forced into receivership in July 1898, James John Hagerman was by far the largest creditor. In the proceedings subsequent to receivership, he accepted the Northern Canal and other property in Chaves County for his equity and in lieu of his claims for money advanced; and the other creditors accepted the Eddy County properties. Subsequent to 1900, Hagerman spent several years developing and marketing the properties he had acquired through the receivership and by purchase. Eventually the Northern Canal was sold to the Hagerman Irrigation Company, a concern organized by the water users of that district; and sales were effected of most of the lands acquired near Hagerman, Dexter and Roswell, with the exception of the old Chisum place.*

The Chisum place, haunted at night by the ghost of old John S. Chisum himself because it was the favorite of all his ranches up and down the Pecos River when he was the cattle king of New Mexico, was conveyed to the South Spring Ranch and Cattle Company, a

---

* To quote from a letter received by the author from the late Percy Hagerman of Colorado Springs, son of James John Hagerman, on August 7, 1945:

"Many of the characters of whom you speak in your book, *The Fabulous Frontier*, were well known to me, my father first of all, C. B. Eddy, Pat Garrett, W. A. Hawkins, Capt. Poe, Capt. Lea and many others. I think you have shown them all in their true light with a real historical spirit. Naturally I was particularly interested in what you said abont my father who was of a very different type from those who preceded him in Lincoln County and of most of his contemporaries during the years when he spent most of his time and the greater part of his money in that country. It goes without saying that I have often regretted that he ever saw the Pecos Valley, and yet when one contemplates the final result of his efforts there, one must admit that they resulted in much good for the valley and for New Mexico at large. You have done well in bring-

Hagerman-owned corporation. On the old Chisum place, in the attractive countryside, James John Hagerman spent the last few years of his life in comparative quiet. His days of feverish efforts at promotion were over. His squabbles with Charles B. Eddy were a thing of the past. He had personally invested in the Pecos River projects two and a half million dollars more than he ever expected to get out of them.

There were some murmurs of criticism and discontent up and down the valley when he sold the Pecos to Amarillo line of railway to what critics referred to as a "soulless corporation." But Hagerman only smiled, for deep down in his heart he felt that no person alive knew the half of the torment he had suffered and the grief that he had been obliged to endure in his efforts to bring about the development of the Pecos Valley country. Here on the old Chisum place, with memories of the old cattle king all about, Hagerman found time to wander along paths among the shade trees; and to browse in his great library, with its many beautifully bound volumes, reading and studying about Napoleon Bonaparte, his lifelong hobby. While a resident of Colorado Springs, James John Hagerman had been generous to Colorado College. He had made substantial cash donations in money and had paid the bills for the construction of two substantial buildings. His fortune depleted, Hagerman was generous to the extent of his ability, with the town of Roswell, now his home. He donated the land upon which the first unit of the New Mexico Military Institute is situated. He assumed leadership and worked hard in the campaign to obtain a Carnegie Library for Roswell.

Hagerman was happy when he learned on January 10, 1906, that his son, Herbert J. Hagerman, had been appointed governor of New Mexico upon recommendation of Ethan Allen Hitchcock, Secretary

---

ing out the fact that he was a straight shooter and never tried to do anything on other people's money more than on his own. As I look back on a rather long life in which I have come in contact with a great many businessmen and promoters of all sorts and descriptions, I believe that in this respect he was the straightest shooter I have ever known. Your picture of C. B. Eddy is a just one. He possessed a hypnotic power which he exercised on others and on himself as well, and I believe he had absolute faith in his visions and had an uncanny ability to make others believe in them. He was an extraordinary character and the picture you show of him exhibits this truly Svengali nature even more than I remembered it."

of the Interior, under whom young Hagerman had served as Secretary of Embassy when Hitchcock was Ambassador to Russia.[17]

James John Hagerman was saddened not long after the inauguration of Governor Hagerman, when political pirates and buccaneers of the Territory conspired to have his son Herbert removed from office. The plot to remove the Governor revolved around the execution and delivery of deeds for territorial timber lands with which Governor Hagerman had little or nothing to do. He had followed the routine of the office and the opinion of the Attorney General of the Territory. Governor Hagerman went to Washington and tried to explain the transactions and the ramifications of the political plot to President Roosevelt. But crafty territorial politicians had seen to it that the President had been heavily inoculated with a dose of "practical politics." The President grudgingly gave young Hagerman an interview in the White House. The Governor expected to do some of the talking. Impatient and angry, the President refused to listen to any explanation, lectured young Hagerman and demanded his resignation, which Hagerman wrote out on April 22, 1907. Roosevelt accepted it by letter dated April 29, 1907. Learning of his son's difficulties with Roosevelt, James John Hagerman telegraphed to his long time personal friend, Elihu Root, Secretary of State, asking that Roosevelt be asked to defer action until a clearer understanding could be developed of the facts and background of the political aspects of the case. Roosevelt promptly wrote a "Rough Rider" letter of thousands of words to Governor Hagerman, dated May 1, 1907. Obviously intended for the press, the letter was a condemnation of the timber deed transactions, a lecture to young Hagerman on certain phases of political science, and an eulogy of George Curry, already chosen as the new governor of the Territory. The final paragraph of the letter, eulogizing George Curry, is as follows:

> No one suggested to me the appointment of Captain Curry as your successor. The idea was my own, because I wished, under the extraordinary circumstances in New Mexico, to find some man whom I knew personally and in whose uprightness, strength of character and knowledge of the people and circumstances I could have entire confidence. Captain Curry was one of the best men in my regiment. He has been away from New Mexico for eight years,

---

17. See *Letters of a Young Diplomat*, H. J. Hagerman, Rydal Press, Santa Fe, 1937.

so that he is in no shape or way identified with any factional trouble therein. I do not even know his politics. During these eight years he has done distinguished military and civil service in the Philippines, not only having shown great gallantry in action, but marked administrative ability when in charge of the Manila police force and afterwards in various other positions, including that of Governor of the provinces. As far as I know, there has been universal approval in New Mexico of his choice; and approval of the choice of Captain Curry as Governor is incompatible with the existence on the part of those approving it of either the hope or the desire to see crooked methods obtain in the New Mexican government.[18]

Fortune had smiled on James John Hagerman in Wisconsin, Michigan and Colorado. He had lost his millions in New Mexico and had endured the humiliation of witnessing his son removed from the governorship of the Territory by Theodore Roosevelt, whom he had always considered a personal friend, on charges that were technical, complicated and shot through and through with political intrigue. But James John Hagerman accepted and endured the touches of adversity with patience and fortitude.

A public spirited man, interested in charitable and educational enterprises, Hagerman had never identified himself with dogmatic religion or sectarianism. He had a strong and enduring faith in a Supreme Being, little sympathy or understanding of the man who paraded his virtues and publicized his charities. Hagerman's old friends never appealed to him in distress without a prompt and generous response.

In the summer of 1909, he and Anna Osborne Hagerman, his wife, left for Europe to travel and to rest. On September 15, 1909, at Milan, Italy in the arms of his beloved wife, James John Hagerman died suddenly of a stroke of apoplexy. His body was brought home and buried in Milwaukee, place of residence in early manhood and scene of many successful ventures; far away from the banks of the Pecos River, the scene of his defeat and despair. The man who had

---

18. For a full explanation of the controversy between Herbert J. Hagerman, the New Mexico old guard Republican politicians and Theodore Roosevelt, from Hagerman's viewpoint, see *Matters Relating to the Administration and Removal of Herbert J. Hagerman, Governor of New Mexico, 1906-1907* privately printed at Roswell, November 1, 1908.

done more, single-handed, for New Mexico than any other man, although he owed it nothing and it gave him little in return, was at rest. James John Hagerman knew nothing of six-shooters, or of yearling steers, or of cow camps or trails up and down the Pecos River. He had taken the dreams of Pat Garrett, Charles B. Eddy and many other Pecos River personalities and by intelligence, force of character and determination, had translated them into actualities.

eight

ALBERT BACON FALL

FOR MANY YEARS in Territorial days and subsequent to statehood, there was no town, village or hamlet in southeastern New Mexico in which the name and fame of Albert Bacon Fall were unknown. There was no ranch house from the Rio Grande to the Pecos, but where he would have been welcomed with open hand and genuine western hospitality. In all southeast New Mexico Fall never closed a door behind him that he could not reopen. He was offered wine where most men would not be asked to take a sip of water. An outstanding character in New Mexico for decades, Albert Bacon Fall still lived on as the autumn leaves of 1944 fluttered to the ground, a prelude to the cold and snows of winter. It was winter time of life for Albert Bacon Fall. He spent as much time as was possible in the New Mexico that he had loved for so long, with occasional stays in El Paso, Texas, where he enjoyed for many years a position of outstanding influence and prestige as a leader of men. An invalid for years before his death, journeying from hospital to hospital for medical treatment, Albert Bacon Fall paid the penalty of leadership, paid his debt to society, waited patiently for the glad tomorrow, conscious that in his day and time he had given generously of his ability and energy to the upbuilding of his state and nation. Some things in his career in the days when, standing at the summit of national eminence, he leaped the heights that were meant to be climbed, could perhaps best be blotted out. Time, the great healer, may yet soften the judgment of many and reverse the verdict of man-made courts before the bar of which Albert Bacon Fall was obliged to appear in the days of his adversity. He died in Hotel Dieu Hospital in El Paso, Texas, at 4:30 P.M., on November 30, 1944, just a few days after his 83rd birthday. Death came peacefully. Propped up in bed, he had been reading a newspaper. The paper fluttered from tired hands, fell to the floor. The earthly career of a nationally known figure was at an end. Judge Fall found comfort in the last months of his life by thinking that he had been vindicated by the events of the war with Japan in his policy to draw vast stores of oil from United States Naval reserves on the mainland and transport them to storage tanks at Pearl Harbor.[1]

Born in Frankfort, Kentucky on November 21, 1861, Albert Bacon Fall came to New Mexico in 1883 at the age of twenty-two years. In less than thirty years after his arrival in the Territory, Fall achieved the height of his early-day ambition, a seat in the United States Senate. Fall's boyhood was spent in Kentucky in the atmosphere and tempo of the years immediately following the Civil War. His formal education was limited, but he received instruction from his school-teacher father, Captain William R. Fall, who had served in the Confederate Army throughout the war between the States. In his youth, Fall was inclined toward the ministry, but deciding to become a lawyer, he studied law in Frankfort in the office of Judge William Lindsley, later United States Senator from Kentucky.

Failing health obliged Fall to leave his native state and he struck out on his own for the west. First in Indian Territory and then in West Texas, Fall worked on cattle and sheep ranches. In his travels in a country that was typical of the far western frontier, he met up with good men and bad men of the day. Employed as a cowboy and chuckwagon cook on a ranch on the Conchas River in Texas, Fall was introduced to Miss Emma Morgan, a Texas born schoolteacher, at the time engaged to marry a young Texan. With the energy, elo-

---

1. Fall was baptized a Roman Catholic during 1935, following instruction in that faith by Rev. Albert Braun, a friend on the Mescalero Indian reservation, and Rev. David J. Kirgan of El Paso. Father Kirgan conducted the funeral services on December 3, 1944, at the Fall residence, 1725 Arizona Street, El Paso, with burial in Evergreen Cemetery. The writer visited Judge Fall at Beaumont Hospital, Fort Bliss, Texas, on November 6, 1937, talked with him about old times in New Mexico and left the hospital believing that Fall had but a few months to live, a belief shared by Mrs. Fall at the time. Mrs. Fall died on March 25, 1943, after a valiant fight carried on for years for the restoration of her husband's good name and for recovery of at least a part of his property.

After having read every available item relating to the Fall case, the writer long since reached the conclusion that the testimony submitted in the various trials had not proved him guilty of wrongdoing "beyond a reasonable doubt" in connection with the Teapot Dome–Elk Hill–Doheny or Sinclair incidents. As indicated by William Allen

quence and persuasiveness that later characterized his life in New Mexico, young Fall prevailed upon Miss Morgan to forget about the Texan she had promised to marry and to become his wife. They were married in Texas in 1883 and moved the same year to Kingston, New Mexico, then a thriving mining camp. Fall spent some time around Kingston, prospecting for gold and silver. For a brief time he worked with hammer and drill in the famous Bridal Chamber mine, which produced from pockets more than 2,500,000 ounces of silver within a few years.

A mining shanty town with a real wild west atmosphere, Kingston offered the kind of life that Fall liked. He met there a number of men who were in later years important and significant in his life, among them Edward L. Doheny, a fellow miner, who hoped to make a fortune in the gold and silver ore in the hills and mountains of the district. Fall was one day an eyewitness to a shooting affair in which Doheny was an unwilling participant. Fall saw Doheny dodge in and out doors on Kingston's main street, seeking refuge from a drunken miner who had run amuck. The drunk was taking potshots at Doheny with a six-shooter. Fall was interested to observe the coolness with which Doheny held his fire, dodging bullets in the meantime intended to take his life. At an appropriate intermission, Doheny took his forty-five from its holster and aiming low, shot the miner in the leg to avoid a fatality. Nerve and courage of the kind exhibited by Doheny pleased Fall. He was one of the first in Kingston camp to congratulate Doheny on his composure and marksmanship.[2]

White of Emporia in *A Puritan in Babylon*, Fall had probably been induced to cadge funds to be used in paying off national Republican committee campaign debts. Fall apparently made the mistake of carrying on at the same time negotiations for a loan from his friend, Edward L. Doheny, something readily understandable by old-timers in New Mexico, and by those who knew Fall intimately. Fall's handling of the business relating to the Doheny loan was careless and inept. The negotiations with Doheny might just as well have been carried on and brought to a conclusion in open and above board transactions, without any necessity for a "black satchel." A note and mortgage on the Fall ranch could have been executed and the mortgage recorded immediately in Otero County, New Mexico. The hundred thousand dollar mortgage money might just as well have been paid over the counter of the best known bank in America. Fall picked an unfortunate time to negotiate the Doheny loan. Subsequent events in the arena of national politics required a defendant. Circumstances pointed to Fall. He was selected to play the leading role in the tragedy of trials and tribulations that ensued.

2. Edward Lawrence Doheny was born in Fond du Lac, Wisconsin, August 10, 1856, and died in Los Angeles, California, September 8, 1935. Doheny went west in

It was in Kingston in those early days that Albert Bacon Fall became acquainted with Frank W. Parker, a scholarly-looking young lawyer, recently from Michigan, later to become a judge of the New Mexico territorial district and supreme court. Fall years later directed his fire in an impassioned accusation against Parker when he was the trial judge at Hillsboro in the famous case of the Territory against Oliver M. Lee, accused of the murder of Col. Albert J. Fountain and his little son, Henry.

If fate had been kind in throwing the dice, Albert Bacon Fall would never have been permitted to go to Kingston, New Mexico, or to strike up a friendship with Edward L. Doheny. The Doheny of Kingston days was the same Edward L. Doheny who had dealings of one sort or another with Albert Bacon Fall, Secretary of the Interior of the United States of America during the Warren G. Harding administration.

But it is not so much of national politics, or of the days when Albert Bacon Fall had become a significant figure in Washington that are of concern here, but the early days of Albert Bacon Fall when he was young and handsome and fearless and a fighter, a political buccaneer perhaps, for in the late eighties and early nineties in New Mexico, the game of politics was played for keeps.

Concluding that Kingston was destined eventually to become a ghost mining camp, an observation confirmed in later years, and convinced that mining was for the most part a slow and tedious business, Albert Bacon Fall decided to go to Las Cruces in neighboring Doña Ana County and take up the law, the profession for which he had fitted himself in Kentucky.

Pleasantly situated on the Rio Grande, not far from the Mexican border, Las Cruces was the county seat of one of the ancient counties of the Territory, the key town in a large area of surrounding country,

---

his teens and as a young man spent twenty years prospecting for gold and silver. When nearly forty-five years of age Doheny switched from his search for precious metals and prospected for oil. One of the pioneers in oil development near Los Angeles and Bakersfield in California, Doheny extended his oil activities to the Tampico Field in Mexico and achieved fame and fortune in the industry. Doheny never forgot his pals of New Mexico mining days. Many of them called on him for help in Los Angeles. He never asked but one question: "How much money do you need at present?" and always complied with any reasonable request for assistance. Doheny's chance meeting with Fall in early day Kingston proved to be of vast significance in the trend of his life in later years.

peopled by miners, cowboys and ranchers. Among lawyers it was soon recognized that Fall was not a profound student of the law or a "book lawyer," but they all agreed that he was a fighting advocate. A lawyer who would go into court and do battle was the kind of a lawyer that the folks in the back country demanded. When Albert Bacon Fall went to Las Cruces he had little or no money, no close friends and only a few acquaintances. However, he had courage, an attractive personality, a world of confidence in himself and a high esteem of his own ability. He soon was known as a fearless man and in the eyes of many people he soon became a hero.

A fervent Democrat, Fall began to take part, soon after his arrival in Las Cruces, in the political affairs of Doña Ana County. Within a few years he was an outstanding figure in the politics of southeastern New Mexico. As his political stature and influence enlarged and extended, he became a recognized leader in the Territory. Fall's entrance into the political field on the Democratic side was hailed with rejoicing by the Democrats in politically-minded Doña Ana County. Republicans were not particularly glum, because Doña Ana County was safely in the Republican column. The Republicans rather welcomed Fall into the political arena. They recognized him as a fighter and took delight in annoying him to see him charge and challenge.

The dominant political leader of Fall's early days in New Mexico was Thomas B. Catron. For a generation Tom Catron, through his "Santa Fe Ring," had been the acknowledged leader of the Republican party in the Territory. The "Ring" was rather a vague and shadowy organization; its personnel varied in different parts of New Mexico, but Tom Catron cracked the whip in all the rings wherever they might be located. Political battles in Doña Ana County in early days involved local offices, the sheriff, assessor, treasurer, probate judge, representatives in the Territorial Legislature, and a lone delegate in Congress from New Mexico. The battles were fought out, however, on lines that were tensely drawn to the accompaniment of much oratory, frequently complicated by personal enmities, sometimes enlivened by hand-to-hand fighting. Albert Bacon Fall was always eager to be a participant in the political battles, great and small. Sometimes by daring tactics, he succeeded in bluffing political enemies, thus bolstering up the courage of his Democratic colleagues.

President Grover Cleveland appointed Albert Bacon Fall on March 21, 1893, to the office of associate justice for the Third Judicial

District of New Mexico. Fall accepted the appointment, but did not care particularly for the title of "Judge" that accompanied it, or the duties required of a member of the judiciary. Judge Fall served on the bench, holding sessions of court in Las Cruces, in Lincoln and occasionally in other county seats by invitation of other judges. He went dutifully to Santa Fe, the capital, to confer with judges of the district court, who sat once or twice a year as an appellate court, and wrote a few opinions of no great significance. However, Fall was by nature and inclination too much of the advocate, too much of the trial lawyer.[3]

Fall resigned from the bench on February 1, 1895, and returned to the practice of law in Las Cruces and to the hurly-burly of political life. In 1897 and again in 1907 Fall served briefly as Attorney General of New Mexico. Each time he was impatient because of the routine of office and irked by its duties. During his early day residence in Las Cruces, Albert Bacon Fall financed a small weekly newspaper, *The Independent Democrat*, ostensibly owned and published by his father, Capt. W. R. Fall. The newspaper gave Fall an opportunity to write an occasional editorial, blasting the Republicans for their sins of omission and commission.

Albert Bacon Fall, lawyer, and Oliver M. Lee, young ranchman, became casually acquainted and their acquaintance developed into a sincere lifelong friendship. Oliver Lee entered Fall's office in Las Cruces one day in 1889 and introduced himself. A fine-looking young man, of good personality, Oliver Lee spent his spare time on the range studying Greek and Latin. He made a splendid impression on Albert Bacon Fall. Fall had heard that Oliver Lee was a dead shot

---

3. In a speech in the United States Senate on May 15, 1912, Albert Bacon Fall referred briefly to his career on the bench. Fall's speech was a castigation of the United States Forest Service and all that it stood for. He made mention of the withdrawals of public domain by President Theodore Roosevelt, which Fall criticized, although professing great admiration for T. R. Fall then blamed Grover Cleveland for inaugurating a policy of "hounding" settlers on the public domain through the Department of the Interior and of withdrawing public domain for forest reserves. Senator Hitchcock twitted Fall saying: "Possibly the Senator from New Mexico will be able to reconcile his great admiration for the ex-president, Theodore Roosevelt with his strong criticism of probably his strongest and most dominant policy." Senator Chamberlain then entered the debate and said: "I do not want to be understood as criticizing Mr. Cleveland or anyone else for the creation of these reserves. I approve them. But while the conditions were so bad in New Mexico, at the time the Senator suggests, I believe he was a part of the Cleveland administration." Fall then absolved himself by saying: "During the

with pistol and rifle, cool and collected in an emergency. Lee knew that Fall was a man of ability and courage. He had been impressed by reports in the range country that Fall had no fear of Tom Catron and his "Santa Fe Ring." In the early months of their acquaintance, Fall told Oliver Lee of his desire to break up the political ring of the Republican party. After they had become better acquainted, Fall confessed to Lee that his greatest ambition in life had been to be a crack shot with a gun, an ambition which he never realized. As their acquaintance ripened into friendship, Fall and Lee came to depend on each other more and more. Threats had been made against Fall's life on many occasions and he needed the assistance of a man who could be depended upon to shoot quickly and effectively. Efforts were being made to diminish Oliver Lee's freedom and independence on the range. He feared unjust accusations and needed a lawyer of nerve and resourcefulness who would come to his aid in an emergency. Both men loved horses and liked cattle. Both loved the open range. The arrangement between Fall and Lee became one in which Fall looked after Lee in courthouse matters, and Lee looked after Fall on the outside.

In the early nineties, in opposition to the regular Republican organization candidates, Fall sponsored in Las Cruces a fusion town ticket composed of Democrats and "citizens." Fall learned that the Republicans had arranged to have the militia called out on election day, ostensibly to preserve order at the polls, but actually, Fall believed, to intimidate honest voters, duly qualified, who wished to cast a ballot for the fusion candidates. Subsequently the Republicans claimed that Fall had brought many men into Las Cruces on election day from outside precincts and voted them at the polls, who were not even citizens of the United States.

Warned in advance that the militia was to be on hand on election day "to preserve the peace," Albert Bacon Fall sent word out on the range to Oliver M. Lee to start at once for town with a half-dozen cowboys. Lee and his cowboys rode all night, arrived in Las Cruces

---

second administration of Mr. Cleveland I was appointed on the bench of New Mexico. If the Senator wants personalities interjected into the debate, I will state that, without my asking for the appointment, but upon the request of certain citizens of New Mexico, Mr. Cleveland did appoint me, without my knowledge, and I resigned just as soon as I could get out of it." See speech of Senator Fall on appropriation bill, U. S. Forest Service, May 15, 1912.

by daylight. They stationed themselves on the roof of Martin Loh-
man's adobe building, opposite the polling place in the old Masonic
Temple. With Winchester rifle in hand, Oliver Lee was in readiness
on the rooftop when the polls were opened for election. Maj. William H. H. Llewellyn and Capt. Thomas Branigan with a company
of New Mexico Territorial militia soon marched up the street and
halted nearby the polling place.

Albert Bacon Fall at once appeared near the election booth, cursed
and damned for a moment and then yelled at Major Llewellyn:
"Llewellyn, get the hell out of here with that dam'd militia inside
of two minutes, or I will have you all killed." Fall pointed toward
the roof of the building where Oliver Lee and his cowboys were
standing by for instructions. Llewellyn and Branigan issued the
necessary orders. The militiamen dispersed. When the polls were
closed in the evening and Fall's crowd had won the election, Oliver
Lee and his men went back to the ranch country. By his participation
in the events of the day, Oliver Lee had made enemies of Llewellyn
and Branigan. Both of these men went with investigating parties
some time later when Colonel Fountain and his son Henry disappeared, presumably murdered. Both of them signed affidavits expressing the belief that Oliver Lee and others had killed the Fountains.
Both of them testified as prosecuting witnesses at Lee's trial for murder at Hillsboro.

Ben Williams, a tough fighter and a good shot of the old days,
made his home in Las Cruces in the early nineties. When Numa
Raymond, with no time or liking for the place, was elected sheriff
of the county, he made Williams his chief deputy. Ben Williams
had served as a United States deputy marshal and had been employed
as an agent for the Singer Sewing Machine Company at a time in
New Mexico when a man had to be a gunman to enforce collections
and undertake repossession of machines sold on the installment
plan. Williams also had been a precinct constable and a detective
for the Southeastern New Mexico Cattle Association. Many years
later the Atchison, Topeka & Santa Fe Railway employed him as
chief in its secret service department, with headquarters in
Albuquerque.

On September 15, 1895, at 10 o'clock at night, Ben Williams was
walking toward home along the main street of Las Cruces. Judge

Albert Bacon Fall appeared on the street accompanied by his brother-in-law, Joseph Morgan, then a United States deputy marshal. Without the exchange of a word by any of the participants, the shooting began. Standing behind an awning post at the edge of the sidewalk in front of R. L. Young's law office, Joe Morgan fired at Ben Williams at close range. The bullet passed through Williams' head above and behind the ear and powder burned his face. Almost at the same instant Judge Fall took a potshot at Williams. The bullet penetrated the Constable's left arm near the elbow, injuring the bone and inflicting a serious wound. Williams recovered, but carried for the rest of his life a badly damaged arm. Williams fired two or three shots at his assailants, one of which struck Morgan in the left arm. The shooting attracted a crowd and the firing stopped. Fall and Morgan were arrested, but released on their own recognizance. Their enemies circulated reports that the shooting started because Williams had been attempting to have Morgan arrested and sent back to Texas to face an old murder charge. Fall's friends claimed that Ben Williams had started the shooting at the instigation of Republican politicans who wanted Fall killed.

Fall himself said the shooting had no political significance; that he had seen Williams coming along the street and suddenly decided to take a shot at him; that he didn't like Williams anyway and that the dislike had recently been intensified because Williams had shot and dangerously wounded a sheepherder from Mexico without just cause. The grand jury of Doña Ana County was convened in special session and heard many witnesses testify about the shooting affray. Instead of indicting Fall or Morgan, the jurors indicted Ben Williams as principal and Albert J. Fountain as accessory before the fact. Democrats pointed out that the grand jury was composed of eleven Republicans and ten Democrats.

During the campaign of 1895, Albert Bacon Fall made his last stand as a fighting champion of the Democratic party in New Mexico. The fight had been unusually bitter in Doña Ana County. The Democrats had been enough interested in the outcome of a close contest to station "a committee" on horseback near San Augustin Pass. The "committee" intercepted a messenger carrying the ballot box from Tularosa to the courthouse at Las Cruces. The "committee" burned the ballot box and its contents. In the election contest that followed, witnesses proved that the Republican candidates had received a majority of the ballots cast at Tularosa on election day. The canvassers decided that if the Tularosa votes had been counted, the Republican county candidates would have been elected. Certificates of election were issued in conformity with this decision. Fall was present as usual at the contest, in a fighting mood, representing the Democrats. His ever loyal brother-in-law, Joseph Morgan, was at his side. Both Fall and Morgan wore guns and cartridge belts. Albert J. Fountain, destined soon to be lost forever in the White Sands, represented the Republicans and he had his gun and plenty of ammunition. Fall made every possible technical objection in the contest proceedings to the introduction of unfavorable testimony. Speaking sometimes in English and sometimes in Spanish, Fountain suavely made up the record for his side. Several times during the proceedings, Democrat and Republican watchers alike reached for their guns to settle things quickly, but no shots were fired.

Soon after the election of 1900, Albert Bacon Fall announced his retirement as a Democrat and his affiliation with the Republican party. Democrats were disheartened and discouraged when Fall dropped out of their ranks. They had honored Fall with leadership of the party in his part of the Territory. Under the Democratic banner he had been elected to the Legislature and had been appointed a judge on the bench, had served as Attorney General. From Fall's viewpoint, he realized that for years to come in New Mexico the Republican party would be dominant. Fall believed that New Mexico would soon be admitted to the Union. He was ambitious to go to the United States Senate. Attempting to justify his apostasy, Fall gave as his reason for leaving his party, a disinclination to follow the national leadership of William Jennings Bryan. Bryan's theories of free and unlimited coinage of silver and his ratio of 16 to 1 offered Albert Bacon Fall an opportunity to resign, as a matter of principle, from the party to which he had given his loyalty and allegiance for so many years. Fall denied that his failure to be nominated for Delegate-in-Congress by the Democratic territorial convention in 1900 was the reason for his resignation from the party, although admitting that he had been willing to accept the nomination.

The Republicans of New Mexico were not overly enthusiastic about Fall's announced conversion to the principles of their party.

Republican leaders soon learned that to some extent at least, Albert
Bacon Fall was, as some Democratic leaders had contended, selfish,
intolerant and egotistical. Fall's identification with the Republican
party soon became an accepted fact. Democrats and Republicans
alike reformed their lines accordingly.

With the outbreak of the Spanish-American War, Albert Bacon
Fall announced that he had offered his services to Governor Miguel
A. Otero in the organization of fifty sharpshooters to be attached
to troops being raised to fight Spain, the "sharpshooters to act in an
independent capacity" and to be headed by the originator of the
plan, Albert Bacon Fall. Governor Otero declined the offer, but
gave Fall a commission as captain in Company "H," First New
Mexico Territorial Regiment. He went south with his company,
but by chance did not get to see service in Cuba, or to strike up
a friendship with Theodore Roosevelt as was the good fortune of
George Curry, Maj. W. H. H. Llewellyn and dozens of other Rough
Riders from southeastern New Mexico and elsewhere in the Territory. After the war, Fall assumed a place of importance in the affairs
of the Republican party in New Mexico. He was elected a member
of the Territorial Council in 1903 and was the orator of the day on
the occasion of the inauguration of George Curry as Governor of
the Territory on August 8, 1907, and served for a brief time as Attorney General during the Curry administration. Now identified
with everything that for many years, as a Democrat, he had criticized
in the Republican party, Fall became a gadfly in the Republican
organization. Many an ambitious Republican leader in New Mexico
saw Fall, a renegade Democrat, as the shadow standing between
him and a seat in the United States Senate.

Growing steadily in stature, knowledge and influence, Albert
Bacon Fall became more and more an outstanding figure in New
Mexico. He became widely known in West Texas and in Old Mexico. Establishing a law office in El Paso, Texas, Judge Fall was prominently identified with many of the more important enterprises of
the Southwest. Almost his entire time was devoted to clients interested in railroads, mines and timber. Although living in a fine home
in El Paso, Texas, he never relinquished his legal residence in New
Mexico. Money that Fall earned in Texas and Old Mexico that did
not go into political channels was used to expand and improve his
Tres Ritos horse and cattle ranch, in southeastern New Mexico,

estimated at one time to contain hundreds of thousands of acres of land.[4]

In the years of his maturity Albert Bacon Fall was a distinguished-looking man. He wore his naturally curly hair long, sometimes reaching almost to his shoulders in the style of Kentucky statesmen in Fall's youth. He preferred to wear a black Stetson fedora type cowboy hat. Substantially built, tall and dignified, with impressive personality, commanding voice, puffing away at a cigar, carrying a cane on his arm with the ever-present possibility that he might use it vigorously if occasion required, Albert Bacon Fall was a leader to be feared and respected. Brushing aside obstacles that would have dismayed most men, Fall, by sheer bluff and personality, dominated many a Republican caucus and convention in New Mexico and for years occupied a post of preeminence in the innermost councils of the party.

Fall's attitude toward men and his ability and daring were never better demonstrated than at Albuquerque on the occasion of the visit there of William Howard Taft, President of the United States, on October 15, 1909. President Taft crossed the Arizona–New Mexico territorial line on that day, en route to Texas from California and the far west. The President's special train was returning from a swing around western and northwestern states. President Taft's visit to New Mexico was an event of major importance to the politicians of the Territory, regardless of party affiliation. They boarded his Santa Fe railway special train at Gallup, New Mexico, kept him in tow in Albuquerque, traveled with him to El Paso, Texas, and to the edge of Juarez, Mexico, where Taft exchanged formalities on the international bridge with President Porfirio Diaz of the Republic

---

4. Albert Bacon Fall became financially interested in cattle raising and ranching in 1907, when he acquired the Pat Coghlan ranch of about 103,000 acres in the Three Rivers country. The ranch extended from El Paso and Northeastern right-of-way on the west to the Mescalero Indian reservation on the east, and from south of the I Bar X on the north to within three miles of Tularosa Creek on the south. Coghlan, old time Tularosa merchant, got into the cattle business by buying Joe Wingfield's ranch and Bar KL cattle. Wingfield had bought the Bud Smith holdings. Bud Smith had owned the Plus outfit, later managed the SLS for George D. Barber and Susie McSween Barber. Mrs. Barber, widow of A. A. McSween, killed in the Lincoln County War, was for many years known as "the cattle queen of New Mexico." The "Rock House," a landmark on Three Rivers, was headquarters for Mrs. Barber's outfit. Judge Fall purchased the Coghlan ranch from Numa Raymond of Las Cruces, who had obtained a deed to it on a mortgage foreclosure. Fall's position in the Three Rivers

of Mexico. Statehood for New Mexico was uppermost in the minds of its political leaders in 1909. Visions of a seat in the United States Senate lured men of both parties on to greater efforts for New Mexico's admission into the Union.

Leaving Gallup, New Mexico, early on the morning of October 15, 1909, the Presidential train stopped at the Pueblo of Laguna, where Taft was greeted by Laguna and Acoma Indians. At Isleta Pueblo, thirteen miles south of Albuquerque, the President held a brief reception for the Indians there. En route from Gallup to Albuquerque, Florence E. Sullivan, a newspaper writer of Chicago on the staff of the Chicago *Journal*, temporarily a resident of Albuquerque, presented all the newspaper correspondents on the train with Navajo blankets, gifts of the Commercial Club of Albuquerque. In Albuquerque the President was given a horsehair bridle, woven for him by a craftsman of great skill.

The program in Albuquerque for the reception to President Taft had been prepared and rehearsed, carefully and religiously, for weeks in advance. The visit of the President, it was believed, would afford New Mexico a magnificent opportunity to deliver telling arguments for statehood.

The Alvarado Hotel in Albuquerque, the then pride of the Fred Harvey system, had made every preparation to extend unusual hospitality to President Taft. Blue point oysters were brought from the Atlantic seaboard and the finest food and drink had been procured for the banquet on the evening of October 15th. The west veranda of the hotel was enclosed to permit the placing of tables for sixty-five carefully chosen guests, selected from the most prominent men in New Mexico. Secret service men were stationed at various places in

---

was greatly strengthened in 1912 when M. P. Everhart, a son-in-law, and the Thatcher Brothers, bankers and business operators of Pueblo, Colorado, purchased the Bar W watering places south and west of Carrizozo, which controlled about 900,000 acres of land. Everhart and Thatchers brought the Hatchet cattle into the range and organized the Hatchet outfit. Soon after 1912, the Hatchet and Fall outfits merged their holdings, bringing the total area of the Hatchet ranches to one million acres, or 1,719 sections. The watering places sold by the Bar W outfit had included Brazil spring and seep and the extreme southern waters, Malpais spring on the west, 7 X well and Mound spring on the northwest, Willow springs between the Malpais and the railroad, and the lower waters of Three Rivers. After the Hatchets and Fall merged to form the Hatchet outfit, Three Rivers, Upper Willow spring, Jake's spring, Chavez spring, Venau and Vera Cruz springs, all east of the railroad, were included in the unit as additional watering places.

the hotel and on the roof during Taft's public address to the crowd that gathered in the afternoon on the lawn in front of the north approach. Santa Fe Railroad detectives, local police and bodyguards patrolled constantly, all anxious to protect the President in his every move from possible harm.

The harm to the President, however, came from an unexpected source. Speakers for the banquet had been selected with utmost care. H. O. Bursum of Socorro responded to the toast "Statehood." O. N. Marron of Albuquerque spoke eloquently on the subject, "The New Era in New Mexico." Thomas Benton Catron of Santa Fe was most effective in his speech, "The Spanish-American People." Bursum (Republican), Marron (Democrat), and Catron (Republican), were all circumspect in their remarks. They praised, eulogized, politely expressed hope of help and favor from the distinguished guest in New Mexico's long fight for statehood. Albert Bacon Fall was the last speaker. He had been chosen to make the most important talk of the evening. He was graciously introduced by Governor George Curry, long-time personal friend of Col. Theodore Roosevelt, former President of the United States. Fall's subject was "Our Guest." Taft's public speech of the afternoon, dealing with the statehood problem, had not aroused much enthusiasm among the politicians. The President had counselled patience and pointed out the necessity of spending adequate time in the preparation of a sane and conservative state constitution.

Fall's opening remarks at the banquet amazed his hearers. They had expected to hear words of praise for the President, of thanks and appreciation for his friendliness toward the cause of statehood. Albert Bacon Fall, however, had plunged at once into an "argument to the jury" type of speech in which he expressed doubt that President Taft was sincere in his purported friendliness toward New Mexico in its fight for a place in the Union of States. Step by step Fall reviewed New Mexico's fight for a star in the flag, going back to the speech of William H. Seward in the United States Senate on July 26, 1850, in which Seward had demanded that the Territory be admitted as a state. Fall recalled the many promises of statehood made by men high in the affairs of the nation and told how those promises had been broken. He specifically cited the national Republican convention of 1908 at which President Taft had been nominated and complained bitterly that the statehood plank in the Republican platform had been intentionally linked with the Gompers' anti-injunction plank for the very purpose of evading and submerging the statehood issue. The afternoon assurances of President Taft's assistance in the statehood cause, Judge Fall insinuated, had been lukewarm and were not as sincere as they might have been. The Republican leaders, who had expected Fall to make the speech of his lifetime, to create a profound and favorable impression on the President, were aghast at the tenor of the speech, dumbfounded at Fall's audacity and boldness. They were crestfallen, humiliated and embarrassed, certain that Taft would resent Fall's speech, that he would be justified in feeling that he had been insulted and would become a bitter enemy to New Mexico, not only in the statehood fight, but in all other matters affecting the Territory.

There had been no place on the program for a response from the President, but as soon as Fall had finished speaking, Taft was on his feet, plainly agitated and disturbed, "warm under the collar," as he later confided to a friend. The President made a spirited reply to Fall, cited numerous instances and examples of his friendship for New Mexico. He categorically denied that his manifestations of interest in statehood were not sincere. President Taft finished his reply to Fall's speech by telling the story of a young lawyer, who had argued his case before a judge; of how the judge had interrupted the argument from time to time to assure the young man that he agreed with him on the law. The young lawyer, however, continued to repeat and insist on his points. At the conclusion of the argument, Taft declared, the judge had said to the young advocate that, in spite of the reasons advanced to support his argument, he still agreed with him. Taft ended his reply to Fall by saying: "Judge Fall, I have heard your argument, and am for your cause in spite of it."

The banquet for President Taft, so carefully planned and arranged by the most competent managers of the two political parties, had apparently been a failure of serious proportions. As the guests filed out of the banquet hall, for many years thereafter called "Taft Hall," they looked at Judge Fall with unfriendly eyes. In controversies with his political cronies after the banquet, Fall stoutly stood his ground and defended his position. He denied that he had insulted Taft, contended that he knew the measure of the man and had adopted the right tactics to awaken Taft from his lukewarm attitude toward statehood. Fall said that he had deliberately and intentionally made

ALBERT BACON FALL IN 1912, IN THE DAYS OF GLORY AND TRIUMPH
WHEN HE WAS ELECTED TO THE UNITED STATES SENATE BY
THE NEW MEXICO LEGISLATURE.

the speech, not to offend Taft, but to provoke him into a definite admission and to compel him to adopt and follow a specific course of action. Fall's explanations received scant approval from most of his friends and associates. Most of the men who had been guests at the banquet and the public generally in New Mexico concurred in the thought that Fall had overstepped the bounds of propriety, that he had not acted with true western hospitality, that he had been discourteous to a great man, that he had offended a distinguished guest in his own home Territory, and that, politically, Fall was slated for oblivion.

The *Tribune Citizen*, a Democratic daily published in Albuquerque, commenting on the incident editorially in its issue of October 16, 1909, said:

> The spectacle of the guest of honor forced to defend himself from an attack by another guest is an unusual occurrence at a banquet in the nature of the one last night, especially when the guest of honor is the President of the United States, and the incident has caused a great deal of unfavorable comment.

The Republican politicians returned to their homes, grumbling about Fall and the unfortunate speech he had made. Democrats joined Republicans in expressing the belief that statehood for New Mexico would not be possible of achievement during the Taft administration. In this thought, however, they were all mistaken, for President William Howard Taft on June 20, 1910, signed the bill enabling New Mexico to be admitted into the Union as a state. They were also mistaken in their prediction that Fall, because of his conduct in "insulting" Taft, would be forced out of political leadership. Albert Bacon Fall on March 28, 1912, was elected by the first State Legislature of New Mexico as one of the first two members from New Mexico to the United States Senate.

The politicians were correct in their predictions that George Curry, Governor of the Territory, an appointee of former President Theodore Roosevelt, would soon find himself out of the governorship. The post of Governor of New Mexico was given on March 1, 1910, to William J. Mills of Las Vegas, a graduate of the Yale Law School in the class of 1877. Taft had been graduated from Yale University, Academic Department, June 27, 1878. Taft and Mills had been friends since their days at Yale. Taft appointed Mills on the representation and in the hope and belief that once he was Governor, Mills would establish himself politically to such an extent that immediately after statehood, he could be elected to the United States Senate by the Legislature of New Mexico. Taft proved a poor political prophet, however, because Governor Mills never came within reaching distance of the great honor which had intrigued many ambitious New Mexico men, far abler, far more adroit than he, from 1850 to 1912. In the final balloting for Senator in the first State Legislature, Governor Mills received only one vote.[5]

Judge Fall was elected a member of the New Mexico constitutional convention in 1911 and was perhaps its most outstanding personality —certainly a dominating factor. The Republicans had two factions in the convention, the ultraconservatives and the mild conservatives, called strangely enough "Progressives." Fall joined in with the so-called progressive wing of the party, but manifested his utter independence on every occasion. Fall's boldness in debate was exhibited during a discussion in a Republican caucus over the merits or demerits of what finally became Sections 7 and 8 of Article 9 of the Constitution, prohibiting the issuance of bonds by the Legislature in excess of $200,000 without a vote by the people. Fall was in accord with the plan, which was finally adopted, but was having difficulty in the caucus. Picking up his hat, ready to leave the meeting, Judge Fall lectured the caucus and walked out for the day. His parting shot:

> Mr. Chairman: It appears that the dividing of the way has come. When this convention began, I agreed to abide by the action of the Republican caucus upon all matters of a purely political nature. I have consistently done that. I do not believe that this proposition is a political question and, therefore, refuse to be further bound by its actions, but, before I leave, I desire to state that I have been

---

5. William Joseph Mills was born in Yazoo City, Mississippi, January 11, 1849, received a degree of LL.B. from Yale in 1877. He practiced law in New Haven, Connecticut, from 1877 to 1885, came to New Mexico and practiced his profession from 1886 to 1893, then returned to New Haven and practiced from 1894 to 1898. He was a member of the Legislature House of Representatives in Connecticut in 1878, and of the Senate in that state in 1881 and 1882. From 1898 to February 28, 1910, Mills was judge of the Fourth Judicial District in New Mexico, residing at Las Vegas. He served as Governor of New Mexico from March 1, 1910, until January 15, 1912, and had the distinction of being the last governor of the Territory. A Republican in politics, Governor Mills died on December 24, 1915.

threatened by certain gentlemen that, unless I submit to the dictates of the caucus on all matters, I shall not be permitted to go to the United States Senate as one of its first members. I desire to state here and now that I am not a candidate for United States Senator, or for any other position. I desire, however, to state that, if in the future, I desire to be a candidate, I will be a candidate without the consent of any person on earth.

I desire to further state that no man can hold the sword of Damocles over my head in such a manner as has been attempted on this occasion. Good day, gentlemen!

Albert Bacon Fall was elected to the United States Senate by the Legislature of New Mexico on March 28, 1912, assisted greatly by the maneuvering of Holm O. Bursum of Socorro County. Bursum was originally for William H. ("Bull") Andrews, but convinced that Andrews could not be elected, undertook management of Fall's candidacy. When Fall was re-elected to the Senate in 1918 by the vote of the people, defeating William B. Walton, the Democratic candidate, Holm O. Bursum traveled for weeks over the State of New Mexico to help assure success of the Republican ticket. When Fall decided to enter Harding's cabinet in 1921 as Secretary of the Interior, Bursum was anxious to succeed him and sought his help. Bursum was chagrined to learn from Fall himself that he was not in sympathy with Bursum's ambition and declined to endorse him for the appointment. Regardless of Fall's attitude, Bursum was appointed by Governor Merritt C. Mechem, longtime personal friend, as Fall's successor in the Senate. Bursum was elected by the people at the special election on September 20, 1921. Bursum could never understand why Fall, in debt to him politically to a great extent, should have told him face to face that he was opposed to having him in the Senate.[6]

---

6. Albert Bacon Fall was anxious to have someone succeed him in the United States Senate who would consult him about matters pertaining to the office. He made a trip from Washington to Santa Fe to protest to Governor M. C. Mechem against the appointment of H. O. Bursum of Socorro as his successor. Fall believed Bursum would be too independent in Washington and would not rely on his suggestions as to what should be done in the Senate. Mechem informed Fall that the matter of the appointment had been referred to the state executive committee of the Republican party, that the committee had been unanimous for Bursum, and that he expected to appoint him. Fall countered with the suggestion that Mechem resign as Governor and assured him that he, Fall, would have Lieutenant Governor W. H. Duckworth of

Albert Bacon Fall became Secretary of the Interior on March 5, 1921, the first New Mexico man in history to obtain a place in the cabinet of the President of the United States. Stephen B. Elkins, for thirteen years a resident of the Territory, served as Secretary of War in Benjamin Harrison's cabinet in 1891 and 1893, but he was a resident of West Virginia at the time of his appointment. Sixty-two years old, Fall was in good health physically, bright mentally and had a definite plan in mind for immediate development of the natural resources of America. He was particularly anxious that the vast mineral and timber resources of Alaska be developed by idle capital. Fall planned to thrust aside prevailing notions of conservation for future generations. He had no earthly use for the United States Forest Service, its officials or policies.[7]

On March 4, 1923, Albert Bacon Fall resigned as Secretary of the Interior and his resignation was accepted immediately by President Warren G. Harding. The President died on August 2, 1923, a few months after Fall left the cabinet. Involved in a scandal over oil leases and bribery charges that rocked the nation from end to end, Fall ran the gauntlet of Senate investigations, grand jury indictments, court trials and gibbeting by the press of America.

On July 21, 1931, at 10:17 P.M., after more than seven years of battling in the courts, defending himself against charges of bribery, Albert Bacon Fall was enrolled as a federal prisoner in the State Penitentiary at Santa Fe, New Mexico. Fall had served in Santa Fe as a member of the Territorial Legislature, as a member of the Territorial

Clovis, who would succeed him as Governor, appoint him, Mechem, to the Senate. Mechem told Fall he was not interested in going to the Senate; that in fact, he was not interested greatly in being Governor and had made up his mind not to run for a second term. While the matter of the appointment was pending, Burton C. Mossman of Roswell telephoned Governor Mechem from Washington that he had talked with Charles Curtis of Kansas, and that Curtis was very anxious to have some one succeed Fall who would be agreeable to Fall. William A. Hawkins conferred with Governor Mechem at the executive mansion soon after Mechem had appointed Bursum to succeed Fall. Hawkins and Fall had been closely associated for many years in business and politics. Mechem explained to Hawkins his reasons for appointing Bursum. Hawkins commented: "Fall is a political desperado. With him it's either rule or ruin."

7. By joint resolution, the Legislature of New Mexico on March 12, 1921, praised President Warren G. Harding's appointment of Albert Bacon Fall to be Secretary of the Interior. The Legislature was . . . "deeply appreciative of the signal honor that has been conferred upon the State and upon its distinguished citizen and Senator in Congress, . . ." and expressed the belief of the Legislature that "the services to be rendered to his country by the Honorable Albert B. Fall in the cabinet of the President

Supreme Court, twice as Attorney General of the Territory. He had sat in the Constitutional Convention there in 1911 which framed New Mexico's organic law. He had been elected by the Legislature in Santa Fe to the United States Senate. Using Santa Fe as a political springboard, he had reached the pinnacle of his career nationally as a member of the Harding cabinet. Albert Bacon Fall was now obliged to endure the humiliation of being the only member of a presidential cabinet in American history to be convicted of a crime. As he entered the penitentiary in Santa Fe, Fall remarked to United States Marshal Joseph Tondre: "I don't give a damn for myself, but I feel sorry for my family."

Fall spent the last few months prior to imprisonment at his ranch house at Three Rivers, New Mexico, where he found refuge among the many books of his library there. Fall was taken from his Tres Ritos ranch near Carrizozo to Santa Fe in an ambulance, ill and suffering, but if he ever lost his nerve, or his courage, there was no outward indication that he had done so. On the trip to the penitentiary, Fall remarked to friends that while the conveyance in which he was riding was called an ambulance, it really should be called a hearse.

Albert Bacon Fall was a prisoner in Santa Fe because he had been unable to gain a reversal of the verdict of a jury which had convicted him of bribery in the United States court in the District of Columbia. The trial judge had fined him $100,000 and sentenced him to serve a year and a day for violation of Sec. 117, U. S. Penal Code. When tried before a jury in the District of Columbia, Albert Bacon Fall was over 70 years old, broken in health, but not in spirit. Each day of the long trial, wrapped in blankets, he entered the courtroom in a wheelchair. Fall went before the jury heavily handicapped. He was obliged to try to explain away a statement he had made regarding the source of a large sum of money he received while Secretary of the Interior, almost coincident with the execution of important leases on oil bearing public lands to companies headed by E. L. Doheny and H. F. Sinclair. The first big pre-trial break in the case developed when it became an open secret that Fall had unexpectedly received from some one, some place, one hundred thousand dollars ostensibly to

---

of the United States will be as faithful in performance and as distinguished in character as those heretofore rendered to his country and his State in the Senate of the United States."

finance New Mexico ranch extensions. Fearful of the possibility of damage to the party, Republican leaders gathered in Florida and in a Miami Beach hotel room persuaded Fall to agree to say that he had received the money from E. B. McLean, newspaper publisher of Washington, D.C. Department of Justice investigators soon proved that Fall had uttered an untruth and it soon became evident that McLean's promise to help him out of the predicament would be unavailing. After he had stated publicly that he received the $100,000 from McLean and McLean had denied in his testimony before the Senate Investigating Committee that he had given Fall the money, Fall wrote a letter to Senator Thomas F. Walsh of Montana, which said:

> I desire to advise you that I have carefully read the testimony which Mr. McLean gave today, and that I endorse the accuracy of the same. I will also say that before giving his testimony Mr. McLean had a conference with me and I told him that, so far as I was concerned, it was my wish that he answer freely, and, in this connection, I will say that it is absolutely true that—I did not finally use the money from Mr. McLean, which he expressed himself willing to give me, because I found that I could readily obtain it from other sources. I wish it thoroughly understood that the source from which I obtained the money which I used was in no way connected with Mr. Sinclair or in any way involved in the concession regarding the Teapot Dome, or any other oil concession.

At the jury trial, there was testimony concerning Fall's great desire to enlarge his ranch holdings in the Three Rivers country in New Mexico and to purchase additional cattle for his ranches.[8] On De-

---

8. When he purchased the Harris-Brownfield ranch holdings, Albert Bacon Fall acquired a property with an historic background. In the early eighties, Bar W cattle ranged over a vast stretch of territory, extending from White Oaks on the north to El Paso on the south. In the summertime the cattle ranged largely from the Malpais to the south and in the wintertime from the Malpais to the north. Bar W roundup wagons ran as far south as the Dog Canyon country, about fifteen miles south of present Alamogordo. The wagons were run to the south in late summer, working the cattle from the south, northward. In the early spring, the cattle were rounded up in the northern portion of the range and driven south to the southern end of the Malpais, where they were turned loose for the summer. The Three Rivers country was settled up in the early days by Pat Coghlan, the Maxwells and others. They were succeeded by Will Ed Harris, A. D. Brownfield, former president of the American Livestock Association, and other men now prominent in the cattle industry. Harris and Brownfield

cember 6, 1923, Fall wrote a letter to the Senate Committee of Public Lands, denying that he had ever received any money from E. L. Doheny or H. F. Sinclair. This letter, read to the jury, was as follows:

> The fact that Mr. H. F. Sinclair came to Three Rivers with his wife and another lady and gentleman on December 31, 1921, or January 1, 1922, just after I had taken possession of the Harris home ranch property and of the Harris-Brownfield cattle has incited some evil minded persons to the conclusions that I must have obtained money from Mr. Sinclair. It should be needless for me to say that in the purchase of the Harris ranch or in any other purchase or expenditure I have never approached E. L. Doheny or anyone connected with him or any of his corporations or Mr. H. F. Sinclair or anyone connected with him or any of his corporations, nor have I ever received from either of said parties one cent on account of any oil lease or upon any other account whatsoever.

Convicted by the jury on the bribery charge, pleading ill health and expressing a desire to return to New Mexico, Fall was permitted to serve his sentence in Santa Fe, most of it in the prison hospital. He was discharged on May 9, 1932.

Millions of words have been spoken and written in respect to the Albert Bacon Fall case and its many ramifications. Briefly, less than ninety days after he had been appointed Secretary of the Interior, Albert Bacon Fall obtained an executive order from President Harding, which transferred from the Secretary of the Navy to the Secretary of the Interior the authority to lease or otherwise develop un-

---

acquired the outfit of the Hyde Brothers, of whom there were four or five, and sold out to the Hatchet-Fall combination. Following the collapse of the Fall cattle empire, the Hatchet Cattle Company properties were taken over by the Palomas Cattle Company. Palomas sold some eighteen to twenty sections in the southeastern portion of the ranch to Albert Burch of Alamogordo, and the rest of the immense property to the big four, Will Ed Harris, A. D. Brownfield, Truman Spencer and Jesse York. This syndicate sold the 7X well and Willow Spring country to George McDonald, the Three Rivers country to Thomas Fortune Ryan, III, and the south end of the unit east of the railroad, known as the old Maxwell ranch, to Al Stover, former sheriff of Lincoln County. The remnant of the Fall-Hatchet empire, approximately 650 sections, eighteen townships, two townships wide, was managed by Truman Spencer. Albert Bacon Fall's difficulties with ranch management began in 1918, during the influenza epidemic, when he lost his son, Jack Fall, who had supervised the affairs of the property. From that time on, it was apparent to old-time friends of Fall that his dreams of empire in the cattle industry began to fade and his kingdom began to crumble.

appropriated lands in Naval reserves known to contain oil and gas. There never was any question but that President Harding signed the order in entire good faith. That transfer order was limited to Naval petroleum reserves numbered 1 and 2 in California, and Naval petroleum reserves numbered 3 in Wyoming, and certain Naval shale reserves in Colorado and Utah.[9] At the time that President Harding

---

9. Those interested in the details of the Teapot Dome lease in Wyoming and of the Elk Hills lease in California in which Albert Bacon Fall, as Secretary of the Interior, Edward L. Doheny and many other prominent men were important figures, are referred to the *Congressional Record* and other official publications of the proceedings. Senator Thomas F. Walsh of Montana assumed leadership in the Senate investigation into the Naval reserve leases and contracts negotiated by Fall, Doheny and others. Walsh demonstrated great ability and sagacity. He died March 2, 1933.

Civil and criminal cases furnishing many interesting facts as well as opinions of the courts, include the following:

For Teapot Dome—see *United States v. Mammoth Oil Co.*, 5 Fed. (2d) 330, in which District Judge T. Blake Kennedy found against the government in its charges of conspiracy between A. B. Fall and Harry F. Sinclair, representing the Mammoth Oil Co.; *United States v. Mammoth Oil Co.*, 14 Fed. (2d) 706, in which the Eighth Circuit Court of Appeals reversed the district court; and *Mammoth Oil Co., Sinclair Crude Oil Purchasing Company, and Sinclair Pipe Line Company vs. United States of America*, 275 U.S. 13, 48 S. C. R. 1, 72 L. ed. 137, in which the Supreme Court of the United States affirmed the decision of the Circuit Court of Appeals.

For Elk Hills lease—see *United States v. Pan American Petroleum Co.*, 6 Fed. (2d) 43, in which District Judge Paul J. McCormick in Los Angeles found that a conspiracy existed and ordered cancellation of the lease. Judge McCormick in his opinion recited many details of the negotiations between Albert B. Fall and Edward L. Doheny providing for development of the Elk Hills lease and the exchange and transportation of crude oil to Pearl Harbor, adjacent to Honolulu, and the erection there of tanks and refineries. Time has demonstrated that Fall and Doheny had a rather comprehensive understanding of the possibilities for trouble with Japan in the Far East. Their contention that they were motivated by patriotism and love of country would doubtless have a more sympathetic hearing before the American people at the present time, subsequent to the Japanese attack on Pearl Harbor, December 7, 1941. Judge McCormick's opinion was affirmed in *Pan American v. United States*, in the Ninth Circuit Court of Appeals, 9 Fed. (2d) 761, excepting that the Circuit Court refused to give Pan American credit for any tanks built or oil already delivered, as directed by Judge McCormick in his opinion. The opinion of the Circuit Court of Appeals was affirmed by the Supreme Court of the United States. See *Pan American v. United States*, 273 U.S. 456, 47 S. C. R. 416, 71 L. ed. 734.

For details of the Fall conspiracy charge, see *Fall v. United States*, 49 Fed. (2d) 506, writ of certiorari denied by Supreme Court of United States, 283 U.S. 867, 51 S. C. 657, 75 L. ed. 1471. Also see *Sinclair vs. United States of America* (Congressional contempt case), 279 U.S. 263, 49 S. C. R. 268, 73 L. ed. 692; also *Harry F. Sinclair v. United States of America*, 279 U.S. 749, 49 S. C. R. 471, 73 L. ed. 938, a case wherein questions were decided as to the right of a defendant to employ detectives to shadow a jury.

For the views of Attorney General Harry M. Daugherty on the Fall case, see *The*

issued the executive order, Edward L. Doheny was the dominant and managing executive officer of Pan American Petroleum Company and Pan American Petroleum & Transport Company. Albert Bacon Fall and Edward L. Doheny had been old-time friends. Their friendship had its inception in Kingston, New Mexico, in the early eighties.

Inside Story of the Harding Tragedy, by Daugherty and Thomas Dixon. In that book Daugherty states: "When Fall's appointment to the Cabinet was delayed by Harding, the westerner, in characteristic fashion, without saying a word to me about it, sent a telegram to the President and signed my name to it." The telegram, according to Daugherty, urged Harding to hurry and make public the news of Fall's selection as Secretary of the Interior.

On July 25, 1955, the author gave to the University of New Mexico Library, for the use of students and scholars, a collection of letters, correspondence, printed briefs, several hundred Albert Bacon Fall items in all, mostly relating to the Teapot Dome difficulties. This collection was purchased by the author through the cooperation of Rev. R. M. Libertini, S.J., of El Paso.

For a comprehensive narrative of the Albert Bacon Fall difficulties, see *Teapot Dome: Oil and Politics in the 1920's*, by Burl Noggle, Louisiana State University Press, 1962.

nine

ALBERT J. FOUNTAIN

I N THE EARLY DAYS of the Territory there lived at Mesilla, and later at Las Cruces in Doña Ana County, New Mexico, a picturesque, adventuresome character in the person of Albert J. Fountain. He had come to New Mexico during the Civil War, when twenty-five years of age, as a soldier in the Carleton California Column. Some thirty years later Fountain disappeared in the White Sands of New Mexico under most peculiar circumstances. The manner of his death was consistent with the life of excitement and adventure that he had lived. No man in New Mexico of his time could match Fountain's life, year for year, for thrills and adventure.

Albert J. Fountain was born on Staten Island, New York, October 23, 1838. Educated in the public schools of New York, he won at New York Academy a scholarship to Columbia College, went on a tour of the world with a tutor and five other Columbia students, traveling in many countries in Europe, in the Nile country, in the Holy Land. The youths deserted their tutor at the Hague, traveled on an East India vessel for Calcutta, left it at Capetown to explore the continent, abandoned this project, went to Calcutta, boarded a schooner for Hong Kong, which proved to be an opium smuggling craft. Fountain and his companions were arrested, sent to Canton, released through efforts of the American consul general, sent on to San Francisco, where the travelers separated. In California, Fountain engaged in newspaper work, was sent by the Sacramento *Union* to Nicaragua as a correspondent to report the Walker Filibuster expedition, was arrested by Walker, ordered to be shot, escaped, put on women's clothes, made his way back to the States.

In California again, Fountain studied law in San Francisco under N. Greene Curtis, was admitted to the bar of that state, enlisted in the army at the beginning of the Civil War in August, 1861; became a First Lieutenant in the First California Volunteer Infantry, marched across the deserts of California, Arizona and New Mexico, had several brushes with marauding Indians, was mustered out of the army in 1864; was later appointed a Captain of Cavalry by General James H. Carleton and ordered to recruit a company of scouts and guides to help fight the Navajos and Apaches.

Wounded in a skirmish with Apaches in Arizona, Fountain was sent to El Paso for treatment, recovered, was made a customhouse officer at the Port of El Paso, obtained a leave of absence, organized the artillery of the army of Benito Juarez, was made a Colonel in his army, helped in the storming of Chihuahua. General Phil Sheridan had Fountain appointed a judge of election under the Reconstruction Act of Congress and he was thereafter made Assessor and Collector of Internal Revenue for the Western District of Texas. In 1868, Fountain was elected a member of the Texas State Senate, representing thirty-two western counties. When Lieutenant General Flanegan was elected to the United States Senate from Texas, Fountain succeeded him as President of the Texas State Senate. Fountain claimed that he drafted the first Texas Ranger bill, helped secure its passage. In 1875 he returned to New Mexico, the scene of his Indian skirmishes, started to practice law at Mesilla, but was diverted from time to time by Indian fights and organized in 1878 and became captain of the first company of militia in southeast New Mexico. He was in the campaign against Chief Victorio and later trailed Geronimo as a Colonel of the First Regiment of New Mexico Cavalry.

Fountain was special counsel under Grover Cleveland in prosecution of federal land frauds; elected to the New Mexico Legislature in 1888 from Doña Ana and Lincoln Counties, he became Speaker of the House. As a soldier in the field, Fountain chased down and arrested cattle thieves and bandits and then went into court as special prosecutor for livestock associations and prosecuted them. In the year 1894 he convicted twenty men in New Mexico courts on charges of cattle stealing. Fountain was a man of a great many qualifications. Whether in military, political or professional life, he was always an outstanding figure. He was ambitious, vain, fond of effect. Always anxious for adventure, he craved the distinction his exploits gave to him. Fountain frequently appeared in court wearing the uniform of a major of the Territorial Militia and at times undertook to prosecute cases in the routine of a court martial instead of a trial at common law. On April 8, 1881, Fountain was appointed by Judge Warren Bristol at Mesilla, Doña Ana County, to defend William H. Bonney on a charge of murder.

With a talent for writing, Fountain wrote a number of articles for the Mesilla *Independent* and other territorial newspapers, which told stories of the days he had spent as a soldier and of Indian fights in which he had participated. In nearly all of the stories, Fountain pictured himself as a leader and as a brave man and a hero. On one occasion Fountain wrote an article for the Mesilla *Independent* telling of a brush with Navajo Indians in 1880 near Ojo de Analla, a small spring on the Jornada about twenty miles from Paraje, on the wagon road leading from that place to Fort Stanton. The scene of the fight, as described by Fountain, was near a place where Surgeon Watson of the First California Volunteers had been waylaid and murdered by the Apaches in the summer of 1863. Fountain's account pictured the narrow pass, bloodthirsty Indians, mounted on galloping horses, armed with rifles and bows and arrows, and the predicament in which he and an unnamed companion found themselves as they hit the malpais. To quote Fountain:

> Just as the sun was sinking we came to a wall of lava rising abruptly twenty feet or more above the plains and extending for miles in each direction. I knew the place and also knew that immediately before us was the only pass though the wall of lava for many miles. Sitting carelessly on my horse, my Henry rifle held in my right hand and resting across the pommel of my saddle, my bridle rein and lariat with which I led the mule grasped in my left, I entered the narrow pass which barely afforded room for horse and rider. The perpendicular walls on either side rose nearly to the height of my horse's head. When about half way to the summit my mule suddenly reared back, jerking my bridle hand and throwing up my horse's head. At the same instant I looked into the muzzle of a rifle not ten feet distant and behind it the head of an Indian. The rifle was discharged, the ball taking effect in the head of my horse; he fell, dead, carrying me with him. The first shot was followed by a volley and as I went down crushed and stunned under my dead horse, an arrow passed through my left shoulder, a bullet entered my left thigh, and an arrow severed the artery in my right fore-arm. As I lay crushed and bleeding the Indians rushed on me. The pass

was so narrow that but one could approach me at a time. Lying on my back under my dead horse I fired shot after shot from my repeating rifle. I had no occasion to look through the sights as my assailants were not three yards from me. In less than a minute it was over. During that brief period I had discharged ten shots. This was perhaps the first time the Navajos had encountered a repeating rifle and its work must have astounded them. The last Indian I saw was a villainous looking rascal whose only garment was a breech clout. He stands before me now, his every feature photographed in my memory. I can see the expression of his countenance as he came upon me with an uplifted lance to give the coup. He was within six feet of me when I fired, extending my rifle in one hand as if it were a pistol, the muzzle not more than six feet from his body, then he disappeared and I saw him no more.

The night came on; how joyfully I hailed the darkness with its protecting cloak sheltering me from further attack. Jammed as I was beneath the dead horse in the narrow passage, the Indians could not reach me without exposing themselves to my fire at short range. They knew I was wounded and desperate, and they must have suffered severely from my fire in the first attack. I felt satisfied they would wait for daylight to finish the work if I were still alive.

I lay on my back, my left leg numbed and without feeling, crushed under my dead horse; I did not then know I had a bullet in my left thigh, but the wound was not a serious one. My left shoulder was jammed in a corner of the rocks bleeding freely from an arrow wound, and the blood was pumping out in jets from the wound in my right arm.

I succeeded in reaching my knife and using my left hand, cut off the right sleeve which I bound around the severed artery and twisting it tight with a section of the steel wiping rod from the butt of my rifle, succeeded in stopping the flow of blood. Then I drained one of the canteens of water hanging to the pommel of my saddle and lay with my head against the wall of rock waiting for the end.

Colonel Fountain, according to his recitation, was rescued just in time and lived to take part in many other adventures. For some years he had been particularly active in the affairs of the Republican party in New Mexico. Political matters in Doña Ana County were taken quite seriously. The Democrats and Republicans had clashed there one Sunday afternoon in 1871, leaving on the field nine dead

MAJOR FOUNTAIN AND HIS STAFF IN 1883. STANDING, LEFT TO RIGHT,
LIEUTENANT PEDRAGON, LIEUTENANT FOUNTAIN, LIEUTENANT BOTELLO.
SEATED, LEFT TO RIGHT, CAPTAIN VAN PATTEN, MAJOR FOUNTAIN,
CAPTAIN SALAZAR.
Photograph by F. Parker, El Paso.

and many wounded, establishing a precedent for lively political procedure.[1]

Doña Ana County had a peculiarly interesting political background.[2] A political significance was attached to many minor happenings in the community. Because Colonel Fountain had resided in southeastern New Mexico for many years, had been active in the prosecution of criminals and had been so militant in the field against the Indians, he was widely known personally and by reputation in that part of the Territory. He had many enemies among cattle thieves and outlaws. He was disliked by political opponents. However, he had many friends and acquaintances who admired his aggressive tactics and considered him an outstanding citizen with but few equals in the field of law enforcement.

On January 31, 1896, traveling in a buckboard, drawn by a team of good horses, Albert J. Fountain disappeared while en route home to Las Cruces after attending a term of court in Lincoln County. Fountain's disappearance was sudden and complete, as if the earth had opened and enveloped him. Henry Fountain, nine-year-old son

1. This occasion was on Sunday, August 21, 1871, when José M. Gallegos was a candidate for Delegate in Congress on the Democratic ticket against Colonel J. Francisco Chaves, the Republican candidate. Gallegos had arranged for a political rally in Mesilla. Not to be outdone, the Republicans arranged for a meeting at the same place and almost the same hour and invited Chaves to be the speaker of the day. Chaves was unable to accept the invitation, but the meeting went on as scheduled. Horace Stephenson, supporting Gallegos, learned of the opposition meeting, hurriedly gathered one hundred men on horseback and took them from La Mesa to Mesilla. The rival political organizations completed their meetings quietly enough and many, including Stephenson and his horseback riders, started for home. The Democrats, with a brass band which had not exhausted its repertoire at the political rally, headed a procession around the plaza at Mesilla playing "Marching Through Georgia." Although they were without a band, the Republicans started a procession around the plaza, traveling in the opposite direction. When the inevitable results of the collision had been calculated, nine men were found to have been killed, forty or fifty injured. Troops from Fort McRae hurried to Mesilla and remained a week to maintain order, during which time Colonel J. Francisco Chaves, the Republican candidate for Congressional Delegate, arrived in town and made a speech at a rally. Because the rioting began almost instantly without any overt acts that could be recollected, probably the result of a long submerged feeling between the two rival political organizations, the Doña Ana County grand jury failed to return indictments. No one was ever held accountable for the deaths of the nine men. For a detailed account of the rioting, see article written by S. M. Ashenfelter, in the Silver City *Independent*, Oct. 1, 1899.

2. The Legislature of New Mexico by an act of January 18, 1855, provided that "all that part of the Territory of New Mexico that was recently acquired by the Gadsden

of Colonel Fountain, was with him as a traveling companion at the time of his disappearance.

The disappearance of Colonel Fountain was sensational. News that little Henry Fountain also was missing, had perhaps been murdered, shocked the Territory from end to end. People in Las Cruces later recalled that on the night of the disappearance of the Fountains, they had seen the reflection of a huge bonfire against the sky in the mountains east of town. The fire, they believed, was a secret signal announcing that a conspiracy to do away with Fountain had been accomplished.

When the Fountains failed to reach Las Cruces, a posse began a search for them which lasted day and night for many days. Neither the body of Colonel Fountain nor his son could be found. No trace could be discovered of a grave in which they might have been buried. To the date of this writing, nearly seventy years later, the mystery attached to their disappearance is as profound as it was a few hours after the tragedy when Apache Indian scouts, on fresh trails, were unable to piece together clues which might discover the bodies of the missing man and his child, dead or alive. Fountain had some acquaintances in New Mexico who openly expressed the hope that he had been killed; if he had been murdered, they heartily approved of it, regardless of time, place or manner. Others, friends and companions of former years, although not surprised that Fountain had at last met with an adventure from which he probably could never extricate himself, nevertheless joined in the search for him, defended his character against assaults.

Serving as special prosecutor, Albert J. Fountain had attended court in Lincoln County for some days before his disappearance. He had conferred frequently with the district attorney, the sheriff and other court officers. On January 21, 1896, the grand jury of Lincoln County handed up a number of indictments. Among them was an

---

Treaty and has been annexed by this Territory by Act of Congress, entitled, 'An Act Designating the Southern Limits of New Mexico,' Approved Dec. 4, 1854, shall be and hereby is annexed to the County of Doña Ana." By this Act Doña Ana acquired many inhabitants, until 1854 citizens of Mexico, who could be amalgamated with adroitness into the body politic and be useful as voters. During the early years of the Civil War the Confederacy, with its eye on Arizona and the ports of San Diego and San Francisco in California, attracted many southern sympathizers, some of whom remained in Doña Ana County and participated in political activities on the Democratic side.

indictment against William McNew and Oliver M. Lee, charging
that on September 24, 1895, they had defaced a brand on a steer
belonging to W. A. Irwin of El Paso, Texas. A companion indictment charged that McNew and Lee, "did on Sept. 25, 1895, steal,
take and drive away feloniously and knowingly deprive the owner of
a steer, the property of W. A. Irwin, and deprive him of the immediate possession thereof." The indictments listed as witnesses Albert
Sanders, C. R. Simms, T. W. Jones, Geo. Bunting, Melvin Lusk,
Clabe Prude, W. A. Irwin, J. Leslie Dow.* In the language of the
layman, the indictments alleged that McNew and Lee had taken
one of Irwin's steers, which had been branded = and changed the
brand to # and had then run it over onto Lee's range. A grand jury
indictment in the year 1896 on a charge of cattle stealing was a
matter of serious concern. Bill McNew heard about the incident
quickly, so did Oliver Lee. The record in Lincoln County shows that
no further action was taken on the indictments by the Territory
subsequent to their return into open court and that they were dismissed on April 13, 1897.

His court business finished, Albert J. Fountain started for home
on January 30, 1896, taking with him a number of affidavits and
other papers relating to the cattle stealing matters he had presented
to the grand jury. Son Henry was particularly happy, because his

---

* James Leslie Dow, widely known as Les Dow, a diligent and courageous law enforcement officer in early day southeastern New Mexico, might have lived to the
proverbial ripe old age if he had not been a witness before the Lincoln County grand
jury which handed up indictments against several prominent men at the instigation of
special prosecutor Fountain. The youngest son in a large family which settled in South
Texas about the time or shortly after the Civil War, Les Dow was born in DeWitt
County, Texas, April 30, 1860. He was married to Mary Neatherlin on January 10,
1884, in Williamson County, Texas. Mrs. Dow died on March 25, 1949. Two children
of this marriage survived the death of both parents, Hiram M. Dow of Roswell and
Robert C. Dow of Carlsbad, both prominent attorneys and leading citizens in their
respective communities.

For some years prior to his marriage, Les Dow worked cattle in the employ of Cap-
tain Hi Millett, a noted Texas rancher and cattle baron, and for whom his oldest son,
Hiram M. Dow, was named. After his marriage, Dow established his own ranch near
Cotulla, Texas, and acquired a small herd of cattle. In the early part of 1885, he dis-
posed of his Texas ranch and trailed his cattle to New Mexico, homesteading on North
Seven Rivers, two miles west of the town of Seven Rivers, which was then in Lincoln
County. In 1896, Les Dow was employed by the Texas-New Mexico Cattle Raisers
Association, at which time he was commissioned as a Deputy U.S. Marshall by Edward
A. Hall, U.S. Marshall for the Territory of New Mexico. Dow's duties were principally

father had bought a pony for him in Lincoln. The pony was tied to the rear of the buckboard with halter and rope. Friends of Colonel Fountain in Lincoln were uneasy. From hints they had heard here and there, they feared that Fountain's life might be in jeopardy. Several friends approached Fountain just before he left Lincoln and urged him not to make the trip to Las Cruces without protection. George W. Prichard, a prominent attorney, perhaps the last man to see Fountain before he left Lincoln, advised him, for his own protection, to wait for the mail carrier and follow behind the buckboard carrying United States mail. With a display of confidence, Fountain picked up a shotgun from the front of the buggy and showed it to Prichard. Patting the gun with his hand, Fountain said: "This will be my protection." With a crack of the buggy whip, the Fountains started for La Luz, where they stopped overnight with David M. Sutherland, leaving the next day for Las Cruces.[3]

Notified by his mother that the father and little Henry had not returned from Lincoln as expected, Albert J. Fountain, Jr., a son of Colonel Fountain, on February 2, 1896, left Las Cruces with Antonio Garcia, Catarino Gallegos, Casimiro Chacon and Pedro Onapa and traveled quickly to Luna's Wells. Saturnino Barela, the mail carrier between Luna's Wells and Las Cruces, had seen the Fountains near the Wells as he had stopped there to water his horse. The searching party soon found the buckboard in which Colonel Fountain and little Henry had been riding. Three shawls, a belt filled with cart-

---

to look out for cattle which had been stolen from Texas ranchers and driven into New Mexico, to apprehend the wrongdoers, and assist local peace officers in suppressing cattle thefts and corralling outlaws wherever they might be found. An alert and diligent law enforcement officer, Dow made some bitter enemies among the lawless element, whom he pursued without fear or favor. Elected sheriff of Eddy County on a law and order platform in the fall of 1896, Dow took the oath of office January 1, 1897. On the night of January 18, 1897, only eighteen days after he had taken over as sheriff, he was ambushed, shot and killed in the town of Eddy (now Carlsbad). The Santa Fe *New Mexican* of January 19, 1897, giving an account of the killing, described Les Dow as "a brave and efficient officer, and a very popular man."

3. Elfego Baca, combination lawyer and gunman, was in Lincoln, attending to legal business on the day of Fountain's departure. Baca had accepted an invitation to ride with him to Las Cruces, enroute to his home in Socorro. As Baca was about to get into the conveyance he was approached by a man who said he wanted to see him about some business. "What business?" inquired Baca. "Business concerning a horse," replied the man. Baca then knew he had an opportunity to defend a horse thief, perhaps earn a good fee. He told Fountain to drive on.

ridges and other items of personal property, all identified as property of Fountain, were found at a point on the public road about forty-five miles from Las Cruces, on the Tularosa–Las Cruces highway. The team and buckboard had left the road near the Chalk Hills. The boot tracks of three men were plainly seen by the searchers, but no sign whatever of Colonel Fountain or of Henry, or any footprint that could be identified as belonging to them. The searchers reported discovery of "tracks of one man made by a cowboy boot with a pointed toe and high heel, the tracks of the two others made with fine cowboy boots with box toes, one with a foot smaller than the others."

The searchers spent hours on the trail, running down every clue. Colonel Fountain and little Henry were not to be found, dead or alive. Maj. W. H. H. Llewellyn, formerly Indian agent on the Mescalero reservation near Fort Stanton, and Thomas Branigan, who had been for some years chief of the Indian scouts on the Mescalero, went on an independent investigating expedition on February 3, 1896, saw the footprints, returned home to Las Cruces and reported that there was not much doubt but that the Fountains had been "foully dealt with and murdered." They had the help of Indian trailers from the Mescalero reservation, but the Indians gave up after trying for several days. They had followed the prints of horses for four miles, then lost the trail for good.

The mystery of the disappearance of Colonel Fountain and his son deepened with the passing of the days. There was much talk and there were rumors that the Fountains had been seen here, there, in many different places. The hunt for the Fountains, dead or alive, was spurred on by offers of large rewards. The Masonic Grand Lodge of New Mexico, of which Colonel Fountain had been an officer, offered $10,000 for information leading to discovery of his body, dead or alive. The late Isidoro Armijo of Las Cruces, for many years a newspaper publisher of Doña Ana County, later an official Spanish Interpreter for the second judicial district in New Mexico, confident that he had an important clue, went to Mexico early in 1896, to search for them.

Armijo spent eighteen months in Mexico, at his own expense, looking everywhere for Fountain and little Henry. Traveling from mountain village to valley town, from town to city, from place to place, following leads which at long last he abandoned, Armijo returned to Las Cruces convinced in his own mind that the Fountains had not gone to Mexico. Thereafter, with characteristic force and energy, Armijo turned his talents to interpreting into magnificent Spanish, to the accompaniment of appropriate looks and gestures, the mediocre speeches of gringo candidates for political office in New Mexico.*

---

*For information concerning Fountain's career in El Paso, Texas, and the controversy between Fountain and W. W. Mills in 1869, see *Forty Years at El Paso, 1858-1898*, by W. W. Mills, El Paso, 1901 (reprint with notes by Rex W. Strickland, published by Carl Hertzog, El Paso, 1962).

ten

OLIVER MILTON LEE

O LIVER M. LEE, for many years a resident of Alamogordo, Otero County, New Mexico, came to the Territory in the fall of 1884, traveling overland with his half-brother, Perry Altman, and a horse herd from Little Elm Creek, Taylor County, Texas. Born in Buffalo Gap about fifteen miles south of Abilene, Texas, on November 8, 1865, Oliver Lee died in Alamogordo on December 15, 1941. He had lived in southeastern New Mexico for fifty-seven years. His life had been colorful and crowded with the action of the frontier. Fate gave Oliver Lee a part to play in southeastern New Mexico and he played it with a zest for life, with dignity, courage and capability.

During the latter years of his life, after all the fighting on the range was over and things had quieted down to something of a normal existence, Oliver Lee participated prominently in public affairs. As state senator in 1922 and 1924, as a director of the Federal Land Bank of Wichita, Kansas, and in other important posts, Oliver Lee contributed valuable services to New Mexico. For decades he was an acknowledged authority on horses and accepted as a leader in the cattle industry. The old ways of the range clung to Oliver Lee and during the time of his service in the State Legislature it was an open secret among his brethren in the Senate that at every session he carried a forty-five in a leather holster, with a well filled cartridge belt nicely concealed beneath the folds of the Prince Albert coat which he wore on all occasions of state.

Perry Altman, over in Texas, had decided in the early eighties to emigrate to New Mexico. He had heard that there was free land, open range and a good demand for horses at substantial prices. Oliver Lee insisted on accompanying him. Born and reared in a country where horseback riding was a natural accomplishment and where marksmanship was absorbed in childhood, Oliver Lee came to New Mexico already a superb horseman and an expert with six-shooter and rifle. When only seven years old Oliver Lee had given one of his earliest demonstrations in the use of firearms. Two steer buyers visited the Perry Altman ranch in Taylor County, Texas, where Oliver spent his boyhood, and complained of the lack of fresh meat on the place. Little Oliver Lee spoke up in a childish voice and declared that if someone would carry them back for him, he would go out and shoot some turkeys. The steer buyers were amused, and to humor him, accepted the boy's challenge. Oliver Lee led them out into the woods nearby the ranch and in an hour the party returned. Young Oliver had shot two turkeys through the neck, with balls fired from an old squirrel rifle. The steer buyers had their fresh meat.

Perry Altman and Oliver Lee and their horses and a few cows came to New Mexico in 1884. With them came "Ed" and "Ef," two Negro boys. Looking for a suitable place to settle down, Oliver Lee met William Kellum ("Cherokee Bill") at Mescalero and talked to him about a location. "Cherokee Bill" told Lee of a canyon on the west side of the Sacramento Mountains where 1,000 head of cattle could be held together with only a little fencing, so abrupt were the walls of the canyon. "Cherokee Bill" guided Perry Altman and Oliver Lee to the mouth of Dog Canyon. On seeing the place, Perry Altman said: "Well, Oliver, this country is so damned sorry, I think we can stay here a long time and never be bothered by anybody else." That was the beginning of the famous Dog Canyon Ranch, located in what was then the eastern part of Doña Ana County, a part of which later became Otero County. Oliver Lee brought with him from Texas the Circle Cross brand and to this day it is one of the brands used by his sons on their New Mexico cattle ranches. There were still rumblings of the Lincoln County War in southeastern New Mexico at the time Oliver Lee reached New Mexico; there was talk of the power of the "Santa Fe Ring," of its ability to first threaten and frighten people and then to act, perhaps with violence, always with serious results.

Sitting around camp fires at night and visiting on Sundays and holidays at the lonely ranches in a new country, Oliver Lee listened to the tales of gunmen and their ability with a six-shooter. To establish his identity in the country, on the Fourth of July in 1885 Oliver

Lee gave a demonstration of his ability with firearms. A few cowboys had done a bit of plain and fancy shooting. Oliver Lee handed a pine board to a youngster, instructed him to ride a mile out on the range, plant the board firmly upright and then get out of the way. With a high-powered rifle, Lee quietly proved his marksmanship, hitting the target five shots out of six fired. Then Lee waved the spectators away to a place of safety, took his pistol and rode in a circle about a cedar hitching post. Firing six shots from a galloping pony, Oliver Lee's bullets split the post into pieces, every shot reaching its mark.

Altman had taken up a place on the range and, as soon as he was twenty-one years old, Oliver Lee filed a homestead entry on a quarter section of land where there was possibility of water and available range nearby. In those days in any part of New Mexico, the man who had the waterhole was the man who controlled the public range. The man who controlled the range had an opportunity to become a cattle king. Having a waterhole and holding it in the open range country, however, was a goal which but few men achieved. To hold a place where cattle could be watered required nerve and intelligence. Most of all, it required a man who was a good shot. In the eighties on the open range in many parts of New Mexico, there was an almost constant warfare over waterholes and grazing lands. Barbed wire fences had hardly reached southeastern New Mexico. If fences were erected on the public domain, they frequently were cut down overnight and cattle of intruders trampled over the grass that had been enclosed. There had been many a murder over waterholes and range rights in eastern and southern Doña Ana County and in adjoining Lincoln County. The authorities were powerless to cope with the situation even if that had been their desire. There was much talk out on the ranges that officers were in league with the big cattle owners—sometimes looked the other way when there was violence over rights to a waterhole.

Southeastern New Mexico was being invaded by men with a craze for cattle and cattle ranches. Their animals stricken with Texas fever and quarantined, cattlemen from Texas were frantically pushing their herds over into New Mexico, a new country where grass could be had free on government lands. Perry Altman and Oliver Lee slowly gathered together herds of cattle in a country where there was little running water and only an occasional waterhole. The life on the open range was hard. Feuds that had started and recessed in Arkansas, Texas and Missouri were continued in New Mexico as men and their families and kinfolk began to settle up the country. Quarrels over rights on the range led to violence. On December 16, 1885, John H. Good shot and killed Charles Dawson at La Luz, nine miles from Tularosa. There had been trouble between the men on the range and a "shoot on sight" ultimatum had been issued. Good shot Dawson three times and he died quickly. Dawson's wife, the former Sue Yonker, who had been accused of killing Robert Black in Socorro a year before, brought a Winchester rifle into play when she saw that Good was about to kill her husband, but Good escaped injury and was acquitted in a hearing before Justice of the Peace Humphrey Hill.

On August 20, 1888, the body of Walter Good, son of John Good, a Texan, was found in the White Sands by his father and fifteen men who had scoured the country for two weeks looking for him. The young man had suddenly disappeared without leaving a clue to his whereabouts. Walter Good's body had been exposed to the sun for many days, a prey to coyotes and carrion. The skeleton was identified from Walter Good's height, six feet, six inches, and from the clothing and jewelry alongside the remains. Near the body lay Good's revolver containing two empty cartridges. In the searching party were John Good, his son Charles, his son-in-law, Hugh Taylor, his nephew, Ed Good, E. O. Rucker and George Swigart, Good's foreman. On their way home, near the Malone ranch, the searching party met up with an opposition crowd on the range, Perry Altman, Oliver Lee, Tom Tucker and William (Cherokee Bill) Kellum. Both parties dismounted on sight and started far off to shoot at each other. One hundred sixty shots were fired, but only two horses were killed in the fracas. The Good party went into La Luz and sent a messenger on horseback to notify Sheriff Ascarate at Las Cruces that they had found Walter Good's body. The Sheriff left for the seat of the trouble with a posse of twenty-five men. The posse was enlarged in La Luz by twenty-five more men. E. O. Rucker of the Good outfit was sworn in as deputy sheriff in charge. The remains of Walter Good were buried in La Luz. That night the ranch house of Perry Altman was burned to the ground. The Good crowd claimed that Perry Altman had lighted the match and started the fire that burned the house to prevent proof of guilt of the murder of Walter Good. They said that Walter Good had been shot and killed at the Perry Altman place and his body dragged to the White Sands and left there to rot in order to conceal clues of the crime.

The Perry Altman crowd claimed that the Good crowd had burned Altman's place out of spite, for no good reason. After Walter Good's death on the range, things tightened up in that part of the cattle country. John Good was running several thousand head of cattle on the open range on shares. Among the ranchers it was generally accepted that the cattle belonged to Riley and Rynerson and Thomas B. Catron of Santa Fe. John Good sent out word that "all little men" in the country "had to" get off the range. Oliver Lee had a friend, George McDonald of Texas, who was employed by John Stewart, a storekeeper of La Luz, to look out for Stewart's cattle grazing on the public domain. In an interview with George McDonald, John Good attempted to get him to move Stewart's cattle out, but McDonald refused to be frightened out of the country. One day George McDonald, resting, perhaps sleeping, on the open range near a spring of water, was shot through the forehead and instantly killed. When McDonald failed to return to La Luz in a reasonable time, Oliver Lee rode out and found the dead body of his friend. Lee enticed two of John Good's cowboys over to the Lee ranch, employed them and persuaded them to agree to give testimony for the Territory against the murderer of George McDonald.

Lee kept the cowboys under his protection for five months, waiting for the next grand jury session at Las Cruces. Oliver Lee and his cowboy witnesses went to the county seat at Las Cruces, saw the district attorney and told him their story. They waited around the courthouse for five days, expecting to be called to testify. The grand jury adjourned without taking up the case of the murder of George McDonald and the crime was never avenged. Convinced that the law enforcing machinery of the county was not interested in him or his difficulties and that he would be obliged to depend on his own resources, Oliver Lee returned to his ranch country, oiled his guns and saw to it that his cartridge belts were always well filled. He carried a six-shooter in a holster by day, slept with one under his pillow at night.

Bit by bit in the Dog Canyon country, his favorite ranch location, and in the Wildey Well ranch country, Oliver Lee expanded his holdings and enlarged his herds of cattle. He developed water in a country which was almost a desert, built tanks, erected windmills and tried to be a good citizen. The years went by in the range country, good years and bad years, years of fair rainfall and almost none, of fair prices and no prices.

Then on February 4, 1896, came the news that traveled swiftly over the White Sands from Las Cruces, from La Luz, from Tularosa, that Col. Albert J. Fountain was missing and that his little son, Henry, nine years old, had disappeared with him. Not many days passed before it was whispered in the range country that Oliver Lee knew something about the Fountains and their disappearance. Oliver Lee smarted under the charges and accusations, but was helpless to do anything about them.

On April 2, 1898, after the Fountain case had slumbered for more than two years, Sheriff Pat Garrett of Doña Ana County, now back from Uvalde, Texas, walked into Judge Frank W. Parker's courtroom at Las Cruces and asked for a bench warrant for the arrest of Oliver M. Lee, William McNew and James Gililland, charged with the murder of Albert J. Fountain and Henry Fountain.

Garrett filed an affidavit with the court, reciting facts and circumstances, "going to substantiate the fact that Lee, McNew and Gililland had murdered Fountain and Son," as the petition for the bench warrant alleged. Pat Garrett's affidavit filed in the office of J. P. Mitchell, clerk of the district court of Doña Ana County, was as follows:

TERRITORY OF NEW MEXICO: COUNTY OF DOÑA ANA.

In the District Court of the Third Judicial District, within and for the County of Doña Ana.

Before the Honorable Frank W. Parker, Associate Justice of the Supreme Court of the Territory of New Mexico, and Presiding Judge of the Third Judicial District Court thereof.

Patrick F. Garrett of lawful age being first duly sworn by the undersigned authority, upon his oath deposes and says: That he knows persons and can have them before the court, who identified the tracks of Oliver M. Lee, William McNew and James Gililland at the first camp where they stopped with Colonel Albert J. Fountain and his little son, Henry Fountain, after the said Lee, McNew and Gililland had captured Colonel Fountain and his little son. He can also bring before the court a witness who saw Lee, McNew and Gililland early on Sunday morning, February 2, 1896, being the very next morning following the supposed murder of Colonel Fountain and his son Henry. This witness will testify that he was at

Oliver Lee's ranch at the time that Lee, McNew and Gililland arrived there and that both the men and horses were in a very tired and worn out condition. He will also have witnesses before the court who will show that William Carr shadowed Colonel Fountain all the way from the town of Lincoln to the town of La Luz; that Colonel Fountain and his son Henry remained at La Luz all night Friday night the last day of January A.D. 1896, and that Carr passed La Luz late in the evening on the same day going in the direction of Oliver Lee's ranch. He will also have other evidence before the court going to substantiate the fact that Oliver M. Lee, William McNew and James Gililland are the parties who murdered Colonel Albert J. Fountain and his son, Henry Fountain.

P. F. GARRETT

Subscribed and sworn to by Patrick F. Garrett before me this 3rd day of April A.D. 1898.

JOHN D. BRYAN
Notary Public

A like affidavit, signed by Thomas Branigan and William H. Llewellyn, filed with the Clerk of the court, was as follows:

TERRITORY OF NEW MEXICO: COUNTY OF DOÑA ANA.

Before me the undersigned personally appeared Thomas Branigan and William H. H. Llewellyn, who being duly sworn upon oath according to law, deposed as follows: Each are of lawful age and residents of the town of Las Cruces in the county and territory aforesaid and have resided therein for the period of over twelve years.

That on the 2nd day of February, A.D. 1896 learning of the disappearance of one A. J. Fountain and his little son Henry Fountain that they organized a party and went on the 3rd day of February A.D. 1896 in the direction of the town of Tularosa with said party and that at a point on the public road between said town of Las Cruces and said town of Tularosa and distant from Las Cruces about forty-five miles that they found indications that the said A. J. Fountain and his son Henry Fountain had been foully dealt with and murdered.

That from examination made at that time on the ground while the SIGN were fresh that the tracks and other evidence found at that time indicate that the said Fountain and his son were murdered and further that from trails followed and other circumstances every indication points to the commission of the crime by one Oliver Lee,

William McNew, one Carr and one Gililland and that the said
Fountain and his said son have never been seen alive since the 1st
day of February A.D. 1896 and that the motive existed at that time
for the said persons named above to commit the said crime.

THOMAS BRANIGAN
WILLIAM H. H. LLEWELLYN

Sworn to and subscribed before me and in my presence this 3rd
day of April A.D. 1898.

JOHN D. BRYAN
Notary Public,
Doña Ana County, N. M.

Never inclined to turn a deaf ear to things that were being gossiped
about in the community and probably not surprised at the turn of
events, Judge Parker ordered the bench warrant to issue, thus circum-
venting the processes of a grand jury, and Pat Garrett went into
action again.

Seventeen years before, on July 14, 1881, Pat Garrett as sheriff of
Lincoln County had fired the shot in a darkened room that ended
the life of William H. Bonney, the Kid, with only Peter Maxwell,
son of the famous land grant king, Lucien B. Maxwell, as the sole
close-range eyewitness. Now, for the first time in the intervening
years, Pat Garrett was to have an opportunity to demonstrate his
ability as an officer of the law in undertaking to arrest a man who
would oblige him to shoot it out with him face to face in broad daylight.

The issuance of an order of arrest of some type had been expected
for some time by those who had closely followed the Fountain case.
Months before it had been expected that the Doña Ana grand jury
would indict Oliver Lee and his companions. Pat Garrett and Oliver
Lee barely knew each other by sight before the disappearance of the
Fountains. Oliver Lee had heard, out on the range, in Las Cruces and
other places, that efforts had been made and were being made to
involve him in the case. Only a few days before the bench warrant
was issued, there had been a sociable game of stud poker in Tobe
Tipton's saloon at Tularosa. Playing in the game were Albert Bacon
Fall, George Curry, Oliver Lee, Tobe Tipton, Jeff Sanders and Pat
Garrett. Poker chips were pushed from player to player as the cards
fell and as deal followed deal. Because he had been losing quite

steadily, hoping to change his luck, Pat Garrett rapped on the table for a new deck of cards. George Curry casually remarked that he had heard on the street in Tularosa that the Doña Ana County grand jury might indict somebody for doing away with the Fountains and that his guess was that somebody in the crowd might be obliged to hire a lawyer before long and that he, Curry, had an idea that the lawyer who might be hired was sitting in the game. Oliver Lee acknowledged the thrust and bowed in the direction of Sheriff Garrett. "Mr. Garrett," said Lee, "if you wish to serve any papers on me at any time, I will be around here or out to the ranch." Equally polite, Sheriff Garrett, in the southern drawl that never entirely escaped him, nodded his head in Lee's direction and said: "All right, Mr. Lee, if any papers are to be served on you, I will mail them to you, or send them to George Curry here to serve on you." [1]

The conversation between Sheriff Garrett and Oliver Lee in Tobe Tipton's saloon at Tularosa was just so much verbal poker playing. Oliver Lee had been told by Las Cruces friends that a warrant was about to be issued for his arrest; that Judge Parker had openly expressed the view that Lee, when arrested for the murder of the Fountains, should be placed in jail and held there without bail until time came for trial. Friends had sent word to Oliver Lee to be on his guard at all times, that they had heard and believed that Pat Garrett was out to kill him while attempting to arrest him. Lee had communicated his fears without delay to Albert Bacon Fall.

---

1. No man who ever lived in New Mexico had a more exciting time than George Curry, Governor of New Mexico in 1907. Among other events George Curry had the distinction of being reported dead on three different occasions. The first false report arose in Trinidad, Colorado, where he had gone from Raton in 1885 to attend a baseball game between Raton and Trinidad. An Englishman stopping at the same hotel as Curry, by mistake took Curry's vest, went out to look at some property, made a display of money and was murdered, found dead with envelopes containing George Curry's name in the vest pockets. The coroner's jury found that the deceased was George Curry, but was mistaken. The second time was in the province of Samar in the Philippine Islands in 1902. Leading a detachment of 51 men in battle, Captain Curry lost 46 of them and was reported killed. President Theodore Roosevelt on learning that the report of Curry's death was a mistake, cabled him: "Hearty congratulations on your miraculous escape. Keep a stiff upper lip: I am with you. Theodore." George Curry was reported dead a third time when the Associated Press sent out through the country the following telegram: "Hillsboro, N.M., April 11: George Curry, 70 former territorial governor of New Mexico, Spanish-American War veteran and ex-congressman, died here Sunday afternoon." The Albuquerque *Morning Journal*, relying on the Associated Press Dispatch, published the report of Curry's death on April 12, 1932. Clifford Curry,

Sheriff Pat Garrett arrested William McNew on April 3, 1898, and put him in jail at Las Cruces without bail. Arresting Oliver Lee was another matter. Sheriff Garrett knew that Lee was not going to submit tamely to arrest. Maneuvering for advantage, Pat Garrett did not go to Oliver Lee's Dog Canyon headquarters ranch, the most likely place at which Lee could be found. Lee decided that Sheriff Garrett was waiting to get the drop on him.

Late in the summer of 1898, Oliver Lee and Jim Gililland left the Dog Canyon Ranch and rode horseback over to the W. W. Cox ranch, remained there all night and spent a part of the next day watching the Cox outfit brand calves. Clint Llewellyn, a deputy sheriff under Pat Garrett, showed up at the Cox ranch, soon followed by another deputy, José Espalin of Garfield. Oliver Lee had known Espalin for some years and greeted him cordially in Spanish. "Where are you going?" inquired Espalin of Lee. "To the Wildey Well Ranch," replied Lee. "Look out, there are strangers in the country," Espalin whispered to Lee, as he mounted his horse and rode away. Oliver Lee and Jim Gililland rode horseback forty miles across the country, reaching the Wildey Well Ranch late at night. On November 7, 1937, nearly forty years later, recalling the Wildey Well fight, Oliver Lee in Alamogordo told the author:

> Gililland and I got to Wildey Well late at night on July 12, 1898, unsaddled our horses and took our camp beds up on top of an adobe house. Wildey Well was west from Turquoise, eight miles east of Oro Grande, not far from where grading outfits were build-

---

son of George Curry, sued the Journal Publishing Company for damages, but the Supreme Court of New Mexico held that the newspaper was not liable. 41 N.M. 318, 68 Pac. 168. George Curry died in the United States Veterans Hospital in Albuquerque on Nov. 24, 1947 (Thanksgiving Day) in his eighty-seventh year. Over a long period of years George Curry had talked to the author on many occasions about the old days, giving generously of his time and recollections to fill in the missing gaps about "old-timers." On one occasion he told the author: "I had many chances to get rich in my time, but I never took a dollar." From time to time he worked on his autobiography, despite the fact that he was seriously handicapped by lack of secretarial help and inability to locate papers which had been lost or mislaid. However, Curry was gifted with a marvelous memory and he succeeded in piecing together much of the story of his life. Death overtook the Governor before his manuscript had been completed. Fortunately for posterity, Horace Brand Hening, an intimate friend of almost fifty years and an accomplished writer, took over after Curry's death and completed the task. The all-important book, *George Curry, 1861-1947*, was published by the University of New Mexico Press in 1958.

ing the El Paso and Northeastern line of railway, about 32 miles due south of Alamogordo. Wildey Well was a part of the Dog Canyon outfit. On the ranch there was a frame building sitting endwise to a shed. As we found out later, Pat Garrett and his outfit followed Gililland and me across the country. We had taken a short cut and reached there quite awhile ahead of them, but never suspected that they were trailing us. Gililland and I went to sleep on top of the roof of the building. The first thing I knew, just about day-break, the Garrett posse was shooting at us from the top of the shed, with Garrett, Kent Kearney, José Espalin, Ben Williams and Clint Llewellyn in their crowd. Garrett, Kearney and Espalin were stand-ing on the roof of the shed. Ben Williams was up on a dirt water tank shooting. The first thing I knew they had shot my bed all to pieces. Garrett had shot at us three times, and he started to shoot without calling on us to surrender. I had understood that Garrett was usually cool, but that day he had lost his head and missed all three shots. I had a man, Madeson, working for me, who was sleeping in the room I usually occupied when at the Wildey Well Ranch. The first thing Madeson knew, as he told me later, was that Garrett was in the room and had a gun rammed against him. When Garrett discovered that he hadn't found me, he said to Madeson, "If I find him, (Lee) I'll kill him." In a few moments Garrett was on the shed roof. Garrett had got his job as sheriff on the strength of the boast that he would kill me. Garrett, in my mind, didn't want an equal break. When he saw what was hap-pening, Gililland and I must have fired at Kearney at the same time because he was hit twice and mortally wounded. When the shooting first began, and I was awakened, I whirled over when I felt the impact of one shot in particular which came against the bedclothes right under my stomach where I was sleeping. I jerked up my Winchester rifle, which I had at the side of my bed, and shot at Pat Garrett, intending to hit him in the head, but he ducked as I fired and I missed him. Garrett jumped. Ben Williams ducked as soon as the shooting began. I had no idea I hadn't killed Pat Garrett, because everything was quiet after we shot Kearney, and I thought I had shot Garrett. I had no idea at the time how many were in the posse, but I called out, "You are a hell of a lot of bastards to shoot at a man when he is asleep." Then much to my surprise, for I thought he had been shot, Pat Garrett called up, "Are any of you hurt?" I said "No." Then I said to Gar-rett, "You have got yourself in a hell of a close place." Garrett then said to me, "I know it. How are we going to get away from here?"

I said, "I don't know." I shot two or three shots through the shed as a demonstration. Finally after considerable powwow with Pat Garrett, I said to him, "You fellows leave your guns and come out in the open and bunch up and start to leave here." Garrett said, "All right." Garrett turned to Llewellyn and Williams. Then I said, "Just hold on a minute. You fellows, Llewellyn and Williams, take the guns with you." They had tied their horses 40 or 50 yards away, to a fence outside. The posse left the ranch. José Espalin, who jumped when the shooting started, had taken his shoes off, probably to sneak up to the house, and had been walking in his stocking feet. Sand burrs had gotten into Espalin's feet and he was having a hard time of it. In spite of the fact that I had been through a hot gun-fight, almost been shot, and Kearney had been seriously wounded, I just had to laugh at Espalin dodging cockleburrs in his bare feet. When the Garrett crowd had left the ranch, Jim Gililland paced off the distance from which Pat Garrett had fired at us, and found it to be exactly thirty-seven feet. How Garrett missed us, I never did know. It just wasn't our time to die. Garrett had been smart too. He had left a guard over my man Madeson, who had been taken by surprise and couldn't warn us, and Garrett so placed his posse that when they shot at us they got the benefit of the morning sun at daybreak, shooting from east to west. When the shooting at Wildey Wells was all over and Garrett found out he was still alive, and I told the posse they could go, Garrett called up to Gililland and me: "You won't shoot us in the back, will you?" and Jim Gililland answered: "You know damn well we won't."

Deputy Sheriff Kearney, a large man, six feet two inches in height, was taken to Tularosa for treatment, but he died soon after reaching there. Within a few days Oliver Lee and Jim Gililland learned that they had been indicted by the grand jury of Doña Ana County on a new charge—the murder of Deputy Kearney.

When Pat Garrett and his posse returned to Las Cruces, they emphasized the killing of Deputy Sheriff Kearney, but could give only lame and unsatisfactory excuses for failure to arrest Oliver Lee.

Oliver Lee was definitely on the dodge after the Wildey Wells gunfight with Sheriff Pat Garrett and his posse. The public had been informed by Garrett that Lee had resisted arrest and had killed Kearney; that he was an outlaw. Now more than ever, Oliver Lee felt that Garrett was out to kill him. Lee could not surrender to Garrett, even in the presence of friends, because he would lose face and there were constant rumors that reached him that if arrested, he would not live to see the day of his trial, but would be lynched in Las Cruces.

After Pat Garrett became a candidate to succeed himself as sheriff of Doña Ana County, the *Independent Democrat* at Las Cruces published several letters, some written by Oliver Lee, which resulted in the arrest of Carlton E. Bull, the publisher of the paper, on a charge of criminal libel. Referring to the fight at Wildey Well Ranch in which Pat Garrett had attempted to shoot him while asleep—as Oliver Lee claimed—one letter dated July 27, 1898, and signed by Lee, charged that Garrett had said "before the Wildey Well shooting occurred, that if he succeeded in finding Jim Gililland and myself, he would kill us."

Lee wrote another letter, published in the *Independent Democrat* on August 16, 1898, in which he declared that Pat Garrett had been employed to assassinate him and Jim Gililland; that Garrett had no intention of making arrests, but that he fully expected to kill both Lee and Gililland in arresting them. Samuel G. Bean, a friend of Oliver Lee, wrote a letter to the *Independent* on September 8, 1898, in which he prodded a sore spot on Pat Garrett's hide. Bean said in his communication that Garrett was the "murderer" of Billy the Kid and that numerous propositions had been made by Garrett to Oliver Lee to induce him to surrender; that it had been Garrett's plan all along to deal out to Oliver Lee the same kind of treatment that Garrett had given the outlaw Kid at Fort Sumner on July 14, 1881. Smarting under the publication of the letters, Pat Garrett had Bull indicted by the grand jury. Released at once on bond, the indictments against Publisher Bull slumbered in the court records until October 19, 1899, when Judge Leland held that there was no such thing in New Mexico as a criminal libel law and sustained a motion to dismiss that had been filed by Albert Bacon Fall.

After the Wildey Well fight, Oliver Lee and Jim Gililland went to the HG Ranch near Engle on the Rio Grande, where Eugene Manlove Rhodes was working as a horse wrangler for Lee's half-sister and brother-in-law, Mr. and Mrs. H. G. Graham. The HG Ranch of thousands of acres of range land became their place of hideout until Lee's surrender. Eugene Manlove Rhodes was their constant companion. Not knowing when Sheriff Garrett and his posse might make another attempt to arrest him, Oliver Lee was on the alert day and night. He and Jim Gililland grew beards, kept away from settlements and avoided strange cowboys. Early every morning Oliver Lee went on top of the HG Ranch house, took a spyglass and swept the country, searching the Santa Fe Railway station at Cutter and in every direction to see if there was any sign of Pat Garrett, or any man who might be suspected of being an officer of the law, on their trail.

The Pat Garrett–Oliver Lee contest was apparently at a standstill. Some outspoken citizens of Las Cruces said publicly that Garrett didn't want to find Oliver Lee, that he knew where he could be found, but was evading another showdown fight. In Santa Fe, however, two men were at work, devising a plan that might solve the entire problem for Oliver Lee and incidentally release Pat Garrett from a position that was becoming very embarrassing to him. These men were Albert Bacon Fall and W. A. Hawkins, the latter to become famous as author in the 1903 Legislature of the famous "Hawkins Law," annulled by Act of Congress. Albert Bacon Fall and W. A. Hawkins devised a plan to have the Legislature of New Mexico create a new county out of portions of Doña Ana, Socorro and Lincoln Counties. The argument was that the El Paso and Northeastern Railway was being built through that strip of territory, that a new county was required to facilitate the business of the Territory and its inhabitants.

The prospects were not particularly favorable for the passage of the bill for the creation of a new county. Thomas Benton Catron, always unfriendly toward Oliver M. Lee and for many years hostile politically and otherwise to Albert Bacon Fall, was in the Territorial Council and virtually in command of that branch of the Legislature. There had been a long standing feud between Tom Catron and Governor Miguel A. Otero. In the lower house, Maj. William H. H. Llewellyn was an important member and personally hostile to Oliver Lee.

Hawkins and Fall, however, were adroit, experienced men in legislative matters. They obtained support from Governor Otero, because of a provision in the bill that the proposed new county should be named in his honor. Never suspecting the scheme behind the new county idea, Tom Catron balked at the name "Otero County," but finally agreed to go along after obtaining from Fall and Hawkins a promise of help for his pet bill to create McKinley County in the western part of the Territory.

After the Legislature adjourned, Thomas Benton Catron and

others were soon aware that the "Otero County" bill had been put
through largely to help Oliver M. Lee out of his difficulties. Examination of the boundary lines of the new county disclosed that the
White Sands country in which Colonel Fountain and Henry had
last been seen alive and in which it was alleged that they had been
murdered, was no longer in Doña Ana County, but in Otero County;
that Otero County and not Doña Ana County would thereafter have
jurisdiction of the cases against Oliver Lee, James Gililland and
W. H. McNew for the murder of the Fountains. Tom Catron
growled when he read that Governor Otero had appointed George
Curry, late of Colonel Theodore Roosevelt's Rough Riders in the
Spanish-American War, as sheriff of the new county. Catron knew
that Lee and Curry were old-time personal friends.

With Otero County created, Oliver Lee and Jim Gililland con-
sulted with Eugene Manlove Rhodes and other friends about surrendering to the new sheriff.[2]

Soon after the law creating Otero County became effective,
George Curry, newly appointed sheriff of the new county received
a letter from Oliver Lee, sent to Curry from the HG Ranch through
Tom Tucker, who was Lee's ambassador on the range. The letter
from Oliver Lee set forth the terms and conditions of a proposal to
surrender. Sheriff George Curry went to Santa Fe and conferred with
Governor Miguel A. Otero in regard to the amenities of the situation.[3] Oliver Lee had offered to surrender to the law upon two conditions: first, that he should not be turned over to Pat Garrett,

---

2. 'Gene Rhodes knew what it was to be on the dodge—to have officers on the trail.
On April 7, 1891, 'Gene Rhodes had been indicted by the grand jury of Doña Ana
County for resisting an officer and drawing a deadly weapon. Learning that he had
been indicted, Rhodes kept under cover, working as a cowhand and horse wrangler
on ranches from Mockingbird Gap to the Ladders until May 16, 1892, when he voluntarily submitted to arrest. "What am I charged with?" asked Rhodes of the arresting
officer. "Drawing a deadly weapon," replied the officer. "Hell," replied Rhodes, "if it
had been a deadly weapon, the grand jury would never have indicted me for resisting
an officer, it would have indicted me for clubbing the dam'd ignoramus to death."
Simon B. Newcomb, district attorney, was determined to prosecute Rhodes, but 'Gene
hired a lawyer to represent him, got a change of venue from Doña Ana to Sierra County
on June 11, 1892, and on June 28, 1893, the indictment was dismissed on a nolle
prosse.

3. Miguel A. Otero, Governor of the Territory for nine years, was one of the most
colorful characters in the history of New Mexico. Born in St. Louis, Missouri, on October 17, 1859, he died in Santa Fe on August 7, 1944. Appointed Governor by President
William McKinley in 1897, Miguel A. Otero served as chief executive of the Territory

sheriff of Doña Ana County, and second, that he should not be placed in the Doña Ana County jail. Governor Otero advised Sheriff George Curry to agree to the conditions and Sheriff George Curry went to Las Cruces and told Judge Frank W. Parker in confidence of the arrangement.

Eugene Manlove Rhodes helped to plan the details of the surrender of Oliver Lee and Jim Gililland to the law. 'Gene Rhodes was delighted, out on the HG range, to be in on the planning, happy to help circumvent Sheriff Pat Garrett. On an appointed day Oliver Lee, Jim Gililland and Eugene Manlove Rhodes left the HG Ranch and rode horseback to the Aleman station, a few miles south of Engle, a place later immortalized by Rhodes' poem, "Engle Ferry." There they got on the Santa Fe train, with Las Cruces as their destination. At Rincon they were joined by Tom Hall, another friend, later killed at the Adobe Ranch on the San Augustin plains in neighboring Socorro County. Oliver Lee and Jim Gililland still wore the long whiskers they had grown on the range. Suddenly 'Gene Rhodes crouched in his seat in the chair car of the train and looked at Oliver Lee out of eyes that sought to convey a message. Pat Garrett, sheriff of Doña Ana County, six feet four inches high, was walking down the aisle of the car, the one man in all New Mexico that Oliver Lee did not want to see at that particular moment. Oliver Lee, too, saw Garrett coming, but decided instantly not to try to reach for his gun, hopeful that Garrett would not recognize him. Eugene Manlove Rhodes held his breath. Pat Garrett walked by Lee, Gililland and Rhodes, on into the next car, where he remained during the rest of the journey. The whiskers had saved Lee and Gililland, and possibly Pat Garrett.

Scouting about in the car, Eugene Manlove Rhodes discovered that sitting only a few seats ahead of them was Capt. J. R. Hughes of the Texas Rangers, en route from Santa Fe to El Paso with a prisoner chained to the seat.* With Pat Garrett in one car and

---

until 1903. Fond of politics, Otero was nevertheless a stickler for honesty and integrity in public office, had great courage in the discharge of his official duties. During the latter years of his life Governor Otero wrote the story of his life in "My Nine Years as Governor," in two volumes, "The Real Billy the Kid" and "My Life on the Frontier."

* Geronimo Parra was the name of the prisoner "chained to the seat." Garrett and Hughes, the latter then stationed at Ysleta, Texas, were returning from Santa Fe, where they had obtained the consent of Governor Miguel A. Otero for the release of Parra to Texas authorities. Parra had been a prisoner in the penitentiary in Santa Fe, serving

Captain Hughes in another, Rhodes decided to get right with the law. He got off the train at Rincon and telegraphed Judge Frank W. Parker at Las Cruces that Oliver Lee and Jim Gililland were on their way to surrender. The telegraph operator at Las Cruces told Ben Williams of the message and Williams, when the train arrived there, was at the station, silent and scowling, as an observer of the developments. Oliver Lee, Gililland, 'Gene Rhodes and Tom Hall went at once from the Las Cruces depot to the home of Judge Parker and there formally surrendered. Lee and Jim Gililland handed their guns to 'Gene Rhodes for indefinite safe-keeping. Oliver Lee had kept his promise that he would never surrender to Pat Garrett. Judge Parker deputized 'Gene Rhodes and Tom Hall to guard Lee and Gililland, while he considered what he should do. He studied for a time and then said he would not admit the prisoners to bail and could not send them to jail in Otero County, because Otero County as yet was just a law, a piece of paper, and had no jail. Finally, Judge Parker decided to have Lee and Gililland placed in jail in Socorro and they were turned over to Special Deputy Vincent May of Socorro County, who in turn took them to Socorro and delivered them to Sheriff C. F. ("Doc") Blackington to remain in his custody until a jail could be built at Alamogordo. While in the Socorro jail Oliver Lee spent leisure time in the jail yard boxing with George Cook, a young lad of Socorro, who many years later became sheriff of the county. When the jail was ready at Alamogordo, Sheriff Blackington started for that place traveling on the Santa Fe from Socorro to El Paso, and from El Paso to Alamogordo on the El Paso and Northeastern.

In El Paso, Sheriff Blackington left his prisoners, on their honor, at the Union Station and went out to see the town. Blackington "saw the town" too enthusiastically, was taken into custody by Constable Manning Clements, who refused to believe Blackington's claim that he was the sheriff of Socorro County, New Mexico. Blackington was obliged to have Clements go with him to the Union Station, where Oliver Lee identified him and the constable turned

---

a seven-year term for larceny, committed in Doña Ana County, and for resisting arrest by Deputy Sheriff Ben Williams, at whom Parra had taken a shot. Texas wanted to try Parra in El Paso County for the murder of Sergeant Fusselman of the Texas Rangers, some thirteen years before. See *Santa Fe New Mexican,* March 13, 1899, Albuquerque *Daily Citizen,* March 14, 1899.

OLIVER MILTON LEE.
*Courtesy of Vincent Lee; art work
courtesy of E. L. Blumenschein.*

him loose. Sheriff Blackington had no fear that his reputation in Socorro County might suffer as a result of the El Paso incident. In his home county of Socorro, Blackington was not only the Sheriff, but he was a roving medical practitioner. From one end of the county to the other, he combined medicine and free services as a physician and surgeon with an occcasional bit of practical politics. Professional politicians recognized that on election day "Doc" Blackington could not be defeated for office.

The trial of the case of the Territory of New Mexico versus Oliver M. Lee and James Gililland for the murder of Colonel Fountain began before Judge Frank W. Parker at Hillsboro, Sierra County, on May 25, 1899, and lasted eighteen trial days.[4] Oliver Lee's difficulties had been transferred from the open range and the six-shooter to the domain of law and lawyers.

The trial was looked upon throughout the Territory to be a showdown between the forces of Thomas Benton Catron on one side, of Albert Bacon Fall on the other. Catron, powerful and able, was determined that Oliver Lee should be convicted and hanged. Fall was equally, if not more determined, that Lee should walk out of the courthouse a free man. The case was tried at Hillsboro on a change of venue from Otero County. Prosecution and defense had agreed that the Territory could not get a fair trial in Otero County, where Oliver Lee had many friends. The Territory conceded that Lee would have sentiment against him in Fountain's home County of Doña Ana. The town of Hillsboro had wanted the Oliver Lee trial. For a time it appeared as if the case would go to Socorro or Silver City. The *Sierra Advocate*, published in Hillsboro, on March 17, 1899, complained in an editorial that it was "hardly fair to give the trial to some other county . . . Judge Parker should do something for Hillsboro, the land of his home and mining interests. He refused to give us the United States Court and our corner lots suffered in consequence. The very least he can do now is to give

---

4. Frank Wilson Parker, the trial judge, was born in Sturgis, Michigan, October 16, 1860, received a degree of Bachelor of Laws from the University of Michigan in 1880. He came to New Mexico in 1881 and started to practice at Kingston, then a wild and riproaring mining camp. Here Parker first became acquainted with Edward L. Doheny and Albert Bacon Fall. A Republican, Parker was appointed a judge in New Mexico in 1898 and served either as a trial judge or was on the Supreme Court from that year until his death, August 3, 1932.

James Robert Gililland. An informal picture taken with his
permission a few weeks before his death on August 8, 1946
at Hot Springs, New Mexico.

us the Oliver Lee trial." The *Advocate* had reference to Parker's refusal to hold a term of federal court in Hillsboro. The territorial judges sat both as district judge of New Mexico and as a United States District Judge.

A picturesque mining town, situated in the Percha Valley, with its broad main street beautified by many shade trees, Hillsboro was an ideal place for the holding of the trial of Oliver Lee and Jim Gililland.[5]

Sierra County had recently finished building a new brick courthouse on a hill commanding an entrancing view of Hillsboro's back country of mines and mining, of great livestock interests. Hidden away in the mountains, twenty miles from the railroad, transportation to Hillsboro was a problem, but not a serious one. There were the stagecoach lines to Hillsboro from Nutt and Lake Valley stations on the Santa Fe railroad. One of the stages was driven by Sadie Orchard, the only woman stage driver in New Mexico. Sadie had her own ideas about the Oliver Lee trial and expressed them emphatically in a vocabulary garnished with fighting words. Theoretically, Sadie's husband, J. W. Orchard, ran the Lake Valley, Hillsboro and Kingston Stage and Express line, but there never was any question as to the identity of the senior partner of the enterprise.

The Little Corner saloon, Tomlinson's place and the Union Hotel and bar were popular places before and during the Oliver Lee trial, while Tom Murphy's "Parlor saloon," with three shifts of bartenders, sold the best of liquor and plenty of it to a select patronage. Hillsboro had its share of assay offices, blacksmith shops and like

5. Sierra County was created by Act of the 1884 Legislature, of territory carved out of Doña Ana, Grant and Socorro Counties. The act established "Hillsborough," as the county seat. The spelling was changed to "Hillsboro" in later acts of the Legislature. The name "Hillsborough" was probably given to the town by its founders, Englishmen and Cornishmen, hard-rock miners. In prehistoric days an Indian village, long since in ruins, occupied a site on the bluff adjacent to Hillsboro. Living water for irrigation attracted the Indians as well as the white men. The first town in present Sierra County was located at the placers some six miles northeasterly of Hillsboro, where gold was panned in the late sixties and early seventies. David Stitzel discovered the Snake mine, causing the hard-rock gold rush to the Hillsboro country. The discovery of the Snake mine was soon followed by development of the Opportunity, Bonanza, Ready Pay, Wicks Gulch and many others, bringing hard-rock miners to supplement the placer miners already in the field. Hillsboro became a thriving and prosperous town, picturesque, replete with the activities of the wild west. The Union Hotel, scene of much of the life of the country, was burned down in 1905. The Legislature tried to move the county seat from Hillsboro to Cutter, near Engle, on the Santa Fe Railroad in 1909.

THE COUNTY COURTHOUSE AT HILLSBORO, NEW MEXICO, AS IT APPEARED IN 1899. IT WAS THE SCENE OF THE FAMOUS CASE OF THE TERRITORY OF NEW MEXICO VS. OLIVER M. LEE, ET AL.

enterprises in a community where ordinarily the talk was of mines and mining, pockets of rich ore, the staking out of claims and of contesting them. The hotels in Hillsboro were unable to take care of the crowds in attendance at the Lee trial. There were seventy-five witnesses altogether, about evenly divided between the prosecution and the defense.

The Territory took care of its witnesses in a camp of tents at the north end of town, with its own cook, waiters, guards and discipline. The defense had a like arrangement, called the Oliver Lee camp, at the south end of town and had a chuck wagon where all the Oliver Lee witnesses took their meals. Urged on by the Associated Press and the Hearst papers, the Western Union Telegraph Company built a telegraph line for the trial from Lake Valley on the Santa Fe railroad to Hillsboro in the hills and provided two telegraph operators at Hillsboro to handle the reports filed each day of the trial by correspondents. The *Sierra County Advocate* carried a front page story saying that, "for the first time in the history of Hillsboro, the busy click, click of the telegraph instrument is heard, connected with a wire that stretches across the mountains and valleys, and unites, twenty miles away, with a myriad of other wires that lead to all parts of the United States and the world." Proudly the *Advocate* added: "A few minutes after the wire was cut in, a message was flashed to San Francisco, New York and Chicago, and operators all over the land added a new 'call' to their list." Belvidere L. Brooks, a son of Manager J. W. Brooks of the El Paso office of the Western Union, was one of the telegraph operators employed at Hillsboro during the trial; and he was to live to see his uncle, Belvidere Brooks, become president of the Western Union Telegraph Company a few years later. The Associated Press, El Paso *Herald*, El Paso *Graphic* and the Hearst papers had their own representatives in Hillsboro for the entire trial. John H. McCutcheon, publisher of the *Graphic*, was called before Judge Parker a few days after the trial began,

---

Hillsboro sent Edward D. Tittman, a fighting advocate, to Washington to fight the removal. He was successful in having the Congress annul the act directing removal. Several years ago the county seat was moved to Hot Springs (now Truth or Consequences), taking away much of Hillsboro's prestige and importance. In its days of glory, many men, later to become prominent in affairs, visited Hillsboro, including A. B. Fall, E. L. Doheny, Frank W. Parker. Doheny worked in Kingston, nine miles up Middle Percha Creek. Eugene Manlove Rhodes was in and out of the Hillsboro country for many years. He drew heavily on the Hillsboro area for local color in "Stepsons of Light."

placed under a five hundred dollar bond for contempt of court, returnable at the next term, and warned to thereafter word his dispatches with greater discretion.

The most important lawyers of the day in New Mexico were present for the trial. For the Territory of New Mexico, there were District Attorney R. P. Barnes of Silver City, Thomas Benton Catron, special prosecutor of Santa Fe, and William Burr Childers, special prosecutor, of Albuquerque. For the defense there were Albert Bacon Fall of Las Cruces, Harvey Butler Fergusson of Albuquerque, late of White Oaks, and Harry M. Dougherty of Socorro.

Tom Tucker, a survivor of the Tonto Basin war in Arizona who had been Oliver Lee's ambassador at large while Lee was hiding out on the HG Ranch, arrived in Hillsboro as a witness and pitched camp with no other baggage than a cowboy saddle and a six-shooter. Tucker was a large man, weighed 220 pounds and friends said he looked like "a cross between a deputy sheriff and a cattle rustler."[6]

The weather in Hillsboro was ideal for the trial. There was an atmosphere present during the trial reminiscent of homecoming week and of an old fashioned prolonged revival meeting, with much visiting and handshaking. For Oliver Lee, in jail behind the bars when not in the courtroom, there was many a sincere handshake from old friends of the range country. Prospectors and miners from the hills and valleys around Hillsboro suspended work for a spell, came into town to attend the trial.

When the trial began, it was obvious that Oliver Lee had more friends in Hillsboro than any other man in attendance at the proceedings. Friends had come from all parts of the Territory, eager to show their friendship and to offer help of any kind. Among the cowboys, miners and cattlemen in Hillsboro there was a feeling that

---

6. While helping Oliver Lee and Jim Gililland dodge the law on the HG range, Tom Tucker was an outlaw himself. Tucker was wanted for the murder of Hipolito Vigil, whom Tucker had shot and killed in 1892 while a deputy sheriff under Sheriff Cunningham in Santa Fe County. After the Oliver Lee trial at Hillsboro, where he had been seen and identified, Tucker was arrested by Sheriff Kinsell of Santa Fe County and taken to Santa Fe to face the charge. Tucker claimed that he had attempted to arrest Hipolito Vigil, accused of complicity in the Borrego cases, that Hipolito had resisted arrest, jumped behind a tree and opened fire on him. Tucker, with a Winchester rifle, returned the fire and killed Vigil. Tucker was arrested January 2, 1899, at Oliver Lee's Dog Canyon Ranch near Alamogordo. The usual self defense plea prevailed at Tucker's trial.

Oliver Lee would never be convicted by a jury, but if convicted, that he would never go to prison. Each day of the trial, three cowboys occupied the same seats in the courtroom, followed the testimony carefully and tried to understand the rulings made by Judge Parker. Neither Oliver Lee nor Albert Bacon Fall was aware of it, but the three cowboys had agreed among themselves that, in the event of Oliver Lee's conviction, they would take him away from the custody of the sheriff of the county at the point of six-shooters, place him on a horse, always saddled and bridled outside the courthouse yard, and start him for the border of Old Mexico not so many miles from Hillsboro and of course outside the jurisdiction of the courts of New Mexico. Relays of horses had been provided to make certain the success of this plan of escape.

Many laymen attending the trial at Hillsboro heard for the first time the Latin words, "corpus delicti." Speculation among defense lawyers revolved around the question as to how the Territory would be able to prove that Colonel Fountain had actually been murdered. Even before Lee's arrest, Albert Bacon Fall had held to the theory that unless the Territory could prove that Fountain and his son were dead by actually producing their bodies, or by producing witnesses who had seen them dead, the Territory would be unable to make out a case.

The Territory rested its entire hope of conviction on circumstantial evidence. Somewhere in the White Sands in Otero County, the prosecution believed, were the burial places of the Fountains, but the White Sands, silent, spectral, had disclosed but few important clues. Barnes, Catron, Childers, able, resourceful lawyers for the Territory, tried hard, day by day, to build up a case that would satisfy court and jury, that Oliver Lee should either be hanged by the neck until dead or go to the penitentiary for life. Fall, Dougherty, Fergusson, the defense counsel, always relying strongly on the belief that the prosecution would be obliged to prove the corpus delicti, were surprised and disappointed at the conclusion of the Territory's case, notwithstanding the prosecution had failed to "produce the body" of Fountain or actually prove him dead, when Judge Parker overruled a motion for a directed verdict and summarily ordered the defense to proceed.

The Territory had relied mainly upon the testimony of Pat Garrett, sheriff of Doña Ana County, Captain Thomas Branigan and

Major W. H. H. Llewellyn, all of them known throughout the Territory to be personal and political enemies of Oliver Lee. The jury had been selected, after many challenges by Territory and defense, and kept together in Galles Hall when not in the courtroom, always in charge of two bailiffs. The jury members were: Thomas Mahar, Henry Patrick, Oscar Greeley, P. Torres, Tomas Chavez, Thomas Inglis, Louis Kluse, Alex Bentley, Abel Chavez, August Reingardt, John E. Wheeler, R. A. Nickel. The first witness called by the Territory was Missouri-born William T. Thornton, Governor of the Territory of New Mexico at the time of the disappearance of the Fountains. Thornton had gone to Las Cruces at the time of the tragedy, had made a personal investigation into the facts and had offered a reward for the arrest of the perpetrators of the crime. Governor Thornton had secured blood-clotted earth and horsehair from one of the searchers for the bodies and had submitted them to Dr. Francis M. Crossman of Albuquerque. Dr. Crossman, offering expert testimony designed to prove that human blood had been found at the Chalk Hill camp, was quite confused under cross-examination by Albert Bacon Fall, who had done research on the medical and chemical issues involved with a view to combatting Crossman's expert opinions.

Thornton remained in Hillsboro several days and endeavored to live up to his name of "Poker Bill," by playing a few hands of stud poker with friends. The San Francisco *Examiner* of May 31, 1899, reaching Hillsboro several days later, contained a story sent out by a Hearst reporter regarding Thornton's testimony. The *Examiner* headline over the story read: "Perjury in the Fountain Case—Ex-Governor Thornton's Evidence Tainted with Suspicion—Blood, Soil and Hair Found. Indications that they may have been manufactured." Thornton threatened to sue the *Examiner* for libel, but he and the Hearst man settled their differences in a poker game and the incident was forgotten.

Plagued by what they called an unfair press, counsel for the prosecution went into a conference, cussed the newspapers for being biased and issued the following announcement:

All newspaper reports, including the Associated Press, sent from Hillsboro, about the trial of Lee and Gililland, are gross misrepresentations of evidence and facts generally. We ask you to publish

this daily until the trial is over, or we notify you that misrepresentations have ceased.—R. P. Barnes, T. B. Catron, W. B. Childers,
Counsel.

Unraveled day by day in the testimony of the witnesses, the thread
of the story told by the prosecution in the form of question of counsel and answer of witnesses was that Colonel Fountain and little son
Henry had been waylaid and their buckboard forced off the main
road between Tularosa and Las Cruces. Tracks of three horsemen
surrounded the place. Footprints were found behind a clump of
bushes by the side of the road at Chalk Hill. Three men on horseback had been trailed to a place where they had built a fire and
camped for supper. The trail of the horseback riders had continued
toward the Sacramento Mountains. The trail had been lost because
it had been obliterated by the stampede of an immense herd of
cattle.

There was no question from facts produced at the trial, but that
the child, Henry Fountain, had been waylaid and badly treated, if
not murdered. Henry's older brother, Albert J. Fountain, Jr., testified
that he had seen and identified at the place of waylaying and had
measured with a blade of soap weed footprints of a child's shoes,
that he was certain that the footprints were those of little Henry.
Other footprints had been measured at the camp near Chalk Hill,
it was claimed by Garrett, Branigan, Llewellyn, and that these footprints included those of Oliver Lee and Gililland. There was admitted in evidence the testimony of Colonel J. Heman of White
Oaks, a foreman of the Lincoln County grand jury in 1896 before
which Colonel Fountain had secured indictments against alleged
cattle rustlers, two of the indictments being against Lee and Mc-
New and these indictments were read to the jury. Major H. S. Van
Patten of Las Cruces, best prepared witness for the prosecution, following his recital by reference to a well drawn map of the area, gave
testimony which left but little doubt that Colonel Fountain and
his son Henry had been killed. On the ground the day following
the disappearance of the Fountains, Major Van Patten testified
that he had made a personal search of the vicinity; that he had
found footprints of the assassins behind soap weeds near the Chalk
Hill cut; had discovered empty cartridges and a large pool of blood;
had picked up a napkin and two pieces of blood stained silver cur-

rency on the spot where the crime was claimed to have been committed and had helped to find one of Fountain's horses. Undergoing a strenuous cross-examination, Major Van Patten failed to waver in his testimony.

Jack Maxwell of Tularosa, testifying for the prosecution, said he had visited Oliver Lee's ranch in Dog Canyon on the Saturday evening the Fountains disappeared and had remained there all night; that Lee, Gililland and McNew were not at the ranch that night, but rode up to the ranch the next day, riding double on two horses, with "Ned," a colored boy. Maxwell's testimony became less valuable on cross-examination when he admitted that he had a written contract, signed by Sheriff Pat Garrett and C. G. Perry, under the terms of which they agreed to pay him $2,000 for evidence that would convict Lee. Maxwell was also obliged to admit that he had lived in No Man's Land in Texas under the name of John Alexander. James F. Gould for the Territory testified that he had worked for Gililland and McNew both before and after the disappearance of the Fountains; that soon after the disappearance of the Fountains he had heard Jim Gililland say that "Old man Fountain had come from Texas in a chicken coop and had pried up hell ever since, but that he guessed he would not pry it up any more." Gould testified further that Gililland had told him in the same conversation that "The Fountain child was nothing but a half-breed and that it was no more harm to kill him than to kill a dog." Under cross-examination the defense was unable to get Gould to change his testimony in any important detail. William R. Baker, a deputy sheriff under Pat Garrett and a brother-in-law or Jim Gililland, testified that "at a point in Grapevine Canyon in the Sacramento Mountains, while gathering cattle with Gililland, the latter showed him a spot where he, Lee and McNew had sat with a spy glass and watched the posse search for the Fountains." Baker also testified that Gililland had told him on another occasion "that if no one could be convicted until the bodies were found, no one would ever be convicted." Baker cracked somewhat on cross-examination and admitted that, as a deputy sheriff, he and others, all fully armed, had watched from a house top in Alamogordo, planning to arrest Lee and Gililland "last election day when they came to vote," and also admitted that he had "done a good deal of searching for the defendants but had never visited or searched their homes in the Sacramento Mountains."

Pat Garrett's testimony was not as sensational as rumor had promised that it would be. Garrett's testimony was to the effect that he had seen the pool of blood near Chalk Hill, "that the place looked to him as if a man had been killed there." Garrett testified that he had carried warrants for the arrest of Lee and Gililland for the alleged murder of the Fountains; and told of his several attempts to serve them, the last being at Wildey's Well where Lee and Gililland were found on top of the house and called upon to surrender, at which time Kearney, one of Garrett's deputies, shot at Lee and Gililland and was fatally wounded in return. Garrett told of the voluntary surrender finally of Lee and Gililland to Judge Parker and on cross-examination produced a copy of the much-talked-of $2,000 contract with Jack Maxwell for evidence that would lead to the arrest and conviction of the Fountain murderers. The contents of the contract, signed by Pat Garrett and C. G. Perry, were read to the jury. Garrett's testimony developed nothing of particular importance and his attitude on the witness stand created no impression of value.

With a map of Dog Canyon, Chalk Hills and vicinity tacked up on the wall for the information of the jury, the battle between prosecution and defense continued day after day, much testimony about the Chalk Hills, places of the campfires, footprints of the Fountains and of three unidentified other men, of trails found and lost. On the fourth day a small girl ran up to Oliver Lee in the courtroom during a recess and pinned a bouquet of mountain flowers on the lapel of his coat. Lee smiled and looked pleased and the little child appeared delighted with her venture. Testifying that he had been in a searching party, Carl Clausen, son-in-law of Colonel Fountain, said that he had followed the tracks of horsemen in the attacking party and had followed the trail particularly of a large-footed horse leading toward Wildey's Well; that he had gone there to fill water casks for the searching party and had seen Oliver Lee and five other men there, all heavily armed, on the defensive. Clausen said he had measured the tracks of Lee's saddle horse and that they were the same dimensions as those made by the big horse on the Fountain trail. Captain Thomas Branigan of Las Cruces, an old Indian scout, testified that "there were evidences of a party having carried a heavy object, and depositing it on a blanket at night; that the tracks of a child's shoe were light and only of one foot." Branigan testified:

I measured the tracks of three men about the camp and at other camps along the trail of seven horses from this point, and the next day found tracks on Lee's dirt roof exactly like the one having a heel run over that I found in the camps. When McNew came to Las Cruces a short time later I waited for a chance and measured his tracks. These gave the same measurements as the other about the camp. The track of Lee's horse also corresponded with those of the largest horse on the trail from the camp.

The testimony of Maj. W. H. H. Llewellyn, expected to be of importance to the prosecution, failed to provide anything of unusual value, tracking that of other witnesses who had been with searching parties.

The defense began with the testimony of Albert Blevin, a Texas and Pacific fireman turned rancher, who said that he was with Lee and Gililland at Lee's ranch, sixty-five miles from the scene of the murder during the time Fountain and little Henry were supposed to have been killed. Blevin testified that he arrived at the Lee ranch at two P.M., Saturday, February 1, and remained there until Monday. Three hours of vigorous cross-examination by the prosecution failed to shake Blevin's story.

Oliver Lee took the stand in his own defense, told a straight-forward story of his actions, stood up well under cross-examination. He had been preceded by Mrs. Mary Lee, his mother, who said that her son Oliver was at home on the ranch the day that Colonel Fountain and his son disappeared. Oliver Lee said that he did not learn for several days after the Fountain disappearance that he was being suspected of knowledge or complicity; that he went at once to Las Cruces and offered to surrender and stand trial, but his offer was refused by the authorities. While in Las Cruces, Lee testified that an extra edition of a newspaper was published there, containing inflammatory accusations that he had killed the Fountains; that in Las Cruces he also learned that a posse was being organized to capture him and that among the members of the posse was to be Ben Williams, whom Lee believed to have a mania for murder, and that others to be included in the posse were known to be his sworn enemies.

Albert Bacon Fall, chief of defense counsel, then undertook to have the extra edition of the newspaper offered in evidence to substantiate Lee's testimony. The prosecution, through Thomas Benton Catron, vigorously objected. In reply to the objection, Fall said to Judge Parker that he, Fall, could point in the courtroom to the man "who wrote that article, and he is not the editor of that paper either." Judge Parker ruled that the paper could not be introduced as an exhibit, or displayed to the jury, but permitted Oliver Lee to testify as to the manner in which he had been affected by the publication of the articles. Oliver Lee testified also that he had been advised by friends in Las Cruces that the members of the posse then being formed there would kill him, "with warrants for the murder of Fountain as an excuse." Lee said he heeded the advice of his friends, hurried out of Las Cruces and remained on his ranch, although later he visited Las Cruces on several occasions and learned at one time that the warrants had been withdrawn.

Asked about the killing of Kearney, deputy sheriff under Sheriff Pat Garrett at Wildey's Well, Oliver Lee testified that he slept on the roof because he was afraid that Pat Garrett and his crowd would kill him while asleep. "I was asleep when fired upon," testified Lee. "Kearney fired twice and Garrett also fired before I fired. I heard no commands of hands up, but Garrett was talking while shooting. We killed Kearney. We took care of him and made him as comfortable as possible while dying. We made the Garrett party ride away, but agreed to surrender on condition that Garrett would tell the truth about the matter. I was waiting for a new sheriff to be put in Doña Ana County before surrendering. We were at Dog Canyon almost every day soon after Fountain's disappearance and neither Pat Garrett nor any other officer came after us at that place."

Oliver Lee had made a favorable impression on the jury. His testimony bore the earmarks of truth. It became increasingly apparent that Lee was the center of a political feud, with Tom Catron furnishing the leadership for one crowd, Judge Fall for the other. The disappearance of Colonel Fountain and little Henry became rather incidental. Pat Garrett, Major Llewellyn, Captain Branigan, makers of affidavits which prompted the arrest of Oliver Lee, promising in them strong evidence of guilt had failed to make good their promises. After eighteen days, with many evening sessions, the trial finally came to an end.

The trial judge instructed the jury in a courtroom that was tense with submerged excitement. Albert Bacon Fall, chief counsel for the defense throughout the trial, listened attentively to Judge Parker's instructions. Worn out physically and mentally by the legal battle of many days, Fall asked Harvey B. Fergusson and Harry M. Dougherty, his associate counsel, to make the closing arguments to the jury and left for his hotel room to rest. Oliver Lee soon noticed that Fall had left the court and learned from Harvey Fergusson that he had gone for the day. Lee sent a note to Fall, asking him to return at once. When he returned, Oliver Lee said to him: "Fall, I want you to make an argument before the jury, even though it is not more than ten minutes long. I want you to appear before this jury." Fall pleaded exhaustion and said that both Fergusson and Dougherty were more able and more eloquent orators before a jury. Lee was firm with Fall, however, saying: "Fall, they are trying to hang me for something I'm not guilty of, and you know what I would do for you if you were in trouble."

Conceding to Oliver Lee's request, Albert Bacon Fall agreed to make a short argument to the jury. The argument was without precedent in the history of the Territory. Beginning in a low voice, which gradually increased in volume and pitch, with his hands resting on the jury railing, Fall said:

> "Gentlemen of the Jury: The prosecution of Oliver Lee is the result of a conspiracy to send an innocent man to the gallows. The District Attorney is involved in that conspiracy; the Honorable Thomas B. Catron is involved in that conspiracy. His honor on the bench is involved in that conspiracy."

At the reference to the court, Judge Parker jumped to his feet, excitedly pounded his gavel on the bench and said:

> "Mr. Fall, unless you withdraw your remarks about this court from the jury immediately I shall send you to jail for contempt."

Fall replied:

> "Your honor will not send me to jail for contempt until I am through addressing this jury. When I finish my argument you may do whatever you wish."

Fall knew, Judge Parker knew and Tom Catron must have known that any attempt to stop Fall from addressing the jury through a contempt proceeding would have been construed by the cowboys in the courtroom, nearly all Lee's supporters, as an attempt to prevent their friend from having a fair trial. Bullets from every direction would have been quite a definite possibility. Parker did not pursue his contempt threat. Fall finished his brief argument to the jury and walked out of the courtroom. The hours of lawyer oratory ended, the jury filed out, selected Alexander Bentley as foreman and in a few minutes reached a verdict of not guilty. Oliver Lee was a free man and so was Jim Gililland,* his co-defendant.

When the trial was all over, Oliver Lee and Gililland called on Albert Bacon Fall in his office in Las Cruces, thanked him again for the efforts he had made on their behalf, said they were ready to settle up and asked how much money they owed him. Fall took a slip of paper from his vest pocket, figured a moment and said: "My bill, gentlemen, is $62.25, the money I am actually out, traveling

---

* James Robert Gililland, who probably knew more about the Fountain mystery than any man then living, died in Hot Springs (Truth or Consequences), Sierra County, on August 8, 1946. Several months before his death, the author called upon "Jim" Gililland by appointment in his Hot Springs home, in what might be called an "eleventh hour" attempt to persuade him to make a statement which would clear up some of the mysterious aspects of the cases. The visit was prompted by suggestions from Gililland's close friends that "some day, before it was too late, Jim would tell all he knew about the Fountain case." Polite, courteous and responsive up to a certain point, Gililland skirted and evaded all efforts on the author's part to get him to talk about pivotal points in the case. Jim's secret knowledge passed away with him. It is doubtful if he had ever really "talked" to a living soul about the actual facts of the mystery, whatever they might have been.

Gililland was born in Brown County, Texas, March 22, 1874. The Gililland family packed their belongings in a prairie schooner when Jim was twelve years old, and with a small herd of cattle, made their way to the Mimbres river country, some miles from Deming. The next year the family moved to the Sacramento Mountains country, near present-day Mountain Park. Young Jim worked as a cowboy on several cattle ranches in the White and Sacramento Mountains and in the Tularosa Valley, most of the time in association with Oliver M. Lee, with whom he was implicated in the Fountain case. On June 15, 1902, Gililland was married to Adella Gould, daughter of Jim Gould, a well known ranchman of the Sacramentos. With his wife, Gililland established a cattle ranch in the San Andres Mountains in Socorro County, operating it successfully for 37 years. In 1940 the Gilillands sold the ranch property, traveled about for a year, then located in Hot Springs, the hub of the country they knew so well, and within reach of friends. Old-timers served as pallbearers at Gililland's funeral: W. W. Threadgill, Frank Martin, W. W. Brazil, Oliver Lee, Jr., Lealon Miller, Ed Sanders, Bert Bookout, George Shipley. Of Jim Gililland, it was said by the Sierra County *Advocate*, August 15, 1946: "James Robert Gililland was as typical a pioneer western cowman as any author of scenario, song or story could ask for."

expenses from Las Cruces to Hillsboro and return and my hotel bill in Hillsboro. I took most of my meals at the chuck wagon during the trial and saved you some money that way." Judge Fall waved aside insistent efforts of Lee and Gililland to settle with him on a basis which would compensate him for the services he had rendered. Many years later when Albert Bacon Fall resigned as Secretary of the Interior from the cabinet of President Warren G. Harding, and became involved in Teapot Dome charges, one man from the range country of New Mexico was at Fall's side during the many months of his difficulties. That man was Oliver M. Lee.

eleven

CHARLES BISHOP EDDY

IFFERING over men and management, over methods
and policies, unable to reconcile their differences, James John Hagerman and Charles B. Eddy, co-promoters of the Pecos River railroad and irrigation projects, came to the parting of the ways in
eastern New Mexico in the early nineties. A wealthy man with con-
tacts that were not available to anyone else in New Mexico, James
John Hagerman assumed responsibility for the continuation of the
operation and completion of the enterprises then under way. Eliminated as a factor in the development of the valley, Charles B. Eddy
was obliged to look elsewhere for a market for his talents and ambition. Barely forty years old at the time, he was a powerfully built
man, barrel-chested, vigorous, energetic, restless, ambitious, a man
of nerve and imagination. The county of Eddy, which had been
named after him, was to see him thereafter only occasionally and
the town of Eddy, named in Charles B. Eddy's honor in the days
of his popularity there, was to have its name changed to Carlsbad.[1]

---

1. Charles Bishop Eddy, for twenty years a resident of New Mexico of territorial
days, was born in 1857 in the village of Milford, Otsego County, New York, eight
miles from Cooperstown of baseball fame, adjacent to Cooperstown Lake, in which
the Susquehanna River heads. J. Fenimore Cooper wrote of the country and its characters in the "Deerslayer" of the Leatherstocking Tales. Eddy's father, "Squire" John
Eddy, was a well-known citizen of the community, a part of which was called Eddyville.
Charles B. Eddy left New York state in the early eighties, engaged in the cattle business
in Colorado, where he owned two ranches, "The High Lonesome," and "El Dorado."
He left Colorado and went on the Santa Fe railroad to Las Vegas, was a stagecoach
passenger to the lower Pecos Valley country. Eddy acquired a ranch, which he called
Halagueno, and a bunch of cattle in the Black River country in southeast Lincoln
County, present-day Eddy County. His brother, John Arthur Eddy, joined him in the
enterprise. Although he extended his ranches and increased his herds, cattle raising was
not Eddy's ambition in life. Within a few years he turned his hand to promotion and
remained a promoter until the day he died. Eddy lived dreams, fastened on ideas, pro-

Reluctantly leaving the Pecos Valley country, Charles B. Eddy went to Salida, Colorado, remained there for a time, became interested briefly in a mining promotion. He visited Denver, Leadville, Cripple Creek and other places where mines and mining were the all important subjects of conversation. Unlike James John Hagerman, his late associate in the Pecos River country in New Mexico, Charles B. Eddy had no great interest in mining. The opportunities available to him in Colorado did not appeal to him. His mind kept turning back to New Mexico and a consideration of the possibilities there. Eddy resented that fact that he had not been able to complete the plans and schemes that he and Pat Garrett and others had matured to a point where they were obliged to invite James John Hagerman and other capitalists to become associates and partners. Eddy was anxious to return to New Mexico and try again. He knew the Pecos River country intimately from the Texas line to Fort Sumner. He had every confidence in the ultimate success of the valley railroad venture and the interlocking irrigation projects and land schemes now being administered by Hagerman, in the promotion of which he had assumed leadership for a number of years.

During the time he had helped to promote and build the railroad line from Pecos, Texas, to Carlsbad and on to Roswell, Charles B. Eddy had been urged on a number of occasions to undertake the promotion of a railroad that would serve western Lincoln County and eastern Doña Ana County. Now that he was divorced from his Pecos Valley enterprises and a free agent, Charles B. Eddy began to visualize a line of railroad that would start at El Paso, Texas, skirt the Sacramento Mountains, where there were immense areas of timber lands, take in the ranch country and have its terminus at White

---

moted them, got men and capital interested, lived to see many of his dreams come true. His promotional ability was summed up by William A. Hawkins, for many years general counsel for Eddy and his enterprises, by the statement: "Eddy could dream up something, begin talking about it, would soon begin to believe in it himself, was then irresistible and could convince any skeptic." Many enterprises in New Mexico today owe their existence to Eddy's resourcefulness, tenacity, capacity to think up schemes and develop them into actualities. After a life of great activity, Charles B. Eddy died in New York, April 13, 1931. Affable enough, but never an entertainer nor inclined to boast, Charles B. Eddy was not a "mixer" among people, nor a "hail fellow well met" type of man. He was interested in projects, not in people. He selected men with whom he wished to be associated in his schemes and enterprises. Then he aimed at the target, directed to the kill in his money-raising ventures. In his dealings he preferred the single shot from a rifle, rather than many pellets from a shot gun. Absorbed in his promotional

Oaks, with its gold mines and its coal fields. Eddy blinked his eyes when he remembered that on the proposed route there would be encountered the White Sands and alkali flats, the lava fields and the great areas of land that had been laid waste through volcanic eruption. He preferred to think of the fact that for twenty years the mining camp of White Oaks had been clamoring for a railroad, that White Oaks ore and coal had to be hauled to El Paso, its only substantial market, in wagon trains pulled by horses and mules, an impossible haul, or to the Santa Fe Railroad by way of Carthage, over to San Antonio, a hundred miles away. He preferred to think of the fruit trees of the Mescalero country and of the streams of Tularosa and La Luz affording irrigation for many acres, than of the unsolved problem of water supply for the range country. Never a man to be discouraged by the liabilities of a project, Charles B. Eddy persuaded himself that a railroad could be, and should be, promoted into the White Oaks country. He recognized that over on the Pecos River side of the country, east of the Sacramento and Guadalupe Mountains, there was water in great abundance and that an almost exactly opposite condition existed in the country through which he proposed to construct a line. But, he argued to himself, there would be the satisfaction of demonstrating to all of New Mexico and to the Southwest that he could build a railroad through a country, in some parts of which, at least, a lizard and a horned toad could survive only with difficulty.

Just as barbed wire fences were becoming rather popular in Lincoln County and windmills were being thought about as something other than a new fangled contraption of little practical use, Charles B. Eddy threw doubt to the winds and started on his second big venture in railroad promotion. He knew enough about the background of the railroad situation to profit by the failures of the men

---

work, both in the Pecos River valley and in the White Sands country of New Mexico, Charles B. Eddy had little time for the niceties of life. Frequently on the wing, raising capital, directing enterprises, Eddy never found time for love or marriage. After his early pioneering days, Charles B. Eddy found friends and acquaintances among the prominent men of the nation. He belonged to the Union League Clubs in New York and Chicago and held membership in a number of other exclusive clubs throughout the country. Although he had been interested in cattle ranching in Colorado and New Mexico, Eddy never affected the sombrero or cowboy boots of the West, always clinging to the well tailored business suits to which he had been accustomed in the New York of his young manhood.

who had gone before him in attempting to build a road into south-east New Mexico. He recalled that Morris R. Locke and associates had started to build a railroad from El Paso to White Oaks in 1889, that they had put $170,000 into the enterprise and were then obliged to seek the aid of the courts in receivership. Eddy knew that Locke and several friends had gone broke in attempting to finance the enterprise; that Locke had spent seven years in going from one broker and banker to another in Europe and America, in unsuccessful efforts towards refinancing. Eddy knew also that George Jay Gould, the greatest speculative railroad financier of his day, had gone to El Paso and bought the defunct El Paso & White Oaks Railroad at a receiver's sale for fifty thousand dollars, expecting to resume construction within a short time. He recalled that Gould, after complete investigation into the possibilities, had washed his hands of the deal and pocketed his loss. Eddy knew that the Santa Fe Railroad had considered building into the White Oaks country in 1881 by constructing a line from San Antonio, south of Socorro, but had abandoned the plan as impractical and excessive in cost when measured against the potential freight tonnage. However, Eddy visualized a line of railroad that would pay its way by hauling coal from the mines at White Oaks and from the Salado fields to El Paso, where it could be sold to the railroads, to the mining and smelter enterprises in Texas, Arizona and Mexico.

Promoter Eddy could see profits for the rail line because it would pass nearby Fort Bliss, then a large cavalry post near El Paso; would pass through many miles of cattle raising country; would skirt the White Sands and gypsum dunes near Alamo ranch, which could be utilized for the manufacture of plaster and kindred products; could tap the immense stands of timber in the Sacramento Mountains, accessible from La Luz. There were the thriving towns of Tularosa, Three Rivers and Oscura, to be considered, with great back countries of ranching and mineral development. There were Fort Stanton and the Mescalero Indian reservation, maintained by the federal government, located not far from the proposed line of railway; there were deposits of iron ore, fire and potter's clay near Ancho. Eddy quoted figures to prove his assertions that the railroad would offer employment to many people. He had statistics to show that the railroad would develop an immense country presently without any adequate transportation facilities, from El Paso to White Oaks and perhaps beyond. Certain in his own mind of the feasibility and advisability of the project, Charles B. Eddy, promoter extraordinary, had little difficulty in persuading others to join him in the promotion of the enterprise. He had learned a great deal about business matters from James John Hagerman during his association with him in the promotion of the Pecos River railroad and irrigation projects.

Charles B. Eddy went to New York, interviewed George Jay Gould, acquired from him the ten miles of track of the El Paso & White Oaks Railroad and the ten miles of roadway that had been graded and then abandoned when Morris R. Locke and his associates became involved financially in 1889. Smart enough to know that when George Jay Gould let him have the defunct El Paso & White Oaks property, that the Texas and Pacific Railroad was no longer interested in the possibility of an extension to the north and east, Charles B. Eddy went to the Rock Island Railroad people, placed a map before the board of directors, pointed out that a line could be built from Liberal, Kansas, the then western terminus of Rock Island lines, to Clayton, New Mexico, to connect with the proposed El Paso & White Oaks road which Eddy promised to build eventually to Clayton. Rock Island executives were quick to see the possibilities for them to get a line into El Paso. Eddy said that it would not only mean a 250-mile shortening of the distance between Chicago and El Paso over any competing route, but would also give the Rock Island a connection with the Mexican Central at Juarez, a direct line to the City of Mexico. The Rock Island negotiators were non-committal, but they did not discourage Eddy's plans. He went to El Paso, posted ten thousand dollars with the City Council on September 20, 1897, as evidence of good faith, in return for a railroad franchise through El Paso, the money to be forfeited if construction was not started on the line to White Oaks within ninety days.[2]

Before he went east to interview capitalists, Charles B. Eddy worked for more than two years on the plans looking toward the rehabilitation of the El Paso & White Oaks Railroad. He and his associates acquired the Three Rivers ranch of George B. Barber,

---

2. Texas and Pacific interests were active in 1895 in efforts to take over the abandoned El Paso & White Oaks project, but finally gave up the idea of building into New Mexico.

CHARLES BISHOP EDDY.
Courtesy of Archaeological and Historical
Society of the Carlsbad, New Mexico, Museum.

took an option on coal mines at Salado, supervised diamond drilling on the Carrizozo flats and in the "Mal Agra" country, had
miners open up one hundred or more coal seams at various places
along the route of the proposed railway, made a reconnaissance of
the Tularosa and Three Rivers Valleys. Careful study was made of
the gold mining properties at White Oaks. Reports were prepared
on the possibilities of the Old Abe, South Homestake, North Homestake, Rip Van Winkle, Little Mac, Boston Boy and Lady Godiva.
Experts compiled data on the White Oaks coal field[3] and made a
note of the fact that in the White Oaks gold mining properties
shafts had been sunk to a depth of over 1,000 feet underground
without striking water.

The cattle industry, at the time of Eddy's survey, was in a thriving condition. El Capitan Cattle Company ran over 40,000 head
of cattle on its ranges, the Carrizo Company about 30,000, the
Angus VV outfit about 20,000 head. Many smaller ranches ran
from 500 to 5,000 head. Cruisers confirmed reports of millions of
feet of virgin timber, pine and spruce, accessible in the Sacramento
Mountains, some of it owned by the Mescalero Indians because
it was on their reservation, some of it privately owned and large
areas owned by the federal government.[4]

Charles B. Eddy was successful in his efforts to interest important
eastern capital in his El Paso & White Oaks project. On April 16,
1897, the private car, "Newport," was placed on a side track at
San Antonio, New Mexico, a few miles south of Socorro, on the
Santa Fe line from Isleta to El Paso. Eddy chaperoned a party of
distinguished visitors to New Mexico to examine into the possi-

---

3. The first coal opening at White Oaks was made by J. W. Kelly in 1880. In 1884
coal was discovered about 20 miles south of White Oaks at a place known as Salado.
Development of the mines at the Salado field was carried on through the backing of
James A. Alcock, one of the owners of the Carrizo cattle ranch.

4. The El Paso & Northeastern built a standard gauge line to Russia in the Sacramento Mountains to get out the timber, developed an important industry. An escarp-
ment just below Cloudcroft offered an apparently insurmountable obstacle. Engineer
Sumner, loaned by the D. & R.G., solved the problem by recommending a switchback.
The five per cent grade on the Cloudcroft branch was the steepest grade used by any
standard gauge road in America. Special locomotives were used for a time, then replaced
by Shays, but these were unsuitable because the gears wore out too rapidly. At Cloudcroft a fine hotel was built at an elevation of some 9,000 feet. For many years Cloudcroft has been a widely known summer resort. The hotel was opened to the public on
June 1, 1901.

bilities of the El Paso to White Oaks Railroad. In the party were Colonel Henry M. Boles, a capitalist of Scranton, Pennsylvania; W. A. Lathrop, General Superintendent of the Lehigh Valley Coal Company of Wilkes - Barre, Pennsylvania; Benjamin H. Harmon, an attorney of New York City; Clarence D. Simpson, coal operator of Scranton, Pennsylvania; George Dickinson, former general manager of the Union Pacific, with offices in Omaha, but representing New York capitalists on the inspection trip; Commodore G. C. W. Lowrey, president of the Vanderbilt Mining Company, a large stockholder in the Rock Island and other railroads; John A. Eddy, brother of C. B. Eddy; and M. M. Gillam, who had been for six years city editor of the Boston *Post*, seven years managing editor of the Philadelphia *Ledger*, and for eight years public relations expert for John Wanamaker and other prominent men of the east. Oliver M. Lee and Andrew H. Hudspeth, in charge of a roundup outfit especially selected for the occasion, greeted the easterners in San Antonio, piloted them across the country east of the Rio Grande. Albert Bacon Fall, George Curry and William A. Hawkins joined Eddy at San Antonio, helped to entertain his guests. The capitalists rode in splendidly equipped hacks and coaches, drawn by four horses, slept in the open at night on bed rolls, took their meals from a chuck wagon, lived for days in typical western style. The party visited White Oaks, Nogal, Salado, the Mescalero Indian reservation, Tularosa, the Sacramento timber, Black Mountain gold camp, Slack's wells and other places along the route of the proposed railroad. The trip ended in El Paso, to which place the luggage of the visitors and their car, the Newport, had been forwarded. The easterners stopped at the Vendome Hotel in El Paso, shocked the natives by dressing in evening clothes for dinner. By October 1, 1897, the eastern capitalists notified Charles B. Eddy that they would back his railroad enterprise from El Paso to White Oaks or a nearby point. By October 28, 1897, Eddy had incorporated the El Paso & Northeastern Railroad Company.[5]

---

5. The incorporators were Clarence D. Simpson of Scranton, Pennsylvania; Charles B. Eddy of Eddy, New Mexico; G. C. Lowry, Rudolph T. McCabe, Benjamin S. Harmon and John Davis, all of New York City. The officers elected included Charles B. Eddy, president; C. D. Simpson, vice-president; John A. Eddy of Denver, secretary; W. A. Hawkins, counsel. It was announced that the road was to be 170 miles in length, of which 26 miles would be in Texas and about 150 miles in New Mexico. From El

Construction work of the El Paso & Northeastern Railroad was prosecuted vigorously. Hundreds of men and teams were put to work building the grade and laying the track. The tents and cook shacks of the construction outfits were moved to a new camp every few days. Mule skinners, proud of their ability to drive "sixup," looked down on men occupying less responsible places, pushing on the lines of teams of horses drawing fresnos and scrapers. By February 1, 1898, the construction gangs had crossed the Texas line into New Mexico, twenty miles from El Paso. John A. Eddy opened a bottle of champagne to celebrate the occasion as the first spike was driven into a tie to fasten a steel rail on the New Mexico side. Before the railroad reached New Mexico, Attorney W. A. Hawkins filed for record in Las Cruces and Lincoln a $5,000,000 mortgage to secure a bond issue on all the company's property in Doña Ana and Lincoln Counties.

From the Texas–New Mexico line, the El Paso & Northeastern Railway followed a survey that went along the foothills on the east side of the Jarilla Mountains, passed within three miles of the old Wildey Well. On April 13, 1898, Oliver Lee sold his Alamo ranch and water rights to Eddy Brothers for $5,000. Surveyors laid out and platted a townsite named Alamo Gordo, shortly contracted to "Alamogordo," and the railroad reached that place at 10 A.M. on June 15, 1898. Petitions were signed requesting the establishment of a postoffice at Alamogordo and Silas D. Pollock was named the town's first postmaster. Everybody connected with the railroad construction from high officials to mule skinner was happy when the work was finished into Alamogordo, because there for the first time water could be obtained in abundance. From the time they had left Fort Bliss the construction outfits had been plagued and ham-

---

Paso the road would be built to Fort Bliss, thence to the Tularosa Valley, on to the foothills of the Sacramento Mountains and thence north to the coal fields of Salado and White Oaks. The primary object of the railroad project, it was announced, was to get coal. John A. Eddy, a brother of Charles B. Eddy, was to be in charge of construction. Charles B. Eddy immediately purchased 27 miles of steel rails that had been laid on the Chispa railroad, built to reach the San Carlos coal properties in San Presidio County, Texas. The Chispa coal fields had been abandoned. Eddy used the rail in the El Paso & Northeastern. The contract for the first 85 miles of line was let to Geo. S. Good & Co. of Lock Haven, Pennsylvania, and 100 teams started to work on November 30, 1897. The contract for ties and timber was let to William Cameron & Co., of Waco, Texas. Eddy rented engine 38 from the Santa Fe Railroad and an engine from Kansas Midland, which was repaired in the T. P. shops at El Paso.

pered by lack of water for man, beast and machine. Well drillers went ahead of the tracklayers, searching for water, and developed it, even in small quantities, with the greatest difficulty. As the railroad was being built toward La Luz, it began to become a boom town. Men worked day and night shifts in the Sacramento Mountains on contracts for 300,000 railroad ties to be used in construction of the railroad. There was a wild scramble for government land. Homesteaders filed on four thousand acres of public domain near La Luz within a few days after the railroad reached that place. Representatives of the railroad company took options on seventy-five ranches in the Sacramentos, expecting to sell them to Pennsylvania farmers who were to be brought in to settle up the country.

Tularosa, nine miles from La Luz, had a population of from 600 to 800 people in 1898. Excitement over the coming of the railroad unbalanced for a time Tularosa's usual interest in politics and saloons. Construction work out of Alamogordo lagged for many months, but by June 29, 1899, the track of the El Paso & Northeastern had been laid to Three Rivers, some eighteen miles above Tularosa, and a month later was within thirty-two miles of White Oaks. On August 3, 1899, the track had been completed to White Oaks junction in the Carrizozo flat. Only an hour away by team, on horseback, or on foot, from the railroad line down in the valley, the people on the mountain up at White Oaks were enabled to leave that camp in the morning to reach El Paso by 7 o'clock the same evening. This extraordinary possibility prompted the White Oaks *Eagle* to remark, that "this seems incredulous almost, to persons who little more than a year ago, made the trip to El Paso and return in two weeks."

The people of White Oaks, having patiently waited for twenty years for a railroad to reach that camp, were disturbed by rumors that the railroad would be built to other places, but not to White Oaks. The White Oaks *Eagle* of November 9, 1899, spoke rather frankly on the subject, accused the promoters of the road of insincerity and contended that the use of the name White Oaks as a terminal point on the line of the proposed road had been merely for promotional purposes. It was soon apparent that White Oaks was to be by-passed by the railroad, for the time being at least, because construction was started on a branch line from the Carrizozo flats to the Salado coal fields.[6] Soon after the eastern capitalists had agreed to back Eddy in his El Paso to White Oaks railroad enterprise, Eddy and his associates incorporated the New Mexico Railroad & Coal Company, with an authorized capital of $4,000,000. The Eddy brothers sold to a syndicate for $200,000 the Salado coal mining properties which they had acquired several years before for a comparatively small sum of money. On February 1, 1900, the Eddys bought acreage from S. T. Gray, platted a townsite on the old Safford place just across the Salado and named it "Capitan." White Oaks people from time to time had declared it was folly to build a railroad to the Salado country in expectation of finding coal there in commercial quantities, that the Salado field simply did not have the coal. Eddy's coal experts advised him to the contrary. The railroad was built from Carrizozo to Capitan. The mines were opened, adequate equipment was installed and experienced coal miners were brought in from Pennsylvania. Widely advertised "white ash coal" was for a time mined in Capitan in substantial tonnage, hauled to El Paso and marketed there. Faults and dikes were encountered in the mines at Capitan. Miners began to experience difficulty in mining the coal. Slabs of volcanic rock interfered with digging. New veins were opened up, but the same conditions prevailed, apparently throughout the field. Thirty-six coal miners, most of them from Pennsylvania, were discharged on October 3, 1899. They talked frankly, said the coal was "pinching out," that in their opinion the Salado country was so broken up that coal never would be found there in paying quantities. The news that the coal was "pinching out" at the Salado mines, if true, was of tremendous importance and would be a terrific blow to Charles B. Eddy and his associate promoters of the El Paso & Northeastern. The White Oaks Eagle was not slow to comment on the rumor about the coal situation in the Salado field. In the issue of October 10, 1899, the Eagle carried an "I told you so" editorial. Referring to the Eddys, the Eagle commented:

---

6. White Oaks had promised a subsidy to the railroad promoters of $50,000 and forty acres of land for terminals and a right-of-way nine miles long from the mouth of the canyon to the top of the divide. Black Mountain people had pledged $40,000; La Luz, $7,500; Tularosa, $35,000; Three Rivers, $10,000 and 140 acres of land. J. L. Bell, associated with Eddy Brothers in the railroad promotion, had charge of obtaining subsidy pledges. Bell rode a mule over most of the country west of the Sacramentos in his campaign to obtain subscriptions.

The Eddys are all right. They occupy an easy position. They have mortgaged the Salado coal fields, or that portion of them under their contract, for a million and a half dollars, and the railroad for two and a half million dollars, making a total of four million dollars, out of which they should at least clear two millions of dollars, which pays them pretty well for the work they have done in the development of the country. . . . They have already demonstrated their strength in handling both people and things, and in this side of New Mexico, as in the Pecos Valley, they will get what they are after, and the other fellow will get the rest.

In El Paso, Charles B. Eddy, president of the El Paso & Northeastern, was quick to defend the integrity of the Salado coal field and said in an El Paso *Herald* interview of October 11, 1899:

There is no trouble about the coal; it is there in abundance. All we need is time to fully open a mine. As a matter of fact, the term pinching applies only to minerals and not to coal. Coal veins do not pinch out. It is true that what are known specifically as faults, under the general term of "troubles," and which are in effect, a seemingly abrupt termination of the vein, exists in ours as well as in all other coal fields. The Salado deposit is all right. The coal is there and we will have an output up to our most sanguine expectations when the headings are driven deep enough to permit regular mining.

Coal experts, however, soon rendered an opinion that was the death blow for the Salado coal mines. Charles B. Eddy was forced to admit privately the complete failure of the Salado coal field as a substantial producer, a thing he had denied publicly. With coal in great quantitites simply not available, with no other tonnage of importance, the railroad would be nothing but a liability, a streak of rusted steel in a few years.

On June 26, 1900, the Eddy Brothers, associated together for more than fifteen years in various promotional enterprises dissolved their partnership. Charles B. Eddy paid his brother one hundred thousand dollars in cash as his share of the profits. John A. Eddy was free to go his separate way. By May 1, 1901, there was no longer any use in pretending that stoppage of work in the Salado mines was of a temporary nature. The coal field was abandoned and the machinery was pulled out of the mines.

When Charles B. Eddy had engineers confirm for him that the Salado coal at Capitan had "pinched out," or was so shut off by dikes that it would never develop into a commercial field, he turned resolutely toward the White Oaks coal mines. White Oaks people had sat on the side lines, disgruntled because Eddy had built his railroad to the Salado field, instead of to White Oaks, still suspicious that he might leave White Oaks isolated. They were confident that Eddy was on the right trail at last, when he visited their camp on May 17 and again on May 31, 1900, inspected the coal fields and their gold mines. They were quite elated when a survey gang started on July 5, 1900, with rod, chain, transit and level to take measurements and run levels between the head of White Oaks Canyon and Carrizozo station.

Regardless of the critical situation in regard to the availability of coal, Charles B. Eddy obtained assurance from New York capitalists that they would finance an extension of the railway north and east from the White Oaks country. The White Oaks and Kansas City Railroad Company was incorporated under the laws of New Mexico, with incorporators and objects identical with those of the El Paso & Northeastern. Charles B. Eddy spent many months in New York City, at the turn of the century, negotiating with the officials of the Chicago, Rock Island and Pacific Railroad, urging them to commit the Rock Island to extend their line from Liberal, Kansas, to Clayton, New Mexico, to which latter point he expected to build. Eddy's arguments were so persuasive that the Rock Island decided to build into New Mexico and started to survey to Clayton on July 11, 1900, from a point about 100 miles west of Liberal. The work was carried on under the direction of Chief Engineer W. D. Worral of the C.R.I.&P. Sixteen men with an outfit consisting of a half dozen wagons, sixteen horses and camp supplies, finished the job in ten months. The surveyors abandoned the original plan of running a line to Clayton and the line was run to a point near the present town of Tucumcari. Following the location engineers, the Rock Island completed a line from Liberal, Kansas, to Dalhart, Texas, near the New Mexico line, a distance of 111 miles, by June 20, 1901. On January 15, 1901, Charles B. Eddy began construction of the El Paso and Rock Island Railroad from Carrizozo to the Pecos River. White Oaks was left off the main line, waited patiently month after month for a branch line to provide transportation for its ore to smelters and its coal to market. The railroad branch was never built. White Oaks was deserted by all but its most staunch supporters, became a ghost mining camp.[7]

White Oaks had been left without a railroad because of an idea that came to Charles B. Eddy at a time when it seemed as if he faced certain defeat through the failure of the Salado coal fields and the difficulties he expected to encounter in mining coal at White Oaks. The mines at White Oaks were owned by people who could now dictate the royalty on every ton of coal produced. The cost of constructing a railroad to the White Oaks coal field was almost prohibitive.

Eddy knew of the Maxwell Land Grant in Colfax County, New Mexico, had heard that there was a coal field on the grant of considerable importance, claimed by John B. Dawson, that there had been litigation over the property between Dawson and the Maxwell Land Grant Company. Eddy sent W. P. Thompson, a mining engineer, to make an examination of the coal deposits on Dawson's ranch. Thompson spent many days in looking over the property. He learned that as far back as 1873 it had been known that there was coal on the ranch. Old-timers in the area believed that there were coal veins underground from three to thirty feet in depth

---

7. John Y. Hewitt, born October 11, 1836, in West Farmington, Trumbull County, Ohio, took up his residence in White Oaks in 1880, lived to be 94 years old, was loyal to the camp for more than a half century as lawyer, newspaper editor, owner and operator of the "Old Abe" and other properties. John Y. Hewitt bequeathed his earthly possessions and traditions to his longtime friend and law partner, Andrew H. Hudspeth. Born in Greenville, Texas, on October 23, 1874, "Andy" Hudspeth studied law at Cumberland University, in Tennessee. He came to Lincoln County, New Mexico, in 1894 and was admitted to the bar in the same year.

From 1894 until his death in Los Angeles on March 10, 1948, Hudspeth had a colorful career in New Mexico. From 1894 until 1902 he was secretary of the Angus VV Ranch in Lincoln County, a position which enabled him to know personally many cattlemen and cowboys. In 1902 Hudspeth formed a partnership with Judge Hewitt, and they practiced law together in White Oaks for many years.

Hudspeth served as United States Marshal for New Mexico from 1913 until 1921. In office as Marshal for only a few days, Hudspeth was obliged to deal with a serious uprising of Navajo Indians. Some 150 Navajo braves went on the warpath, conducted a raid on the Indian Agency at Shiprock, on the San Juan River, fired many shots, but wounded no one. However, the Navajos took their children from the Shiprock school and led a thousand men and women, many of them armed, to Beautiful Mountain, from which historic tribal place they defied Marshal Hudspeth and other government officials, and seriously threatened to go on the warpath. The First Squadron, 12th U.S. Cavalry, was rushed from Fort Robinson, Nebraska, to Gallup, New Mexico, in a

and that the coal covered about 1,200 acres. Charles B. Eddy read Thompson's report on the Dawson field, left at once for Santa Fe, where he borrowed from the Clerk of the Supreme Court a transcript of the record in litigation then pending in that court over ownership of the coal field. He took the record to Alamogordo, delivered it to his long-time counsellor and personal friend, William Ashton Hawkins, asked him to read it over, study the law of the case, give him an opinion as to how the legal battle would terminate. Lawyer Hawkins took the papers, pored over them for hours and for days, studied his law books. Finally he told Charles B. Eddy that in his opinion the law was on the side of John B. Dawson and that he would finally prevail over the Maxwell Land Grant Company. Eddy asked Hawkins to leave at once for the Dawson ranch in Colfax County, interview Dawson, get an option from him on the coal field, contingent upon the outcome of the lawsuit. Attorney Hawkins went by railroad to Springer, New Mexico, and from there by team as fast as he could travel to the Dawson ranch, where he interviewed Uncle Johnnie Dawson, one of the oldest settlers on the Maxwell Land Grant. Hawkins learned that Charles Springer, a keen and astute lawyer, represented Dawson and it later developed that Springer owned an interest in the Dawson property. Knowing that the Salado mines had "pinched out" and that great difficulties would be involved in a railroad extension to White Oaks and operation of

---

special train. The cavalrymen began the march from Gallup to the Beautiful Mountain country. General Hugh F. Scott, an experienced Indian fighter, accompanied by Marshal Hudspeth and J. R. Galusha, one of his deputies, went in advance of the troops, had a talk with the Navajo leaders, and agreed upon a treatry of peace and friendship.

On March 9, 1916, Pancho Villa raided Columbus, New Mexico, which resulted in the Pershing expedition into Mexico. As United States Marshal at the time, Hudspeth went to Columbus, where he assumed many burdensome duties, including the supervision of patrols on the boundary line between Mexico and the United States. Many Mexicans were arrested for violating the neutrality laws. One of Hudspeth's most famous prisoners was General José Ynez Salazar, a Mexican general who crossed over the line, was arrested and placed in jail in Albuquerque, only to escape in a sensational prison delivery.

In 1930 Hudspeth was elected a justice of the Supreme Court of New Mexico. He served on the court six years, a part of the time as Chief Justice. When Judge Thomas J. Mabry resigned from the Supreme Court in 1946 to run for Governor, Hudspeth was appointed by Governor John J. Dempsey to fill out Mabry's term.

His days on the Supreme Court at an end, Hudspeth returned to Lincoln County and resumed the practice of law in Carrizozo. To the end of his life, Judge Hudspeth looked forward with great confidence to the day when White Oaks would regain its old time splendor as a great gold mining camp.

coal mines there, Hawkins did not quibble about prices with Dawson or Charles Springer. He obtained an option, under the terms of which Dawson agreed to give Hawkins, or his nominee, the right to buy the Dawson property for $400,000, contingent upon the successful outcome of the pending litigation.

William Ashton Hawkins remained in the vicinity of Raton, Springer and Cimarron for many weeks, waiting for final disposition of the litigation affecting the Dawson ranch. Finally there was an end to the fight between the Maxwell Land Grant Company and John B. Dawson. Dawson was free to deal with Hawkins and his associates, Charles B. Eddy and Clarence D. Simpson.

When it became generally known that Dawson had won his lawsuit over the Maxwell Land Grant people, there was a rush to his ranch of men anxious to purchase the property because of the coal mining possibilities. But Hawkins, careful painstaking lawyer, and Eddy, the idea man, had won the race for the prize.[8]

The Dawson coal field was located twenty miles from Springer, eighteen miles from Maxwell City. The title to the property was conveyed to the Eddy interests on March 1, 1901. The sum of $100,-000 was paid down, and the balance of $300,000 paid shortly afterward. "Uncle Johnnie" Dawson conveyed land for a townsite for an additional $5,000, reserving out of his ranch his home, some farming land, the orchard and a bit of grazing land. With the Dawson coal field in his possession and under his control where, as time demonstrated, there was ample coking coal as good as any known in America, the nightmare of the "pinched out" Salado coal fields faded from Charles B. Eddy's memory. He quickly abandoned the idea of building a railroad to White Oaks and attempting to operate mines there. Plans were made to build a line of railway to the Dawson coal field from either a point on the El Paso & Northeastern, or the Rock Island. It was decided to run the line from Tucumcari, instead of Santa Rosa as had been originally contemplated. Before long men and teams and scrapers were busy throwing dirt on the

---

8. On January 17, 1869, Lucien B. Maxwell, owner of the immense Beaubien-Miranda Land Grant, known as the Maxwell Land Grant in modern times, sold a tract of land of indefinite description, carved out of the grant, to John B. Dawson. Maxwell sold the entire grant to a syndicate in 1870. The new owners of the grant sought to eject Dawson. For details of the litigation see *Maxwell Land Grant Company vs. Dawson*, 7 N.M. 133, 151 U.S. 586. Also see *The Maxwell Land Grant, a New Mexico Item*, by W. A. Keleher, Rydal Press, Santa Fe, 1942.

branch line to Dawson, a distance of 132 miles from Tucumcari. The new line crossed the Atchison, Topeka & Santa Fe Railroad at a point now known as French. Santa Fe officials were obliged to sit idly by and permit the Rock Island interests to invade the Santa Fe's own territory, watch a competing carrier acquire a vast annual freight tonnage.[9]

Fate intervened in the crises of the promotional affairs of Charles B. Eddy. From time to time he drew picture cards from the deck of destiny. If it took aces to beat kings, Eddy held them. The Dawson coal field emerged as an Eddy triumph just about the same time that the Copper Queen mine at Bisbee, Arizona, began to exhibit unmistakeable evidence of greatness as a producer of copper. Two entirely unexpected factors had been introduced into the affairs of the El Paso & Northeastern Railroad—a great demand for coking coal by the Phelps Dodge interests for their mines and smelter operations in southern Arizona and the availability of adequate sources of coking coal at Dawson, in northeastern New Mexico. Coking coal of good quality and in great quantity was essential for the success of the copper property.

A railroad line to transport the coke and coal from Dawson to Bisbee was an absolute necessity. The earnings of the Copper Queen mining property were fabulous, reaching into the millions each year. There were rumors that in one particular year of sensational production the property had netted forty millions of dollars. Anxious to get the Dawson coking coal, the Phelps Dodge people constructed a line of railroad in 1901, connecting Bisbee, Arizona, and El Paso, Texas. Charles B. Eddy built the line from Tucumcari to Dawson. The Rock Island extended its line from Dalhart, Texas, to Tucum-

---

9. Some years after Charles B. Eddy and his associates disposed of their interests in the El Paso & Northeastern Railroad and the Dawson coal field, they acquired from A. H. Hilton (father of Conrad N. Hilton, famed hotel man) and the Santa Fe Railway the coal mines at Carthage, Socorro County, New Mexico, built the New Mexico Midland Railway, a few miles of track, to San Antonio, where it made a junction with the Albuquerque–El Paso branch of the Santa Fe Railroad. For a number of years the Carthage Fuel Company operated the mines successfully, then the coal played out. Bartley Hoyt Kinney, then a young mining engineer who had worked in the mines at Bellair, Ohio, and Dawson, New Mexico, prospected, found valuable veins of coal east of Carthage, began to mine coal, shipped it to El Paso, founded the mining town of Tokay, a name selected at random for the establishment of a postoffice, became a very successful operator. Born in Belmont, Ohio, on December 28, 1884, Mr. Kinney died in Albuquerque on October 8, 1959.

cari, on to Santa Rosa, New Mexico, and across the Pecos River at that place. Eddy's line from Carrizozo was completed to a point near the Pecos River to a junction with the Rock Island.

Eddy's railroad enterprises were financed through bond issues; the Rock Island extensions were financed through bond issues and borrowings. The Phelps Dodge people paid cash as they went along for the El Paso to Bisbee road, named the El Paso & Southwestern. It was inevitable that Charles B. Eddy, the promoter of the El Paso & Northeastern Railroad, and the line from Tucumcari to Dawson, should meet and negotiate with Dr. James Douglas, the man who was directing the affairs of the Phelps Dodge Company. Dr. Douglas was a genius, if there ever was one, in the handling of copper and copper mines.[10]

Early in 1905 Charles B. Eddy recognized that the time had come when he should undertake to promote a deal to sell the El Paso & Northeastern Railroad, the Dawson coal mines and the Dawson to Tucumcari line to the Phelps Dodge interests. He began negotiations with Dr. James Douglas, placed a special train at his disposal upon his arrival in New Mexico. Dr. Douglas left the examination of the railroad property to others, but spent many days at the Dawson mines. He recognized the importance of owning the mines which produced the coal, which made the coke upon which the Copper Queen mine, smelters and allied properties depended, and of owning the railroad which hauled the coke from the coal mine to the copper properties.

Snowbound in Carrizozo, New Mexico, for ten days during his inspection trip, housed in the private car, "Alamogordo," Dr. Douglas had time to ask for detailed information about the El Paso & Northeastern properties from Charles B. Eddy and his associates, took time to tell them of his early day experiences in Arizona min-

---

10. Born in Quebec, Canada, in 1837, James Douglas, of Scotch descent, was educated beyond the rank and file of his day, lived to become one of the outstanding copper men of the world. He took an A.B. degree at Queen's University in Kingston, Canada, in 1858, and was given an LL.D. by McGill in 1899. He was settled for life as a professor of chemistry at Morrin College in Quebec, but friends discovered his ability and prevailed upon him in 1875 to accept a place as manager of the copper works at Phoenixville, Pennsylvania. A volume would be required to tell the story of the part played by Dr. Douglas in connection with the discovery, development and extension of the famous Copper Queen mine at Bisbee, Arizona, of the purchase of the Calumet & Arizona and other mining activities. He became the dominating figure in the Phelps

ing. As a result of the inspection trip, Dr. Douglas recommended to his board of directors that the Phelps Dodge Company purchase the Dawson coal mines, the railroad line from Dawson to Tucumcari and the El Paso & Northeastern and its affiliate enterprises from Santa Rosa to El Paso. Eddy had calculated the mortgage indebtedness on the property, the debts of the various corporations involved in the enterprises, the number of shares of stock outstanding, the profit he and his associates expected to make in the deal. He asked a price for all of the properties which rather shocked the Phelps Dodge crowd. Negotiations incident to the sale of the property lagged for weeks and months. Charles B. Eddy became impatient, requested action. The Phelps Dodge directors asked Eddy to come to New York for an interview. Eddy traveled to New York in a private car. The Phelps Dodge people told Eddy after several conferences that the asking price for his property was much too high, that they had decided to decline his offer and had completed all arrangements to get coal for their Arizona and Mexican properties from the San Juan County coal fields in New Mexico; that they planned to construct a line of railroad from near Farmington to either Albuquerque or Gallup, where it would connect with the Santa Fe.

Charles B. Eddy listened attentively to the talk of San Juan County coal, was silent for a moment and then said quietly: "Gentlemen, your proposal sounds all right, with one exception. San Juan County coal won't coke!" Dr. Douglas, spokesman at the meeting of the board of directors, leaned forward and exclaimed: "Won't coke! Eddy, how do you know it won't coke?" Charles B. Eddy replied: "Dr. Douglas, when you people were so slow about reaching a decision in this deal, I suspected that you were considering an alternate proposal. I knew you had to have coking coal. The only big available coal field that I knew about in New Mexico that might offer coking coal possibilities was in San Juan County. So I went there, took samples of coal from all over the field, had my engineers make tests and satisfied myself that there was no real coking coal in that county." Dr. Douglas and the other directors went into an

---

Dodge Company, with its mines, smelters, railroads and other important properties in the Southwest. Dr. Douglas, grandfather of Bisbee-born Lewis Douglas, one-time president of the Mutual Life Insurance Company of New York, died on June 25, 1918. No one man did more in a constructive way for the mining industry in Arizona and the Southwest, generally, than did James Douglas.

executive session, then told Charles B. Eddy that they would accept his proposal; suggested that the attorneys representing buyer and seller cooperate in the preparation of the necessary papers to effect the transfer. The deal was closed on July 1, 1905.[11] Charles B. Eddy was a multimillionaire. The Phelps Dodge people took over the Dawson mines, installed new equipment, made Dawson a model camp at a cost of hundreds of thousands of dollars. Dr. Douglas personally supervised the construction of coke ovens of an elaborate and expensive design. Coking coal, by trainload after trainload, was sent to Bisbee to permit the Copper Queen and other copper producing and smelting properties in that area to continue the production which meant showers of gold when converted into money.

In and out of New Mexico on promotions for twenty years, Charles B. Eddy, with millions at his command, played the big money game consistent with his pattern of life. Always and incurably a promoter, he was identified with many big and daring schemes requiring substantial sums of "risk money." He became financially interested in early day automatic telephone prospects in Chicago. He was the man who had the idea which resulted in the enlargement of the underground conduit for the telephone wires to sufficient size to accommodate not only the cables but underground freight traffic; he traded and trafficked in mines and smelters in Mexico; he promoted the construction of a railroad in Spain; was the negotiator between American capitalists and General Venustiano Carranza in promoting the Carranza revolution in the Republic of Mexico. He met the General by appointment at Newman, New Mexico, on May 1, 1910, on the occasion of the delivery of assurances to him of financial assistance in exchange for promises of concessions in Mexico at a future day. With his mind ever eager for new schemes, Charles B. Eddy was always willing to take a chance with fate. He was willing to invest time and money in any constructive plan or enterprise offering fair promise of success. Years ahead of his time he became interested in a gasoline-cracking formula, an operation

---

11. The Phelps Dodge interests (El Paso & Southwestern) acquired the Eddy interests (El Paso & Northeastern) and the mining properties at Dawson on July 1, 1905. The El Paso & Southwestern owned and operated the Northeastern lines north and east of El Paso, as well as its own properties west of El Paso, until November 1, 1924, when the Southern Pacific company took over the whole El Paso & Southwestern system by lease of the railroad lines and purchase of its stock.

in which others subsequently made great fortunes. During the Burk Burnett and Ranger boom days in the twenties, he dabbled in oil ventures in Texas oil fields. Before his hair had turned white, Charles B. Eddy had traveled a long distance from the days of his boyhood in Otsego County, New York, and from cowpunching days on a cattle ranch in southeast Lincoln County, New Mexico.

During the latter years of his life Charles B. Eddy visited New Mexico several times, traveling to Carthage, a coal mining camp near San Antonio, in which he was financially interested. In San Antonio, he spent many hours at mid-day in retrospection, resting in a comfortable chair, backed against an adobe wall, bareheaded, drinking in the New Mexico sunshine, eyes directed toward Mockingbird Gap and far horizons to the east, to the Guadalupes and the Sacramentos, beyond which the Pecos River flowed through a marvelous valley.[12]

Tired, aging, his fortune pretty well spent, Charles B. Eddy, always a gentleman and a loyal friend, a man of courage and outstanding ability as a promoter and builder, died in St. Vincent's Hospital in New York City on April 13, 1931. Funeral services and burial were in Milford, New York, the town in which he was born. His imagination, his energy, his planning, his resourcefulness had brought to New Mexico a transcontinental railroad. He had obtained the orderly development of the great Dawson coal field in Colfax County. He had conceived and executed plans that in many respects had changed the map of New Mexico. New Mexico, particularly southeast New Mexico, owes gratitude, respect and admiration to the name and memory of Charles Bishop Eddy.

----

12. The adobe wall formed the south side of the Hilton Hotel in San Antonio, New Mexico, then owned and operated by August Holver Hilton, born near Oslo, Norway, August 15, 1854, who emigrated to the United States with an older brother in 1860. lived for a time in Fort Dodge, Iowa, went to Denver in 1880, to New Mexico in 1881. A. H. Hilton acquired a coal mine at Carthage, sold it to Charles Bishop Eddy for a substantial sum. A. H. Hilton's son, Conrad Nicholas Hilton, born in San Antonio, New Mexico, on December 25, 1887, became well acquainted with Charles B. Eddy, who told him in his youth: "Connie, if you want to launch big ships, you must go where there is deep water." Eddy had reference to the Rio Grande, only a stone's throw from the hotel, at some seasons only ankle deep. Connie Hilton's imagination was fired by Eddy's talk of the big things the future held for men of vision. The present-day far-flung Hilton Hotel empire stems in part from Eddy's enthusiasm, communicated to Conrad Nicholas Hilton, for enterprises of daring and magnitude.

twelve

WILLIAM ASHTON HAWKINS

WITH MOST LAWYERS, the professional achievements of a lifetime are wrapped up in bundles of legal papers and documents, filed away in cabinets, marked down in entries in minute books at courthouses in which they pleaded cases before courts and juries, or recorded in opinions printed in bound volumes in the state reporter system. Engaged in service, dealing with mental processes and opinions, lawyers cannot claim credit in the twilight of their careers for the erection of a structure of steel or stone, of a skyscraper or a bridge or a railroad. The credit for such things must go to the architect, engineer, builder, the financier, the promoter. Limited in their field to paperwork, to advising clients, perhaps encouraging them to a course of action, attorneys at law seldom have the satisfaction of translating the intangible into the tangible.

Occasionally, however, there are lawyers whose professional pathways lead to places where their work is not perishable, where they dominate enterprises of clients to such an extent that they may justly claim a fair share of the credit and acclaim for successfully completed projects. It fell to the lot of William Ashton Hawkins, long-time New Mexico lawyer, to play such a role in connection with the development of many important enterprises in southeast New Mexico. For decades before and after statehood, the name of W. A. Hawkins was known all over southeastern New Mexico, in El Paso, Texas, and generally throughout the Southwest. It is extremely doubtful if the ventures in New Mexico of Charles Bishop Eddy could have succeeded without the help of W. A. Hawkins, lawyer. Eddy, the promoter, needed Hawkins, the lawyer and administrator. William Ashton Hawkins was the indispensible man to Charles B. Eddy.

William Ashton Hawkins was born in Huntingdon, West Tennessee, on April 6, 1861; he died in Albuquerque on June 22, 1939.
Known to boyhood friends in his native state as "Ashton" Hawkins,
he attended the common schools in Huntingdon, began the study
of law in the office of Alvin Hawkins, a power in politics in the state
of Tennessee before, during, and after the Civil War.[1] When Alvin
Hawkins stumped the state of Tennessee in his campaign for governor, his nephew, Ashton Hawkins, went with him and got to
know and understand something of politics. When Uncle Alvin
was elected Governor, Ashton Hawkins went to Nashville, got a
job in the State House, attended law school at Vanderbilt University, became a Phi Delta Theta. Nephew of Governor Hawkins or
not, Ashton Hawkins' boss obliged him to work hard at his job
at the capitol. Ashton was missing so many lectures at Vanderbilt
that he induced his brother, Horace Norman Hawkins, later a very
prominent lawyer in Denver, Colorado, to leave the Hawkins farm
near Huntingdon and help him out with his work at the capitol
building. For this assistance, Ashton Hawkins paid his brother's
board at the St. Cloud Hotel in Nashville. Horace attended business
college at night, hopeful to learn shorthand, but failing to grasp the
intricacies of the subject, he abandoned the enterprise after attending a few sessions.*

When he ran for Governor of Tennessee a second time, Uncle
Alvin Hawkins was defeated. Ashton Hawkins, who had campaigned
with him, felt the defeat more keenly than the candidate himself.
He decided to get away from Tennessee forever and go west. Judge
Ridgely, publisher of the *Tennessee Republican*, obtained a railroad
pass for Ashton Hawkins from Huntingdon to El Paso, Texas. He
arrived in El Paso on July 4, 1883, with little money and no definite

---

1. Alvin Hawkins, uncle of William Ashton Hawkins, was born in Bath County,
Kentucky, on December 2, 1821. His family moved to Maury County and later to Car-
roll County, Tennessee, in 1828. Alvin worked on a farm, helped his father at black-
smithing, taught school, studied law, was admitted to the bar in 1843. He was elected to
Congress as a Unionist in 1862, but was not seated because of claimed irregularities in
the election. He served as United States District Attorney for the western district of
Tennessee in 1864-1865, went to Havana, Cuba, as consul general in 1868 after serving
three years on the Supreme Court of his state. He was elected Governor of Tennessee in
1881, serving until 1883, when he was defeated for a second term. He died in 1905.

* As of 1962, there are seven surviving children of William Ashton Hawkins: Ashton
W., John, Gardner, Clara Hawkins Nellen, Julia Hawkins Sloane, Betty Hawkins Sey-
mour, David.

knowledge of what he expected to do. He was employed for a time on the El Paso *Times*. After a few months as newspaper reporter in El Paso, Hawkins decided to go to Silver City, where he had a friend, John Somers of Dresden, Tennessee, a brother Phi Delta Theta, who had been obliged to travel west for his health. Somers had graduated with the class of 1881 at Vanderbilt and had started to practice law at Silver City. Arriving in Silver City late in 1883, Hawkins found Somers ill of the smallpox, nursed him day and night. He finally closed the eyes of his young friend in death on December 2, 1883. Wandering about Silver City, then a wild west town from Whiskey Creek to Tumbledown Alley, Hawkins was thinking about going to California to join John M. Hawkins, a brother, who had gone to that state in 1878, settling first in Marysville, later in Sacramento, where he worked as a reporter for the Sacramento *Bee*, covering the Senator Sharon trial.

Reports came to Silver City that Geronimo and his Apaches were on the warpath near Pinos Altos, nine miles from Silver City, riding up the hills and down the valleys, scalping men, carrying off women and children, burning and plundering. Back in Tennessee, Hawkins had heard many stories about people being scalped by Indians in the days when the frontier was being settled up. Now, Hawkins felt, he was on the frontier in person, with an opportunity to participate in spectacular Indian fights. He joined Company B, 3rd Regiment, New Mexico Volunteers in Silver City, was given a gun, rounds of ammunition and field rations. Mounted on a cayuse, Hawkins went on the chase with many other men from Silver City and nearby country, looking for Apaches, firing at them, running them toward the mountains of Old Mexico. Indian scares over, Hawkins was discharged from the militia as a sergeant, went back to Silver City, found out that he had made friends among the militiamen and people of the town and was accepted as almost an old-timer. Admitted to the New Mexico Bar in 1885, Hawkins went into the office of Conway & Posey, a substantial law firm in Silver City. After serving a brief apprenticeship with the firm, the name was changed to Conway, Posey & Hawkins.[2] Hawkins practiced law in Silver City for several years, demonstrating ability and capacity that

2. Thomas F. Conway was personal attorney for John S. Chisum. C. G. Posey, from Wilkinson County, Mississippi, was one of the attorneys for Joel A. Fowler, tried at Socorro for murder, lynched by a mob there on January 22, 1884.

gave assurance of future professional success. During the eighties there was great business activity in Grant County, New Mexico, especially in cattle and mining. The firm of Conway, Posey & Hawkins had all the legal work that it could attend to properly. Political experience gained in Tennessee, campaigning with Uncle Alvin Hawkins and about the capitol at Nashville, became a worthwhile asset in Hawkins' hands when he was retained to go to Santa Fe in the late eighties, and again in the early nineties, to oppose measures introduced in the Legislature designed to divide Grant County into two counties, or in the alternative to remove the county seat of Grant County from Silver City to Deming. Always an ardent Republican, Hawkins became initiated into the mysteries of the New Mexico Territorial Legislature, with Sig Lindauer of Deming giving him a few lessons in practical politics. Collections were taken up in Silver City, Deming and several of the mining camps to fight for or against the county division and county seat removal measures. Some forty to fifty thousand dollars went to Santa Fe to participate in the fight. The lawmakers, happy to have struck pay dirt, taught both Hawkins and Lindauer things about political manipulation that disillusioned them, left them wondering about men in public life.

William Ashton Hawkins suffered the loss of his first wife in Silver City in 1888 and decided to leave that part of New Mexico. Charles B. Eddy, a cattleman from New York, who had settled down in the Black River country in southeast Lincoln County, retained William L. Rynerson of Las Cruces as his personal attorney. Eddy and Rynerson met in Lincoln occasionally to discuss legal affairs, each man traveling a long distance to keep the appointment. The arrangement was difficult for both men. Eddy's affairs were broadening out. He was extending his cattle ranch holdings. He was on the defensive in land fraud charges brought by the United States government in connection with homestead entries and final proof. He was associated with Pat Garrett, C. D. Bonney and others in schemes to impound the waters of the Pecos River in reservoirs, to construct canals and irrigate the lands in the valley from the Texas line to the village of Roswell. Charles B. Eddy needed the services of a lawyer nearly every day. He wanted Rynerson to leave Las Cruces and settle in the Pecos River country.

Rynerson preferred, however, not to leave the Rio Grande. He

WILLIAM ASHTON HAWKINS IN 1917.

recommended that Eddy undertake to procure the services of William A. Hawkins, a young attorney at Silver City, who was thinking of a new location. Charles B. Eddy arranged for a meeting with Hawkins. They made a deal. Hawkins was to be Eddy's lawyer. He would have an office with Eddy in the town of Eddy, a hamlet carved out of one of Eddy's cattle ranches. The arrangement between Eddy and Hawkins resolved itself into an attorney and client relationship that lasted for many years. If Charles B. Eddy had looked over the entire country and had interviewed hundreds of lawyers, it is doubtful if he could have made so fortunate a choice as his selection of William Ashton Hawkins. Eddy was a rare combination of a man of imagination and a man of action. Hawkins was keen minded, realistic, with a definite bent for business and corporation law. He had studied about corporations; he knew how they worked; he believed in them. Hawkins was convinced that a corporation was the instrumentality through which capital could best be utilized and protected for the development of the country and the advancement of the people. Notwithstanding his belief in corporations and his reverence for them, Hawkins never believed in corporate manipulation, nor in stock jobbing. His respect for corporations was limited to the legal and legitimate uses to which they might be put. Throughout his life, he held sharply defined ideas about the rights of stockholders and believed that their rights should be interpreted strictly in conformity with legal and moral principles. After leaving Silver City[3] and its memories, William Ashton Hawkins in 1889 began the practice of law at Eddy in the far southeast corner of New Mexico, almost in Texas. Most of his work was done for Charles B. Eddy, or for one of the corporations Eddy and associates had organized. The Eddy enterprises were strung up and down the Pecos River, one of which was the railroad from Pecos, Texas, to Eddy, later extended to Roswell and which, still later under James John Hagerman's administration, was extended to Amarillo, Texas. An-

---

3. William L. Rynerson, who brought Charles B. Eddy and William Ashton Hawkins together, resulting in a fateful combination for New Mexico, was born in Mercer County, Kentucky, February 22, 1828. He went to California in 1852 during the gold rush, enlisted in 1861 in General Carleton's California Column, serving in Company C throughout the war, was discharged as a lieutenant colonel. He was admitted to the bar in New Mexico in 1870, served two terms in the Legislature, served as District Attorney of the third judicial district with residence in Las Cruces.

other enterprise was the townsite in Eddy, as well as townsites at other places up and down the river. Eddy's cattle ranches, irrigation projects, land schemes, all required the attention of an attorney. There was plenty of legal work for Hawkins to do and he did it, carefully, intelligently.

Eddy soon recognized that in Hawkins he had not only a lawyer, but a business associate and confidante of exceptional value. Eddy had little concern for what a statute meant, or how it might be interpreted. He wanted action, wanted the thing done, regardless of what the printed words might be or what they might mean to some people. Hawkins was guided by the words in the law book and the meaning they intended to convey. Hawkins, lawyer and business-man, was brilliant; whereas Eddy was sometimes vague when it came to close consideration of financial problems. Hawkins, with mental acumen, realized in the middle nineties, even before Eddy, that the Eddy enterprises in the Pecos Valley country were headed for financial disaster.

Hawkins became acquainted with James John Hagerman soon after Hagerman became identified with the Eddy promotions in the Pecos Valley. Hawkins was realistic enough to believe that Hager-man and Eddy, two strong men with divergent thoughts on many things, would eventually fall out and go their separate ways. Conse-quently he was not surprised when Charles B. Eddy announced that he was retiring from activities in the Pecos Valley, that Hager-man would carry on. With his head full of facts and figures about the Pecos Valley enterprises, Hawkins would have been a valuable man for Hagerman. But Hawkins, associated now for several years with Eddy, preferred to retire with him.

In the town of Eddy, later Carlsbad, William Ashton Hawkins became acquainted with John Franklin, an able young lawyer from Mississippi. They formed a partnership, started to practice law in El Paso in 1895 under the name of Hawkins & Franklin, an associa-tion that lasted until Franklin's death. When Eddy smashed up financially in the Pecos Valley country he told Hawkins that he had other ideas for New Mexico's development; he told him confiden-tially of a plan he had in mind of giving railroad connections to Lincoln and Doña Ana Counties west of the Guadalupes and the Sacramento Mountains through rehabilitation of the long aban-doned El Paso & White Oaks Railroad. Moving to El Paso, William

A. Hawkins continued to serve as attorney for Charles B. Eddy.

Eddy's plan to rehabilitate the El Paso & White Oaks met with enthusiasm in El Paso. For some time after the panic of 1893, the town had been marking time in the affairs of business and commerce. Assurance of another railroad centering in El Paso stimulated business, encouraged citizens who had begun to doubt El Paso's claim to greatness. Ostensibly the El Paso & White Oaks road, resurrected under the name of El Paso & Northeastern, was to be a coal hauling line from White Oaks to El Paso, with promise also of ore shipments from the White Oaks gold mines for smelting at El Paso. There was talk, however, that the El Paso & White Oaks line would be extended beyond White Oaks and that Promoter Charles B. Eddy had assurance from the Rock Island interests that they would build a line to the Pecos River in New Mexico to make a junction with the Eddy road there, which would give El Paso another transcontinental line. Hawkins accompanied Eddy to New York, talked to bankers and capitalists, outlined plans for formation of corporations and discussed intelligently things pertaining to mortgages, bond issues, and common and preferred stock.

In New York, "Judge" Hawkins as he was introduced by Charles B. Eddy, became acquainted with Arthur Curtis James, director in the Phelps Dodge, later to become the largest individual owner of railroad stocks in America, and with George Jay Gould, heavily interested in the Texas & Pacific, Missouri Pacific, and other railroads. When Charles B. Eddy acquired the abandoned El Paso & White Oaks line from Gould, Hawkins examined the papers, and approved the transaction.

William Ashton Hawkins guided and advised Charles B. Eddy through the legal trials and tribulations incident to the promotion and construction of the El Paso & Northeastern from El Paso to Alamogordo to the Carrizozo flats; the building of the spur to Capitan to tap the Salado coal fields and the building of the extension from Carrizozo to the Pecos River near Santa Rosa.

When the coal fields near Capitan "pinched out" and it appeared that Eddy's venture was a disastrous failure because without coal to haul there was no need for a railroad, William Ashton Hawkins encouraged Eddy in his belief that the John B. Dawson ranch in Colfax County might offer the solution of his coal mining problem.

Hawkins went to the Vermejo country and literally camped on the trail of John B. Dawson and Charles Springer, his attorney. After much negotiating Hawkins obtained an option on the Dawson property, which turned out to be a great coal field and the salvation of the Eddy enterprises.

Before the El Paso & Northeastern reached the present town of Alamogordo in present Otero County, Promoter Eddy and his associates acquired from Oliver M. Lee enough land for a townsite. The blueprints of the engineers specified that Alamogordo was to be a division point and the junction of a line to run into the Sacramentos to haul out logs felled from the millions of feet of timber in the mountains. Long before the railroad was finished into Alamogordo, all of the necessary legal documents had been prepared by William A. Hawkins for the organization of a municipal government. A map of the townsite had been filed showing the streets and avenues, the numbering of the lots and blocks. Subsidiary corporations had been organized and the necessary franchises and permits prepared for the companies to operate proposed public utilities.

A long time prohibitionist, Charles B. Eddy wanted a clause inserted in every deed conveying a lot in Alamogordo prohibiting the sale of intoxicating liquors on the premises. Experience had taught Eddy, however, that such a clause in every deed would create a bootlegging problem just outside of the town limits. Consequently, he requested Judge Hawkins to see that every deed, with the exception of deeds in one block, should contain such a clause. Hawkins tied the liquor traffic legally to one block, suggested that Eddy select the number of that block. Eddy took the map of the town, placed his finger on a block located a considerable distance from the space indicated for the terminal buildings of the railroad. "There's the place for liquor, if we've got to have it," declared Eddy. But William Ashton Hawkins told Eddy it would be a mistake to place a saloon in an obscure place. The place for a liquor establishment, Hawkins said, was right down in the center of things. Hawkins pointed to Block 50 as the ideal location for a liquor establishment, a short block just across the way from the proposed location for the superintendent's office. "We might as well admit that some of the railroad employes are going to take a drink of liquor now and then," commented Hawkins. "With a liquor establishment right across the street from the superintendent's office, a man is going to think twice before he goes into a saloon for a drink and a lot of them are never going in."

Eddy agreed that the lots in Block 50 should be conveyed without a restriction in the deed against liquor and began to talk about the price for the ground involved. Hawkins had thought about that, too. He argued that the ground should not be sold, but conveyed to a subsidiary corporation, which would lease it to an operator, the lease to contain stringent provisions. Eddy agreed. Finally Hawkins said, one-tenth of all the revenue produced by the liquor traffic should be set aside in a fund for the beautification of Alamogordo, to aid in planting trees, in the establishment of parks and in helping the citizens build a model town. Again Charles B. Eddy agreed. The plan was carried out as Hawkins had suggested. Hawkins drove the legal nails into the deeds and leases and contracts, clinched them on the other side. Time and again in subsequent years, shrewd lawyers had attempted by every device known to the law to circumvent the Hawkins liquor restriction and reversion clauses in the deeds of conveyance to Alamogordo lots, but without permanent success.[4]

The El Paso & Northeastern road had a difficult time in building a line as far as Alamogordo and a more difficult time in raising money to build on to a place later known as Carrizozo. The construction of the line from Carrizozo to the Salado coal fields was an uphill task topographically as well as financially. However, Charles B. Eddy had powerful friends in the east and eventually the line was extended from Carrizozo to the Pecos River in order to make a junction with the Chicago, Rock Island and Pacific. Hawkins prepared the papers for each new railroad corporation, and each subsidiary, kept their minutes correctly, and fought and defended damage suits brought against them in New Mexico and Texas. New York lawyers hardly ever criticized the papers that Hawkins prepared. He was a corporation man at heart. He thought in terms of corporations by day, dreamed of them at night.*

---

4. See *Alamogordo Imp. Co. v. Hennessee,* 40 N.M. 162, 56 Pac. 2d 1127; *Alamogordo Imp. Co. v. Prendergast,* 43 N.M. 245, 91 Pac. 2d 428, 122 A. L. R. 1227; *Alamogordo Imp. Co. v. Prendergast,* 45 N.M. 40, 109 Pac 2d 254.

* David Hawkins, youngest son of William Ashton Hawkins, presently teaching Philosophy at the University of Colorado, wrote an appraisal of his father's political

Charles B. Eddy and his associates acquired the Dawson coal mining property, demonstrated that it produced coal that could be made into coke, proved that the supply of coking coal was adequate for a great many years. The Phelps Dodge Company, owners of the Copper Queen and other properties at Bisbee, Arizona, had been obliged to bring coke for their smelters from West Virginia, a long and expensive haul. With Dawson coking coal available, the Eddy interests built a road to the mines from Tucumcari, a distance of 132 miles. The Phelps Dodge Company built a line from Bisbee to El Paso to meet the El Paso & Northeastern line.[5] Trainloads of coke and coal were transported from the Dawson coal mines to the smelter at Douglas and the Copper Queen, Calumet and Arizona,

---

views and the motivation behind them in a letter to the author, written from Santa Fe on Sept. 24, 1945. To quote the appraisal in part: "My father stood for many things now commonly regarded as reactionary. In their time and context they were, I believe, an essential aspect of Lincolnian radicalism. He was a man of strong principle, although not doctrinaire. In the short run he was a loyal 'corporation man,' in the long run he was that because of a conviction of the fruitfulness and progressive character of corporate enterprise. What makes his public life interesting is the fact that the actual nature of the corporation was in his day changing from his idyllic conception of the pool of individual capital to the contemporary self-living financial giant. Indeed, he and countless others like him were the unwitting agencies of this development. Because his views were principled, he was repelled not only by the character of New Mexico politics, but also by the Eastern financial men whom he met. Ignorance of the social niceties and protocol of the latter and a certain condescension from them toward the amusing Westerner, contributed of course. But basically he felt that the predominant interest of many Eastern capitalists in profit blinded them to the proper function of capital, the material development of society. An exception among these men was William Church Osborne of Phelps Dodge, who became one of my father's life long friends."

5. The story behind the building of the lines of railway to bring New Mexico coal and coke to the copper mines in Arizona might well challenge the abilities of a graduate student ambitious to earn a Ph.D. degree. The El Paso & Northeastern, the so-called Eddy line, linked up with the Rock Island line at Santa Rosa, New Mexico, on the Pecos River, on or about February 1, 1902. Some time in 1901, Phelps Dodge Company finished a line from its smelter at Douglas, Arizona, running eastward through Hachita and Hermanas, thence to a connection with the Santa Fe railroad at Deming, New Mexico. It was through this gateway that Phelps Dodge received most of its coal and coke from the West Virginia fields before the development of the mines at Dawson, New Mexico. Dissatisfied with the rates charged by the Southern Pacific for freight over the line running to Benson, Arizona, and equally dissatisfied with the rates charged by the Santa Fe Railroad upon reaching Deming, the Phelps Dodge people resorted to a flank movement. When the Eddy line connected with the Rock Island at Santa Rosa in 1902, they built a line eastward from Hermanas to El Paso,

and other Phelps Dodge properties beyond the Mexican border.* Charles B. Eddy decided to try to sell the El Paso & Northeastern and all of its subsidiary properties to the Phelps Dodge, with vast interests in the Southwest and ample capital. The Phelps Dodge interests were represented by Dr. James Douglas, chairman of the board, a noted chemist and metallurgist. Dr. Douglas entered into negotiations for the property, but there was one serious drawback, the scarcity of good water on almost the entire line of the El Paso & Northeastern. The water situation had proved to be an almost insurmountable problem. The most capable water experts in America had been employed by Charles B. Eddy to study the water problem and to make recommendations for a solution. Wells drilled all along the right-of-way produced water that contained gypsum, alkali and other foreign elements in such quantities that it was impossible

---

thus obtaining an outlet, independent of either the Southern Pacific or Santa Fe, for their ore shipments over the newly completed El Paso & Northeastern—Rock Island route. The Hermanas—El Paso line was finished and opened for business on December 10, 1902.

* The linking together of Dawson coal with Arizona copper, with the El Paso & Northeastern and allied railway lines providing the transportation between coal mine and copper mine and involving an investment of many millions of dollars, proved after all to be only a temporary arrangement. Coal and copper mining and railway construction considered as a unit project, was one which had challenged the abilities of the finest talent in engineering and finance. Peering into the forseeable future in the early 1900's, experts would have been justified in predicting that coal would be mined indefinitely in the Dawson field to produce copper in Arizona. The time came, however, when the Dawson mines were abandoned, when feeder railway lines were torn up, when not a ton of Dawson coal was burned in the operation of the Copper Queen mine in Bisbee, or in the smelter in Douglas. The Dawson mines were abandoned following tests conducted over several years by Phelps Dodge, owner of all the properties directly involved, which demonstrated that it would be cheaper to use natural gas, piped in from west Texas and eastern New Mexico, than to continue to mine coal, transport it and burn it in the Arizona facilities.

As of May 1, 1950, the coal mining town of Dawson, for forty years and more a model camp, was to all intents and purposes extinguished and eliminated, literally wiped off the map of New Mexico. At the Phelps Dodge fiat, wreckers moved in on Dawson and, within a few months, like Jerusalem of old, there was not left in the town a stone upon a stone. In no time at all, or at least so it seemed, the Dawson hotel had been razed; the postoffice, tavern, bowling alleys, recreation building, churches, and the great general store building, said to have been erected at a cost of $250,000, were knocked down and the debris hauled away. The railway depot, scene of happy meetings and sorrowful partings for so many years, was left untouched for a time for purely sentimental reasons. All underground machinery, trackage and facilities worth salvaging were brought above ground, sold and otherwise disposed of, some shipments being made to West Virginia mining camps. Dawson was left without sufficient structures

to use either as drinking water or for use in engines. Railroad men were frantic because of engine failures.[6]

A million dollars expended by the Eddy group in searching for water, in drilling wells and in the use of chemicals in treatment of the water, seemed just that much money thrown away. As a last resort, water trains made up entirely of tank cars, were run from El Paso, for use on the road, mostly between Carrizozo and Santa Rosa.

William Ashton Hawkins was bothered, day and night, by the water problem. He had nothing to do with it really, because it was an operating and not a legal problem, but anything that concerned his client concerned him also. For once, Charles B. Eddy had no solution to offer. He was a promoter, not a water witch. Hawkins reasoned, however, that there must be some way to get around the water situation. He knew, and had known for years, that there was no water worth mentioning in the flats along the White Sands, or the gypsum dunes, the alkali country, or near the lava beds, through and near which for many miles the railroad extended.

While the water men looked for water in the flats and engineers treated water with chemicals, Hawkins turned his thoughts toward the mountains east of the railroad right-of-way. He became convinced that the water problem would be solved in the heights, not in the lowlands. He was familiar with the topography of the Sacramento Mountain country and of the sources of water there. His idea was to trap the water in the mountains and bring it down hill to the railroad, instead of trying to bring it up from below the

---

to justify its claim to distinction as a ghost town. Long to be remembered in Dawson's history: The great explosion of Oct. 23, 1913, in which 286 miners lost their lives.

6. The water problem on the El Paso & Northeastern was without parallel in the history of railroad construction and operation in the Southwest. Wells were drilled every few miles between Carrizozo and Santa Rosa, but the water encountered was a saturated solution of gypsum. The company purchased treating plants, but the water could not be treated effectively for use in locomotives. Coal cars were converted into water cars and several of them were attached to each train, behind the engine, in order to get a train over the road. The water in the engines churned and foamed in the boilers, blew over and washed the oil off the valve seats and cylinder walls. Ordinarily the engineer could not tell how much water he had in the boiler, because the water glass would show full of water when actually the crownsheet was dry. The water used in the boilers loosened flues and staybolts in the firebox. The fire would be put out despite the efforts of the fireman. On most trips, from three to six engines were required to haul a train from Santa Rosa to Alamogordo. Frequently a train would be set out on a siding, and the dead engines pulled in to Alamogordo for repairs.

surface of the earth. Hawkins had an idea that never occurred to Charles B. Eddy, the man of dreams and ideas. At the first opportunity, Hawkins suggested to Dr. James Douglas the possibility of using water from the mountain tops, but warned him of the many problems that would interfere, such as the purchase of land and water rights of many settlers with prior rights, procurement of concessions from the federal government and from the Territory of New Mexico, of the huge cost involved in projects designed to impound and transport the water to the railroad.

The problems Hawkins mentioned did not appear insurmountable to Dr. Douglas, who told him at once that he believed his plan for obtaining water was the one and only practical plan that had been suggested. Dr. Douglas had his engineers make a reconnaissance survey. The Hawkins plan was reported feasible. The Phelps Dodge Company purchased the El Paso & Northeastern and its subsidiary properties, tied them into the El Paso & Southwestern Railroad. William Ashton Hawkins went to New York with Charles B. Eddy to close the deal. Phelps Dodge capital made possible the construction of a wooden pipeline from high up in the Sacramento Mountains, by means of which the water of mountain streams was conveyed to points parallel to the railroad line for many miles eastward from Carrizozo. The great pressure of the water caused the wooden conveyor to weaken in places, leaks developed and some years after the original wooden installation a steel pipe line was substituted.[7]

---

7. The W. A. Hawkins plan for bringing water from the mountain tops involved great expenditures of money, engineering skill and a vast amount of legal work. All of the legal procedure was handled by Hawkins, or under his direction. Some years after the entire job was finished Hawkins wrote an exhaustive report entitled, "Report Concerning Acquirement and Ownership of Bonito and Eagle Creek Waters by El Paso & Rock Island Railway Company." The report was finished on October 16, 1929, after the Rock Island had acquired an interest in the El Paso & Northeastern property. The deal between the Eddy interests and the Phelps Dodge Company was completed July 1, 1905, and the El Paso and Southwestern took over operation of the El Paso & Northeastern. Under the supervision of W. A. Hawkins, the Phelps Dodge interests acquired lands on the Bonito River and with the lands, the water rights, and in many instances, leased the lands back to the former owners. The Nogal reservoir and Bonito pipe line were constructed and water transported to Carrizozo. The Southern Pacific acquired the El Paso & Southwestern property in 1924. Hawkins advised the S.P. that the water system was inadequate, recommended a larger reservoir. As a result the Bonito reservoir was constructed in 1932. Hawkins spent weeks and months in Washington on the water problems, because government lands and water rights were involved, appeared

William Ashton Hawkins was a busy man throughout most of his life in New Mexico. He devoted so much time to his professional work that it was only occasionally that he took a fling at politics. His name was linked politically from time to time with the names of Albert Bacon Fall, Holm O. Bursum, John Sully and other men, prominent a generation ago in the councils of the Old Guard wing of the Republican party. Whether he wished it or not, Hawkins was looked upon as a leader in the party, a spokesman for corporate wealth. Hawkins never manifested any ambition for high public office, but he was persuaded to run for the Territorial Legislature in 1902. He was elected and sat in the Council for the counties of Doña Ana, Grant, Luna and Otero. Hawkins was willing to serve in the Legislature because he had drawn a bill he wanted to introduce and to have passed. The bill became famous as the "Hawkins Bill," and received national attention.

During the many years that Hawkins and his associates had fought battles in connection with the construction of the El Paso & Northeastern Railroad, the company had been sorely afflicted by damage suits, seeking money judgments for personal injuries alleged to have been sustained in New Mexico. Nearly all the suits were brought in

---

many times before departments, carried on extensive litigation. It is doubtful if any lawyer in New Mexico practice at any time conceived and pressed to a successful completion a project as important to New Mexico as did W. A. Hawkins in connection with the Bonito-Nogal water rights transaction. The Phelps Dodge people were not ungrateful. When they sold the property in 1924, they sent Hawkins a check for thirty thousand dollars, with another check for twenty-five hundred dollars for income tax purposes, as a gesture of their gratitude and good will. Until within a few years before his death, Hawkins was the general counsel for all the railroad companies involved in connection with matters pertaining to water rights along the line of the old El Paso & Northeastern.

The magnitude of the water transmission project may be realized by considering that it involved the construction of 170 miles of fourteen-inch line. From Carrizozo to Pastura, a distance of 107 miles, the pipeline parallels the railway. With the advent of the Diesel engine as a replacement for steam engines on the Southern Pacific lines, there was no further need for water in connection with railroad operations between Tucumcari and Alamogordo. As a result, the Southern Pacific, over a period of several years beginning in the 1950's, disposed of its water properties. Alamogordo profited greatly by the transaction, obtaining important water rights, reservoir facilities and pipelines, assuring that community a greatly increased water supply. Carrizozo and other towns along the railway also obtained important water rights and property on a reasonable basis. After many years, the one all-important problem of how to obtain water for railroad steam engines, which so greatly concerned William A. Hawkins and other pioneers, was solved by the use of Diesel engines on the railroad.

courts in El Paso, Texas. Excessive verdicts were rendered in a number of cases. Determined to stop what he called a damage suit racket, Hawkins introduced a bill in the 1903 New Mexico Legislature which he believed, and continued to believe during the rest of his life, was a meritorious measure.

On March 4, 1903, at Santa Fe, on the forty-fifth day of the 35th Legislature Assembly, Honorable W. H. H. Llewellyn, of Doña Ana County, chairman of the judiciary committee of the House, made a brief report on House Bill No. 155. The report was as follows:

> Mr. Speaker: Your committee on judiciary, to whom was referred H.B. No. 155, have had the same under consideration, and I am directed to report the same to the House with the recommendation that it be passed.

The rules were suspended; the bill was passed by a vote of 17 to 3. The ayes were: Baca, Kilpatrick, Llewellyn, Martinez of Guadalupe, Martinez of Rio Arriba, McCash, McIvers, Pendleton, Romero, Sanchez of Mora, Sanchez of Valencia, Sanchez of Taos, Sandoval, Stockton, Turner, Vargas and Nestor Montoya, the Speaker. Nays: Coleman, Gutierrez and Ortega. The bill went from the House to the Council immediately and was considered there on March 5, 1903. William A. Hawkins took charge of the bill and moved a suspension of the rules. The measure was passed on motion made by Martinez of Taos County, the vote being as follows: Ayes: Albright, Chaves, Duncan, Fall, Hawkins, Hughes, Jaramillo, Martinez, Pinard, J. Francisco Chaves, the Speaker. Charles A. Spiess of San Miguel, voted nay. W. H. Andrews was absent by leave.[8] The bill was enrolled and engrossed and sent to the office of the Governor. On March 11, 1903, Governor Miguel A. Otero refused to approve the bill and returned it to the House with a strongly worded message expressing doubt as to the desirability of the measure and its constitutionality. The veto message from Governor Otero was as follows:

> TO THE SPEAKER AND MEMBERS OF THE HOUSE OF REPRESENTATIVES OF THE 35TH LEGISLATIVE ASSEMBLY OF NEW MEXICO.
>
> Gentlemen: I return herewith to your body, being the House in which it originated, House Bill No. 155, entitled "An Act Estab-

---

8. *Council Journal* of the 35th Legislative Council.

lishing the Law and Procedure in Certain Cases," without my approval. My objections to this bill are that it makes an entirely new and untried innovation in our practice, one which has never been tried in any other jurisdiction, and I can seen no possible advantages to be gained by its passage here as an experiment. It makes a radical innovation in legal practice and procedure everywhere in not allowing the plaintiff the right to select the court in which he litigates. He is compelled to go into a court selected by his adversary, where he is bound without any right of appeal from any judgment that may be rendered against him. Under the provisions of the act there is a practical injunction against the plaintiff bringing a suit in the jurisdiction which he selects and a mandamus compelling him to bring his action in the jurisdiction desired by the defendant. There is no need in this Territory for such an act, for there is no right that cannot be enforced and no wrong that may not be redressed under our present laws; and this act is very drastic and its constitutionality very doubtful. It attempts to exercise by writ of mandamus in other jurisdictions not only to compel the commencement of actions here, but also to compel the courts of such jurisdictions not to take jurisdiction in certain instances, as well as to prohibit the doing of something that is already accomplished.

This act would create great criticism of our people, and I believe it is not for the best interests of the Territory, and after very careful consideration, I have deemed that I cannot give it my official approval.

Very Respectfully,

MIGUEL A. OTERO,
Governor of New Mexico.[9]

The House paid scant attention to Governor Otero's veto message and at once suspended all rules which would otherwise prevent consideration of the bill and passed it over the Governor's veto. Only three nay votes were registered, those of Bowie, Coleman and Kilpatrick.

The action of the House in passing the bill in that branch of the Legislature by the required two-thirds majority, notwithstanding the Governor's veto, was duly reported to the Council and on March 11, 1903, the Council, after receiving the report of the Speaker of the House and hearing the veto message read as a part of that report,

---

9. *Journal of the House,* 35th Legislative Session.

proceeded to override the protest of the Chief Executive of the Territory. Albert Bacon Fall of Doña Ana moved the passage of the bill by the Council, notwithstanding the veto, with ayes voting as follows: Albright, Andrews, Chaves, Duncan, Fall, Hawkins, Hughes, Jaramillo, Martinez, Pinard, J. Francisco Chaves, 11 votes. Charles A. Spiess of San Miguel voted against the passage, consistent with his opposition vote when the measure was originally before the Council. The bill was thus declared passed in the Council over the veto of the Governor.

The enactment by the Legislature of the "Hawkins Act," as it was called, raised a storm of protest throughout the Territory. William A. Hawkins bore the brunt of the fire against the act. He insisted that it was a measure designed only to protect corporations against scheming damage suit lawyers, gave it as his opinion that it was constitutional and predicted that in practice it would work out satisfactorily and afford justice to all litigants. The hue and cry raised against the bill in New Mexico soon attracted national attention.

The bill had been managed in the House in the Territorial Legislature by Major Llewellyn. In the Council it had been in the hands of its friends. Hawkins, Fall, "Bull" Andrews, formerly of Pennsylvania, pupil of Boise Penrose and Matt Quay of that state, were in the heyday of their political power in New Mexico. This time they were not pulling wires on the outside of the Legislature, they were sitting in the seats of the membership, and voting. The Legislature was overwhelmingly Republican. The only one of the Old Guard of that party who voted against the bill in the Council was Charles A. Spiess, a member of the inner circle of the party, a sound lawyer, evidently convinced in his own mind that the passage of the bill was unwise, and that it would not stand against attack in the courts.[10]

---

10. Spiess, chosen as President of the New Mexico Territorial Council in 1909, sent a telegram on March 1, 1909, to George W. P. Hunt, then President of the Arizona Legislative Council, which drew a reply from Hunt, for many terms Democratic Governor of Arizona. Spiess wired Hunt: "Overwhelming majority of New Mexico Legislature by caucus, has agreed not to enact legislation adverse or hostile, or which could be considered adverse or hostile, to capital or investments and ask your cooperation if you agree with us." Hunt promptly replied: "Just what may be your interpretation of 'adverse or hostile' legislation as it relates to 'capital or investment' I cannot say, but from the wording of your telegram I am led to fear that the action of your caucus spells a willing subservience to those self-appointed guardians of the public weal, who by reason of great wealth, are too often, and to the everlasting disgrace of our country, powerful enough to influence the action of legislators elected and sworn to represent

The "Hawkins Act" became Chapter 33 of the Laws of 1903 of New Mexico. Succeeding Legislatures refused to repeal the act and it was not until May 9, 1909, that the national Congress nullified the law.

The Act of 1903 was without a precedent in any state of the Union, violated every then-known rule of court procedure in the Territory, was intended primarily for use by railroads and mining companies. Among other things the act provided: that there should be no civil liability, either at common law or under the statute, of any corporation for any personal injuries or death caused by such corporation in the Territory of New Mexico, unless the person claiming damages should within ninety days after such injury, serve upon the corporation at least thirty days before commencing suit an affidavit made before some officer in the Territory, giving the name of the person receiving the injuries, how they were caused and all the facts in the case. No suit could be maintained against the corporation unless the action was brought within one year in a District Court of the Territory and no suit once instituted could be dismissed without the consent of the defendant. The right was given to a corporation to bring suit against the claimant in the county of his residence, requiring the claimant to appear and file a statement of his cause of action against the corporation and if the claimant did not do so, then the cause was to be tried ex parte in the claimant's absence. The injured party was prohibited from bringing suit against the corporation anywhere except in the Territory of New Mexico. In event the claimant should bring suit anywhere else, the corporation was authorized to apply to the courts of the Territory for an injunction to abate it; and such suit was by the act declared to be a waiver of all rights against the corporation. Under the act, a passenger on a railroad train, living in a foreign state, receiving injuries through the negligence of a corporation operating interstate, would be obliged to institute suit in New Mexico. The person seeking damages was prohibited from making an affidavit concerning his injuries except before some officer qualified to take oaths in New Mexico; he was compelled to submit

---

the whole people. The Arizona law will know neither rich nor poor, king nor peasant, and those who have or may hereafter invest their millions here will have to content themselves, as well as they can afford to, with statutes moulded with an eye single to the welfare of the whole people. I commend these sentiments to the thoughtful consideration of the 'overwhelming majority' of your legislative caucus."

the facts of the case to the corporation in advance of resorting to court. He was obliged to furnish the corporation with the names of his witnesses, their place of residence, the facts to which they would testify.

When the "Hawkins Act" was considered in the Congress of the United States for nullification, it aroused much speculation, was looked upon as a masterpiece of legal procedure. In the House, Mr. Crumpacker of Indiana wanted to know if the Railroad Company, ordinarily the defendant in a personal injury case, the company that inflicted the injury, could become the plaintiff in "this peculiar and extraordinary proceeding." He was told that it could. "And against the party injured?" inquired Crumpacker. He was answered in the affirmative. Mr. Butler wanted to know whether the law was passed in a railroad office. Mr. Birdsall, who had the resolution in charge, answered: "It was born in iniquity. I do not know how it was passed." Mr. Clayton said: "No lawyer, no layman, can read this law which it is proposed to repeal by this joint resolution. without being horrified by its outrages." The House committee of the Congress in its report favoring the resolution for the annulment of the law said: "The law is entitled, 'An Act Establishing the Law and Procedure in Certain Cases.' In the judgment of the Committee, the title should be, 'An Act to Prevent Persons Receiving Injuries Through Carelessness of Railroads and Other Corporations in the Territory of New Mexico from Recovering Damages Therefor'." When the report of the committee for annulment came before the House for adoption, there was not one vote against it.

Careful study of the "Hawkins Act," almost sixty years after its passage, will disclose that William A. Hawkins was many years ahead of his time. Some provisions of the bill were, and still are, objectionable. However, many ideas contained in the bill have been incorporated in present-day legal procedure. Defendants in a damage suit today can take the depositions of the injured party in advance of trial, can compel the plaintiff to disclose the facts upon which he proposes to prove his case and can insist on knowing the names of witnesses by whom certain facts will be proved. Pre-trial conferences, permissible in many states and in federal courts, eliminating to a large extent the element of surprise, accomplish some of the things Hawkins was attempting to remedy through his bill. The declaratory judgment, now common in New Mexico and in many states, was apparently one of the reforms Hawkins had in mind in drafting his bill. The provision prohibiting the dismissal of a suit once filed, has its counterpart, within limitations, in present-day New Mexico procedure. Hawkins, in drafting the bill, demonstrated great legal ability and a forward-looking mental outlook in some directions, but at the same time indicated his great confidence in and loyalty to corporations.[11]

For a number of years following his retirement from active law practice, William Ashton Hawkins made his home at La Luz, a picturesque village a few miles from Alamogordo, not far from the tracks of the old El Paso & Northeastern Railroad. For nearly fifty years he had contributed to his clients, and through them to New

---

11. From his viewpoint W. A. Hawkins was entirely justified in sponsoring the so-called "Hawkins Act" in the Legislature of New Mexico. He had impatiently observed damage suit lawyers in El Paso encouraging clients to bring suits in Texas courts on injuries occuring in the Territory of New Mexico. He had appealed for relief, without result, to bar committees in New Mexico and Texas. Strong anti-corporation sentiment prevailed in Texas in his day, reflected not only in jury verdicts, but in decisions of trial and appellate courts. Heavy awards in damages against the El Paso & Northeastern, coupled with the great expense incurred by the railroad in attempting to develop a satisfactory water supply, were rapidly forcing the railroad toward either abandonment of its enterprise or bankruptcy. Hawkins undertook the work of saving the railroad company from being "bled white" by excessive verdicts in damage suits, by procuring the enactment of the so-called "Hawkins Act." Soliciting support for the measure, Hawkins argued that the principal capital of the railroad company was invested in New Mexico, that verdicts of juries had to be paid out of monies derived chiefly from New Mexico patrons of the railroad; that inasmuch as their interests were principally involved in the question of the survival of the El Paso & Northeastern, New Mexico jurors rather than Texas jurors should determine when and how much money should be paid from the resources of the El Paso & Northeastern for personal injuries sustained by persons on the line in New Mexico.

The 90-day notice claim for personal injuries, provided for in the act, was borrowed from analogous provisions of the federal act to regulate commerce, providing that as a condition precedent to recovery in case of loss or damage by carriers, the claimant must serve written notice of claim upon the carriers within a given number of months after the loss, damage or injury occurred. It was designed to curb the practice of filing delayed actions against the railroad after witnesses had vanished or records had been lost or destroyed and compelling a settlement for lack of refuting evidence. The provisions, giving the defendant the right to file an action in court in advance of anticipated litigation and compel the claimant to then come forward with his evidence while the facts were fresh, had their origin in similar principles of law which authorize an owner of real estate to file a suit and compel another person making claim to or asserting some interest in the property, to come into court and adjudicate it, or disclaim interest. As to this feature of the Act, Hawkins contended that a claim for personal injuries was but a "chose in action" or property right; and that a "claim for a mashed thumb was not entitled to greater sanctity before the law than a claimant seeking to establish a hundred thousand dollar claim against an estate," that it was but the incorporation into law of

Mexico, the best that his legal ability and business sagacity could offer. He had been a part of the early days in Grant County. He had seen insignificant prospect holes become important mining properties. He had seen the development of great cattle ranches. He had participated in the early day development of the Pecos Valley. He had helped Charles B. Eddy and James John Hagerman in the early days of empire building along the Pecos River. He had lived to see the realization of his dreams. He had done more than his full share in bringing railroad facilities and affiliate enterprises of great importance to Doña Ana, Lincoln and Otero counties. He had served his corporate clients faithfully, but in that service, he had been careful not to wrong knowingly any man. He had been able in the business matters entrusted to him; he had been powerful in politics. He had

---

claims for personal injuries, the doctrines applicable to actions to quiet title to real property.

The section in the "Hawkins Act" authorizing issuance of writs of injunction to restrain residents of New Mexico from going to Texas to prosecute suits against New Mexico corporations had its source in the decision of the Supreme Court of the United States in the case of *Cole v. Cunningham*, 133 U.S. 107, and similar cases following its reasoning, *Wabash R.R. v. Peterson*, 175 N.W. 523; *Kern v. Ry.* 185 N.E. 446; *Reed's Adm'x. v. I. C. R.* 206 S.W. 794, and other cases. In three decisions, Texas courts upheld the main features of the "Hawkins Bill." *Buttron v. E. P. & N. E. Ry.*, 93 S.W. 676 (writ denied); *Southern Pacific Co. v. Dublason*, 106 S.W. 766 (Tex. Civ. Apps.); *Sawyer v. E. P. & N. E. Ry.*, 108 S.W. 719 (Civ. Apps.). The New Mexico statute of 1903 was annulled by Act of Congress (35 Stat. at Large pt. 1, p. 573) shortly before the Supreme Court of the United States reviewed some of the fundamental questions concerning its validity. See *Atchison, Topeka & Santa Fe Railway Co. vs. George A. Sowers*, decided on March 1, 1909, reported in 213 U.S. 55, 53 L. Ed. 695, on appeal from the Texas Court of Civil Appeals, 99 S.W. 190. Sowers, a citizen of Arizona, was injured while riding on the pilot of an engine at Gallup, New Mexico. He sued the Santa Fe in El Paso, Texas, recovering a judgment for $5,000. The majority of the Supreme Court of the United States in the Sowers case held in substance that a state or territory might not create a cause of action and confine right of recovery to the state of enactment. Justice Oliver Wendell Holmes dissented, saying that he agreed with "pretty much everything that is said on behalf of the majority of the court, except the conclusion reached."

The practice of litigants against railroads "going shopping" for favorable courts in distant forums was freely discussed by the Supreme Court of the United States in the case of *Miles vs. Illinois Central R. Co.*, 315 U.S. 698, in construing the venue provisions of the Federal Employer's Liability Act. In *Miles vs. Illinois Central*, Mr. Justice Frankfurter wrote a strong dissenting opinion in which he expressed views in harmony with the reasoning employed by W. A. Hawkins many years before in his defense of the "Hawkins Act." During federal control of railways, the Director General prohibited "shopping around" in damage suit litigation. See *Davis vs. Farmers' Coop. Equity Co.*, 262 U.S. 312.

been an outstanding success in the practice of the legal profession.[12] But modesty, always a predominant trait with William Ashton Hawkins, asserted itself time and again in conversations with old-time friends during the latter years of his life. He argued that he had accomplished nothing great in life; that he had only done the best he could with the gifts with which he had been endowed.

One thing always kindled a light in his eyes and brought joy to his heart, as he prepared to face the sunset. That was his recollection of the days he had spent as a militiaman in the Gila and Mimbres River country, riding a horse up one canyon and down another, looking for Geronimo and his renegade Apaches.

---

12. For nearly fifty years, William A. Hawkins was one of the undisputed leaders of the Bar in the Southwest. He was a profound and constant student of the law. He was a specialist in corporation law, had no superior in New Mexico as an authority on water rights. Hawkins served as general counsel for the El Paso & Southwestern Railroad for many years, retiring from that position on November 1, 1924, when the property was taken over by the Southern Pacific. His junior law associates in El Paso affectionately called him "Squire" Hawkins. For over half a century, Hawkins was almost continually identified with important affairs in New Mexico.

FRONTIER DAYS in southeastern New Mexico, fabulous, glamorous, adventuresome, have come to an end. The old-time cowboy has vanished with the mist of the years; the tales seem incredible of standing night herd with orders never to light a cigarette in the darkness for fear of starting a stampede. The cowboy's horse, saddle and bridle are no longer of first importance. The buckboard has disappeared from the scheme of things with a finality from which there is no appeal. Cattle brands are all recorded, giving no room for argument as to identity or ownership. Cattle and sheep men have long since settled their feuds. Livestock men run both sheep and cattle on the same range. Federally-owned lands are partitioned and allotted under United States statutes. Rules and regulations govern their use and tenure. New Mexico public domain is leased for long terms of years. The six-shooter, once so important in settling range feuds, is an ornament, a symbol of the days that are no more. Sheep and cattle men dress like bankers and a good many of them own or control banks. Some of them are college graduates, can do algebra and differential calculus, recite poetry and are signed up by the year, in a steady drive toward culture, for at least one new book a month. The branding iron of the old days is gone and in its place is a newfangled contraption that can be applied gently and effectively with little damage to the critter's hide.

With few exceptions, the men who settled up southeastern New Mexico have gone to that other and better land. Along the Pecos River, in the Sacramentos and in the Guadalupes, in the White Sands country, and down near Mockingbird Gap, the descendants of the pioneer settlers have taken up where the old-timers said farewell to things of this earth, and are carrying on somewhat in accordance with the customs and traditions of those other and better days. Stories of the pioneers have become fables and sagas. The men who settled up the country were strong men, physically and mentally, men of courage and conviction. Some of them lived to see the day when old-time revivals were crucified between railroads and recreation.

The roll call is a long one of men who made possible the glamor and adventure of southeastern New Mexico. There are many who deserve a place in the hall of fame of old Lincoln County. Among them it has been possible to name only a few who have walked and talked through these pages, Pat Garrett and Ash Upson, John W. Poe, John Y. Hewitt, Charles B. Eddy, James John Hagerman, William Ashton Hawkins, Emerson Hough, Eugene Manlove Rhodes, Oliver Lee, Albert Bacon Fall, Tom Catron. These men were all New Mexicans at one time or another. They all had an intense loyalty and devotion to New Mexico. Most of them sleep their last long sleep in New Mexico soil and those who found a resting place elsewhere loved New Mexico and its people. With a great many of the men whose names are mentioned in this volume, it was the writer's good fortune to be personally acquainted. No attempt has been made to fictionize any of them, or to distort their true character or personality.

The men who pioneered in the development of southeastern New Mexico built their enterprises on foundations of greater potentialities than they realized. The Lincoln and Doña Ana counties of the old days have been subdivided. It is no longer necessary to travel a hundred miles on horseback to get to a county seat. White Oaks, which offered great promise as a gold producer more than a half century ago, is presently a ghost town. The White Sands country has not yet produced materials that can be utilized in industry. The coal fields at White Oaks and Capitan that were expected to furnish steam for important industries have failed of their objective. The basic industries on the Western slopes of the Sacramentos and Guadalupes, livestock production and lumbering, have justified the prediction of early-day promoters. The El Paso & Northeastern Railroad, originally envisaged as a coal-carrying road between El Paso and White Oaks, is now the transcontinental Southern Pacific. Many freight and passenger trains pass over it each day, something that Charles B. Eddy never anticipated even in his most optimistic moments. East of the Sacramentos and Guadalupes, where the Pecos River hurries along to meet the waters of the Rio Grande in Texas, there is today an inland empire of great resources, tried and demonstrated, decades beyond the experimental stage. Both Charles B. Eddy and James J. Hagerman, had they lived to view it, would have been immensely proud of that great development. Originally a flickering dream in the mind of Sheriff Pat Garrett, improved and enlarged upon by Eddy, brought to fruition by Hagerman, the Pecos Valley development has far surpassed the most ambitious hopes of its early promoters. The Pecos Valley railroad, originally intended to serve the country along the Pecos River between Pecos, Texas, and Roswell, has many years since become an important part of the Atchison, Topeka & Santa Fe. Oil derricks by the thousands now dot the southeastern part of Lincoln County of seventy odd years ago, replacing the drift fences and the cattle corrals of the old days. Where cattle roamed at will by the thousands in the seventies and eighties in Lincoln County, stampeded and choused about at times by reckless cowboys, there are now great underground workings of the potash mines. The magic names, oil, gas, and potash, all representing vast industrial enterprises today, doubtless never were spoken by early-day promoters or even considered remote possibilities in connection with the future development of southeastern New Mexico.

An event of overwhelming importance, the explosion of the first atomic bomb, took place at Trinity Site, on July 16, 1945, changing for all time the face of the land in southeastern New Mexico. The bomb was exploded in the heart of the Eugene Manlove Rhodes country, roughly bounded on the north by the public highway which runs from San Antonio to Bingham, on the south by the White Sands, on the east by the Carrizozo lava beds, and on the west by the Rio Grande as it flows from Socorro. The explosion of the bomb marked the end of one era, the beginning of another. Many people living in the bomb area were obliged to move from the country. Ranch owners, willingly or unwillingly, surrendered their property, and moved their livestock elsewhere. Some few, reluctant to give up their ranches without a fight, learned of the power and might of the federal government in eminent domain proceedings. In no time at all after the explosion, or so it seemed, cattle ranches had been converted into testing grounds; the military had installed and placed in operation devices and facilities designed to function in accordance with the dictates and mandates of a new day. Vast underground testing was undertaken by scientists in the area of the Carlsbad Caverns and potash mines, many miles away from Trinity Site. With the coming of the bomb era to southeastern New Mexico, the days of John S. Chisum, of James J. Hagerman and Charles B. Eddy seemed far off indeed; and the pioneers of the more modern period of oil, gas and potash developments were a bit bewildered by the emergence and introduction of an entirely new factor in the scheme of things in an area in which for generations isolation and a sense of timelessness had been precious, and most cherished possessions.

Seventy years and more ago in Lincoln County and thereabouts, old-time cattlemen sagely predicted that the day would come in southeastern New Mexico when every man, whether he liked it or not, would eat his own beef. That day, too, has come in southeastern New Mexico. A man with ability and ambition to change a brand or steal a cow has vanished along with the colorful days of long ago.

Some day the people of New Mexico, sensing an obligation long past due, will build a monument dedicated to the memories of the pioneers of southeastern New Mexico, to the men and women who blazed the trail and reclaimed the waste places in a bleak and desolate country, bringing happiness and prosperity to the thousands who followed in their footsteps.

SOME SOURCES AND REFERENCES

An Introduction to the Study of Southwestern Archaeology, Vincent Kidder. Yale University Press, 1924.

Appropriation Bill, U.S. Forest Service, May 15, 1912, "Speech of Senator Fall."

Bureau of Ethnology, 29th Annual Report, 1907, pp. 338-50.

Council Journal of the 35th New Mexico Legislative Council.

Executive Document No. 106, 48th Congress, 2d Session, Title to Land in New Mexico.

Final Report on Hemenway Expedition, A. F. Bandelier. Part 2, p. 123.

Geology and Water Resources of Tularosa Basin, O. E. Meizler and R. F. Hare.

Handbook of American Indians, Frederick Webb Hodge, ed., Vol. 2, page 220, Government Printing Office, 1906.

History of Arizona and New Mexico, 1530-1888, Hubert Howe Bancroft. San Francisco, 1889; facsimile edition published by Horn and Wallace, Albuquerque, 1962.

History of Spanish and English Missions from 1850 to 1884, Rev. Thomas Harwood. El Abogado Press, Albuquerque, 1910.

Journal of the House, 35th New Mexico Legislative Session.

Letters of a Young Diplomat, Herbert J. Hagerman. Rydal Press, Santa Fe, 1937.

Matters Relating to the Administration and Removal of Herbert J. Hagerman, Governor of New Mexico, 1906-1907, Herbert J. Hagerman. Privately printed, 1908.

Narrative of the Texas–Santa Fe Expedition, George Wilkins Kendall. 6th Ed., Harper and Brothers, New York, 1847.

New Mexico Legislature Joint Resolution, March 12, 1921.

New Mexico Session Laws, 1882, ch. 101.

Peñalosa, Eugene Manlove Rhodes. Writers' Editions, Rydal Press, Santa Fe, 1934.

Record No. 375, Supreme Court of New Mexico (Kirby Benedict), p. 99.

Regional Planning, Part X. National Resources Planning Board, Government Printing Office, 1942.

Report to Secretary of Interior, 1881—Gov. L. Bradford Prince.

Report to Secretary of Interior, 1883—Gov. Lionel A. Sheldon.

Report to Secretary of Interior, 1886—Gov. Edmund G. Ross.

Report to Secretary of Interior, 1895—Gov. W. T. Thornton.

Resolution, House of Representatives, New Mexico Legislature, Feb. 24, 1868 (Gov. Robert B. Mitchell).

Senate Document Executive No. 60, 30th Congress, 1st Session.

Senate Document No. 70, 30th Congress, 1st Session, p. 18.

Senate Document No. 442, 56th Congress, 1st Session.

The Pecos River Joint Investigation. National Resources Planning Board, Government Printing Office, 1942.

NEWSPAPERS AND PERIODICALS

Albuquerque Daily Citizen, Oct. 17, 1895.

Albuquerque Tribune Citizen, Oct. 16, 1909.

American Journal of Anthropology, Oct. 1, 1886, article by Frederick Webb Hodge.

American Archaeology, No. 1, El Paso Archaeological Society.

Atlantic Monthly, Aug. 1940.

Century Magazine, Dec. 1882; Feb. 1883.

Columbus Courier, Mar. 12, 1916; May 26, 1916.

El Paso Herald, Oct. 11, 1899.

El Paso Sentinel, July 25, 1875.

Evening News, Ada, Oklahoma, April 19, 1909.

Golden Era, Feb. 6, 1884; May 31, 1884; Oct. 23, 1884; Jan. 1, 1885; June 18, 1885; Nov. 5, 1885; Dec. 17, 1885; Dec. 24, 1885.

Inland Magazine, Mar. 1875.

Las Cruces Democrat, Sept. 8, 1895.

Las Cruces Independent, Sept. 8, 1898; Aug. 16, 1898.

Las Vegas Gazette, April 19, 1873; Nov. 25, 1875; Dec. 25, 1875; May 6, 1876; Aug. 4, 1877; Feb. 2, 1878; Mar. 9, 1878; Apr. 13, 1878; Aug. 17, 1878; Sept. 13, 1879; Mar. 28, 1880; Nov. 30, 1880; Dec. 24, 1880; Nov. 11, 1882.

Las Vegas Optic, July 15, 1881; July 16, 1881.

Lincoln County Leader, May 13, 1885; June 6, 1885; Aug. 1, 1885; Nov. 20, 1886; Oct. 6, 1888; Dec. 8, 1888; Oct. 12, 1889; Dec. 7, 1889; July 28, 1892.

Mesilla Independent, Sept. 8, 1877.

News and Press, Cimarron, June 15, 1880.
Out West, Feb. 1902; Feb. 1903.
San Francisco *Examiner*, May 31, 1899.
Santa Fe *New Mexican*, Mar. 2, 1874; May 16, 1921; May 21, 1921.
Saturday Evening Post, Jan. 26, 1916; Aug. 10, 1929; Aug. 20, 1938.
Sierra Advocate, Mar. 17, 1899.
Silver City Independent, Oct. 1, 1899.
White Oaks Eagle, Oct. 10, 1899; Nov. 9, 1899.

TABLE OF CASES CITED

Alamogordo Imp. Co. v. Hennessee, 40 N.M. 162; 56 Pac. 2d 1127; 267 fn.
Alamogordo Imp. Co. v. Prendergast, 43 N.M. 245; 91 Pac. 2d 428; 122
    A.L.R. 1277; 267 fn.
Alamogordo Imp. Co. v. Prendergast, 45 N.M. 40; 109 Pac. 2d 254; 267 fn.
Baxter Gold Mining Co. v. Patterson, 3 N.M. (Johnson) 179, 3 Pac. 741;
    32, 134.
Borrego, In Re, 8 N.M. 655, 46 Pac. 211 (affirmed 164 U.S. 612, 41 L. ed.
    572, 17 Sup. Ct. 182); 106.
Brunswick v. Winters Heirs, 3 N.M. 241; 5 Pac. 706; 33.
Buttron v. E.P.&N.E.Ry., 93 S.W. 676; 277 fn.
Carter vs. Territory, 1 N.M. 317; 87 fn.
Catron, In Re, 8 N.M. 253; 106.
Catron, In Re, 8 N.M. 275; 106 fn.
Cole v. Cunningham, 133 U.S. 107; 277 fn.
Crabtree v. Segrist, 3 N.M. (Johnson) 278; 6 Pac. 202; 67.
Cunningham, Cole, v., 133 U.S. 107; 277 fn.
Davis vs. Farmers' Coop. Equity Co., 262 U.S. 312; 277 fn.
Dawson, Maxwell Land Grant Company v., 7 N.M. 133; 151 U.S. 586;
    253 fn.
Dublason, Southern Pac. Co., 106 S.W. 766; 277 fn.
E. P. & N. E. Ry., Buttron, v., 93 S.W. 676; 277 fn.
E. P. & N. E. Ry., Sawyer v., 108 S.W. 719; 277 fn.
Fall v. United States, 49 Fed. (2d) 506; 201 fn.
Farmers' Coop. Equity Co., Davis v., 262 U.S. 312; 277 fn.
Gililland, James, Oliver M. Lee, Territory of New Mexico v., 117, 227.
Harry F. Sinclair v. United States of America, 279 U.S. 749; 49 S.C.R. 471
    73 L. ed. 939; 201 fn.
Hennessee, Alamogordo Imp. Co. v., 40 N.M. 162; 56 Pac. 2d 1127; 267
    fn.
Hughes, Thomas and W. T. McCreight, In the Matter of Contempt vs.,
    8 N.M. 225; 107.

I. C. R., Reed's Adm'x v., 206 S.W. 794; 277 fn.

Illinois Central R. Co., Miles v., 315 U.S. 698; 277 fn.

In the Matter of Contempt vs. Thomas Hughes and W. T. McCreight, Respondents, 8 N.M. 225; 107.

In Re Borrego, 8 N.M. 655; 46 Pac. 211 (affirmed 164 U.S. 612, 41 L. ed. 572) (17 Sup. Ct. 182); 106.

In Re Catron, 8 N.M. 253; 106.

In Re Catron, 8 N.M. 275; 106 fn.

Kern v. Ry. 189 N.E. 446; 277 fn.

Lee, Oliver M. and James Gililland, Territory of New Mexico v., 117, 227.

Mammoth Oil Co., United States v., 5 Fed. (2d) 330; 201 fn.

Mammoth Oil Co., United States v., 14 Fed. (2d) 706; 201 fn.

Mammoth Oil Co., Sinclair Crude Oil Purchasing Company, and Sinclair Pipe Line Company v. United States of America; 275 U.S. 13, 48 S.C.R. 1, 72 L. ed. 137 201 fn.

Maxwell Land Grant Company v. Dawson, 7 N.M. 133; 151 U.S. 586; 253 fn.

McCreight, W. T., In the Matter of Contempt vs. Thomas Hughes and, 8 N.M. 225; 107.

Miles v. Illinois Central R. Co., 315 U.S. 698; 277 fn.

Miller, James v. State of Texas, 18 Texas Court of Appeals, 232; 79.

Pan American v. United States, 273 U.S. 456, 47 S.C.R. 416, 71 L. ed. 734; 201 fn.

Pan American Petroleum Co., United States v., 6 Fed. (2d) 43; 201 fn.

Patterson, Baxter Gold Mining Co. v., 3 N.M. (Johnson) 179; 3 Pac. 741; 32, 134.

Peralta Reavis Case, 8 N.M. Sup. Ct. Rep. p. 27; 112 fn.

Peterson, Wabash R. R. v., 175 N.W. 523; 277 fn.

Prendergast, Alamogordo Imp. Co. v., 43 N.M. 245; 91 Pac. 2d 428; 122 A.L.R. 1277; 267 fn.

Prendergast, Alamogordo Imp. Co. v., 45 N.M. 40; 109 Pac. 2d 254; 267 fn.

Reavis, Peralta, 8 N.M. Sup. Ct. Rep. 27; 112 fn.

Reed's Adm'x v. I. C. R., 206 S.W. 794; 277 fn.

Sawyer v. E. P. & N. E. Ry., 108 S.W. 719; 277 fn.

Segrist, Crabtree, 3 N.M. (Johnson) 278; 6 Pac. 202; 67.

Sinclair v. United States of America (Congressional contempt case), 279 U.S. 263, 49 S.C.R. 368, 73 L. ed. 692; 201 fn.

Southern Pac. Co. v. Dublason, 106 S.W. 766; 277 fn.

State of Texas, James Miller v., 18 Texas Court of Appeals, 232; 79.

Territory, Carter v., 1 N.M. 317; 87 fn.

Territory of New Mexico vs. Oliver M. Lee and James Gililland; 117, 227.

United States, Fall v., 49 Fed. (2d) 506; 201 fn.

United States, Pan American v., 273 U.S. 456, 47 S.C.R. 416, 71 L. ed.
    734; 201 fn.

United States v. Mammoth Oil Co., 5 Fed. (2d) 330; 201 fn.

United States v. Mammoth Oil Co., 14 Fed. (2d) 706; 201 fn.

United States of America, Mammoth Oil Co., Sinclair Crude Oil Pur-
    chasing Company and Sinclair Pipe Line Company v., 275 U.S. 13, 48
    S.C.R. 1, 72 L. ed. 137; 201 fn.

United States v. Pan American Petroleum Co., 6 Fed. (2d) 43; 201 fn.

Wabash R. R. v. Peterson, 175 N.W. 523; 277 fn.

Winters' Heirs, Brunswick v., 3 N.M. 241; 5 Pac. 706; 33.

INDEX

Abeel's Ranch, 72
Abert, Lt. J. W., 52n
Alamitos Grant, 130
Alamogordo, 94, 164, 167n, 170, 172, 175, 244, 253, 254, 260, 271, 292, 311n, 313n, 319; townsite, 286, 307-08, 308n
Albuquerque, xi, 18, 26, 46, 47, 79, 80, 83, 89, 107, 128, 135, 144, 166, 168, 172n, 176, 216, 219, 224, 267, 292n
Adamson, Carl, 88, 92, 93, 94-96
Ahumada (train), 79
Alcock, James A., 77, 114-16, 284n
Aleman, 49, 50, 50n, 51-52, 259
Altman, Perry, 244-48
American Occupation of N. M., x, 3-7, 10, 11, 22n, 24, 48-49, 104-05, 106n, 117, 121, 130
Ancheta, Joseph Arthur, 134-36; profile, 135n
Andrews, William H. (Bull), 125, 134, 226, 314, 316; profile, 125-26n
Anton Chico, 33, 61, 68, 75, 184; grant, 182
Apaches, see Indians
Armijo, Isidoro, x, 242-43
Arms, George, 175
Ascarate, Sheriff, 247
Ashenfelter, S. M., 238n
Atomic Energy Commission, 96n, 173n, 323
attorneys regulated, 11
Austin, Mary, 172

Baca, Elfego, 241n
Baca, Jesus, 144; profile, 144n

Baird, Jim, 55, 87
Baker, W. R., 271
Bancroft, Hubert Howe, 142, 143
Bandelier, Adolph F., 138, 139n, 142-43, 182n
Barber, Susie McSween, 44, 219n
Barnes, R. P., 267, 268, 270
Baxter, John J., 36-38
Bayer, William A., x, 132-34, 137-38
Bean, Sam, 256
Beard, Jud, 42
Beaubien-Miranda land grant, 73, 293n; see Maxwell Land Grant
Bell, J. L., 288n
Bell, O., 35
Benedict, Judge Kirby, 29, 118; profile, 118-19n
Bent, Gov. Charles, 5n, 6, 6n, 24
Bentley, Alexander, 269, 276
Billy the Kid, see Bonney, William
Blackington, Sheriff C. F., 260-62
Blanchard, Judge Charles, 33
Blazer's Mills, 46
Blevin, Albert, 273
Block Ranch, 72, 174
Boggs, Thomas O., 119-20; profile, 119-20n
Bond, Ira M., 144
Bonney, C. D., 200, 302
Bonney, William H. (Billy the Kid), 40, 43, 54, 63, 67, 68, 79, 80, 84n, 86, 101, 155, 178, 184, 186, 235; death of, 53, 73-76, 85n, 89, 189, 251, 256; Greathouse and Kuch Ranch battle, 69-72; litigation over grave, 73-74n; meets George Curry, 72-73; Upson book, 146-47

Borrego murder case, 126-28, 130n, 267n; profile, 128n
Bosque Grande, 34, 58, 60, 62
Bosque Grande Ranch (Chisum), 60, 61
Botts, Clarence M., xi
Bowdre, Charles, 74n
Branigan, Capt. Thomas, 50n, 215, 242, 250-51, 269, 270, 272, 274
Brazil, Wayne, 77, 81, 276; Garrett's death, 79, 80, 87-88, 97; ranch, 81-82; trial, 92-95
Breece and Sons, 116
Bristol, Judge Warren, 148, 152, 235
British investors in N. M., 81, 114, 197, 252n, 264n
Browne, Mrs. Lina Fergusson, 39n
Browne, J. Ross, 39n
Brownfield, A. D., 229-30n
Bull, Charles, 44
Burch, Albert, 230n
Burke, William Smith, 107-08, 129; profile, 107n
Bursum, Holm Olaf, 80, 176, 221, 226, 313; *photo*, 78
Butterfield Trail, 50n, 169

Caffrey, Maj. William, 42, 69, 144, 149, 155-57
Calhoun, Gov. James S., 169
California Column, x, 3, 3n, 57, 233, 234, 304
Campbell, George W., 19
Cañon del Agua grant, 130
Capitan, 288, 290, 306
Carleton, Brig. Gen. James H., *see* California Column
Carlsbad, 184, 190, 199, 200, 202n, 241n, 279, 305; Eddy renamed, 192n
Carlyle, James, 69, 71-72
Carr, William, 250, 251
Carrizo Ranch, 77, 114, 115, 116, 284, 284n
Carrizozo, 53, 156, 168, 220n, 228, 288, 290, 292n, 295, 308, 311, 311n, 312, 313n
Carson, Kit, 24, 82n, 114n, 120n, 169; and Tom Boggs, 119-20n
Catron, Charles C., x, 62, 138
Catron, Fletcher A., 138
Catron, John W., 131, 138

Catron, Thomas Benton, 114, 116, 214, 221, 248, 257, 258, 262, 267, 268, 270, 323; assassination averted, 134-36; attorney for Borregos, 126-30, 130n; biog., 117-18n; comes to N. M., 117-18, 118n; death, 117, 138, 139-40; and Elkins, 118n, 122-23, 137-38; and Fall, 125, 212, 214, 221, 274-75; and Lincoln County War, 123-24; politics, 119-22, 124, 131-32, 139-40; U. S. Senator, 117, 122, 124-26, 132-34, 137-38, 139; *portrait*, 127
Chandler, Eli H., 38, 157
Chavez, Col. J. Francisco, 35n, 82, 238n, 314, 316; profile, 82-83n
Chavez, Francisco, 128n, 269
Chavez, Tomas, 232
Childers, William Burr, 38, 129, 267, 268, 270
Chisum, John S., 34, 123, 185, 325; banker 62; comes to N.M., 58; death, 65-66; rancher, 58-65; in stage robbery, 61
Chisum Ranch, 58-60, 186, 193, 200, 202, 203-04
Cimarron, xi, 19, 74n, 123
Civil War, 12n, 13, 14, 17, 35n, 38n, 57, 82n, 94n, 107n, 114, 117, 118n, 120, 121, 121n, 122, 134, 157, 177, 189, 209, 239n, 240n; *see also* California Column
Clancey, Capt. J. G., 63
Clark, J., 99
Clements, Manning, 260
clergy reprimanded, 11
Cleveland, Pres. Grover, 80, 107, 212, 213-14n, 234
Cody, William F. (Buffalo Bill), 177
Coghlan, Maxwell, 229n
Coghlan, Pat, 219n
Colfax, Schuyler, 121n
Collins, Sam, 65
Columbus, 137-38n
Congress, *see* U. S. Congress
Conway, Thomas F., 61, 62
Cook, George, 260
Cooper, James, 55
Corn, Harton, 35
Corona, 70n
Cox, James Webb, 94-96n

Cox, William Webb, 55, 89, 92, 94-96n; photo, 95
Cox Ranch, 87, 93, 253; profile, 93-94n
Crawford, John Wallace, "Jack," 176-78
Crist, Jacob, "Jake," 134, 136; profile, 136n
Curry, Gov. George, x, 72-73, 79, 87, 88, 131-32, 173n, 205-06, 218, 221, 251-52, 258-59, 285; profile, 252-53n
Cushing, Frank Hamilton, 141-42, 143

Dale, A. K., 35
Davis, Henry Gassaway, 122, 122n, 123n, 137
Dawson, see mining, coal
Dawson, Charles, 247
Dawson, John B., 291-93, 306-07
Dickerson, B., 35
Dog Canyon Ranch, 245, 248, 253, 254, 267n, 271, 272, 274
Doheny, Edward L., 210, 211, 228, 230, 231n, 232, 262n, 266n; profile, 210-11n
Dolan, J. J., 80
Dougherty, Harry M., 39n, 231, 267, 268, 275
Douglas, Dr. James, 295-97, 310, 312; profile, 295-97n
Dow, Hiram M., 35n, 240n
Dow, James Leslie, 240; profile, 240-41n
Dowlin's Mills, 46, 61
Duckworth, Lt. Gov. W. H., 226n
Dudley, Maj. N. A. M., 124

Eddy, 192n, 241n, 305, see also Carlsbad
Eddy, Charles B., 79, 108-10, 169, 197, 204, 203-04n, 297, 320, 325; biog., 188, 278n; employs Hawkins, 302-05; death, 279n, 298; Pecos Valley promotions—with Pat Garrett, 185, 188, 189n, 190;—with Hagerman, 190-94, 195-97, 278, 324 (feud, 197, 200-01); El Paso & Northeastern R. R. promotion, 201, 201-02n, 279-87, 297, 305-12, 323 (see also mining, coal; Phelps Dodge Co.; railroads); photo, 283
Edison, Thomas A., xi
education in N. M., 7-8, 11-12, 12n, 17, 19, 107

Elkins, Stephen Benton, 118n, 120, 122, 137, 227; profile, 122-23n
Elkins, Mrs. Stephen Benton, 137-38
Ellis, Noah, 116
Ellis, William R., 80, 159
El Paso, Texas, 47, 86-87, 96n, 101n, 137n, 143n, 155n, 189, 201n, 208, 209n, 218, 219, 232n, 234, 243n, 260, 297n, 299, 300, 305-06, 314, 319, 323
Engle, 50n, 161, 162, 163, 167, 172, 256, 259, 266n
Engle, William, 23
Espalin, Jose, 253-55
Espiritu Santo land grant, 130

Fall, Albert Bacon, 39n, 79-80, 285, 316, 323; and Catron, 125-28, 134, 136, 139, 212, 262, 274-75; biog., 209-11; death, 208-09, 209n; and Lee, 139, 211, 214-15, 251, 252, 256-57, 262, 267-69, 273-77; politics, 212-13, 217-19, 228, 313; rancher, 218, 219-20n, 229, 229-30n; Rhodes on, 170-71; Secretary of the Interior, 226-32, 277; Senator, 218, 226, 226-27n, 228, 228n; statehood speech, 219-25; Teapot Dome scandal, 209-10n, 227-32; photos, 78, 223
Fall, Mrs. Albert Bacon, x, 209-10
Fergusson, Harvey Butler, 38, 267, 268, 275; profile, 38-39n
Fergusson, Erna, 39n
Fergusson, Francis, 39n
Fergusson Harvey, 39n
Field, Dr. W. C., x, 88, 92
Forts: Craig, 14, 15, 50n, 177; Cummins, 50n; Defiance, 160n; Filmore, 33, 94n; McRae, 49, 50n, 168, 238n; Selden, 33, 50n; Tularosa, 103, 104n; Union, 8, 8n, 10, 14, 15, 61, 114n, 124, 154; Wingate, 18, 141
Fort Stanton, 33, 34, 42, 45n, 46, 47, 50n, 57, 58, 72, 77, 94n, 102, 103, 114n, 124, 143, 144, 149, 235, 242, 281
Fort Sumner, 34, 58, 60, 68, 69, 73, 74n, 75, 183, 184, 185, 189, 190, 256, 279
Fountain, Col. Albert J., 211, 216, 217; biog., 233-34; disappearance, 86, 215, 238-43, 249-51, 258, 270-73; military career, 234; politics, 237-38; trial, 262-77; writer, 235-36; photo, 237

Fountain, Albert J., Jr., 241
Fountain, Henry, 211, 215, 238-42, 249-50, 258
Fountain, Lt., *photo*, 237
Fox, Marion L., x, 130
Fulton, Maurice Garland, 85n
Fritz, Col. Emil, 77, 114n
Frost, Max, 111n, 189n

Gadsden Treaty, 238-39n
Gaines, George, 43, 44
Galisteo Co., xi
Gallegos, Jose M., 238n
Garner, John Nance, 85, 85n, 86
Garrassu, Father Robert, 153-55
Garrett, Elizabeth, 85n, 91n
Garrett, Juanita, 68-69, 73, 77
Garrett, Patrick Floyd, 35, 35n, 53, 79, 80, 101n, 160n, 165, 203n, 207, 259n, 260, 268, 323, 324; biog., 67-69; death and burial, 87-93, 100; family, 91-92n; and Garner, 85, 86; gravesite, 91-92n, *photo*, 90; Lee trial, 249-58, 268-72, 274, 279; *Life of Billy the Kid*, 146-47, 164; kills Bonney, 73-76; Pecos Valley development, 184-90, 200, 207, 302; rancher, 77, 81, 83-84, 86, 87, 92-93; ranches, 116, 146; Sheriff of Lincoln County, 53, 69, 70-77, 258, 259n, 260; Texas Ranger, 77-81, 83; U.S. Customs Collector, 86-87; *photo*, 78
Gay, George, 43, 44
Gerhardt's Ranch, 34
Gilbert's Ranch, 182
Gililland, James Robert, x, 35n, 55, 86, 139, 164, 249-51, 253-56, 258-60, 264, 267n, 270-72, 276, 277; profile, 276; *photo*, 263
Good, John H., 247, 248
Good, Walter, 247, 248
Goodnight Ranch, 174
Gould, George Jay, 281-82, 306
Graham, H. G., x, 163-64, 256
Gran Quivira, 53, 56
Grant, Pres. Ulysses S., 121
Greathouse (James) and Kuch Ranch battle, 69-72
Greene, Charles W., 189-90; profile, 189-90n

Griffin, John Gerald, 79; *photo*, 78
Griffin, Marcus, 79
Grumbless, Jeff, 115
Grumbless, Rock, 115
Guadalupe Hidalgo, Treaty of, 5n, 105-06
Grzelachowski, Alexander, 63

Hagerman, Anna Osborne, 191n, 194-95, 206
Hagerman, Gov. Herbert J., 191n, 204-05, 206n
Hagerman Irrigation Company, 203
Hagerman, James John, 79, 84, 190n, 205, 323, 324, 325; biog., 191-92n, 195; death, 206; meets Eddy, 190, 192; Pecos Valley development, 190-200, 304-05; railroad promotions, 197-203, 282, 320; *photo*, 193
Hagerman, Percy, x, 191n, 203n
Hall, Tom, 259, 260
Hamilton, Humphrey B., 128
Hanna, Mark, 195
Haptom, James, 35
Hardin, John Wesley, 94-96n
Harding, Pres. Warren G., 80, 211, 226, 227, 227n, 228, 230-31, 277
Harrison, Pres. Benjamin, 227
Harwood, Rev. Thomas, 12n
Hatch, Gen. Edward, 25
Hawkins Act, 257, 313-19, 319-20n; nullified, 317-18
Hawkins, Alvin, 300, 302; profile, 200n
Hawkins, William Ashton, 79, 203n, 227n, 257, 285, 285n, 286, 292-93, 323; biog., 300; and Eddy, 299, 302-05; El Paso & Northeastern R. R., 306-13; and Hagerman, 305; in legislature, 313-20; retirement, 320-21; *photos*, 78, 303; see Hawkins Act
Heath, H. H., 121n
Henderson, Alice Corbin, 166, 181n
Hening, Horace Brand, 253
Hervey, James M., x, 88-89
Hewitt, John Y., 44, 291n, 323
HG Ranch, 163, 256-57, 258, 259, 267
Hill, Humphrey, 247
Hillsboro, 86, 139, 215, 252n, 262-70, 277; courthouse, *photo*, 265
Hilton, August Holver, 294n, 298n
Hilton, Conrad, profile, 298n

Holland Syndicate, 130
Holloman, William L., 35, 84
Holt Cattle Company, 65
Holt, Herbert B., 79; *photo*, 78
Homestead, 34, 52, 53, 57, 175, 197, 240n, 246, 287, 302; laws, 104, 106, 111-12
Hough, Emerson, 38, 88-89, 144, 157-60, 160n, 323
Hubbell, Frank A., 126n
Hudgens, William H., 43-44, 81
Hudson, Henry R., 34-35
Hudspeth, Andrew H., x, 79, 285; profile 291-92; *photo*, 78
Hughes, Capt. J. R., 259
Hughes, Thomas, 128-30, 130n
Huning, Franz, 39n
Hunt, Charles F., 79; *photo*, 78
Hunt, George W. P., 316n
Hunter, Mark, 55
Hunter, Col. R. D., 62, 63, 64
Hunter, William, 55
Hutchison, W. H., 166n

Ilfeld, Louis, 155n
Indians, 6, 6n, 10, 13, 16, 17, 19-20, 22, 23, 36, 43, 47, 48, 52n, 56, 58, 60, 102, 105, 142, 149, 177, 181, 184-85, 234, 238, 264n, 301; Apaches, x, xi, 6, 45, 45n, 50n, 74n, 104-05, 144, 177, 185, 186, 234, 239, 301, 321, profile, 45n; Apaches, Mescalero, 10, 19-20, 45-46, 56, 102-04, 149, 161; Apaches, reservation, 50n, 81, 102-03, 209n, 219n, 242, 281, 284, 285; Arapahos, 10, 14n; Cheyennes, 10, 14n; Kiowas, 10, 14n, 149; Navajos, xi, 6, 10, 13-14, 34, 73, 74n, 82n, 104-05, 141, 160n, 185, 191n, 234, 235-36, 291-92n; Pueblos, 6, 17, 56, 143, 143n, 181n, 182n, 220; Utes, xi, 6, 45n, 74n
Ingersoll, Robert Green, 89-91
irrigation, 6, 34, 45, 46, 52, 54, 84, 185-200, 203, 264n, 305
Irwin, W. A., 240

Jacobs, Thomas, 115
James, Emil, 165
Jewett, Col. D. J. M. A., 40, 44

Johnson, E. Dana, 169-72; profile, 172n
Jornada del Muerto, 9, 48-50, 54-55, 160, 162, 166, 167, 235

Kearney, Kent, 254, 255, 272, 274
Kearny, Gen. Stephen Watts, 3-5, 5n, 7, 21, 104-05, 106
Keithly, Judge, 31-32n
Kellum, William (Cherokee Bill), 245, 247
Kimball, Sheriff, 69, 72-73
Kingston, 210-11, 232, 262n, 266n
Kinney, Bartley Hoyt, 294n
Kirby, Capt. Brandon, 81, 83, 84, 116
Kistler, R. A., 189, 190n
Kline, August, 36
Koogler, J. H., 15, 64
Kuch, *see* Greathouse and Kuch

Lackey, G., 35
La Luz, 241, 247, 248, 249, 250, 280, 281, 287, 288n, 319
Lamy, Father Antonio, 152-53
Lamy, Archbishop John B., 25, 152-55, 155n
land acquisition, 108-11; preemption laws, 107, 112, 116; scrip, 83, 107-08, *see* homestead
land grants, xi, xii, 8n, 22n, 46n, 73, 105-06, 111, 122, 123, 123n, 182-83, 291-93, 293n; Catron owned, 130, 139; frauds, 234
land offices and titles, 106-12
Las Cruces, 33, 43, 45, 47, 47n, 57, 86, 87, 88, 89, 91, 92, 94, 97, 100, 103, 106, 126, 161, 164, 173n, 211-12, 213, 233, 238-39, 241, 241n, 242, 247, 248, 249, 250, 253, 256, 259, 260, 269, 272, 273, 274, 286, 302, 304n; election day row, 214-17
Las Vegas, 4-5, 8n, 18, 20, 21, 23, 24, 26, 33, 43, 61, 64, 70, 75, 105, 123, 144, 224, 278n
Laughlin, Judge Napoleon Bonaparte, 128n, 129
Lava Gap, 33, 54, 55
Lea, Capt. J. C., 35, 77, 80, 147-48, 187, 203n; profile, 35-36n; *photo*, 37
Lea, Sally Wildey, 35n.

Lee, James, 55
Lee, Oliver Milton, x, 35n, 55, 86, 94n, 164, 240, 285, 286, 307, 323; attempt to arrest, 249-57; biog., 244-45; death, 244; feud with Good family, 247-48; friendship with Fall, 213-14, 257; marksmanship, 245-46; Otero County created, 257-58; surrender, 258-60; trial, 92, 139, 211, 215, 262-77; photo, 261
Lincoln (town), xii, 19, 26, 33, 34, 36, 44, 45, 46, 52, 62, 69, 71, 82, 114, 143, 148, 149, 150, 156, 241, 286, 302; photo, 58
Lincoln County War, 35n, 46, 53, 60n, 62, 64-65, 114, 120, 123-24, 149, 245
Llewellyn, Clint, 253, 254-55
Llewellyn, Maj. William H. H., 35n, 46, 47-48, 50n, 52, 131-32, 215, 218, 242, 250-51, 269, 270, 273, 274, 314, 316; profile, 47n
Lloyd's Crossing, 183
Lloyd's Ranch, 58
Longwill, Robert H., 125n; see Santa Fe Ring
Lummis, Charles Fletcher, 143, 164-65

Magoffin, James, 3-4
mail, see U. S. Mail
Martin, Jack, 49-50, 54
Martin, Robert, 168-69n, 173n
Martinez, Felix, 80; photo, 78
Matthews, A. B., 63
Matthews, Washington, 141, 143
Maxwell, Deluvina, 73-74; profile, 74-75n
Maxwell Land Grant, xi, 22n, 45n, 291-93, 293n; see also Beaubien-Miranda grant
Maxwell, Lucien B., xi, 22n, 73, 74n, 251, 293n
Maxwell, Peter, 73, 75n, 251
McCreight, William T., 128, 130, 130n
McDonald, Gov. William C., 44, 79, 81, 174-75; photo, 78
McGinnis, Dick, 43, 44
McKinley, Pres. William, 195
McLean, E. B., 229
McNew, W. H., 55, 86, 165, 240, 249, 250, 251, 253, 258, 270, 271, 273
McSween, A. A., 62, 123, 219n

Mechem, Merritt C., 80, 226, 226-27n
Mescalero Apache, see Indians
Mesilla, 18, 33, 45, 49, 51, 61, 118n, 143, 144, 145, 162, 233, 234, 235, 238n
Mesita de Juan Lopez land grant, 130
Metcalf, Charles, 43
Miller, Jim P., 92-93, 96-100
Mills, Gov. William J., 224-25; profile, 225n
mining in N.M., xi, 26, 202n, 210, 211, 262, 262n, 264n, 266, 279, 296n; coal, 43, 284; Bridal Chamber Mine, 210; Dawson mines, 291-97, 298, 309, 309-10n, 311n; gold, 36-44, 135n, 157, 199n, 210, 211n, 264n, 280, 284, 285, 290, 292n; Homestake mines, 36-39, 40n, 42-43, 284; Old Abe Mine, 39, 284; Salado mines, 281, 284, 284n, 286n, 288-90, 292, 306, 308, 323; silver, 197, 210, 211n
mining, Chapin & Molly Gibson mines, 195-98, 199n
Mitchell, Gov. Robert Byington, 120, 145; profile, 120-21n
Mockingbird Gap, 33, 54, 166, 258, 298, 322
Monnecom, Padre P. J., 22n
Mora Land Grant, 8n, 123, 130
Morgan, Joseph, 216, 217
Mossman, Burton C., 227n
Murphy, Maj. Lawrence Gustave, 114; profile, 114n

Navajos, see Indians
New Mexico Constitutional Convention, 47n, 136, 225, 228
New Mexico fight for statehood, 124, 126n, 136, 136n, 145, 220-25
New Mexico state song, 85n
New Mexico Territorial Legislature, 22, 25, 35, 35n, 47n, 118, 119, 120, 122n, 124, 134, 135, 145, 173n, 224, 225, 226, 228, 244, 257, 302, 304n, 313; —Acts (1855), 238-39n; (1857 & 1859), 29-32; (1869), 29, 33, 50, 51; (1882), 75; (1893), 35, 35n; (1903), 314-19; —Memorials, 17-18, 49, 51, 121
Nogal, 26

Ocate, 24
O'Folliard, Tom, 43, 73, 74n
Orchard, Sadie, 264
Ortiz Land Grant, xi
Oscuro, 53
Otero, Gov. Miguel Antonio, 32n, 83n, 126n, 131-32, 218, 257-58, 259, 314-15; profile, 258-59n

Paraje, 50, 235
Parker, Judge Frank W., 92, 211, 249, 251, 252, 259, 260, 262, 266n, 268, 272, 274-76; profile, 262n
Parks, Judge Samuel A., 62
Patron, John B., 60, 60n
Patterson, Henry J., 40
Peck, Lt. W., 52n
Pecos, 24, 181, 182
Pecos River, description, xii, 180-85; promotion, 84, 196-200, 203, 302
Pedragon, Cesario, x, 89; photo, 237
Perea, Jose Leandro, 63
Perea grant, 183
Pershing, John J., 137-38n, 292n
Phelps Dodge Co., 294-95, 306, 309-10, 312-13n
Picacho, 33, 82
Poe, John W., 53, 76, 77, 81, 82, 84, 115-16, 202, 203n, 323; profile, 85n
Preston Beck grant, 182-83
Prince, Gov. L. Bradford, 25, 65, 111
Pueblos, see Indians
Puerto de Luna, 33-34, 60n, 63, 183, 184

Railroads, 15, 19, 23, 24-26, 169, 186, 191, 194, 218, 279; Colorado Midland, 195, 198n, 203; El Paso & Northeastern, 52n, 175, 201n, 219n, 254, 257, 260, 284-85n, 285, 286-90, 293, 294, 294n, 295-96, 297n, 306-13, 319, 319n, 323; El Paso & Southwestern, 52n, 295, 297n, 312, 321n; El Paso & White Oaks, 281-82, 284-85, 305-06; Pecos Valley, 197, 198, 199, 200-03; Rock Island 52n, 200, 201-02n, 293-95, 306, 308, 309-10n, 313n; Santa Fe, xi, 4, 21-22, 23, 50, 70, 155n, 189n, 198n, 200, 202n, 203, 215, 219, 221, 257, 259, 260, 264n, 280, 281, 286n, 294, 294n, 296, 309n, 310n, 320n, 324; Southern Pacific, 297n, 320n; Texas & Pacific, 282, 282n
ranchers and ranching, 11, 26, 46, 52, 54-55, 58-65, 69, 81-84, 96n, 109, 112-16, 124, 165, 186-87, 246-47, 280, 281, 284, 322; see individual names
Raton, 26, 252n, 293; Pass, 4, 4n, 21-22, 22n; tunnel, 21-23, 25
Raymond, Numa, 85, 215, 219n
Reavis, James Addison Peralta, 133-34
religion in N.M., 11, 12n, 19; see also Lamy
Rhodes, Eugene Manlove, 48, 96n, 144, 160-72, 174, 256, 258, 258n, 259, 260, 266n, 324; burial, 172-73
Rhodes, Col. Hinman, 48, 160-62
Rhodes, May D., 163-64n, 173n
Richardson, Andy, 72
Richardson, Judge Granville A., 72
Riley, John H., 45, 248
Riley, William, 79; photo, 78
Rio Bonito, 33, 42
Ritch, W. G., 17, 160, 161-62; profile, 160n
Roberts, "Buckshot," 46
Rodey, Bernard S., 126n
Roosevelt, Pres. Theodore, 47n, 79, 86, 87n, 174, 205-06, 206n, 213n, 218, 221, 252n, 258
Root, Elihu, 205
Ross, Gov. Edmund Gilbert, 107, 112
Roswell, 34, 35n, 36, 63, 82, 84, 88, 89, 91n, 109, 145, 148, 149-50, 162, 179, 184-87, 190, 194, 196, 200, 202, 203, 204, 227n, 279, 304, 324
Rudabaugh, Dave, 43, 69, 70
Rudolph, Milnor, 34
Rynerson, Col. W. L., 45, 248, 302; profile, 304n

Safford, Charles V., 79; photo, 78
St. Vrain, Col. Ceran, 24, 82n, 114n
Salado mines, see mining
San Augustin Pass, 45, 54
San Augustine Ranch, 93-94n, 96n
San Cristobal Land Grant, 130
San Jose de Anton Chico, see Anton Chico
San Miguel, 24

Santa Fe, 5, 10, 14, 18, 20, 21, 23, 24, 25, 26, 29, 33, 62, 75, 106, 114, 114n, 117, 118n, 119n, 120, 121, 123, 125, 128, 130, 131, 132, 135, 136n, 138, 144n, 147, 151, 151n, 152, 153, 154, 155, 155n, 160n, 170, 172n, 173, 179, 183, 188, 189n, 213, 227, 257, 258, 259, 267, 267n, 292, 302

Santa Fe Ring, 125, 125n, 161, 212, 214, 245

Santa Fe Trail, xi, 23-24

Seven Rivers, 26, 58, 65, 77, 82, 108, 110, 145, 184, 240n

Sganzini, Ilda B., ix

Sheldon, Gov. Lionel A., 111

Shield, D. P., 150

Silver City, 19, 36, 61, 133, 135, 262, 301, 304

Sinclair, H. F., 209n, 228, 230, 231n

Siringo, Charles A., 135, 144, 171, 178-79

Slaughter, Charles H., 110

slavery in N.M., 29-32, 74n

Smith, Thomas, 128-29

Socorro, 33, 42, 61, 176, 241n, 281, 324

Spiess, Charles A., 314, 316, 316-17n

Springer, Charles, 125n, 292-93, 307

Staab, Abraham, 25, 125n, 154-55; profile, 155n

stagecoaches, 4, 5, 6, 8-9, 17, 18, 20-22, 33-34, 36, 43, 45, 50, 67, 70, 123, 169, 182, 264; robbery, x, 61

Staked Plains, x, 33, 35n, 57, 60, 64, 145

Starr, Charles, 43, 44

Stone, Judge E. S., 13, 35

Swiss immigrants, 192-94n

Taft, Pres. William Howard, 145, 219-25

Taliaferro, Jones, 40, 44

Tansill, Robert Weems, 190, 192, 200

Teapot Dome lease, 80, 227-28, 231-32n

Telfer, Lois, 73n

Texas: fugitives, 26n; invasion, 13-14, 33, 182; Rangers, 77, 81, 83, 98, 99, 234, 260n

Thompson, Mark B., 80; *photo*, 78

Thornton, Gov. W. T., 38, 112, 155n, 269

Thorp, Nathan Howard (Jack), 173-76

Three Rivers, 53, 56, 58, 82, 115, 143,

151, 171, 219, 220n, 228, 229, 229n, 230, 281, 287, 288n

Tierra Amarilla Land Grant, 130

Tucker, Tom, 247, 267, 267n

Tularosa, xii, 34, 45, 52, 61, 79, 102, 137n, 167, 172, 217, 242, 247, 249, 250, 251, 252, 255, 271, 280, 281, 284, 285, 287, 288n; origin of name, 103n

Tularosa Basin, description, 52-53

Tunstall, John H., 123, 150

Ulrich, George, x, 151; profile, 151n

Upson, Marshall Ashmun, 35, 76, 85, 109, 144-49, 185, 323

U.S. Congress, 4, 31-32n, 105n, 107n, 111n, 122, 122-23n, 125-26n, 226, 226-27n, 228, 228n, 231n, 234, 257; *see also* Catron, Fall, Fergusson, Otero, Andrews

U.S. Mail, xii, 9-10, 12-13, 17, 18, 23, 33, 42, 44, 47, 49, 103, 145, 241; postmasters, 145, 147, 149, 162, 286

Utes, *see* Indians

Victorio, Chief, 19, 177, 234

Villa, Pancho, raid, 136, 136-38n, 292n

Waldo, Judge David, 23-24

Waldo, H. L., 125n

Wallace, Gov. Lew, 25, 46, 75, 75n

Walter, Paul A. F., 83n

Walz, E. A., 114, 116

water, 52-55, 61, 65, 109, 111-14, 220n, 246, 248, 286; artesian, 109, 109n, 183n, 200; Jornada del Muerto, 49-55; Tularosa Basin, 47, 102-03, (and railroad, 175, 310-12)

White Oaks, xii, 26, 33, 34, 36-44, 69, 70, 71, 77, 79, 97, 114, 143, 151, 155-57, 201, 270, 279-91, 293, 306, 323; *photo*, 41

White Sands, 53, 55, 167, 217, 233, 247, 248, 249, 258, 267, 268, 280, 280n, 323

Wildey, Maj. W. W., profile, 35n

Wildey's Well, 35n, 55, 248, 272, 286; 311, 322, 323, 324

Wildey's Well fight, 251, 253-56, 272, 274
Williams, Ben, 215-16, 254-55, 260, 260n, 273
Wilson, Billy, 59, 69, 70; hanging, 152

Wilson, Pres. Woodrow, 80
Winters, Jack, 36-38, 43, 44
Wootton, Richens Lacy (Uncle Dick), 22, 24; profile, 22n
Wootton, R. L., Jr., 22n